Endorsements

As the Facilitator for North Africa and Middle East Partnerships, I have been involved in reaching the least reached for almost thirty years. Millions and millions of lost people are a reality all around me. My passion has been to see God's people work in unity to reach them, "so that the world may believe that You sent Me" (John 17:21). We need to plan, strategize, and pray together about how best to finish the Great Commission. So it is thrilling to see the global collaboration involved in the production of *People Vision*! I strongly believe that this book is both a major resource as well as an urgent invitation to all key players and leaders at every level in the church. *People Vision* is a call to rethink approaches and to explore imaginative and fruitful ways to collaborate in mission. I recommend that everyone who is interested in missions—indeed, every believer!—should get a copy of this book and catch the vision presented in it.

Edwin Caruana
Vision 5:9 Operations Team
Facilitator for North Africa and Middle East Partnerships, Malta

Here it is! Practical missiology and research we can effectively use. As a former missionary, global organizational leader, and now a local church mission leader, these writers are trusted practitioners, researchers, and academic leaders you can rely on. Whether you are serving locally, globally or both, this will help. Urban or rural, developed or developing communities, complex cultural issues, oral peoples, evangelism, disciple-making movements, compassion and justice, or all the above, least reached peoples must be on your radar screen. Most mission initiatives demand focus and good intel to experience lasting fruit, reproducing disciples, community impact, and great commission acceleration. This is a valuable resource as you "focus" on or "add" a least reached peoples initiative utilizing good missiology, updated research, and better practices.

Mike Constantz
Pastor, The PEACE Plan, Saddleback Church

What a timely, hope-filled call to the church today to "reimagine" the "peoples" in our complex world who have yet to hear and experience Jesus. From the beginning pages of key biblical reminders of God's heart for the lost, to a historical sweep of men, women, and groups from around the world moved and "compelled" to reach the unreached, the book gave me several more "lenses" through which to see, pray for, and relationally engage with "peoples." As a former field worker who labored in a Muslim megacity for over twenty years, I greatly appreciated the challenge to reconsider and reconstruct my own missional efforts in light of today's social, economic, and structural realities that confront the missions enterprise today. We have a creative, imaginative, loving God who continues to call his people to believe in and give of themselves to his unchanging plan and future of a great multitude, from every nation, tribe, people, and language standing before the throne of the Lamb. Read and be ready for your heart to be stirred, your faith to grow, and your hope to increase.

T. Woo Dong
International Directors Team, Frontiers

This book started out as an edition of Evangelical Missions Quarterly but has become the most comprehensive review of the unreached people group paradigm available. It arrives at an important time in contemporary missiological thinking. It is an invaluable resource as the global church seeks to obey Jesus's command to disciple the nations.

TED ESLER, PhD
President, Missio Nexus

Half a century since the inception of the unreached peoples movement, *People Vision* brings together experts from across the globe to pave the way for the next era of outreach. It transcends the confines of a mere contextualized Western gospel, instead championing a gospel that emanates from thousands of peoples to all peoples. This compilation stands as an indispensable roadmap for the evolving landscape of global frontier missions.

TODD JOHNSON, PhD
Professor of Mission and Global Christianity, Gordon-Conwell Theological Seminary

In the Bible, God's salvific program through His Son Jesus Christ aims in creating a kingdom of redeemed people from every tribe, every tongue, every people and every nation (Rev 5:9). This makes Christian mission among unreached people groups—those without access to the gospel—a priority. *People Vision: Reimagining Mission to Least Reached Peoples* underscores this timeless biblical message of God's salvific program through His Son to the nations. The significance of the mandate in our time is strengthened through the writings of these seasoned global leaders based on their biblical and missiological perspectives and their labor among the least reached people groups. This is a must-read for all earnestly seeking the coming of God's Kingdom among the nations until all the peoples, nations and men of every language worship him.

SAMUEL KEBREAB
Horn of Africa Coordinator, Movement for African National Initiative (MANI)
Vision 5:9 Global Team and Training Task Force
Horn of Africa Partnership Director, Partners International

This book should be read by everyone concerned with frontier missions in the twenty-first century. As we engage in renewed focus on and discussion about the least reached peoples with no sign of the gospel taking root, let's give special note to a subset of UPGs called Frontier People Groups. These largely neglected peoples will require special focus, as they comprise 25 percent of humanity. God's heart for them, their families, and communities is shown from Genesis to Revelation. He not only promised "every family (ethne) of the earth will be blessed" but also that every tribe, tongue, and ethne will be represented before his throne.

TIMOTHY LEWIS
Former International Director, Frontiers

In *People Vision*, Len Bartlotti pulled together an amazing team of mission visionaries and practitioners from across the globe to produce a timely book on a critically important subject that has truly astonishing global scope. I am confident that *People Vision* will prove to be of immense value as we celebrate the fifty-year milestone in global mission advance since Lausanne 1974 and renew our vision for the Father's missions mandate through the heart of this twenty-first century. We in Pioneers are in the midst of reenvisioning and enlarging our vision for the unreached and asking God for fresh vision as we increase our efforts to engage with even more of the remaining thousands of unengaged peoples around the world. The rich resources collected together in *People Vision* will serve us very well at this critical juncture as we seek to strengthen our agency's pioneering vision. I expect that *People Vision* will not only be used by God to help the global church reimagine what missions will look like in the next fifty years, but act as a catalyst to greatly increased mobilization, countless creative new endeavors, and fruitfulness in the God-ordained task of discipling all of the hidden peoples of the earth to know, love, and serve the Savior of whom they have not yet heard.

DON LITTLE, DMin
Missiologist-at-Large, Pioneers; Director, Lilias Trotter Center

When I learned that the leadership of the Lausanne Movement asked my colleague, one of my heroes actually, Len Bartlotti, to produce an update on missiological thinking, I mused, "What can be said that hasn't been?" Then, when I received the manuscript of *People Vision*, I was stunned. This is not a book—it's a library!—from a professor of missiology who is also a seasoned field worker. It is available to us who are still in the smoke of the battle! This book is a call to "come up higher" with direction to sit with those who have "laid down their lives" to wrestle with what it might take to actually fulfill the Great Commission of our Lord. This is not merely another book on world mission; it's a missiological collection of thinking and observing of the best of wrestling with the issues. After my sixty years of daily wrestling with the question of "what will it take," I urge all "make-it-happen" leaders and our younger aspirants to seriously examine what you've assumed. And then wrestle with this collection of lessons learned by others hungry to see our Lord's mandate fulfilled exceedingly abundantly beyond all we ask or think.

REV. GREG LIVINGSTONE, PhD
Founder, Frontiers

While other belief systems may spread largely due to demographic factors, the Christian gospel is propelled by a love-fueled mandate to take the good news to everyone, everywhere. We call this the Great Commission. But in a rapidly changing world, what does this look like in practical terms? What is the terrain yet to be traversed? Here is where *People Vision* harnesses the reflections of some of the best thinkers in missions today to sharpen our thinking as we press into the remaining task.

STEVE RICHARDSON
President, Pioneers USA

Amazing! It is not a coincidence that *People Vision: Reimagining Mission to Least Reached Peoples* comes during the emergence of Arise Asia, a growing movement of young people in Asia who are called "to go to where there is no gospel" among unreached and least reached peoples. With the rise of young people prioritizing their lives to go where Christ is not known in Asia, the priority on Least Reached Peoples within the Lausanne Movement comes at the right time!

REV. DR. DAVID L. RO
Executive Director, Arise Asia 2023
Regional Director, Lausanne Movement, East Asia

People Vision is a powerful and impacting read from people who are taking seriously Jesus's commission to take the gospel of the Kingdom into all nations. The editor of this book, Len Bartlotti, is a friend of mine. When he became a member of the group of churches I was pastoring several years ago in Oxfordshire, UK, it changed our thinking about mission, and launched us into new adventures of sending pioneering teams amongst some of the least reached people in the earth, with amazing results! This book encapsulates some of that thinking and lessons that Len and his friends have learned along the way. It is a "must read" for local church pastors, and leaders of church networks who want to be missional in the way Jesus taught us.

STEVE THOMAS
International Team Leader, Salt & Light Ministries

People Vision

Reimagining Mission to Least Reached Peoples

Leonard N. Bartlotti

Editor

visit us at missionbooks.org

People Vision: Reimagining Mission to Least Reached Peoples

© 2024 by Leonard N. Bartlotti. All Rights Reserved.

No part of this book may be reproduced, stored in a retrieval system, or transmitted in any form or by any means—electronic, mechanical, photocopy, recording, or otherwise—without prior written permission from the publisher, except brief quotations used in connection with reviews. This manuscript may not be entered into AI, even for AI training. For permission, email permissions@wclbooks.com. For corrections, email editor@wclbooks.com.

William Carey Publishing (WCP) publishes resources to shape and advance the missiological conversation in the world. We publish a broad range of thought-provoking books and do not necessarily endorse all opinions set forth here or in works referenced within this book.

The URLs included in this workbook are provided for personal use only and are current as of the date of publication, but the publisher disclaims any obligation tso update them after publication.

The following chapters were previously published in *EMQ* 56, no. 4 (Fall 2020): 2, 4, 5, 6, 12, 29, 30, 31, 33, 34, and 38. Chapters 2, 29, and 38 were slightly revised. Used with permission.

Scripture quotations marked NLT are taken from the Holy Bible, New Living Translation, copyright ©1996, 2004, 2015 by Tyndale House Foundation. Used by permission of Tyndale House Publishers, Carol Stream, Illinois 60188. All rights reserved.

Scripture quotations marked NIV are taken from the Holy Bible, New International Version®, NIV®. Copyright © 1973, 1978, 1984, 2011 by Biblica, Inc.™ Used by permission of Zondervan. All rights reserved worldwide. www.zondervan.com. The "NIV" and "New International Version" are trademarks registered in the United States Patent and Trademark Office by Biblica, Inc.™

Scripture quotations marked ESV are taken from the ESV® Bible (The Holy Bible, English Standard Version®), Copyright © 2001 by Crossway, a publishing ministry of Good News Publishers. Used by permission. All rights reserved.

Scripture quotations taken from the NASB® New American Bible®, Copyright © 1960, 1971, 1977, 1995, 2020 by The Lockman Foundation. Used by permission. All rights reserved. lockman.org.

Scripture quotations marked RSV are taken from the Revised Standard Version of the Bible, Copyright © 1946, 1952, and 1971 the Division of Christian Education of the National Council of the Churches of Christ in the United States of America. Used by permission. All rights reserved.

Published by William Carey Publishing
10 W. Dry Creek Cir
Littleton, CO 80120 | www.missionbooks.org

William Carey Publishing is a ministry of Frontier Ventures
Pasadena, CA | www.frontierventures.org

Cover and Interior Designer: Mike Riester

ISBNs: 978-1-64508-600-0 (paperback)
       978-1-64508-602-4 (epub)

Printed Worldwide
28 27 26 25 24   1 2 3 4 5   IN

Library of Congress Control Number: 2024941549

Contents

Figures and Tables x
Foreword I by Robert A. Blincoe xi
Foreword II by Rev. Samuel E. Chiang xii
Preface by Mary Ho xiii
Introduction by Leonard N. (Len) Bartlotti xv
Visualizing the Task by R. W. Lewis and Robby Butler xxii

Part 1: Impetus for the Unreached Peoples Movement: Biblical and Missional Foundations

1: To the Ends of the Earth by Leonard N. Bartlotti 3

2: A Biblical Understanding of People Groups by Steven C. Hawthorne 13

3: *Panta ta Ethne*: All Peoples and Nations by David E. Datema 19

4: The People Group Approach: A Historical Perspective
by David E. Datema and Leonard N. Bartlotti 29

5: Foundations of Frontier Missiology: Core Understandings
and Interrelated Concepts by Alan R. Johnson 39

——Reflection and Discussion——

Part 2: Impact of People Group Thinking on Agencies: Painful and Purposeful Adjustments

6: Run with the Vision: The Impact of the Unreached People Groups Concept on Students, Churches, and Sending Agencies
by Greg Parsons 51

7: Re-envisioning the World: The Southern Baptist IMB Transition
to People Groups by David Garrison and Zane Pratt 59

8: Assemblies of God World Missions and the Unreached
by Dick Brogden, Alan R. Johnson, and Leonard N. Bartlotti 67

9: The Holy Vision Conceived in a Prayer Cave: The Korean Frontier Missions
Movement by Jungkook Han and Mark Kim 81

10: Sub-Saharan Africa: Taking the Gospel to "Where the Smoke Is Seen"
by Peter Oyugi with Mary Ho, Clara Litzsinger, and Zazá Lima 91

11: A Latin American Perspective on Unreached People Groups
by Abraham Duran 101

——Reflection and Discussion——

Part 3: Impact of People Group Thinking on Field Workers: Voices from the Field

12: Voices of Pioneer Workers on the Challenge of "People Groups" 117

Central Asia	Pakistan	Turkey	Southeast Asia
South Asia	Transnational	Eurasia	
India	Middle East	Horn of Africa	

——Reflection and Discussion——

Part 4: Impact of People Group Thinking on Local Churches: Mobilizing for Strategic Engagement

13: The Local Church and Adopt A People by PCC — 135

14: An Ecosystem for Sending:
Austin Stone and the 100 UPG Cooperative by Todd Engstrom — 139

15: Robust Commitment: The Well by Pastor C. C. — 141

16: The Sending Process by Canyon Hills Community Church — 143

17: Sowing Broadly Together: Swedish Pentecostal Churches
by Bo Lundin, Hans Olofsson, and O. K. — 145

18: Where Mountains Inspire Poets: Oitava Church, Brazil
by Célia Margareth Oliveira Laranjo and Luís Fernando Nacif — 147

19: Everyone Leaves, Everyone Is Sent Onward:
Koinonia International Church, Middle East by Brian McSwain — 149

20: The Role of Existing Churches in an African Movement
by Aychi B. R. — 151

—Reflection and Discussion—

Part 5: International Multiplication: Polycentric Pioneers and Collaboration

21: Iberoamerican Missionary Partnership: The Journey of COMIBAM
by Cristian Castro, Zazá Lima, and Allan Matamoros — 157

22: Sub-Saharan Africa: The Sahel by John Becker — 163

23: "Lord, Stir Us Up!": The Acceleration of the Nigerian Missions Movement
by Mike Adegbile and Adeoluwa Olanrewaju — 167

24: When Collaboration Blooms: Reaching India's Muslims
by Martin Hall — 173

25: Facing Roadblocks on the Indian Road: A Closer Look
by Sushil Tyagi — 177

26: From Research to Movement: Partnership in Southeast Asia
by Yahya Ilyas — 179

27: Diaspora Peoples in Europe by Simon Lunt — 181

28: Networking Networks by Ryan Emis and Allan Matamoros — 185

—Reflection and Discussion—

Part 6: Issues Affecting Progress: Challenges, Changes, and Trends

29: Fog in the Pews: Factors behind the Fading Vision for Unreached Peoples
   by R. W. Lewis — 191

30: Rethinking the People Groups Concept:
   Globalization, Urbanization, and Migration by Minh Ha Nguyen — 199

31: Ferment in the Church: Missions in the Fourth Era
   by Alan McMahan — 207

32: Unleashing Next Gen Pioneers by Clara Litzsinger and Lisa Pak — 213

33: The Making of Lists by Dan Scribner — 221

—— Reflection and Discussion ——

Part 7: Imagining Fulfillment: Purpose and Promise of People Vision

34: A Church for Every People: A Retrospect on Mapping Peoples
   by Brad Gill — 233

35: Pioneer Apostleship: Twelve Principles by Daniel Waheli — 239

36: The Unengaged: First Engage, Then Reach by Mike Latsko — 245

37: The Rise of Muslim-Background Churches:
   An Eleventh-Hour Workforce for the Harvest?
   by Patrick Brittenden and Parsa Zarin Ghalam — 249

38: Reimagining and Re-envisioning People Groups
   by Leonard N. Bartlotti — 257

Afterword: People Vision and the Beatific Vision
   by Leonard N. Bartlotti — 271

—— Reflection and Discussion ——

Appendix 1: FAQs about People Groups and UPGs — 275

Appendix 2: Visualizing the Task:
   Maps, Graphs, Figures, Charts, Lists — 282

Appendix 3: Resources — 293

Acknowledgments — 296

Contributors — 298

Figures and Tables

Figure 1: Distribution of International Workers	xxii
Figure 2: Global Status of Evangelical Christianity	xxiii
Figure 3: The World in 1974: 4 Billion People	xxiv
Figure 4: The World in 2024: 8 Billion People	xxv
Figure 5: 300 Largest FPGs as of April 2024	xxvi
Figure 6: The Making of a Movement	35
Figure 7: Granularity versus Complexity in People Group Lists	225
Figure 8: Multi-level Model of Ethnicity	260
Figure 9: Social Bonding	263
Figure 10: Multiple Affinities	263
Figure 11: Re-envision People of God	265
Figure 12: The Accelerating Growth of Jesus's Kingdom	282
Figure 13: The Increasing Progress of the Gospel	282
Figure 14: 2010 Distribution of Foreign Missionaries	283
Figure 15: Top Primary Languages of FPGs and UPGs	284
Figure 16: Top 10 Countries of Largest FPGs and UPGs	284
Figure 17: 110 Mega-cities Map	285
Figure 18: Top Cities of UPGs	285
Figure 19: Layered Journey	286
Figure 20: The Challenge of India	287
Figure 21: Distribution of Workers and Funding	288
Figure 22: Largest Muslim and Hindu FPGs	288
Figure 23: Church Movements Needed in Sub-Saharan Africa	289
Figure 24: Sudan	289
Figure 25: Countries with the Most Unengaged Unreached People Groups, by Religion	290
Figure 26: Religions with the Most Unengaged Unreached People Groups, by Country	291
Figure 27: Twenty Countries with the Largest Number of Unengaged Muslim Peoples	292
Table 1: Terms Designating Human Grouping in Scripture	22
Table 2: A Comparison of the Three Global People Group Lists	222
Table 3: Comparing People Segmentation Levels	223
Table 4: Comparing Traditional and Dynamic Groupings	225

Foreword I

Ralph D. Winter gave his seminal address on unreached peoples at Lausanne in 1974 when he was fifty years old. This year, the hundredth anniversary of Winter's birth, I have the feeling that, were he with us today, Dr. Winter would still be the youngest person in the room, unwilling to let things stay as they are when the needs in the "regions beyond" are so great. Some people see things as they are and say "Why?" Ralph Winter dreamt things that never were and said, "Why not?"

"Probably the most influential few minutes of Ralph Winter's life," remembers Greg Parsons, "was when he gave his talk at the Lausanne meeting in 1974." That speech, Scott Moreau said, was "a bombshell that was dropped at Lausanne." Jim Reapsome and others admitted that, until Winter delivered that address, we had been busying ourselves with "maintenance missions," nurturing churches where they already existed.

Descending the steps after delivering his address, Dr. Ralph D. Winter thought, "I may not have convinced anyone else, but I have convinced myself." His message spread to a younger generation through the "Perspectives" movement and the *Global Prayer Digest* and by word of mouth. New maps opened our eyes to "see" people groups instead of countries. Applicants to mission agencies asked to be sent to unreached peoples, forcing the agencies to adapt and creating entire new agencies specializing in making disciples *"panta ta ethne."* Most of all many people began rereading the Bible and realizing that, in addition to revealing "the chief end of man," the Bible reveals "the chief end of God." That is, "that the Gentiles might glorify God for his mercy" (Rom 15:9 ESV). Everything that Ralph D. Winter did and said was so that more unreached peoples would glorify God for his mercy.

However, by using the term "unreached peoples" we do not all mean the same thing. Some contributors to this book present differing points of view on the meaning of "people groups." Two things have changed in fifty years: first, churches and mission agencies have sent thousands of missionaries to unreached peoples. What did they find that they want us to know? Second, missionaries born in Latin America, Africa, and Asia are rereading the Bible and planting churches among unreached peoples. We have much to learn from them. Let the reader keep the end in mind through it all: building up the church where it is "too small a thing." "I will make you as a light to the Gentiles, that my salvation will reach the end of the earth" (Isa 49:6).

As such, this is the most important book in many years. You need to study it and tell others about it.

This book is for those who, like Ralph D. Winter, call for greater partnerships between congregations and mission agencies—what Winter called "the two structures of God' redemptive mission." This book is for mission leaders, theologians, and thousands of Christians who want their lives and their prayers to change the world in the way that matters most.

I remember when Dr. Winter said, "Love finds a way," and the pause that followed affected me considerably. It still does. With the love of God compelling, let us not lose heart. Let us force ourselves, for that is where the force is most needed, to make the invitation to unreached peoples everywhere. Our Lord's table must be filled before the banquet can begin.

ROBERT A. BLINCOE, PhD
President Emeritus, Frontiers US

Foreword II

As I traveled to China and India, I eagerly devoured this book, and my heart was stirred. Len Bartlotti, author, editor, and the visionary behind this project, along with catalysts Mary Ho and Zaza Lima, invited a global cast of passionate practitioners, researchers, and missiologists to reimagine what it means to bring the gospel to the least reached peoples in a globalising, urbanising, and migration-fuelled world.

Google's Endangered Language Project aims to preserve culture, protect smaller languages, and connect future generations to their heritage, requiring intentionality! *People Vision* also calls for intentionality.

In Revelation 7:9–10, a vast crowd from every nation, tribe, people, and language stands before the throne and the Lamb, clothed in white robes and holding palm branches. "And they were shouting with a great roar, 'Salvation comes from our God who sits on the throne and from the Lamb!'" This vision reminds us of the urgent importance of reaching all people groups with the message of salvation.

For fifty years, the missions movement has worked to understand unreached people groups, but only 4 percent of cross-cultural workers are allocated to the unreached. Undeterred, God has moved, and tremendous advances have taken place! The awakened next generation is demanding sharpened clarity about God's heart, the need, and the call.

In the last fifty years, the global population has doubled from four to eight billion. God has used meager and faith resources to reduce humanity's people groups with no Christward movement from 60 percent to 25 percent. This is astonishing! Data science shows that our remaining frontier task involves reaching:

- 97 percent of the total population of remaining people groups who are Muslim (56 percent) or Hindu (41 percent)
- One billion of them live in India
- 80 percent of the 2 billion people are living in the three hundred largest groups, each greater than 1 million

Due to the size and spiritual needs of these largest groups, we must consider prioritized collaborative strategies for impact.

Ever wonder how to participate in an idea that gets birthed, rooted, spread, and embedded into multiple expressions of denominations, movements, and networks? We hold a precious volume describing what the Holy Spirit has done in UPGs and church planting. We are invited to join God's plan to yield lasting Kingdom fruit. There are still 25 percent of the world's population, mostly Muslims, Hindus, and Buddhists, living in globalized and city contexts. Each one longs to hear a message of hope. Each ones needs to understand and experience for themselves, as beloved sons and daughters, the grace and embrace of God our King.

We have technology, communications support, and transportation means. What we need are intentional Christ followers who will tell them, "you are my beloved." Will you be intentional about accepting this invitation?

REV. SAMUEL E. CHIANG
Deputy Secretary General, World Evangelical Alliance
Orality Catalyst, Lausanne Movement, Beijing, China and Mumbai, India

Preface

We restarted to reimagine. In 2023, we relaunched the Lausanne Least Reached Peoples Issue Network to reimagine Christ's timeless mandate to the church to "Go and make disciples of all people groups (*ethne*)" (Matt 28:19–20). Proclaiming the gospel as a witness to all peoples is the central tapestry of God's story from the beginning to the end. It is the meta narrative of the entire Scripture from Genesis to Revelation, not a side narrative. It is the chronicle of God's own mission, from the ancient past to the future, not an epilogue patched to the end of the Gospels.

After relaunching the network, we began to envision this book to retell God's story together; to recapture his heart towards us; and to rekindle in us his driving passion to bless us—and through each of us, to bless each family and people group on earth that they might know and enjoy him!

If the ink of this book could bleed, it would bleed the blended colors of the global church. These pages throb with the heartbeat of the global church from Asia, Africa, Latin America, and the West … the viewpoints of key influencers, global mission leaders, and networks … the perspectives of the young and the seasoned, both men and women … voices from the field, those leading and laboring on the frontiers of the gospel, for the glory of his name.

For us, making Christ visible among every people group compels us to awake in the morning, to trek the roads to unknown places during the day, and to dream at night of Christward church movements unleashed among every people. Every other good mission initiative must align with God's core mandate for us to be his witnesses to the very ends of the earth.

We are humbled and inspired by the Lausanne legacy. At the 1974 Lausanne Congress, Ralph Winter articulated the breakthrough "people groups" paradigm. As a sequel to this biblical legacy, we humbly offer this book as a gift to the body of Christ to reimagine the ancient charge of our missionary God to bless all the peoples of the earth. The chronicle of Jesus to be worshiped by all peoples continues.

MARY HO, o*n behalf of the Catalysts and Steering Team of the Lausanne Least Reached Peoples Network*

Leonard N. (Len) Bartlotti, Co-Catalyst (Vision 5:9)

Mary Ho, Co-Catalyst (All Nations International)

Zazá Lima, Co-Catalyst (PMI, COMIBAM)

Steering Team:

Mike Adegbile (NEMA)

John Becker (AIM)

Patrick Brittenden (Hikma Partnership)

Samuel Chiang (Global Evangelism Network)

Dave Datema (Frontier Ventures)

Abraham Duran (Frontiers)

Dick Grady (Global Church Planting Network)

Alan Johnson (Assemblies of God World Missions)

Allan Matamoros (Vision 5:9)

Peter Oyugi (Movement for African National Initiatives)

Lisa Pak (Finishing the Task)

Stan Parks (24:14)

Bekele Shanko (GACX)

Sushil Tyagi (Vision 5:9)

Daniel Waheli (Frontiers)

Clara Litzsinger (Executive Assistant/All Nations International)

Introduction

The concept of seeing the world as people groups is arguably the most significant thought innovation in twentieth-century missiology. Yet almost fifty years after the launch of the frontier mission movement, fewer than 4 percent of global missionaries work among "unreached people groups" (UPGs). Does the people group paradigm have relevance for the twenty-first-century church? In a fractured world with myriad, sometimes contested, mission priorities, why should cross-cultural disciple making and church planting among least reached peoples still be the highest priority of the global church? Given the turbulent confluence of urbanization, migration, racialized ethnic tensions, interreligious conflict, globalization, and resultant mixed and multiple identities, what does *panta ta ethne* and "disciple the nations" mean today?

Executive Summary

People Vision: Reimagining Mission to Least Reached Peoples is an exciting, informed, global overview of people group thinking, the priority of least reached peoples today, and innovative efforts to reach them. The book brings together the voices and imaginings of experts and practitioners, church and mission leaders, and the influencers whose ideas, organizations, images, and gatherings have changed the world of missions. In *People Vision*, you will hear the perspectives of Asian, African, Latin American, European, and North American leaders engaged in frontier missions. Starting with core articles on "Rethinking People Groups" republished from the *Evangelical Missions Quarterly* (Fall 2020), the book has expanded to a timely and vibrant global conversation about the unreached involving over sixty contributors.

People Vision surveys the foundational biblical and missiological concepts of the unreached peoples movement; details its impact through the painful but purposeful transitions of agencies, local churches, and field workers; presents regional models from around the world of polycentric pioneers and collaboration; explores critical issues and trends that hinder and/or accelerate gospel advance; and imagines changes and initiatives needed to bring about a future where every tribe, people, language, and nation surround the throne.

Filled with case studies, reports, reflections, and creative thinking from the West and Majority World, *People Vision* is essential reading for every pastor, church and mission leader, mission scholar, student, and serious Christian whose heart beats with a passion for Christ, compassion for the spiritual needs of neglected peoples, places, and nations, and a desire to see Christ glorified among all peoples.

Why This Book?

The passion for reaching "all peoples" has fluctuated over time, sometimes becoming more salient because of conferences, mobilization campaigns, influential leaders, and world events (e.g., turmoil in Islamic countries) or decreasing in importance due to shifting missional interests (e.g., social justice, development) and theological slippage (e.g., relativism, universalism).

Critics claim that "the most significant issue with defining *panta ta ethne* as ethnolinguistic people groups is simple: to do so adopts a modern anthropological definition over a biblical-theological one."[1]

---
1 Carlson and Clark, "The 3 Words." Cf. Lee and Park, "Beyond People Group Thinking," 212–25.

Other counterarguments seem to betray a fear that prioritizing pioneer mission comes "at the expense of" support for one's own or other fields in Europe or Latin America. While framed biblically, some criticisms appear to function as an indirect defense of the value of other ministries and priorities. Here is a recent criticism:

> With all the emphasis on people groups over the last fifty years, however, we've made a course correction at the expense of our mission. Specifically, the focus hasn't been on making disciples of all nations (evangelizing, baptizing, teaching, establishing churches, and training leaders) but instead on finishing the task (i.e., getting the gospel to every last people group). ... And the results? Material and personnel resources have been redirected out of areas no longer deemed strategic. Reached nations have been abandoned, along with their seminaries.[2]

Such opinions are understandable. Let's be clear: Nothing said in this book should be interpreted as devaluing any organization or ministry dedicated to training leaders, responding to crises and needs, and strengthening the global church!

However, the notion of neglect and sense of injustice seems both misinformed and misplaced. As R. W. Lewis points out in her chapter, "Fewer than 4 percent of global missionaries work among UPGs, where 60 percent of the world's nonbelievers live."

Despite the on-and-off visibility of the UPG movement, over 95 percent of the cross-cultural workers—and most of the resources—still go elsewhere. It would be more factually correct to say that, if anyone has been "abandoned" in terms of mission matériel and personnel, it is the least reached UPGs.

Thus, considering the narrative, language, and the plain meaning of key biblical texts, the rejecting of the "peoples" paradigm as unbiblical does not seem justified to many. A reasoned exploration of the biblical, missiological, and anthropological issues, and the passionate and innovative responses of the global church to the needs of the unreached, seems justified and needful.

People Vision: An Overview

Part 1 lays out the biblical and missiological foundations, the *impetus* for the "people group" concept. Chapters by Bartlotti and Hawthorne ground the "all peoples" vision in the grand story of Scripture and God's eternal purpose to have a "people from all peoples" for the sake of his name, "that my salvation may reach to the ends of the earth" (Isa 49:6).

Datema's analysis of Old and New Testament terms related to "nations" confirms that "*panta ta ethne* ... refers to all the particular, diverse, segmented parts of that whole world," a conception he describes as "universal particularism." Far from being a new or modern idea that people group proponents are reading into Scripture, "it is rather an ancient understanding flowing naturally from the Old to the New Testament. ... There is no getting 'beyond' people groups because people groups have always been and ever will be. They are a biblical category and are found literally from Genesis through Revelation."

Bartlotti and Datema collaborate to describe the historical development of the people group approach as a "perfect storm" created by "the coalescence of *ideas* relating people groups to world evangelization; the synergy of *influencers* (thought leaders) and *institutions*

---

[2] Carlson and Clark, "The 3 Words."

(research agencies); the simultaneous juxtaposition of the unreached (computer technology, data, and media); amplified by a vibrant international *interchange* (of ideas, people, data, and organizations at consultations and events); all of which together helped ignite and sustain a global movement."

Equally foundational is Alan Johnson's discussion of Ralph Winter's original insights that launched the frontier mission movement. Regrettably, in our "wrangling over notions of 'peoples,' 'groupness,' and 'reached/unreached,' and the various lists that attempt to document them," Johnson observes, "too often Winter's critical insights have been lost."

Johnson revives these essential concepts, arguing that "the notion of 'people groups' who need the gospel … cannot be understood in isolation. The people group concept is at the center of a *constellation of interrelated concepts* and understandings that serve to clarify these original insights." This constellation includes notions of "access," "peoples," "barriers," "culture," "breakthrough," "church," "movements," "focus," and "hope." Johnson maintains, "None of these concepts stand alone!" These "human constructs" are "useful for strategy development and are best understood only in relationship to Winter's clear-sighted focus" and "larger vision of gospel access."

Parts 2–4 trace the *impact* of people group thinking on (a) mission agencies, (b) regional partnerships and field workers, and (c) local churches, through a series of textured and instructive case studies. Following Parsons's sweeping overview "Run with the Vision," two major denominational agencies describe their "painful but purposeful" transition toward prioritizing unreached peoples. Garrison and Pratt relate the journey of the Southern Baptist International Mission Board (IMB), while participant observers Brogden, Johnson, and Bartlotti narrate the dramatic shift in the Assemblies of God World Mission (AGWM) leading to today's Live Dead movement of sacrificial, disciple-making teams among the unreached. There are important insights and lessons here for leaders and mission agencies, new and established.

Three substantial studies describe the impact of the unreached peoples movement on agencies and churches in very different regional contexts. Jungkook Han and Mark Kim tell the story of the frontier missions movement in Korea, notable because it was UPG focused from the beginning. Korea is now the third-largest missionary-sending country. After an overview of African cross-cultural missions, Mary Ho, Clara Litzsinger, and Zazá Lima interview Peter Oyugi, opening a window into African cross-cultural UPG missions, and the mind and soul of an important East African leader. Abraham Duran's well-documented study reveals key factors that led to the development of the Latin American frontier missions movement. He describes the convergent fault line between "integral" missions and "frontier" missions and the dynamic interactions between influential church and mission leaders that led to a kind of *holistic apostolic* approach to gospel advance that characterizes Latin American initiatives.

These and other narratives here point to ways the global church and its sending agencies have adopted, adapted, and adjusted the "unreached peoples" approach as a mission priority. Far from being "imposed" by the West, these accounts suggest a conception of frontier missions wholly "owned" by Majority World churches and agencies, shaped by biblical, cultural, and contextual dynamics, and reflecting unique responses to the challenges of least reached peoples near and far from them.

"Voices from the Field" (Part 3) is comprised of fifteen brief case studies submitted by field workers in Central Asia, South Asia, Middle East, Pakistan, Horn of Africa, Turkey, and Southeast Asia, and it is one of the most moving and sobering chapters in the book. It's one thing to list unreached people groups, caricature them in a "people profile," and romanticize and fantasize about ways to reach them. Ethnographic reality is often far different! How "people groups" behave, mix with others, and construct and contest identities in different contexts is extremely complex. This has implications for church planting and disciple making (as well as our missiological theorizing and training). The combination of barefoot ethnographic observation and honest personal narratives "from the coal face" will touch your heart.

Part 4 highlights innovative responses of churches that have chosen to *mobilize strategically* for engagement with unreached peoples. These eight case studies—from the US, Sweden, the Middle East, East Africa, and Brazil—challenge the notion of local churches as passive partners in support, sending, and strategy. Unique and creative in their individual approaches, these churches share a common DNA of being *purposeful, prayerful, strategic, collaborative, and focused* in their mission vision and efforts. Training, sending, support, and partnering are aligned to ensure that unreached and unengaged peoples have priority access to the gospel.

Part 5 celebrates *multiplication*, the emergence of polycentric and collaborative frontier mission sending in sectors of the global church. Three influential Latin American leaders, Cristian Castro, Zazá Lima, and Allan Matamoros, describe the joyful collaborative journey of COMIBAM, the Iberoamerican Missionary Partnership that is energizing churches across Latin America. John Becker zooms in on the Sahel, a troubled and desperately needy region of UPGs in Sub-Saharan Africa, while Mike Adegbile and Adeoluwa Olanrewaju report on how the energized Nigerian missions movement is accelerating missions to unreached peoples in Nigeria, North Africa, and beyond. Their prayer "Lord, stir us up!" must become our prayer!

In Asia, Martin Hall and Indian leader Sushil Tyagi provide complementary, personal descriptions of the yearslong journey of Indian mission leaders to reach UPGs in northern India. They are honest about the relational roadblocks, distrust, and competition that had to be overcome on the road to collaboration. Yahya Ilyas relates how robust collaborative efforts to map, research, and engage the scores of UPGs in a large Southeast Asian country have led to gospel breakthroughs. Simon Lunt describes a similar move toward collaboration at the local level in his case study of ministries among "Diaspora Peoples in Europe." Seemingly behind the scenes, but very much in the scene, of this polycentric sending are the growing networks of relationships among local, national, regional, and international partners described and celebrated by Ryan Emis and Allan Matamoros in their case study on "Networking Networks." Taken together, the spiritual energy and intentionality in these collaborative movements are humbling, electrifying, and worth emulating!

Astute readers will notice gaps in our coverage. Limitations of space constrain us from including case studies among Hindus, Buddhists, the Deaf, and Ethnic Religionists; models of multiethnic churches and urban disciple making; and critical issues like orality, Bible translation, church multiplication, and movements; and coverage of the burgeoning prayer movements that lie behind the surges described here. We hope that other Issue Networks and

Regional Networks in the Lausanne Movement will explore ways to collaborate in advancing the conversation about least reached peoples. Each of them provides a valuable "lens" by which to view, understand, and shape responses to UPGs.

Part 6 explores some of the issues and trends affecting progress toward reaching neglected peoples. One critical issue is what R. W. Lewis calls "fog in the pews," a discussion of factors behind "the fading vision for unreached peoples" in the church. Clara Litzsinger and Lisa Pak voice the perspectives of Next Gen followers of Jesus, particularly those in Western contexts, whose unique character, concerns, connections, and longings must be understood, nurtured, and welcomed into mission. In an interconnected, online world, regional readers may see generational attributes to compare and contrast or apply broadly. Clearly, both the fog in the church and the fog between generations must be addressed if together we are to pass the torch and "serve the purposes of God in this generation" (Acts 13:36).

Minh Ha Nguyen (who died in a tragic accident while this book was in process) examines how issues and megatrends like globalization, urbanization, and migration impact our thinking and approach to people groups. Similarly, urban missiologist Alan McMahan zooms in on the dynamics and complexities involved in disciple making and church planting in urban contexts. In cities, ethnicities are compressed, hybrid identities emerge, and urban dwellers move deftly among multiple affinity groups. What is the "glue" that holds people in social networks? How can we discern "pockets of receptivity"? Over 55 percent of the world's population lives in urban spaces (projected to increase to 68 percent by 2050). We need to envision innovative means for disciple-making among UPGs and affinity groups and reimagine new models of what it means to be and do "church" in the city. The megatrends explored by Nguyen and McMahan underline the need to forge better connectivity, communication, and strategic cooperation, between between personnel working with UPGs in the homelands and those working in pluralistic migrant and diaspora settings.

Dan Scribner, a leading figure behind Joshua Project, closes this section with an irenic and transparent look "under the hood" of the lists and databases associated with the unreached peoples movement. Alternatively respected and valued, spurned or ignored; representing heaven's catalog of earth's peoples or the detritus of colonial ethnic stereotypes—however you view them, use them, or abuse them, there is no question that "the making of lists" and tracking the "reachedness" of "all peoples" has been a distinctive mark of the frontier mission movement. They also have been a stimulus to its advance. With characteristic simplicity, clarity, and tech expertise, Scribner explains the genesis of, rationale for, and annoying but understandable differences between people group lists.

Part 7 of *People Vision* looks toward the future, "imagining fulfillment" of God's promise to "bless all nations" in Christ. Brad Gill, longtime chairperson of the International Society for Frontier Missiology and editor of its journal (*IJFM*), looks forward by looking back. Gill offers a "Retrospect on Mapping Peoples" through insights and anecdotes from his experience among the Berbers of North Africa. Seasoned by years of familiarity with cutting-edge scholarship, thought leaders, and the reflective praxis of field workers, Gill's eyes opened to the limitations of our outside categorizations, compared with the "indigenous maps" by which Berbers distinguished group identities. Nonetheless, our "useful abstractions" have both value and "strategic limitations." Gill concludes by reaffirming Donald McGavran's core principle, "Men like to turn to Christ without crossing ethnic and linguistic barriers"—an implicit notion at the heart of many contributions to this book.

Former international director of a major mission agency, Daniel Waheli, reflects on Scripture, his field experience among UPGs, and oversight of pioneer church-planting teams, to outline twelve principles of "pioneer apostleship" today. Mike Latsko, head of the Engage Network, reminds us that there are still hundreds of "unengaged" people groups (UUPGs), large and small, among Hindus, Muslims, Buddhists, and Tribal peoples who still have no identifiable witness among them. Unengaged peoples are not merely "unreached" (no indigenous church movements), but "we have yet to make an intentional, purposeful effort to 'engage' them with the message and messengers of the gospel." UUPGs "lack access to the gospel," and it will take intentionality to reach them.

Pat Brittenden and Parsa Zarin Ghalam's paper on "The Rise of Muslim-Background Churches" initially posed a conundrum for this editor: Where do I position this discussion of one of the most promising signs of gospel progress among Muslims in the last fourteen hundred years? In personal correspondence, Brittenden rightly argued that their paper is more than a case study, report on progress, example of collaboration, or contemporary issue or trend. What is happening is nothing less than a partial but stunning fulfillment of God's ancient promise to Abraham to bless "all peoples"! A new "wing" has opened in the "household of God"! Not only so, but as they "imagine fulfillment," Pat and Parsa envision Believers from a Muslim Background (BMBs, aka MBBs) as God's "eleventh-hour" workforce for the harvest!

Part 7 closes with my capstone chapter "Reimagining and Re-envisioning People Groups." In a wide-ranging discussion, I suggest that we move from a "baseline" understanding of peoples as fixed ethnolinguistic groups (the current default in UPG circles) to an updated understanding of ethnicity, ethnic groups, and ethnic identity in the light of more recent thinking and research. We need "a flexible, multilevel model of people groups," one that takes into account models of interaction between peoples, social bonding, social change, and affinities, especially in multiethnic, urban, and diaspora contexts.

This "reimagining" will require "ethnographic imagination," a shift from a static and reductionist view to a more dynamic view of peoples. Using a chemical metaphor, I suggest that "like elements and molecules, members of a people group bond with others in different ways, depending on the attractive forces and the context." Tracking peoples in an ecosystem that includes globalization, urbanization, migration, social media, and other forces will require new levels of collaboration, information sharing and analysis, and engagements based on multiple tiers of data that are "multi-perspectival, dynamic, and field based."

For UPG enthusiasts, we must admit that this reimagined vision of mission to least reached peoples may require a relative deconstruction of categories and theoretical approaches. This includes a recognition that to engage and penetrate UPGs, "church movements need not be monoethnic. Gospel freedom allows and celebrates, but does not demand, homogeneous ethnic churches." Some field workers and partners will celebrate the freedom to explore new models.

Finally, this book is an invitation to the church to reimagine itself in light of global and spiritual realities. These include the presence and persistent needs of human groupings without access to the gospel or to an indigenous church. God desires a people from all peoples. The chapters of this book reveal hopeful possibilities and responses.

My esteemed co-catalysts, Mary Ho and Zazá Lima, members of the Steering Team of the Lausanne Movement Least Reached Peoples Network, and the gifted contributors to this compendium invite you to do your part to help mobilize and leverage the full spiritual, cultural, and evangelistic potential of your church and agency to share the good news and make disciples among the remaining least reached peoples. *People Vision* is your invitation to this stimulating, thought-provoking, prayerful, and hope-filled journey together.

May the result of this conversation be that every people group will soon have a vibrant disciple-making church movement among it, and that as many individuals as possible within each group join in singing praises to the One who was slain yet lives. Worthy is the Lamb!

Rev. Leonard N. (Len) Bartlotti, PhD
Editor
May 2024

Bibliography

Carlson, Darren, and Elliot Clark. "The 3 Words That Changed Missions Strategy—and Why We Might Be Wrong." *The Gospel Coalition*, September 11, 2019. https://www.thegospelcoalition.org/article/misleading- words-missions-strategy-unreached-people-groups/.

Lee, Peter T., and James Sung-Hwan Park. "Beyond People Group Thinking: A Critical Reevaluation of Unreached People Groups." *Missiology: An International Review* 46, no. 3 (2018): 212–25.

Visualizing the Task
Progress, Imbalance, and Need
R. W. Lewis and Robby Butler

Reached people groups, in which the vast majority of believers live, currently receive 96 percent of international Christian workers. The other 4 percent go to unreached people groups (UPGs), defined as still needing outside assistance to reach their own people group. Some UPGs have indigenous believers whom outside workers can partner with, but other UPGs need pioneer workers to win the first households to Jesus. This subset of UPGs, called frontier people groups, contains one-fourth of humanity (2 billion people) yet receives just 1 percent of workers.

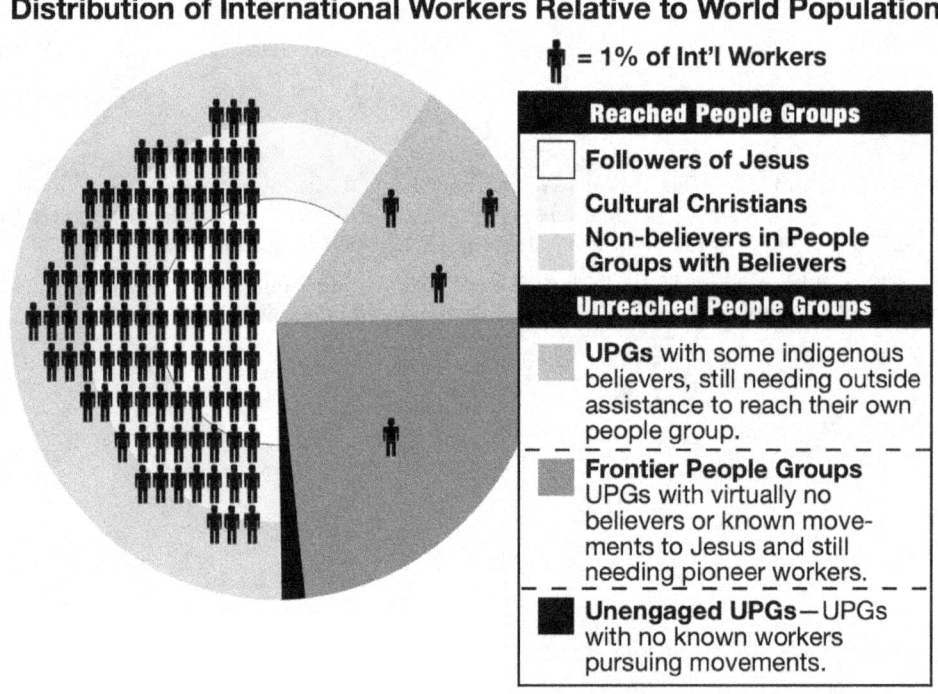

Figure 1: Distribution of International Workers.
From JoshuaProject.net/GreatProgress. Used with permission of RW Lewis.

International Workers Received: India vs. Africa & Latin America

India's population (1.4 billion) is nearly equal to Africa's (1.5 billion), and more than double the population of Latin America (0.67 billion). India has 40 percent of the remaining UPGs but receives far fewer global workers than these other continents.

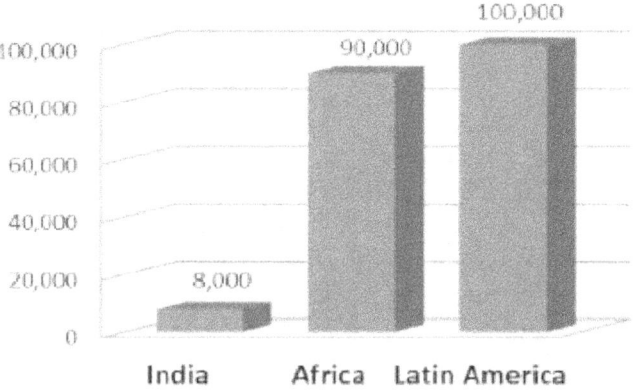

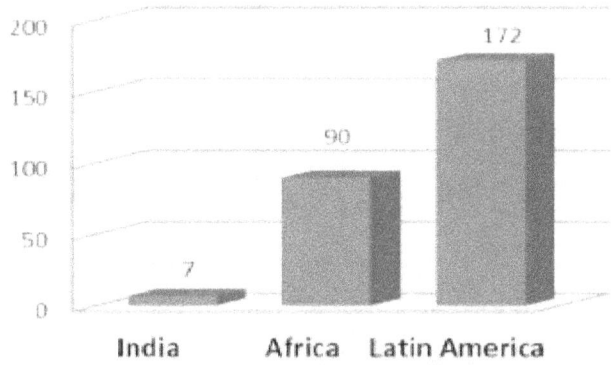

Figure 2: Sources: JoshuaProject.net, Global Status of Evangelical Christianity (IMBTSBC), *Atlas of Global Christianity* (Todd Johnson), Operation World (Jason Mandryk)

The 50 Unbelievable Years

Pursuing God's promise to bless all the families of the earth (Gal 3:8) has led to the greatest gospel advance in history! The first Lausanne Congress in 1974 showed that seventeen thousand people groups (60 percent of humanity) had no indigenous community of believers. By 2024, people groups with no indigenous believers had decreased to less than five thousand people groups (just 25 percent of humanity). These charts show the global population doubling in fifty years. At the same time, followers of Jesus increased 400 percent, and the percentage of global population in people groups with no Christward movements decreased from 60 percent to just 25 percent.

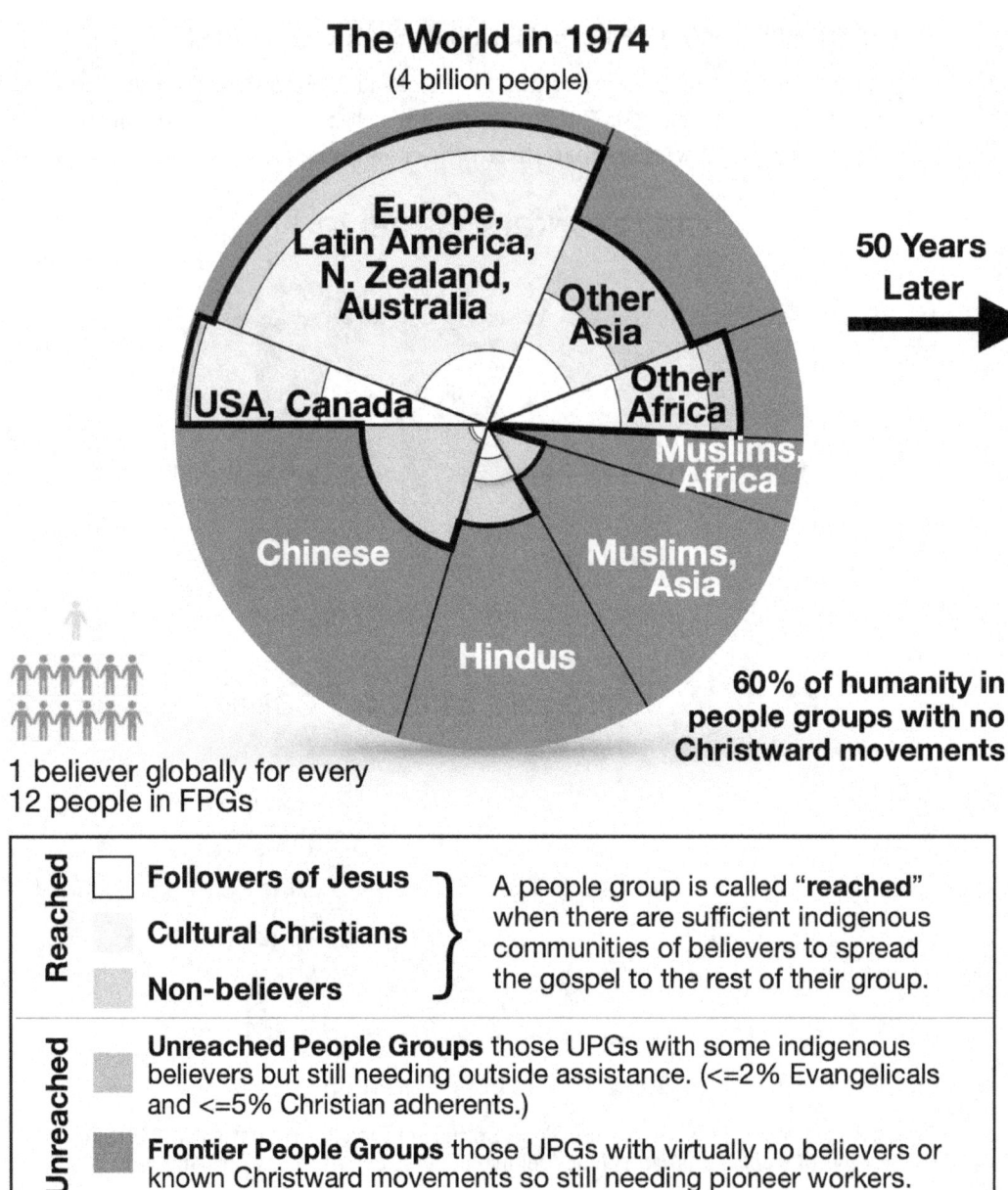

Figure 3: The World in 1974: 4 Billion People.
From JoshuaProject.net/GreatProgress. Used with permission of RW Lewis.

The Highest Priority

All unreached people groups (UPGs) need more outside help. The least reached of the UPGs are called frontier people groups (FPG) and have few or no believers and no known Christward movements. Pioneer workers are urgently needed to birth the first indigenous households of believers.

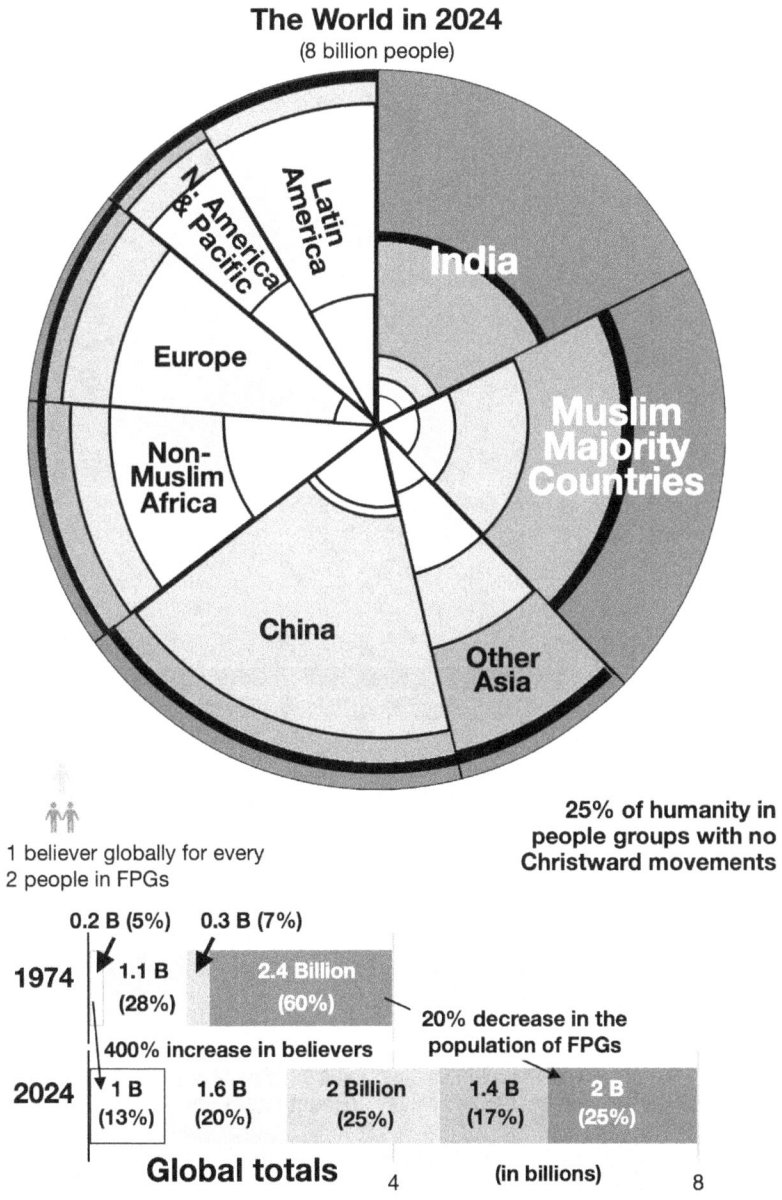

Figure 4: The World in 2024: 8 Billion People from JoshuaProject.net/GreatProgress. Used with permission of RW Lewis and Chris Maynard. Video versions in multiple languages available at JoshuaProject.net/frontier.

300 Largest Frontier People Groups by Religion and Language

They are shown below by their geographic location, religions, and top five languages by population.

- 97 percent of the total population in FPGs are Muslim (56 percent) or Hindu (41 percent).
- 1.4 billion people live in FPGs in South Asia—one billion of them in just India.
- 80 percent of the 2 billion people in FPGs live in the three hundred largest groups, each greater than 1 million. Because of their size and spiritual need, these largest groups are strategic and a top priority.

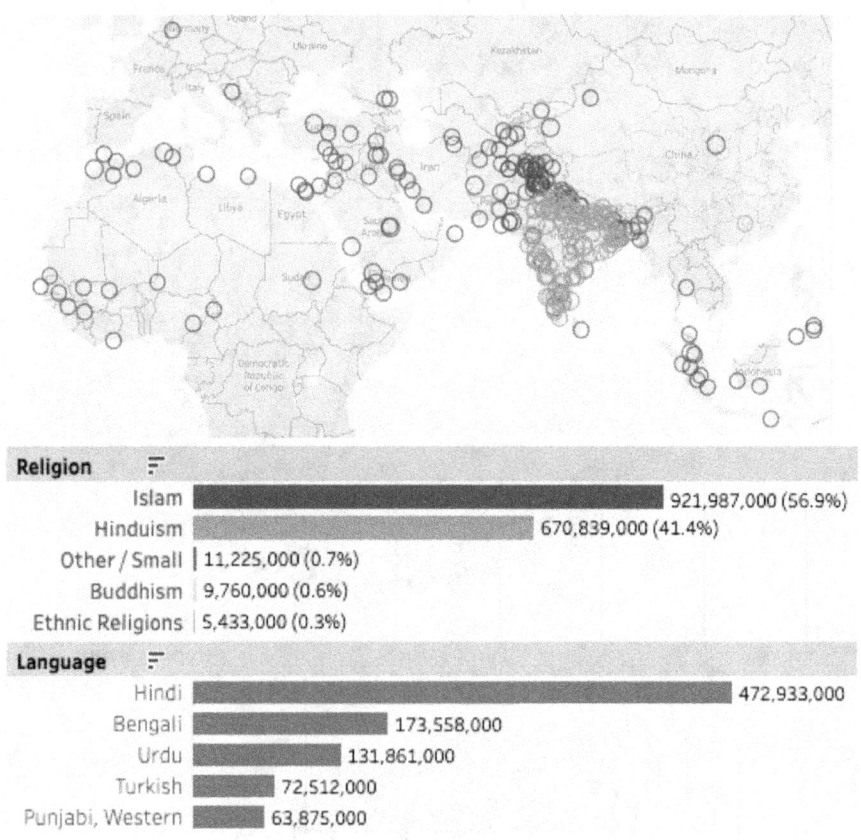

Figure 5: 300 Largest FPGs as of April 2024.
Used with permission by Joshua Project. JoshuaProject.net/frontier/interactive.

Part 1

Impetus for the Unreached Peoples Movement

Biblical and Missional Foundations

1
To the Ends of the Earth[1]

Leonard N. Bartlotti

Christ's power-packed commission in Acts 1:8 compels us to look beyond where we are now—our own church, community, nation, and "people like us"—to see a world full of other peoples, places, and nations that God loves. "The problem," according to international researcher Chris Maynard, "is that most Christians are where most Christians are." That is, "85 percent of Christians live in countries where more than 50 percent of people consider themselves Christians." So for 85 percent of Christians, "if they literally lift up their eyes, they will see Christians."[2]

> But you will receive power when the Holy Spirit comes on you; and you will be my witnesses in Jerusalem, and in all Judea and Samaria, and to the ends of the earth.

In light of our global mandate, how can we rediscover God as a missionary God, our identity as a missionary people, and "see" what most Christians don't see—a world of peoples without Christ? What is our Spirit-empowered part in God's plan? What do we need to understand to help us re-prioritize our mission to "all nations" and the "ends of the earth"?

One temptation is to treat Acts 1:8 as a "multiple choice" question: "Pick one: Jerusalem, Judea, Samaria, ends of the earth?" Another approach reduces the verse to a gradual, sequential witness strategy: "First Jerusalem, *then* we'll get to 'the uttermost parts.'" Missions becomes an appendix, an exotic add-on to which we make forays. "This approach often is used by Christians to avoid moving out of their comfort zones to spread the Gospel of Christ. They will say, 'I have to reach my family (my Jerusalem) before I can reach anyone else.'"[3] However, the verse says "and," not "then" (i.e., all contexts in no particular order).

More commonly, we take a series of hermeneutical leaps: Jerusalem represents "my people, my locality"; Judea is "our region"; Samaria is "the despised other"; and the "ends of the earth" or "uttermost parts" equals global mission. The bothersome fact, however, is that the disciples were from Galilee, not Jerusalem! "Jerusalem" was not their home, neighborhood, or people. I admit, the metaphors are a useful preaching device (I've done it!) but are not supported exegetically. Jesus was speaking of literal historical places and cultural spheres; by Acts 10, the Spirit is advancing the word and stirring the church into "ends of the earth" mode, that is, the Gentile world. That's where we are now!

One antidote for our nearsightedness is to keep the end in view. God begins his redemptive plan with the end in mind. "I make known the end from the beginning, from ancient times, what is still to come. I say: 'My purpose will stand, and I will do all that I please'" (Isa 46:10). In this sense, "the ends of the earth" should arguably be the first topic, not the last, on the agenda of a missions gathering.

---

[1] Originally published for Lausanne Movement (www.lausanne.org). Used with permission. Unless otherwise noted, all Scripture quotations in this chapter are from the NIV.
[2] Maynard, "Shining a Light."
[3] S, Justin. "One Passage, Two Views."

Our strategies should "work backwards" from the end goal. What has God revealed about his endgame plan for the nations? To begin this Missions 101 exploration, let's "work backwards" in Acts 1:8 and consider what the Bible says about God's plan for peoples and nations at "the ends of the earth," then close with a few brief observations about the unfinished task today.

The "Hinge" Verse of the Bible

Isaiah 49:6 has been called the "hinge verse of the Bible." God the Father and the Servant Son discuss the weightiness and ultimate intention of Messiah's coming mission. Here we listen in on their throne room board meeting:

> It is too small a thing for you to be my servant
>   to restore the tribes of Jacob
>   and bring back those of Israel I have kept.
> I will also make you a light for the Gentiles,
>   that my salvation may reach to the ends of the earth.

"It is too small a thing."

Other English translations say: "It is too light a thing" (ESV, ASV); "it is a light thing" (KJV); and "it is not enough for you to be" (CSB) or "to be merely" (CEV) a redeemer of Israel alone. However great God's love for his people, the sense of the Hebrew evokes a stark contrast: It is so "small" and "light" as to be "trivial" (LEB)," or "too trifling a thing" (TLV) in comparison with God's larger master plan of salvation!

Yahweh reveals that "the mission is not to Israel only, but to all the nations of the world. Redeeming Israel alone was too easy; Yahweh wishes for a greater display of His sovereignty."[4] That greater display is revealed in the next phrases.

"A light to the nations."

Israel's corporate mission as a light to the nations (Isa 42:1–9) is "reassigned to the Servant individually, who fulfills Israel's obligations to Yahweh in order to restore their relationship" and fulfill God's mandate.[5]

"My salvation to the ends of the earth."

Through the Servant (cf. Isa 53), "the entire world—not just Israel—will have access to Yahweh's salvation. ... Nations would one day be included in the people of God."[6] Foreigners would be welcome to offer joyous worship, acceptable sacrifices, and prayer inside the temple as a part of God's holy people, "for my house will be called a house of prayer for all nations" (Isa 56:7).[7]

---

4 Barry, et al., "Isaiah 49:6."

5 Barry, et al.

6 Barry, et al.; cf. Isa 2:2–4; 56:3–8.

7 Note that, in context, the house of prayer "for all nations" does not refer to a place of intercession for those outside the temple (eunuchs, foreigners) but to prayers offered inside by people previously excluded but now welcomed by God; this house is "for all nations" to offer joyful, acceptable worship.

The Ends of the Earth

The phrase "ends of the earth" is used forty-six times in the Bible. Sometimes the phrase speaks of approaching judgment on God's people, as when God "stirs up from the ends of the earth" an army from Babylon or "from the north" (Jer 6:22; 50:41). Other times it forecasts foreboding, all-inclusive judgment on sinful humanity:

> The tumult will resound to the ends of the earth, for the LORD will bring charges against the nations; he will bring judgment on all mankind and put the wicked to the sword. … This is what the LORD Almighty says: "Look! Disaster is spreading from nation to nation (*goy*); a mighty storm is rising from the ends of the earth." (Jer 25:31–32)

Conversely, the prophets foresee a great salvific reversal! Gentile nations will one day "come from the ends of the earth and say, 'Our ancestors possessed nothing but false gods, worthless idols that did them no good.' … Therefore I will teach them—this time I will teach them my power and might. Then they will know that my name is the LORD" (Jer 16:19–21).

Metaphorically, "ends of the earth" means "as far as one can go." All the world. All humanity, and all compartments of humanity. Every race, nationality, ethnic and language group. All peoples everywhere.

"As far as one can go"—that's something to think about! It is likely far, far away from our home zone or comfort zone, and Christianized contexts where the church is domestic, and the gospel (often) domesticated by one cultural group or setting. "The ends of the earth" challenges us to consider: "How far" are we willing to go—geographically, culturally, socially, in prayer, service, suffering, and sacrifice—to ensure that all peoples everywhere have a witness to the gospel?

Note, too, the Hebrew parallelism in the above verses: the near equation of "nations" (Hebrew, *goyim*) and "ends of the earth." The "uttermost part" (KJV) or "ends of the earth" are the dwelling places of Gentile "nations," non-Jewish peoples (*goyim*). "The ends of the earth" encompasses all peoples in all places across time and space. No person, in any ethnolinguistic or social grouping, anywhere, escapes God's scrutiny. This is critical for understanding the importance of the "people group" paradigm and prioritizing "unreached" or "least reached peoples"—those sociocultural, linguistic, or ethnic groups with no viable, indigenous, church-planting and disciple-making movement among them.

Dave Datema explains that in the Old Testament, "*goy* can be applied to human groupings defined by a diversity of affinities/boundaries (ancestry, language, land, government) and became synonymous with non-Israelite Gentiles. In the Septuagint, *goy* is usually translated as … *ethnos*," the Greek term Jesus used in Matthew 28:19, "disciple *panta ta ethne*."[8] These ethne or nations, universally, collectively (non-Jewish peoples), and individually (human groupings or people groups) are the focus of our commission and God's redemptive plan.

"All the nations" was understood by both Matthew and his readers as a reference to both universality (everyone everywhere) and particularity (in all their diversity), meaning that it was impossible for them to conceive of the world as a collective whole without simultaneously seeing it in its many and diverse constituent parts. *Panta ta ethne* is both/and not either/or. It means the inclusion of all the nations/Gentiles in all of their

---

8 Datema, "*Panta ta Ethne*."

God-given diversity. *Ethne* does include in its semantic range the idea of various human groupings and boundaries, including ethnicity. It is not a new or modern idea that people group proponents are reading into Scripture. It is rather an ancient understanding flowing naturally from the Old to the New Testament.[9]

Swing Back: The Original Great Commission

The Isaiah 49:6 "hinge verse" swings back to the original "Great Commission" and "all peoples" mandate of Genesis 12:1–3 (long before Matthew 28:18–20):

> The LORD had said to Abram, "Go from your country, your people and your father's household to the land I will show you.
>
> "I will make you into a great nation,
> and I will bless you;
>
> I will make your name great,
> and you will be a blessing.
>
> I will bless those who bless you,
> and whoever curses you I will curse;
>
> and all peoples on earth
> will be blessed through you."

The late John R. W. Stott, a founding leader of the Lausanne Movement, called these verses, "The most unifying verses in the Bible; the whole of God's purpose is encapsulated here."[10] "The Living God is a Missionary God," he declared, not a petty tribal deity, but the Creator of the universe, of earth, and all humankind. In Genesis 12, God sets in motion a plan to defeat the powers of darkness (cf. Gen 3:15) and redeem a people for himself from among the fallen and scattered peoples of the world (Gen 3–11). Stott says, "God chose one man and his family in order, through them, to bless all the families of the earth."[11] Through one chosen people, blessing was to flow to "all peoples on earth," all nations, all places.

This unfolding story forms the backbone of Scripture from Genesis to Revelation, what Steve Hawthorne calls "the story of His glory": "God reveals His glory *to* all nations that He might receive glory *from* all nations."[12] God's purpose and desire, for the praise of his glory, is to have a "people from all peoples," a "family from all the families of the nations." "The ends of the earth" have been in view from the very beginning!

Missionary God, Missionary People

The people of God are a missionary people, "set apart from the peoples" and their idolatry, immorality, and customs (Lev 20:26; Exod 19:6). Israel was "consecrated" to God, a "chosen people, a royal priesthood, a holy nation"—an identity applied to the church in 1 Peter 2:9–10. This "priestly people" has a "priestly duty" to mediate blessing to the nations (cf. Rom 15:18).

---

9 Datema, "Universal Particularism of *Panta ta Ethne*," 9.
10 Stott, "Living God Is a Missionary God," 3.
11 Stott, 4.
12 Hawthorne, "Story of His Glory."

God displays his holiness, power, and majesty through the obedient love and loving obedience of his covenant people. This challenges us to ensure that our lives, ministries, relationships, and witness display God's holiness, glory, and power.

The Exodus revealed God's power and righteousness "in the sight of the nations" (Ps 98:2 ESV). Israel's deliverance from Egypt was not done in a corner! The story was trending on "social media" in the ancient Near East—all nations "trembled in anguish" (Deut 2:25)! God told Pharoah, "I have raised you up for this very purpose, that I might show you my power and that my name might be proclaimed in all the earth" (Exod 9:16).

In Israel's temple, Yahweh's name, presence, and power were a missional attraction for foreign peoples and nations. Solomon prayed,

> As for the foreigner who does not belong to your people Israel but has come from a distant land because of your name —for they will hear of your great name and your mighty hand and your outstretched arm—when they come and pray toward this temple, then hear from heaven, your dwelling place. Do whatever the foreigner asks of you, so that all the peoples of the earth may know your name and fear you, as do your own people Israel. (1 Kgs 8:41–43)

The heart, hopes, and prayers of every leader should imitate Solomon's world-sized faith and intentionality: "So that all the peoples of the earth may know you!"

Through the prophets, God reminded the people of their identity as "witnesses" to his lordship. When called to the stand in a court of law, a witness cannot remain silent! A witness testifies about what he/she knows, has seen, or has heard. God calls his people to a witness that is bold, clear, unashamed, God-centered, and global: 'I have revealed and saved and proclaimed—I, and not some foreign god among you. You are my witnesses,' declares the LORD, 'that I am God' (Isa 43:12; cf. 43:10; 44:8).

Missions is a melody. We go to the nations with songs in our hearts! It's easy to worship in a sanctuary, hall, or stadium filled with passionate believers and a spirited band. But in the hard places, we may cry, "How can we sing the songs of the LORD while in a foreign land?" (Ps 137:4). But even there, in the dark hours and lonely places, God is with us. "About midnight Paul and Silas were praying and singing hymns to God, and the other prisoners were listening to them" (Acts 16:25). How can we develop in our own souls and in Next Gen "goers" and "senders," the kind of perseverance, resilience, and dependence on the Spirit's power needed to "sing a new song to the Lord" in a strange land?

Swing Forward: The Coming Savior and the Ends of the Earth

Just as the Isaiah 49:6 "hinge" swings back to Genesis 12 and God's unfolding mission in the Old Testament, it swings forward to the coming of the Messiah. Isaiah 49:6 connects the end with the beginning by revealing the means by which God's purposes will be fulfilled, as well as the redemptive end, namely, "salvation to the ends of the earth."

What is the means? God sends his chosen Servant, his only Son: "I will make you a light for the nations." This was the Christ's self-understanding: "The Spirit of the LORD is on me, because he has anointed me to proclaim good news to the poor" (Luke 4:18; cf. Isa 61:1–2). He came not only as Israel's Messiah, but as the Lamb of God, the Savior of the world:

"For even the Son of Man did not come to be served, but to serve, and to give his life as a ransom for many" (Mark 10:45; Matt 20:28). "He is the atoning sacrifice for our sins, and not only for ours but also for the sins of the whole world" (1 John 2:2). Christ's sacrifice is not only sufficient; it is effective: "He shall see the fruit of the travail of his soul and be satisfied; by his knowledge shall the righteous one, my servant, make many to be accounted righteous; and he shall bear their iniquities" (Isa 53:11 RSV).

The Great Commission in Matthew 28:18–20, then, is neither a new thought nor the afterthought of an exiting Messiah! It is an affirmation, reiteration, and authority-packed mandate to carry forward and fulfill God's original "ends of the earth" purpose. "Make disciples of all nations (*panta ta ethne*), baptizing them in the name of the Father and of the Son and of the Holy Spirit, and teaching them to obey everything I have commanded you."

The difference now is that the cross and resurrection guarantee the fulfillment of God's redemptive plan by defeating sin, death, and the powers of darkness over the nations! "I will build my church (*ecclesia*) and the gates of hell will not prevail against it" (Matt 16:18 ESV). "With your blood you purchased for God persons from every tribe and language and people and nation" (Rev 5:9).

Empowered Witness

The book of Acts recounts the inexorable progress of the word of God through a people empowered and sent by the Holy Spirit. "The word of God spread; and the number of the disciples multiplied" (6:7 KJV). "The word of God increased and multiplied" (12:24. ESV). "So the word of the Lord continued to increase and prevail mightily" (19:20. ESV). Religious opposition, imperial decrees, repression, persecution, tribulation, or death—nothing can stop the gospel "because it is the power of God that brings salvation to everyone who believes: first to the Jew, then to the Gentile" (Rom 1:16). As Gamaliel advised the Sanhedrin, "I advise you: Leave these men alone! Let them go! For if their purpose or activity is of human origin, it will fail. But if it is from God, you will not be able to stop these men; you will only find yourselves fighting against God" (Acts 5:38–39). Driven by the Spirit, the gospel has today advanced such that in every country on earth, there are believers in Christ and communities of faith! But there's still work to be done.

In Acts 1:8, the risen Christ promises the "power" to be "my witnesses." This power compels us to get out of our home zone and comfort zone, and cross every geographical, cultural, linguistic, and social barrier to "the ends of the earth." Without the abiding power of the Holy Spirit, our efforts are fleshly and ineffective: "Apart from me you can do nothing" (John 15:5). "'Not by might nor by power, but by my Spirit,' says the LORD Almighty" (Zech 4:6). "Compelled by the Spirit I am going to Jerusalem, not knowing what will happen to me there" (Acts 20:22). Compelled, going, not knowing—the order of the verbs is important! This is the faith and Spirit-filled journey of believers sent to be witnesses even "to the ends of the earth."

Today, especially in cities, the nations are not "far off," but near, at our doorstep! From Dubai, Singapore, and Sao Paulo, to New York, London, Brussels, and Marseille, the church must now impart the basic knowledge, understandings, and relational skills needed for cross-cultural witness as an essential component of discipleship. Ministry among unreached peoples includes diaspora and immigrant ministry among nations that are now our neighbors, many of whom maintain transnational connections.

"Sending," however, is still needed. Some data suggests that many of the largest "frontier people groups" are only minimally represented in diaspora and migrating populations. Pioneer workers are still needed in the homelands. This is not a colonial or Western activity, a form of cultural imperialism, or ideological hegemony. Today's mission is polycentric: "from every nation to every nation." Sending begins with the triune God. We need cross-cultural disciple makers "where Christ [is] not known" (Rom 15:20–21). May God give us eyes to see those "hidden peoples" who are not yet incorporated, or not "incorporable," in existing churches and fellowships (due to barriers of understanding or acceptance).

Our calling to transformation does not negate our calling to world evangelization. We are called and privileged to declare—to testify, speak up, tell the story, proclaim—the good news of salvation in Christ! Transformation without proclamation is abdication. The synergy of word and Spirit is a theme throughout Scripture. The Spirit inspires, compels, and brings forth anointed speech. As "ambassadors for Christ," we have ambassadorial authority and a duty to announce, implore, and appeal in wise, winsome, and heartfelt ways, in the heart languages of all peoples, the "message of reconciliation": "Be reconciled to God" (2 Cor 5:19–20). "How beautiful are the feet of those who bring good news!" (Rom 10:15).

Breathtaking Vision

The least reached peoples and the "ends of the earth" take us to the heart of the biblical narrative. As we embrace God's desire for "a people from all peoples," we see new global realities and the persistent needs of the unevangelized.[13]

The final vision is breathtaking: "Then I saw a Lamb, looking as if it had been slain, standing at the center of the throne" (Rev 5:6). The incense prayers of God's people and a new song fill the atmosphere:

> "You are worthy to take the scroll
>   and to open its seals,
> because you were slain,
>   and with your blood you purchased for God
>   persons from every tribe and language and people and nation." (Rev 5:9)

In this scene, the people of God are one, but many—multinational, multiethnic, multilingual. United in faith and worship, with distinctions both visible and audible! Every ethne has its place in the heavenly stadium.

New Testament scholar Gordon Fee outlines this panorama of radiant worship: the "new song" acclaims the *means* of his redeeming act ("with your blood"), the *effect* of that sacrifice ("you purchased for God"), the *breadth* of redemption ("members of every tribe and language and people and nation"), its *goal* ("made ... to be a kingdom and priests to serve our God ... they will reign on the earth"), and God-centered, God-ordained *climax*, "To him who sits on the throne and to the Lamb be praise and honor and glory and power, for ever and ever!"[14]

---

13 Bartlotti, "Reimaging and Re-envisioning," 46–49.
14 Fee, *Revelation*, 88.

We are invited to respond both with *wonder* and adoration and with faithful cruciform *witness* (Rev 6:9–11; 19:10) to "the word of God and the testimony of Jesus" (1:2; 20:4).

- *The Dimensions of the Task.* Forty percent of humanity—3.4 billion people—in 7,300 unreached people groups (UPG) (less than 2 percent evangelicals and 5 percent professing Christians). Two billion of these in "frontier people groups" with virtually no Christians of any kind and no known gospel movements. Sixteen hundred "unengaged UPGs" with no known initiatives to reach them. Without access to the gospel and church movements. Pioneer cross-cultural workers needed.[15] "This is the land that remains" (Josh 13:2).

- *The Complexity of the Task.* Thirty-five hundred Muslim unreached people groups (UPG), 2,203 Hindu UPG, 511 Buddhist UPG, and 925 Tribal UPG (ethnic religionists). Cultural, social, religious, political, prejudice, and linguistic barriers. Urbanization, globalization, migration, affinity groups, multiple identities, deaf, global youth culture, persecution.

- *The Do-ability of the Task.* Global church—1 billion Great Commission Christians (living faith), 13 percent of humanity. Progress through movements in China, among Buddhists in Asia, tribal groups in Oceania and Latin America, some movements among Muslims and Hindus in Southeast Asia. Growing partnerships between agencies, collaboration between Western and Majority World, regional and international networks. Media and diaspora ministries. Vibrant prayer movements. "Ask of me and I will make the nations your inheritance, the ends of the earth your possession" (Ps 2:8 ESV). "All authority has been given to me in heaven and on earth" (Matt 28:18 CSB). "You will receive power when the Holy Spirit comes upon you, and you will be my witnesses" (Acts 1:8).

- *The Priority of the Task.* Ninety-nine percent of international workers serve among the three-quarters of the world's population where 99.99 percent of all followers of Jesus live. One percent of all international workers serve among the one-quarter of the world with 2 billion people, 5,000 people groups, and 0.01 percent Christians. Jesus left the ninety-nine to find one lost sheep. "It has always been my ambition to preach the gospel where Christ was not known, so that I would not be building on someone else's foundation. Rather, as it is written: 'Those who were not told about him will see, and those who have not heard will understand'" (Rom 15:20–21). "Our hope is that … we can preach the gospel in the regions beyond you" (2 Cor 10:15–16).

- *The Urgency of the Task.* "'Everyone who calls on the name of the Lord will be saved.' How, then, can they call on the one they have not believed in? And how can they believe in the one of whom they have not heard? And how can they hear without someone preaching to them? And how can anyone preach unless they are sent? As it is written: 'How beautiful are the feet of those who bring good news!'" (Rom 10:13–15). "Faith comes from hearing the message, and the message is heard through the word about Christ" (10:17). "And this gospel of the kingdom will be preached in the whole world as a testimony to all nations (ethne), and then the end will come" (Matt 24:14).

---

15 Figures from https://joshuaproject.net, Dan Scribner, R. W. Lewis, and Chris Maynard. For a helpful theology of data and the importance of data in missions, see Maynard, "Honouring Data in Missions."

- *The Motivations for the Task*[16]
    - Glory—Love of God and passion for his glory (John 17:4; 1 Pet 2:9; Rev 4:11; 5:12).
    - Obedience—The mandate to proclaim the gospel of Christ and make disciples (Matt 28:18–20; Acts 1:8).
    - Love—Desire for the salvation and good of others (Luke 15:11–31; Rom 9:1–3; 2 Cor 5:14–15).
    - Need—Compassion for the spiritual and physical needs of the lost (Matt 9:35–38; 10:1; 14:13–31; Luke 19:41).
    - Reward—God's pleasure and approval (1 Cor 3:11–15; 2 Cor 5:10–11; 1 Thess 2:19).
    - Hope—Vision and passion for the fulfillment of God's purposes (John 4:34; 17:4; Rev 5:9; 7:9).

Bibliography

Barry, J. D., D. Magnum, D. R. Brown, M. S. Heiser, M. Custis, E. Ritzema, M. M. Whitehead, M. R. Grigoni, and D. Bomar. "Isaiah 49:6." In *Faithlife Study Bible*. Bellingham, WA: Lexham, 2012. https://app.logos.com/books/LLS%3AFSB/references/bible.23.49.6.

Bartlotti, Leonard N. "Reimaging and Re-envisioning People Groups." *Evangelical Missions Quarterly*, 56, no. 4 (2020): 46–49.

Datema, David Earl. "*Panta ta Ethne*: All Peoples and Nations." In *People Vision*, edited by Leonard N. Bartlotti. Littleton, CO: William Carey Publishing, 2024.

Datema, David Earl. "The Universal Particularism of *Panta ta Ethne*: A Biblical Case for the Continued Viability of the People Group Concept in Mission." *Missiology: An International Review* 50, no. 2 (2021): 9.

Fee, G. D. *Revelation: A New Covenant Commentary*. Eugene, OR: Cascade Books, 2011.

Hawthorne, Steve. "The Story of His Glory." In *Perspectives on the World Christian Movement*. Pasadena, CA: William Carey Publishing, 2009.

Maynard, Chris. "Honouring Data in Missions." WEA Missions Commission, August 26, 2023. https://weamc.global/archive/reimagining-data.pdf.

Maynard, Chris. "Shining a Light into a Dark Corner: Looking at Mission Information Work." Global CMIS, 2018. https://www.globalcmiw.org/node/52.

Packer, J. I. *Evangelism and the Sovereignty of God*. Downers Grove, IL: IVP Books, 2012.

S., Justin. "One Passage, Two Views." *Missions in the Bible: Your Jerusalem, Judea, and Samaria* (blog). The Traveling Team. N.d. https://www.thetravelingteam.org/articles/your-jerusalem-judea-and-samaria.

Stott, John. "The Living God Is a Missionary God." In *Perspectives on the World Christian Movement*. Pasadena, CA: William Carey Publishing, 2009.

---

16 See, for example, Packer, *Evangelism and the Sovereignty of God*, 45ff.

2
A Biblical Understanding of People Groups

Steven C. Hawthorne

What does the Bible say about people groups in God's mission? Far from being a recent construct of social sciences, the Bible speaks of the peoples, languages, and lineages of humanity, with all their diverse cultures, as God's creation and as greatly valued covenant partners.

The initial burst of interest in people groups decades ago was all about breaking down the task of world evangelization into doable endeavors. While there are ample biblical grounds for clear, strategic gospel communication in every cultural setting, in the biblical account peoples are much more than mere objects of our messaging. Instead of focusing on our outreach to humanity, the Bible emphasizes the outcome of God being loved by every people. The Bible speaks of each of the world's peoples as having vast worth, and even glory, as greatly desired, much-beloved worshipers.

God Creates All Peoples

Paul declares that God had "made … every nation (*ethne*) of humankind to live on all the face of the earth, having determined their appointed times and the boundaries of their habitation" (Acts 17:26).[1] How did this story of nation making unfold?

God's promise to Abram in Genesis 12:1–3 is often cited as the beginning of mission to humanity as families or peoples. Before Abram, however, we find the story of Babel (Gen 11:1–9). God is often presented in the story of Babel as judging and punishing humanity by scrambling their one language into many. But in fact, there is no explicit mention of sin or judgment in the Babel account. God simply intervened, interrupting the construction of the one-culture project before it went too far: "This is what they began to do, and now nothing which they purpose to do will be impossible for them" (v. 6).

Instead of inflicting punishment, the myriad of languages can be seen as God's way of helping and accelerating humankind to "be fruitful and multiply, and fill the earth" (1:28; 9:1). The fullness of humanity on earth is more than mere geographic habitation. God created humanity in his image, which means, in part, that humanity was endowed with creative ability to form diverse cultures. Instead of being a curse, different languages gave each of the peoples capacity to cultivate distinctive intergenerational communities, flourishing with the glories and burdens of diverse cultures.

The Babel account describes the beginning of humankind being scattered "abroad over the face of the whole earth" (11:9). In the previous chapter, the so-called "Table of Nations" describes the dispersion in genealogical format, which means that it all unfolded over many generations. Four specific factors of ethnic formation are repeated four times (10:5, 20, 31,

---

[1] All Scripture translations are the author's own, unless otherwise cited.

32): according to their clans (*mishpachah*), according to their languages (*lishan*), by their lands (*eretz*), and according to their nations (*goy*).

As people scattered "over the face of the whole earth" (11:9), their languages and family groupings were constantly changing along with their locations. Ethnolinguistic factors were prominent, but the cultures and peoples were not fixed and unmixed realities. Even though we see specific names in the Genesis 10 "Table of Nations" genealogy, humanity then, as now, was not separated into discrete, unchanging entities. The peoples were morphing and blending as they were moving throughout the earth.

One Family to Bless Every Family

In the midst of this massive diasporic array of tribes, languages, and peoples, we meet Abram. He was told to depart "from your relatives and from your father's house" (12:1). Abram may be the only one in the Bible who was clearly called to separate from his family in order to obey God.

It must have been bewildering for him to hear God's promise that in him "all the families (mishpachah) of the earth will be blessed" (12:3). A common custom of that day was that a father's blessing, or inheritance, would reveal the extent of his own family. How was it possible that Abram, one man, would be able to bless many families? Later, God would change Abram's name to Abraham, "for I will make you the father of a multitude of nations" (17:5).

This promise of becoming God's blessing to all peoples was repeated twice more to Abraham, but with a key difference. Instead of all nations being blessed by one person (12:3), the nations would be blessed by Abraham's descendants (18:18–19; 22:18). God repeated this same forward-looking promise directly to Isaac, and yet again to Jacob, that all the peoples of earth would be blessed by their descendants (26:4; 28:14). Still, it was a mystery how one family would bring about blessing to all.

One People, Many Tribes

Near the end of his life Jacob recounted God's promise, "I will make you a company of peoples" (*amim*, 48:4), before bestowing a distinctive blessing on his twelve sons and the tribe that descended from them—"every one with the blessing appropriate to him" (49:28). Before leaving Egypt, Israel was one people consisting of multiple tribes.

At Sinai, God established a covenant with the twelve tribes, addressing them as "the house of Jacob ... the sons of Israel" (Exod 19:3). Keeping the covenant would bring forth God's purpose—to be served, loved, and worshiped by a special, or holy, people among all the peoples of earth. The language is extravagant, describing the people as a "special treasure" to God: "If you will ... keep my covenant, then you shall be my own special treasure among all the peoples (*amim*), for all the earth is mine; and you shall be to me a kingdom of priests and a holy nation (*goy*)" (19:5–6).

God's purpose is relational, seen in the easily overlooked words "to me." The phrase "kingdom of priests" was a poetic way of describing their essential identity as worshipers. The primary task of biblical priests was to serve God, standing before him and helping God's people give themselves to him by their offerings and praise. To coin a word, the people were to bring a "God-ward" service, pleasing God as they came near in worship.

The Twelve Tribes and the All Peoples Throng

The God-ward purpose of the Sinai covenant shines in John's opening words of Revelation: Christ has "made us to be a kingdom, priests to his God and Father" (Rev 1:5–6). This kingdom of priestly worshipers is heard again in the "new song," exalting the slain Lamb: "Worthy are You ... for You were slain, and purchased for God with Your blood people from every tribe and tongue and people and nation. You have made them to be a kingdom and priests to our God; and they will reign upon the earth" (5:9–10).

As the new song extols the worthiness of the Lamb, John also hears of the worth of the diverse peoples. At the tremendous cost of the blood of the Lamb, men, women, and children from every tribe (*phulē*), language (*glōssa*), people (*laos*), and nation (*ethnos*) have been purchased "for God" in order to become priests, or worship-servants, "to our God" (5:9–10).

John continued to hear, not a song, but a numbering of "those who were sealed from every tribe of the sons of Israel" (7:4). The enumeration of the twelve tribes specifically mentioned the twelve tribal names (7:5–8). Then John saw what he had only heard. He must have been stunned by the sight of a vast expanse of people. "After these things I looked, and behold, a great multitude which no one could count, from every nation (*ethnos*), tribe (*phulē*), people (*laos*), and language (*glōssa*), standing before the throne and before the Lamb" (7:9).

It was an immense, uncountable multitude, but John recognized that there were some from every ethnicity—every which way that humanity continues life together in any abiding way. Every. All. The fullness of humanity, ever-enduring as diverse, and yet united in the Lamb.

Israel's many tribes had been formed together as one worshiping people, foreshadowing this great multitude comprised of persons of every people glorifying God in full-hearted worship.

We have jumped from the beginnings in Genesis to the end of days. But of course, there is more to the story of how God called to himself a people from all peoples, tribes, and nations.

Prophetic Expectations: The Pilgrimage of Nations

Many songs and prophecies of Israel lifted an expectation that many, or even all of earth's peoples, would come to his house—the temple—to worship him. More than a dozen texts describe the nations streaming toward the mountain, the city, or the temple of the Lord to worship and learn to walk in his ways. This eschatological movement of the peoples in worship has been described as "the pilgrimage of the nations."[2]

The psalter resounds with this hope: "All nations (*goyim*) whom You have made shall come and worship before You, O LORD, and they shall glorify Your name" (Ps 86:9).

Zechariah describes many peoples not just coming to the temple but becoming part of God's people. "Many nations (*goyim*) will join themselves to the LORD in that day and will become my people (*am*). Then I will dwell in your midst" (Zech 2:11). Note that the foreign peoples will not be merely mingling in public gatherings; they will actually somehow "join themselves to the Lord."

---

[2] The promised coming of many peoples to worship the God of Israel was called "the pilgrimage of the nations" by Joachim Jeremias in *Jesus' Promise to the Nations*. A few of the important texts: 1 Kgs 8:41–43; 1 Chr 16:23–30; Pss 22:26–31; 47:1–9; 102:15–22; Isa 60:1–12; Jer 3:17; Zeph 3:8–13; Hag 2:7; and Zech 8:20–22. See also Goldingay, *Israel's Faith*, 818–33; and Wright, *The Mission of God*, 478–79.

Isaiah wrote of a coming day when non-Hebrew people, described as "foreigners," would "join themselves to the Lord" in order "to minister" as worship-servants "to him" (Isa 56:6).

> The foreigners who join themselves to the LORD, to minister to him, and to love the name of the LORD ... even those I will bring to my holy mountain and make them joyful in my house of prayer. Their burnt offerings and their sacrifices will be pleasing on my altar; for my house will be called a house of prayer from all the peoples (amim). (Isa 56:6–7)

The phrase "to love the name of the LORD" means that they would come to love God truly by embracing all that they heard about him. Take note of the relational splendor of their worship: As they offer themselves to God by their offerings, God himself is pleased, gladdened as they give themselves in worship, and he will make them joyful. Ultimately, this will not be limited to a few select foreigners. God promised to draw men and women "from all the peoples" of the earth to enter this relational fullness.

At a climactic moment of his life's work, Jesus expounded Isaiah 56 before the crowds at the temple (Mark 11:15–18). It is common to hear the phrase "house of prayer" as referring to local churches that focus on intercessory prayer for other countries. But Isaiah 56 does not speak of intercessory prayers. When read in context, the phrase "house of prayer" must refer to the temple, not a congregation or church. The foreigners bring sacrificial offerings intended to express honor and thanks. Jesus was announcing God's purpose to receive worship from "all the peoples (ethne)" of the earth (Mark 11:17).

The Mandate to Disciple All Peoples

These promises perplexed Jewish leaders before Christ's day. Would the nations come spontaneously? Or should Jewish people take initiative to become the promised "light to the nations (goyim)" (Isa 49:6)?

For years some streams of Judaism had sent emissaries who traveled "on sea and land" to help Gentiles become Jewish proselytes (Matt 23:15). Proselytes were those who had passed through a twofold process of conversion. First was the ceremony of circumcision and washing, thought to bring a ritual purity or holiness. This was followed by rigorous training to follow one of the traditions of Torah observance. By doing so, proselytes essentially renounced their family and ethnic identity.

Christ's mandate in Matthew 28 calls for incorporating non-Jewish people into God's people in a radically different way than converting individuals as proselytes. Jesus's description of discipling involved two things that correspond to the twofold process of proselytizing. Instead of circumcision as an initiation rite, baptism brought disciples into covenant belonging with the triune God ("baptizing them into the name"). Instead of learning a package of Torah-keeping traditions, the new communities learned to obey Jesus ("teaching them to obey all that I commanded you").

Neither baptism nsor obeying Jesus as Lord necessarily involves renouncing one's family or ethnic identity. Instead of being divorced from family and culture, it is possible for disciples to continue with their people. Sincere followers repudiate sinful ways and learn lifestyles of obedient love, bringing changes to their behavior and often to their culture. In this way the risen Christ has been redemptively changing diverse cultures without imposing something like a universal kingdom culture.

Communities of disciples are to be formed in "all the peoples (*panta ta ethne*)" (28:19). The word for "peoples," ethnos, can sometimes refer to non-Jewish individuals. But in this grammatical construct in plural form (*panta ta ethne*) refers to collective entities with generational depth, such as ethnicities, languages, or sometimes countries.[3]

Affirmed by the Apostles: One People of Many Peoples

In the first movement of Christ followers a few tensions arose amidst the different cultures and familial loyalties of the regathered diaspora in Jerusalem. But we see those difficulties resolved by acknowledgment of the ethnic differences (Acts 6:1–5). As the movement expanded to other places and cultural spheres (11:19–20), we see indications that the blend of Jews and Greeks took on a generalized nonethnic identity as "Christians" (11:26). Their leaders came from different backgrounds that matched the diversity of the movement (13:1).

At the Jerusalem Council of Acts 15 leaders came to recognize and affirm the magnitude of what God was doing to form one people that would include all peoples.

What about the Gentiles who had recently been turning to God in Christ? Some were insisting that proselyte conversion was essential for these non-Jews: "It is necessary to circumcise them and to direct them to observe the Law of Moses" (15:5). Others, including Peter, asserted that God "made no distinction (*diakrino*, to discriminate) between us and them, cleansing their hearts by faith" (15:9). Peter was referring to a circumcision of the heart since circumcision was considered a ritual of cleansing. The Spirit that fell upon them was "holy," thus demonstrating them to be clean. Peter had already heard from heaven: "What God has cleansed, no longer consider unholy" (10:15; 11:9).

James then declared that God had begun to accomplish the long-promised greater exodus that would bring about the expected pilgrimage of all peoples to God. "God first concerned himself about taking from among the peoples (ethne) a people (laos) for his name" (15:14). Here James was quoting well-known texts in which God had said that he was so "concerned" about the plight of his people in Egypt (Exod 3:16; 4:31), that he was determined to "take you to myself for my people (laos in the LXX)" (6:7).

The allusion to the exodus, in which multiple tribes served God together as one people, was clear. But James also quoted a medley of different prophetic promises (Acts 15:15–18).[4] This proved decisive: Men and women from many peoples (ethne) were being received as worshipers of God and wearing his name. They were becoming one global covenant people (laos, a covenant people). What Gentile followers had in common with Jewish believers was the life and lordship of Jesus: "We [Jews] are saved through the grace of the Lord Jesus, in the same way as they [Gentiles] also are" (15:11).

---

3 John Piper's careful lexical work shows that in the New Testament the word *ethnos* in singular form always refers to a collective entity, something like an ethnicity, language, or country. In plural form the word can refer to ethnicities or it can refer to non-Jewish individuals. But when used in the phrase *panta ta ethne*, in any of the cases, the word *ethne* "virtually never carries the meaning of 'Gentile individuals' but always carries the meaning 'all the nations' in the sense of people groups" (Piper, *Let the Nations Be Glad*). This assessment is supported by over a hundred occurrences of the full phrase, *panta ta ethne*, in the Septuagint, which always refer to peoples or nations.

4 In addition to Amos 9:11–12, there are possible allusions to Zech 2:11, Jer 12:15, Isa 45:21, and Hos 3:5.

Gentiles were becoming covenant worshipers of the living God in Christ but were not becoming Jews or expected to adopt Jewish culture.[5] They were retaining, not renouncing, their family and ethnic identity.

The Glory of the Peoples

In our day ethnic identities are not static. Surges of migrants, a globalized economy, urban complexities, and ever-changing technologies are constantly shifting and hybridizing ethnic identities. It would seem that attempting to reach the world one people group at a time is an archaic, bygone idea. But now, more than ever, ethnic group identities matter.

Some leaders claim that churches flourish best as multiethnic congregations. Others make a case for people-specific gatherings to enhance fruitful evangelism in compartmentalized urban settings or rural and tribal communities. Either way, it matters that mission and church leaders recognize and respect every kind of group identity.

I have argued that people groups are important in mission primarily because of the value of each people group to the living God. The blood of the Lamb was shed to purchase men, women, and children so that he would receive whole life, culturally enriched worship from every people.

At the first exodus God called forth a covenant people consisting of multiple tribes. This prefigured a later, greater exodus, initiated in Christ, in which a global people is now being formed from every people. In some larger celebrations we enjoy diverse ways of worship. But our church gatherings only foreshadow the great multitude. Only on the final day will we behold one covenant people consisting of some from every one of the peoples. "Behold, the tabernacle of God is among people (*anthrōpōn*), and he will dwell among them, and they shall be his peoples (laos plural)[6] and God himself will be among them" (Rev 21:3).

As we finally come home together, the heaven-on-earth city will shine with "the glory of God" (21:11). But there will be other glories: "The kings of the earth will bring their glory into it … and they will bring the glory and the honor of the nations (ethne) into it" (21:24, 26).

The glory of the peoples includes the distinctive music and literature, the diverse artistry, the various inventions and industries, all of the gorgeous and soul-stirring creations of culture—they will have been purged and redeemed by the Lamb. We labor in hope of beholding God's joy as he is loved extravagantly by the peoples.

Bibliography

Goldingay, John. *Israel's Faith*. Downers Grove, IL: InterVarsity Press, 2006.

Jeremias, Joachim. *Jesus' Promise to the Nations*. Philadelphia: Fortress Press, 1958.

Metzger, Bruce. *A Textual Commentary on the Greek New Testament*. New York: UBS, 1975.

Piper, John. *Let the Nations Be Glad*. 3rd ed. Grand Rapids: Baker Academic, 2010.

Wright, Christopher. *The Mission of God*. Downers Grove, IL: IVP Academic, 2006.

---

5 The four prohibitions (Acts 15:19–12, 28–29; 21:25) were the only four practices that were forbidden for visiting foreigners while living among the Jewish people (Lev 17:8, 10–14, 15; 18:6–18). No other part of the Torah was required. The fact that these were mentioned at all supports the idea that Gentile followers of Jesus were, in a sense, sojourning in the midst of the Jewish people, but remained Gentiles.

6 Metzger, *A Textual Commentary*, 763. Variant manuscripts contain both singular and plural forms, with the plural having slightly better evidence. The singular matches the oft-repeated covenant formula with three elements— "your God," "my people," "I will dwell among you"—making it more likely that the original was plural.

3

Panta ta Ethne

All Peoples and Nations

David E. Datema

Within the evangelical mission movement, the concept of reaching unreached people groups (UPGs) has been the dominant way of promoting the missionary endeavor over the last fifty years. The UPG movement began with a recognition that national identity—and the corollary national church—is insufficient to represent the dynamic and complex ways human beings group themselves in each country or nation-state. This led to long lists of people groups. The evangelistic goal widened from reaching the world's 195 countries to reaching approximately seventeen thousand unreached peoples!

However, in recent decades the anthropological and biblical support for this notion has been challenged.[1] Critics argue that the people group concept does not correlate with "the reality of the fluid and porous nature of social boundaries as well as the reality of globalization and hybridization of contexts."[2] They go on to ask: If the people group concept is losing credibility in social science, does it still have a basis biblically?

This second criticism is the focus of this chapter—namely, the biblical support for the use of the people group concept. First, I give an overview of the way human grouping is understood in the Old and New Testaments by exploring relevant Hebrew and Greek terms. I then examine exegetical issues related to *panta ta ethne* in Matthew 28:19, the most well-known passage related to the people group concept. I counter arguments that render the people group concept false, unreliable, and unbiblical, and conclude by urging refinement of the people group concept rather than replacement.

Human Grouping in the Old Testament

The OT portrays the people of the world with a diversity of terms that describe very large human groupings to relatively small subgroups or segments of them. The largest human grouping would be humankind without distinction, as in Genesis 1:26, "Let Us make man (אָדָם, *adam*)[3] in Our image,"[4] and 6:5, "Then the LORD saw that the wickedness of man (adam)

---

[1] This view began with a book edited by Fredrik Barth, *Ethnic Groups and Boundaries* (1969), and has grown each decade since into a place of prominence. Among evangelicals, the most significant voices calling for change along these lines within missiological circles have been Radcliffe, Howel, Zehner, Rynkiewich, and Yip. Constructivist notions of ethnic formation and maintenance emphasize change to the neglect of stability. I prefer a view of ethnicity that holds the poles of fixity and fluidity in tension (Stoler, 1997: 198) and recognizes that ethnicity can be both malleable and durable (Ozgen).

[2] Lee and Park, "Beyond People Group," 2. Other writers in this compendium respond to social science and biblical critiques (e.g., Bartlotti, "Reimagining"; Johnson, "FAQ").

[3] All biblical words will be introduced in the Lemma or dictionary form (singular) in Hebrew and Greek followed by a transliteration in parentheses. Subsequent references to words will include only the transliteration. Exceptions to this will be observed whenever words are presented as part of a quote.

[4] All verses of Scripture are in NASB 1995 version.

was great on the earth." In these cases adam refers to "humankind, mankind, a class of being created by God without regard to sex, with a focus as a class of creature, distinct from animals, plants, or even spiritual beings."[5] Another example is in Genesis 11:1, "Now the whole earth (אֶרֶץ, eretz) used the same language and the same words." This is an anthropomorphic use of eretz to refer to all humankind.

The next layer of human grouping found in the OT is the idea of nations or peoples. It is well known that גּוֹי (goy) and עַם (am) are the most common words for nations/peoples. In one dictionary they are defined similarly[6] as "a people group sharing a common ancestry and/or sociopolitical identity" with an addendum for am, "also used for groups of people smaller than a nation, such as the inhabitants of a city." Note the phrase "people group" in the very definition and the variety of group size the word am covers. Goy indicates "a common sociopolitical identity that can be defined by ancestry, language, land, and government … as Israel's national identity becomes clearer in the OT the majority of the occurrences use some form of the plural to refer to the surrounding non-Israelite nations."[7] Thus goy can be applied to human groupings defined by a diversity of affinities/boundaries (ancestry, language, land, government) and became synonymous with non-Israelite Gentiles. In the Septuagint, goy is usually translated as ἔθνος (ethnos), while am is generally used to denote God's people Israel and is usually translated as λαός (laos).[8]

The fact that language was a major defining element of nations and peoples can be seen in Daniel. Seven times reference is made to "peoples (am), nations (אֻמָּה, ummah) and men of every language (לִשָּׁן, lishan)" (3:4, 7, 29; 4:1; 5:19; 6:25; 7:14). It would seem fair, in a very general sense, to equate the modern term "ethnolinguistic" to this level of grouping, especially since the OT is full of specific examples of such, both small (Kenites, Kenizzites, Jebusites, etc. of Gen 15:19–21) and large (Assyrians, Babylonians, Egyptians—Israel's major enemies).

A third and smaller layer of human groupings can yet be found. In Genesis 12:3 we read, "And in you all the families (מִשְׁפָּחָה, mishpachah) of the earth will be blessed." Although mishpachah has a wide range of meanings (people, kingdom, tribe, clan, family, group, genus, kind),[9] the overwhelming majority of its occurrences in the OT are translated as "clans" (NIV, 253 of 296 occurrences) or "families" (NASB95, 289 of 303 occurrences).[10] The word refers to "a family group larger than an individual household but smaller than an entire tribe."[11] Another example of such grouping is found in the account of Achan in Joshua 7:14–18,

---

5   Swanson, "132 I. אָדָם ('ā·ḏām).''

6   Speiser (1960) sees major distinctions between goy and am. Am is personal and subjective, goy impersonal and objective. Am denotes family connections and emphasizes blood ties, goy signifying groups held together more from without than from within. Israel was both am and goy. Genesis 12 uses goy because they were already an am in the process of becoming a goy. "Consider too that this nation (goy) is your people (am)" (Exod 33:13).

7   Minard, "Gentiles."

8   Minard, "Gentiles." I note other less common words used for non-Israelites, those outside the covenant YHWH made with Israel: נָכְרִי (nokri) foreignness, זָר (zar) someone strange or foreign, עָרֵל (arel) uncircumcised, and גֵּר (ger) and תּוֹשָׁב (tosab) sojourner or alien.

9   Swanson, "5476 מִשְׁפָּחָה (miš·pā·ḥā(h))."

10 Logos, "mishpachah." See especially the census of Israel in Numbers 26 (ex: v. 7) and tribal land allotments in Joshua 13 (ex: v. 15) and 15.

11 Blair, "Family."

where God first chooses the tribes (שֵׁבֶט, *shebet*), then the families (*mishpachah*), then the households (בַּיִת, *bayit*), and finally Achan himself. The people of Israel in the Bible are thus presented in segmented groupings and the references to such (tribes, families, households) in the OT are numerous. A good example of these distinctions is found in the phrase "families (*mishpachah*) of the nations (*goy*)" in Psalm 22:27 and "families (*mishpachah*) of the peoples (*am*)" in Psalm 96:7.[12] As early as Genesis 10:5, 20 and 31, the descendants of Noah's sons are each described in terms of families (*mishpachah*), languages (*lishan*), lands (*eretz*), and nations (*goy*). In this case there is a mixture of terms representing smaller (*mishpachah*) and larger (*lishan, eretz, goy*) groups.[13]

Human Grouping in the New Testament

The NT contains a similar diversity of words to describe humanity. The top layer once again consists of humanity as a whole, such as John 1:29, "Behold, the one on the Throne who takes away the sin of the world (κόσμος, *kosmos*)!"[14] Also Luke 2:1, "Now in those days a decree went out from Caesar Augustus, that a census be taken of all the inhabited earth (οἰκουμένη, *oikoumenē*)." In both cases, the "world/earth" is a reference to all the people in the world.

The next layer of human grouping can be seen in the use of ethnos, nation or people, which is the NT equivalent of goy. Importantly, "in the majority of NT occurrences ... it appears in the plural and takes on a more technical sense that is usually translated 'Gentile,' contrasting non-Jews with Jews."[15] It is this technical usage of the word that is the focus of Lee and Park. These first two layers of human grouping can be seen in Matthew 24:14: "This gospel of the kingdom shall be preached in the whole world (*oikoumenē*) as a testimony to all the nations (*ethnos*), and then the end will come." Another word of note is laos in significant ways is the NT equivalent of am. While the singular form normally refers to the Jewish people, it is often used for non-Jews in the plural, as is the case in Revelation 5:9, 7:9, 11:9, 13:7, and 14:6, all of which refer, in differing order, to nations (*ethnos*), tribes (φυλή, *phylē*), peoples (*laos*), and tongues/languages (γλῶσσα, *glōssa*).[16] These phrases are used to describe the entire breadth of humanity in all its forms and varieties. The word phyle is used whenever the NT speaks of the tribes of Israel. In Revelation it takes on an eschatological sense and "means generally people (as an ethnic collective)."[17] As for glossa, in addition to its basic meaning for the tongue, "it could denote a particular language (Acts 2:4) and could thus be used as a distinguishing mark of a people group (Rev 7:9)."[18]

---

12 Psalm 96 possesses three levels of description for human groupings in the first seven verses: all the earth (eretz), nations (goy), peoples (am), and families (mishpachah).

13 Minard, "Gentiles."

14 Also Rom 5:12–13; 1 Cor 1:27–28; 2 Cor 5:19.

15 Minard, "Gentiles." Similar to the OT (see footnote 6), the NT employs other less common words to describe the Gentile world: ἐθνικός (*ethnikos*) a pagan or heathen person; ἀκροβυστία (*akrobystia*) the uncircumcised; Ἕλλην (*Hellen*) of Greek descent or a non-Jew living in Greco-Roman culture; σέβομαι (*sebomai*) devout non-Jew or God-fearer; προσήλυτος (*proselytos*) a proselyte or convert to Judaism; ξένος (*xenos*) a foreigner.

16 Revelation is significantly dependent on Daniel, thus this grouping of words parallels that in Daniel referenced earlier.

17 Paulsen, "φυλή, ῆς, ἡ," 442.

18 Lookadoo, "Body."

The tribe, clan/families, and household segments in the OT are not as clearly defined in the NT, not because they ceased to exist but because they simply were not as prominent in a nation subjugated under Roman rule. The tribe, clan, or extended family was usually designated by πατριά (*patria*), as in Luke 2:4, "Joseph also went up from Galilee … because he was of the house and family (*patria*) of David." Similarly, συγγενής (*syngenēs*) is used to describe the idea of extended family relatives: "And behold, even your relative (*syngenēs*) Elizabeth has also conceived a son in her old age" (Luke 1:36). But the main social unit in the NT is the οἶκος (*oikos*), the house or household, an equivalent to the OT *bayit*. In Acts 16:31, the Philippian jailer is told, "Believe in the Lord Jesus, and you will be saved, you and your household (*oikos*)." In Mark 6:4, these segments are put together, "A prophet is not without honor except in his hometown and among his own relatives (*syngenēs*) and in his own household (*oikos*)."[19]

The following table (Table 1, not exhaustive) summarizes this overview of how human groups are described in the biblical record.

Table 1: Terms Designating Human Grouping in Scripture

Group Types	Hebrew Terms Used	Greek Terms Used	Affinities/ Boundaries	Modern Terms[20]
All Humanity	adam, eretz	kosmos, oikoumenē	human	homo sapiens
Nations/Peoples	goy, am	ethnos, laos	ancestry, language, land, government	race, ethnicity, language, ethnolinguistic, nation-state, cultural blocs, mega-peoples, macro-peoples
Non-Israelites, Gentiles	nokri zar arel ger tosab	ethnikos akrobystia Hellen sebomai proselytos xenos		
Tongues/ Languages	lishan	glōssa		
Tribes	shebet ummah	phylē	kinship, lineage	tribe, socio-peoples, mini-peoples
Families/Clans	mishpachah	patria, syngenēs	smaller kinship segment	unimax peoples, micro-peoples, extended family
Households	bayit	oikos	smallest kinship segment	family

---

19 Blair, "Family."

20 These are only rough comparisons and by no means an attempt to suggest exact equivalence of concepts with the biblical terms. For instance, there seems to be no biblical equivalence of the modern idea of a nuclear family.

Biblical writers understood (1) the basic unity of all humankind, (2) human difference based on various and diverse affinities/boundaries that created separate nations/peoples (horizontal segmentation, the first two types above), and (3) segmentation within each nation/people based on kinship/lineage (vertical segmentation, the last three types above). I believe the overview of Scripture above shows that human grouping is an ancient phenomenon and was not introduced by people group proponents in the twentieth century.[21] People are always seen as members of such a variety of groups that many terms are needed to fully explain the subsets and segments. The Bible highlights particularism in its universal treatment of humanity. NT writers such as Matthew would have understood these human groupings in all their variety and complexity.

Panta ta Ethne in Matthew 28:19

After looking at human grouping in broad strokes as seen throughout Scripture, I want to now focus on one single text. There is present debate about whether the phrase "*panta ta ethne*" refers to "people groups" or simply "Gentiles?"[22] While this may seem a minor difference, it highlights the importance of the dual emphasis of the unity of humankind (universalism) and the many groups that make up the whole (particularism). The Bible always emphasizes both, and the translation of "Gentiles" does not do justice to the pattern we have just seen. It would have been impossible for Matthew to contemplate "the Gentiles" only as a monolithic non-Jewish mass; rather, he would have envisioned a mosaic of nations/peoples, languages, tribes, clans, and households. In what follows, I claim that while the technical usage of ethne as a reference to Gentiles is undoubtedly a reality in the NT and Matthew,[23] this is not the way it is being used in 28:19. Instead, I propose five reasons why *panta ta ethne* in Matthew 28:19 is better understood as a reference to all human groupings ("nations" or "peoples"), not individuals ("Gentiles").

First, the continuity of the salvific purpose of God in the Bible favors nations over Gentiles. I believe Matthew 28:19 is a repetition of the OT promise to Abraham "that the blessings promised to Abraham and through him to all peoples on earth (Gen 12:3) are now to be fulfilled in Jesus the Messiah."[24] As earlier sections show, the thread of God's purpose in Scripture has in mind all the human groupings (nations, peoples, tongues, etc.) in the world, peoples more than people. The use of "Gentiles" obscures this continuity.

Second, the history of exegesis favors nations over Gentiles. "The ancient church, the medieval exegesis, and the interpreters of the early modern period almost uniformly interpret παντα τα έθνη in the universal sense of 'all nations.'"[25] In terms of present scholarship, "nations" is the majority view over against a large minority who favor "Gentiles."

---

21 Hawthorne, "Biblical Understanding."

22 Luz, *Matthew 21–28*, 629. Luz notes, "Εθνη is not a homonym that means either 'nations' or 'Gentiles'; in the Judaism of that day it meant both. … The alternative between 'Gentiles' and 'nations' is created only when one translates the text into the languages of Christian European nations that make a distinction between these two meanings." If Luz is correct, then I am not against "Gentiles" as a translation if particularism is understood, but rather against how those in America and Europe conceive it.

23 According to Hare and Harrington, in the Persian and Hellenistic periods when nations in the Levant were subsumed under large imperial rulers, *goyim* began referring not to national groups but to "one overarching collective—non-Jewish mankind" (Hare and Harrington, "Make Disciples," 360).

24 Carson, *Matthew*, 1066.

25 Luz, *Matthew 21–28*, 629.

Third, lexicographers favor nations over Gentiles. While both Bertram and Schmidt reference the technical usage of ethne as Gentiles, neither of them attach this meaning to Matthew 28:19.[26] Rather, they view ethne in this passage as a continuation of the OT usage found in the Abrahamic promise—what Schmidt termed "an ethnographical sense." Therefore, although ethne as Gentiles is indeed a correct translation in many cases, it is decidedly not the case in Matthew 28:19.

Fourth, the use of *panta ta ethne* in Matthew favors nations over Gentiles. When it comes to the use of ethnos/ethne in Matthew, there are

> seven cases where it clearly means "Gentiles," one case that is doubtful, and five cases where the sense cannot be limited to "Gentiles." ... The latter five cases ... contain three out of the four occurrences of ethne modified by panta ta. The fourth occurrence is precisely Matt 28:19. ... I would submit, then, that the weight of preponderant evidence is in favor of taking the fourth occurrence of panta ta ethne, like the other three, to mean "all the nations," or "all peoples."[27]

Fifth, the use of diverse human groupings in Revelation favors nations over Gentiles. Revelation 5:9 and 7:9, which most scholars agree were written decades after Matthew and are considered among the final writings in the NT canon, confirm the continued relevance of particularism in the early church's understanding of salvation history. Matthew 28:19 and Revelation 5:9 and 7:9 can be seen as NT bookends for the concept of peoples. If Matthew 28:19 serves as a mission statement, a precise directive telling the disciples what it is that they should do, Revelation 5:9 and 7:9 are more of a vision statement, a general description of the promised future. These passages in Revelation are a powerful reminder that particularism does not cease in the eschaton, even as all peoples worship one Lord. In fact, the redundancy used in these passages to emphasize particularity, coupled with their importance in portraying the culmination of redemptive history, suggests that they may be an even greater argument for the continued relevancy of human groupings than Matthew 28:19. At the very least, their correlation, which can rightfully be extended all the way back to Genesis 12:3, represents a golden thread of universal particularism running through the entire sweep of Scripture.[28]

By rejecting the technical usage of ethne as meaning "Gentiles" in 28:19, I am not saying that the Gentiles as a representation of the non-Jewish world are not in view. The inclusion of the Gentiles in God's salvific purpose is an unquestionable and shocking NT theme. The problem is that although "all the Gentiles" portrays humanity as a whole (universalism), it does not portray well, at least in English, the equally important idea of humanity in all its parts (particularism). Ethne must include both meanings or the diversity of human groupings (so extensively portrayed in Scripture) is obscured.

Having argued for a reading of "nations" or "peoples" instead of "Gentiles," I reiterate what I think is most important: that *panta ta ethne* in Matthew 28:19, whether translated as "all the Gentiles" or "all the nations," was understood by both Matthew and his readers as a

---

26 Bertram, "εθνος, εθνικος," 367; Schmidt, "εθνος, εθνικος: εθνος," 369; Bietenhard, "People, Nation, Gentiles," 793.

27 Meier, "Nations or Gentiles," 102.

28 Beyond those cited in this section, here is a sampling of scholars who prefer "nations" over "Gentiles": Blomberg, *Matthew*, 431; Bosch, *Structure of Mission*, 237; Carson, "Matthew," 1066; Hagner, *Matthew*, 887; Keener, *Matthew*, 401; Meier, *Matthew*, 371.

reference to both universality (everyone everywhere) and particularity (in all their diversity), meaning that it was impossible for them to conceive of the world as a collective whole without simultaneously seeing it in its many and diverse constituent parts. *Panta ta ethne* is both/and, not either/or. It means the inclusion of all the nations/Gentiles in all of their God-given diversity. Ethne does include in its semantic range the idea of various human groupings and boundaries, including ethnicity. It is not a new or modern idea that people group proponents are reading into Scripture. It is rather an ancient understanding flowing naturally from the Old to the New Testament.

Therefore, *panta ta ethne* cannot simply mean "the whole world." Rather, it refers to all the particular, diverse, segmented parts of that whole world, or "each of those subdivisions of humanity in which people find their identity."[29] Until now, I have used the phrase "human grouping" more than "people group." But "people group" remains the best phrase to describe ethne in modern English, and translating ethne in 28:19 as "people groups" is biblically legitimate. It is better than "nations," which for most people conjures up the idea of modern nation-states and is more descriptive than "peoples."

Conclusion

There is no doubt that new understandings of human groupings are a challenge to traditional people group constructs.[30] People groups as traditionally understood tend toward "a reductionism which employs simplified, managed categories overlaying complex social realities,"[31] a truth seen clearly in Mark Pickett's survey of the Newar people.[32] Nonetheless, there is no getting "beyond" people groups because people groups have always been and ever will be. They are a biblical category and are found literally from Genesis through Revelation. Rather than calling for a replacement of the people group idea, I agree with proposals to reimagine and re-envision them.[33] New awareness of cultural hybridity or people group fluidity does not put an end to human grouping, but rather changes the affinities and boundaries of their formation. We are better served to adjust to their new formations than to question their basic and biblical legitimacy.

Bibliography

Baker, K. "Beyond 'People Groups': Why the Term 'Communities' May Be Preferable." *Evangelical Missions Quarterly* 53, no. 5 (2017).

Barth, F., ed. *Ethnic Groups and Boundaries: The Social Organization of Culture Difference*. Long Grove, IL: Waveland Press, 1969.

Bartlotti, Len. "Reimagining and Re-envisioning People Groups." *Evangelical Missions Quarterly* 56, no. 4 (2020): 46–50.

Bertram, G. "εθνος, εθνικος: People and Peoples." In *Theological Dictionary of the New Testament*, edited by G. Kittel. Grand Rapids: Eerdmans, 1964.

---

29 Showalter, "All the Clans," 126.
30 See Nguyen, "Globalization, Urbanization, Migration"; Undisclosed, "Notes from the Field"; McMahan, "Ferment in the Church"; Tira and Uytanlet, *Hybrid World*; Gill, "Church for Every People."
31 Baker, "Beyond 'People Groups.'"
32 Pickett, "Ethnicity, Kinship, Religion."
33 Bartlotti, "Reimagining and Re-envisioning."

Bietenhard, H. "People, Nation, Gentiles, Crowd, City." In *The New International Dictionary of New Testament Theology*, edited by C. Brown. Grand Rapids: Zondervan, 1967.

Blair, T. "Family." In *The Lexham Theological Wordbook*, edited by D. Mangum, D. R. Brown, R. Klippenstein et al. Bellingham, WA: Lexham, 2014.

Blomberg, C. L. "Matthew." In *The New American Commentary: An Exegetical and Theological Exposition of Holy Scripture*, edited by D. S. Dockery. Nashville: Broadman & Holman, 1992.

Bosch, D. J. "The Structure of Mission: An Exposition of Matthew 28:16–20." In *Exploring Church Growth*, edited by Wilbert R. Shenk, 218–48. Grand Rapids: Eerdmans, 1983.

Carson, D. A., "Matthew." *The Expositor's Bible Commentary, Revised Edition*, edited by T. Longman III and D. E. Garland. Grand Rapids: Zondervan, 2010.

Datema, D. E., "Defining 'Unreached': A Short History." *International Journal of Frontier Missiology* 33, no. 2 (2016): 45–71.

Datema, D. E., and Leonard N. Bartlotti. "The People Group Approach: A Historical Perspective." *Evangelical Missions Quarterly* 56, no. 4 (2020): 8–11.

Gill, Brad. "A Church for Every People: A Retrospect on Mapping Peoples." *Evangelical Missions Quarterly* 56, no. 4 (2020): 43–45.

Hagner, Donald A. *Matthew 14–28*. Dallas: Word Books, 1995.

Hare, D. R. A., and D. J. Harrington. "Make Disciples of All the Gentiles (Mt 28:19)." *The Catholic Biblical Quarterly* 37, no. 3 (1975): 359–69.

Hawthorne, Steve. "A Biblical Understanding of People Groups." *Evangelical Missions Quarterly* 56, no. 4 (2020): 4–7.

Howell, B. M. "Globalization, Ethnicity, and Cultural Authenticity: Implications for Theological Education." *Christian Scholar's Review* 35, no. 3 (2006): 303–22.

Howell, B. M. "Multiculturalism, Immigration and the North American Church." *Missiology: An International Review* 39, no. 1 (2011): 79–85.

Howell, B. M., and E. Zehner. *Power and Identity in the Global Church: Six Contemporary Cases*. Pasadena, CA: William Carey Library, 2009.

Keener, C. S. *Matthew*. Downers Grove, IL: InterVarsity Press, 1997.

Lee, Peter T., and James Sung-Hwan Park. "Beyond People Group Thinking: A Critical Reevaluation of Unreached People Groups." *Missiology: An International Review* 46, no. 3 (2018): 212–25. DOI: 10.1177/0091829618774332.

Logos Bible Software 8.15 (n.d.) Bible Word Study: mishpachah.

Lookadoo, J. "Body." In *The Lexham Theological Wordbooks*, edited by D. Mangum, D. R. Brown, R. Klippenstein et al. Bellingham, WA: Lexham, 2014.

Luz, U. *Matthew 21–28*. Minneapolis: Augsburg Fortress, 2005.

McMahan, Alan. "Ferment in the Church: Missions in the 4th Era." *Evangelical Missions Quarterly* 56, no. 4 (2020): 36–38.

Meier, J. P. "Nations or Gentiles in Matthew 28:19?" *The Catholic Biblical Quarterly* 39, no. 1 (1977): 94–102.

Meier, J. P. Matthew. New Testament Message 3. Wilmington, DE: M. Glazier, 1980.

Minard, M. "Gentiles." In *The Lexham Theological Wordbook*, edited by D. Mangum, D. R. Brown, R. Klippenstein et al. Bellingham, WA: Lexham, 2014.

Nguyen, M. H. "Globalization, Urbanization, Migration, and Rethinking the People Groups Concept." *Evangelical Missions Quarterly* 56, no. 4 (2020): 32–35.

Ozgen, Z. "Maintaining Ethnic Boundaries in 'Non-Ethnic' Contexts: Constructivist Theory and the Sexual Reproduction of Diversity." *Theory and Society* 44, no. 1 (2015): 33–64.

Paulsen, H. "φυλή, ῆς, ἡ phylē tribe, nation, people." *Exegetical Dictionary of the New Testament*, edited by H. Balz and G. Schneider. Edinburgh: T&T Clark, 1990.

Pickett, M. "Ethnicity, Kinship, Religion and Territory: Identifying Communities in South Asia." *International Journal of Frontier Missiology* 32, no. 1 (2015): 23–36.

Piper, John. *Let the Nations Be Glad!: The Supremacy of God in Missions*. Grand Rapids: Baker Books, 1993.

Radcliffe, L. "A Field Worker Speaks Out about the Rush to Reach All Peoples." *Mission Frontiers* 20, no. 1 (1998).

Rynkiewich, M. A. "The World in My Parish: Rethinking the Standard Missiological Model." *Missiology* 30, no. 3 (2002): 301–21.

Rynkiewich, M. A. "Corporate Metaphors and Strategic Thinking: 'The 10/40 Window' in the American Evangelical Worldview." *Missiology: An International Review* 35, no. 2 (2007): 217–41. DOI: 10.1177/009182960703500210.

Rynkiewich, M. A. "Do We Need a Postmodern Anthropology for Mission in a Postcolonial World?" *Mission Studies* 28, no. 2 (2011): 151–69.

Rynkiewich, M. A. "Do Not Remember the Former Things." *International Bulletin of Mission Research* 40, no. 4 (2016): 308–17. DOI: 10.1177/2396939316656792.

Schmidt, K. L. "εθνος, εθνικος: εθνος." In *Theological Dictionary of the New Testament*. Grand Rapids: Eerdmans, 1964.

Showalter, R. "All the Clans, All the Peoples." *International Journal of Frontier Missions* 1, no. 2 (1984): 123–28.

Speiser, Ephraim A. "'People' and 'Nation' of Israel." *Journal of Biblical Literature* 79, no. 2 (1960): 157–63.

Stoler, A. L. "Racial Histories and Their Regimes of Truth." In *Political Power and Social Theory, Vol. 11*. JAI Press, 1997. 183–206.

Swanson, J. A. "132 I. אָדָם ('ā·dām)." In *A Dictionary of Biblical Languages: Hebrew (Old Testament)*. Logos Research Systems, Inc. 1997.

Swanson, J. A. "5476 הַחְפָּשְׁמ (miš·pā·ḥā(h))." In *A Dictionary of Biblical Languages: Hebrew (Old Testament)*. Logos Research Systems, Inc. 1997.

Tira, S. J., and J. L. Uytanlet, eds. *A Hybrid World: Diaspora, Hybridity, and Missio Dei*. Littleton, CO: William Carey Publishing, 2020.

Undisclosed Authors. (2020) "Notes from the Field: Voices of Pioneer Workers on the Challenge of 'People Groups.'" *Evangelical Missions Quarterly* 56, no. 4 (2020): 20–27.

Winter, R. D., and B. A. Koch. "Finishing the Task: The Unreached Peoples Challenge." *International Journal of Frontier Missions* 19, no. 4 (2002): 15–25.

Yip, G. "The Contour of a Post-Postmodern Missiology." *Missiology* 42, no. 4 (2014): 399–411. DOI: 10.1177/0091829613512965.

4
The People Group Approach

A Historical Perspective

David E. Datema and Leonard N. Bartlotti

Confusion reigns among leaders in the world of missions when it comes to assessing the evangelistic responsibility of the church. Every decade or so the wave of a new theory crashes ashore and theoreticians who teach and write books as well as practitioners who lead missions bob about furiously seeking to stem the tide or to ride the wave. The impressive conclaves and private skirmishes seem dominated either by enthusiastic and often uncritical promoters of the new wave or the veterans who scramble to synthesize older, devoutly held verities with the implications of the newly ascendant idea.[1]

In 1983, J. Robertson McQuilkin described the advent of the people group approach as "the current missiological tidal wave." All efforts to stem the tide failed. Most chose to ride the wave. Fifty years later some argue that the wave seems to have spent itself; its remaining impetus rushing backward as if to feed the next surge. Others hold on to people group thinking, seeing nothing on the horizon coming to take its place. In what follows we will attempt to briefly tell the story of the development of the people group approach until 1982, when a consensus on terminology was established.[2]

Precursors to People Groups

In reality, the people group wave of the 1970–1980s was not "new." Missionaries were well aware of humanity's ethnic and linguistic diversity. They were not surprised by the complexity of peoples and ethnicities within single nation-states. An uncritical reader of Ralph Winter's "Three Eras"[3] treatment of modern mission history might conclude that it was not until missionaries went "inland" from the "coastlands" that they suddenly realized this diversity. Yet even William Carey's *Enquiry* (1792) showed appreciation for human difference and variety. Throughout the nineteenth century great strides were made in understanding human groupings. In 1910, Commission One of the World Missionary Conference in Edinburgh presented a survey of the non-Christian world that was over two hundred pages in length, used the phrase "unreached" regularly, and was impressively cognizant of ethnic and linguistic difference.[4]

---

1 McQuilkin, "Assessing the Evangelistic Responsibility." This unpublished paper is used with permission by the Ralph D. Winter Research Center and Archive, Pasadena, CA. McQuilkin's paper was edited and later published as "Looking at the Task Six Ways" in *EMQ* 19, no. 1 (January 1, 1983).

2 For an overview of the frontier mission movement, see Johnson, "Part I: The Frontier Mission," 81–88; "Part II: Major Concepts," 89–97; "Part III: Critical Analysis," 121–27; and "Part IV: The Core Contributions," 129–31. For more detail on people group definitions, see Datema, "Defining 'Unreached,'" 45–71.

3 Winter, "The Concept of a Third Era." Cf. Winter, "Three Men, Three Eras"; more fully developed by Winter in a later version, "Four Men, Three Eras."

4 Mott, *Report of Commission I*.

In the twentieth century this research continued, expanding understanding of the diversity and complexity of human groupings. In Central America, W. Cameron Townsend noted the many tribal peoples often bypassed and in need of their own Scriptures. In India, J. Waskom Pickett wrote a signature book on mass movements, which formed the basis for Donald McGavran's later work on people movements and church growth principles. Most important among these for our purposes was the homogeneous unit principle, which emphasized the human tendency to prefer association with others of similar affinities. In Africa, David Barrett and Patrick Johnstone began research projects on peoples that eventually became global, Barrett representing a more academic investigation and Johnstone creating resources for prayer. All of these efforts represented attempts to identify human grouping at a level below that of nation-states.

Our point here is simply that the people group paradigm was not primarily a new revelation about the existence of diverse people groups. Rather, it was a unique and culminating phase of its development, "engendering a global *awareness* and concerted *application* of the people group concept that created new *approaches* to the task of world evangelization."[5]

Stimuli That Sparked a Movement

The people group approach of the 1970s was triggered by two different but complementary stimuli. First, there was an awakening to the "shattering truth" that "at least four out of five non-Christians in the world today are beyond the reach of any Christian's E-1 [local] evangelism."[6] This stimulus came about through Ralph Winter's provocative and groundbreaking lecture at Lausanne '74, which exposed the inability of near-neighbor (E-1) evangelism to reach these people groups, and called attention to the need to make cross-cultural evangelism (E-2, E-3) "the highest priority."

The second stimulus helped visualize this reality. The emergence of new computer technology enabled mission leaders to effectively display lists of the "hidden peoples" that made up that non-Christian world. It added specificity by naming and listing people groups instead of referring to them with vague general headings like "unevangelized" or "heathen world." The intent was to overcome "people blindness," the inability to see these smaller entities that made up the human population. Thus, an ethnic *representation* of the unevangelized world was wedded to a more detailed *visualization* of that world.

The convergence of these two forces shifted the picture of the world from nation-states to people groups, especially those labeled "unreached." A previously monochrome world was now polychromatic: Variegated unreached peoples, languages, and groupings, previously "hidden" by (what Winter called) the "high grass" of existing national churches, were now projected before the eyes of missionaries and the global church.[7] This placed new emphasis and urgency on the "pioneering" phase of mission in pursuit of "missiological breakthrough" among each unreached people.

---

5 Len Bartlotti, personal communication, May 28, 2020.
6 Winter, "The New Macedonia," 353.
7 Winter, *Penetrating the Last Frontiers*. "The main problem now is that the national church has grown up like high grass which our missionaries can't see beyond" (3). This statement generated heated defensive responses from some denominational mission leaders who felt their national churches and foreign mission programs (the vast majority of which were not pioneering) were being disparaged. See e.g., chapters by Garrison and Pratt, and Brogden, Johnson, and Bartlotti in this volume.

In one sense, the people group paradigm gained traction when it did because computer technology was advanced enough to organize and manipulate already existing data. The *Ethnologue* listing of the world's languages was first computerized in 1971.[8] Across the mission world, computer technology now allowed for faster retrieval, arrangement, and analysis of data than ever before.[9] It was a technological innovation that allowed for the construction and maintenance of people group lists, enhancing Winter's cognitive insight with graphic display. While the insight itself was powerful, when coupled with the lists it proved to be irresistible. Now, individuals could not only hear about unreached peoples but see them more clearly than ever before. In missions, seeing is believing.

The Primary Thought Leaders

Although many were involved in people group research, including David Barrett (*World Christian Encyclopedia*) and Patrick Johnstone (*Operation World*), the people group approach as a full-orbed concept and mission strategy was the product of three main spheres of influence, all emanating from southern California: Fuller Theological Seminary's School of World Mission (SWM); the Missions Advanced Research and Communications Center (MARC) of World Vision; and the U.S. Center for World Mission (USCWM). MARC was established in 1966 as a joint venture of World Vision International and Fuller.[10] Together they had a large influence during the seventies and eighties on unreached peoples research.

Each of these institutions was led by missiological luminaries. C. Peter Wagner, professor at Fuller's SWM, served as chairman of the Strategy Working Group (SWG) of the Lausanne Committee for World Evangelization (LCWE).[11] Working closely with Wagner was Ed Dayton, director of MARC. Dayton was a Fuller graduate and had studied under SWM professors. This collegiality and the close proximity (nine miles) between Fuller Seminary (Pasadena) and the then-headquarters of World Vision (Monrovia) facilitated synergy. According to Wagner and Dayton:

> Since its founding in 1966, ... MARC *centered its philosophy of world evangelization around the people group*. The analysis that was done jointly by Donald McGavran and Ed Dayton, at the School of World Mission at Fuller Seminary, *indicated that the country-by-country approach to mission was no longer viable*. ... McGavran and Dayton worked through an analysis of needed world evangelization, based on McGavran's earlier insight gained from *people movements*. ... *As the analysis continued, it was obvious that the basic unit of evangelization was not a country, nor the individual, but a vast variety of subgroups.*[12]

Note the interconnecting concepts: world evangelization; people group versus country approach; people movements; and vast variety of subgroups. The driving concerns were

---

8 Eberhard, Simons, and Fennig. "History."
9 Samuel Wilson, "SHARE."
10 Samuel Wilson, "SHARE."
11 The LCWE was established in January 1975 to implement the ethos and vision of the International Congress on World Evangelization (ICOWE), July 16–25, 1974. It consisted of the international body, seven regional committees, an executive committee and four working groups: theology and education, intercession, communication, and strategy. The first meeting of the Strategy Working Group was in 1977.
12 Wagner and Dayton, *Unreached Peoples '81*, 24 (emphasis added).

both biblical and strategic: World evangelization could be strategically advanced by fostering Christward people movements among all the identifiable subgroups of the world.[13]

In 1976, Ralph D. Winter reluctantly left his professorial role at Fuller's SWM to found the USCWM (just three miles away in Pasadena) as a cooperative mission center "think tank," research university, and platform to mobilize the church to reach the world's "hidden" peoples. Originally proposed to be a part of Fuller, Winter's ideas and approach were too radical and "out of the box" to fit in a normal educational structure. In faith, he launched an enterprise that became the leading promoter of the UPG concept and movement globally.

There were now three organizations in close proximity, each connected to Fuller's SWM but with unique yet parallel and complimentary purposes. This created a rich environment for robust dialogue and debate among several missiological thought leaders.

Wagner and Dayton

In conjunction with SWM professors at Fuller, MARC put together the first *Unreached Peoples Directory* for the 1974 Lausanne Congress. The *Directory* was an attractive booklet that introduced Congress-goers to the world of unreached peoples. For most, it was surely the first time they had ever seen a list of unreached peoples. It defined a people group as a homogeneous unit. Based on a questionnaire sent to twenty-two hundred people, it presented a list of 413 unreached people groups, using the criterion of "less than 20 percent" professing Christians. The list used the criterion of 20 percent professing Christians as a way to delineate "reached" status.[14] Three years after the Congress, the Strategy Working Group (SWG) was founded. Wagner worked closely together with Dayton and MARC, and they jointly produced the *Unreached Peoples* book series from 1979 to 1984. These books continued the original work that had been presented in 1974, and each volume included an updated list of unreached peoples, the number of which increased each year.

The biggest change made during these years involved the criteria for "reachedness"—an issue that today remains central and contested. Without such a criterion there was no way of determining whether or not a people group was reached or unreached. First, "professing Christians" was changed to "practicing Christians" as the measuring criterion. (Some critics wryly suggested that in doing so all people groups were now unreached!) More important, there was also continuing debate about the appropriate percentage of Christians to represent the "reached" tipping point. It was finally agreed that an unreached people group be defined as "a group that is less than 20 percent practicing Christian."[15]

Winter

Ralph Winter was the antagonist in this debate. He did not like the word "unreached" because of its general connotation as a reference to anyone who was not a Christian. He was also suspicious of quantitative criterion like a percentage. Winter put forth the alternative concept of "hidden peoples": "Any linguistic, cultural or sociological group defined in terms of its primary affinity (not secondary or trivial affinities), which cannot be won by E-1 methods and drawn into an existing fellowship is a Hidden People."[16]

---

13 See Johnson, "Foundations of Frontier Missiology" in this volume.
14 For a fuller discussion of the rationale and problems associated with "percentage" indicators of reachedness, see Datema, "Defining 'Unreached.'"
15 Wagner and Dayton, *Unreached Peoples '79*, 24.
16 Winter, *Penetrating the Last Frontiers*, 42.

A few years later a simple, refined definition for hidden peoples emerged: "Those cultural and linguistic sub-groups, urban or rural, for whom there is as yet no indigenous community of believing Christians able to evangelize their own people."[17] For Winter, it was not about how many Christians or missionaries there were among a people. It was about the quality of the Christian community (the presence or absence of a viable, indigenous, evangelizing church movement), not its quantity.

The issue of affinity or subgrouping was another particular concern of Winter, and it remains to this day the most confusing aspect of people group theory. How far can people groupings be divided into "segments"? What level of affinity (kinship, like-mindedness, attraction) was considered relevant to people group identity? Were "nurses in St. Louis" or "professional hockey players" (these were in the early lists!) distinct people groups? For Winter, this concept of segmentation was of ultimate importance because it was just here where people groups could be "hidden" from view, perhaps existing within a more obvious group. Winter developed four segments to portray these realities. He used the terms Megasphere, Macrosphere, Minisphere, and Microsphere in order to identify the subgroupings that exist as layers or strata within a people group. Segmentation was needed "whenever we discover that a people group is internally too diverse for a single breakthrough to be sufficient."[18]

The 1982 Chicago Consensus

By 1980, the year of the Lausanne Congress in Pattaya and the USCWM-backed meeting in Edinburgh, there were two definitions: one for "unreached peoples" and another for "hidden peoples." There was a pressing need to agree on terminology, in part because these same entities were also trying to figure out how to match churches with agencies in order to "reach," "adopt," or "love" unreached peoples. Note that *mobilization* concerns—how to present field realities and concepts to sending churches—began to take on increased significance.[19]

In the fall of 1981, Wade Coggins, on behalf of LCWE/North America, and Ed Dayton called for a meeting to agree on terminology and discuss how such a matching program might work. First dubbed the "Unreached Peoples Discussion,"[20] it was eventually referred to as the "Reach-A-People Meeting"[21] and took place in Chicago, March 25–26, 1982. It consisted of nineteen mission leaders, most of whom were mission executives. The following definition emerged for *people group*:

---

17 Winter, "Frontier Mission Perspectives," 61.

18 Winter, 63. Winter concedes that "the reality of human diversity is, of course, immeasurably more complex than these four levels imply. One can easily imagine cases where there are far more than four levels."

19 The USCWM's "Adopt-A-Hidden-People" proposal was drafted by Len Bartlotti, then chairman of the Mobilization Division, published in *Mission Frontiers*, no. 11 (November 1980), and discussed at the Edinburgh 1980 World Consultation on Frontier Missions. Concurrently, SWG, MARC, and Lausanne in Pattaya discussed their "reach" a people concept. The Center's proposal involved a three-step process: (1) "Validation"; (2) "Agency decision to initiate action"; and (3) "Church adoption of the Hidden People." The schema reflects Winter's convictions about both data and mission agency initiative in pioneering, and envisioned marshaling all the resources of the U.S. Center behind mission-church initiatives. The AAP proposal (which evolved into the current Global Adopt a People Campaign [GAAPC] based in Manila, Philippines) became part of a call for a comprehensive mission renewal movement: "The time has come for church and mission leaders to unite in promoting a cooperative mission renewal movement embracing the entire home base of the Protestant mission movement, and the rebuilding of pioneer mission perspective within it." See Bartlotti, "A Call for a Mission," 37–56.

20 Letter from Wade T. Coggins to participants.

21 Letter from Ed Dayton and Wade Coggins to participants.

A people group is a significantly large grouping of individuals who perceive themselves to have a common affinity for one another because of their shared language, religion, ethnicity, residence, occupation, class or caste, situation, etc., or combinations of these. For evangelistic purposes it is the largest group within which the gospel can spread as a church planting movement without encountering barriers of understanding or acceptance.[22]

The second sentence was added at Winter's behest, in order to emphasize segmentation caused by social/cultural barriers. But the real issue had to do with the nomenclature (unreached or hidden) and definition of those without access to the gospel. An *unreached people* was also defined: A people group among which there is no indigenous community of believing Christians with adequate numbers and resources to evangelize this people group without outside (cross-cultural) assistance.[23]

Thus, in the end, Winter agreed to use "unreached peoples," while Dayton agreed to Winter's definition that had no percentages. The focus was on the absence or presence of a viable church.

Remaining Difficulties

There have been no official changes to these definitions since. Yet significant problems remained. First, no percentage was given in the 1982 definitions, so there was no official agreement as to when a group became "reached," resulting in different numbers of unreached people groups (UPGs). Second, the consensus did not answer one of the most pressing and practical questions: Which level of segmentation (ethnicity, language, kinship, class, etc.) was the most appropriate one? Differences here also led to different numbers of UPGs. A good example of this uncertainty can be seen in the report of the pre-Congress (1989 Lausanne II Congress in Manila) Statistics Task Force chaired by David Barrett, which gives six categories for peoples: Countries, Macropeoples, Ethnolinguistic peoples, Minipeoples, Micropeoples and Sociopeoples.[24] As a result, different interpretations of exactly what constituted a "people group" led to different lists throughout the 1980s.

It was not until the mid-nineties and the advent of the AD2000 and Beyond Movement that a combined list was attempted that settled on *ethnolinguistic* as the primary category and changed the percentage to "*less than or equal to 2% Evangelical—AND—less than or equal to 5% Christian Adherent*,"[25] which remains in use for the Joshua Project list. Yet even today, people group lists reflect differences in assumptions about what constitutes a cohesive grouping within which the gospel can spread as a church-planting movement without encountering barriers of understanding or acceptance. Consensus on these matters has proven elusive.

Winter continued to promote his "no people group left behind" approach by unveiling the concept of "unimax peoples," which he considered to be the "mission relevant" group and which he also equated with the Minisphere (the second to last of his segmentation levels). Winter was again trying to emphasize smaller groupings. It is clear from Winter's later writings that he felt

---

22 Winter and Koch, "Finishing the Task," 536.
23 Winter, "Unreached Peoples," 36–37.
24 Johnstone, "People Groups: How Many Unreached?"
25 Joshua Project, "Why Include Adherents," (emphasis added). A Christian Adherent is simply anyone who self-identifies as a Christian of any kind.

the 1982 definition was unwisely equated with ethnolinguistic peoples, which were in some cases too large and likely hiding smaller groups. Winter maintained these differences throughout his life, as is evident in the *Perspectives Reader*. In the eyes of most, however, people groups simply referred to ethnolinguistic entities.

Conclusion

This historical overview puts into perspective both positive and negative aspects of this missiological tidal wave. First, a "perfect storm" was created by the coalescence of *ideas* relating people groups to world evangelization; the synergy of *influencers* (thought leaders) and *institutions* (research agencies); the simultaneous juxtaposition of computer technology, data, and media that provided new *images* of the unreached; amplified by the international *interchange* of ideas, people, data, and organizations at consultations and events;[26] all of which together helped ignite and sustain a global movement. (See Figure 6 for a summary.)

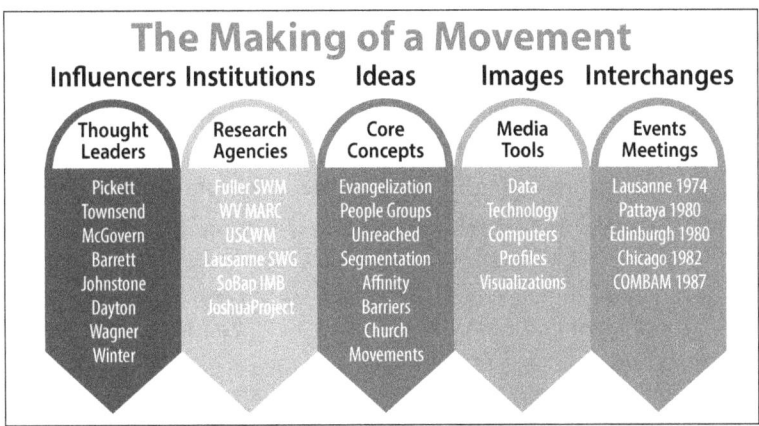

Figure 6: The Making of a Movement

Second, people group rhetoric was always far ahead of people group reality, meaning that even as the paradigm was boldly promoted onstage, there was much backstage confusion. The paradigm was always trying to catch up with its bold assertions and to cover conceptual holes, while keen observers, such as *EMQ* editors Jim Reapsome and Gary Corwin, supplied appropriate and significant pushback. Given the massive amounts of confusion that attended the movement, it is surprising that it ever succeeded at all.

Third, the fact that ongoing confusion continues today, in terms of segmentation levels, debates about which percentage criterion is best, and the rise of hybrid identities as a foil to the discrete people group model, shows that human complexity remains beyond our grasp to fully comprehend. The people group paradigm humbles all advocates.

---

26 Ralph Winter consistently promoted the historical significance of international consultations. These events were venues for the strategic interchange of ideas, people, and organizations focused on world evangelization and the "every people by the year 2000" goal. See Winter, "Report from Brazil," in which he calls COMIBAM '87 (Congreso Misionero Iberoamericano '87 in Brazil), a gathering of three thousand third-world leaders, "the meeting of the century." He writes, "The great hew and cry here at COMIBAM '87 is to transform mission fields into mission forces. And I do not believe the world will ever be the same again. COMIBAM is one unmistakable, indelible evidence of a movement that is gaining strength around the world … the definitive, final public announcement of the coming of age" of third-world missions. In particular, COMIBAM gave "significant attention to the unique instrument of global evangelization—namely, the missionary and the mission society."

The concept of seeing the world as people groups is arguably the most significant thought innovation in twentieth-century missiology. Still today, the people group remains the unit of analysis most people think of when contemplating world evangelization. As the contributions to this compendium confirm, things are changing. Whether the paradigm is simply adjusted or replaced altogether, it is likely that the same elements that brought it into existence will be significant in paving the way forward. New awareness of the social realities of the unevangelized world and new abilities to depict that world in ever-increasing clarity will change once more how we think about the Great Commission.

Bibliography

Bartlotti, Len. "A Call for a Mission Renewal Movement." *IJFM* 1, no. 1 (1984): 37–56. https://www.ijfm.org/PDFs_IJFM/01_1_PDFs/Bartlotti.pdf.

Datema, Dave. "Defining 'Unreached': A Short History." *IJFM* 33, no. 2 (Summer 2016): 45–71. https://www.ijfm.org/PDFs_IJFM/33_2_PDFs/IJFM_33_2-Datema.pdf.

Eberhard, David M., Gary F. Simons, and Charles D. Fennig. "History." *Ethnologue: Languages of the World*. 27th ed. Dallas, TX: SIL International. http://www.ethnologue.com/history.

Johnson, Alan. "Part I: The Frontier Mission Movement's Understanding of the Modern Mission Era." *IJFM* 18, no. 2 (Summer 2001): 81–88. https://www.ijfm.org/PDFs_IJFM/18_2_PDFs/AJFrontier.pdf.

Johnson, Alan. "Part II: Major Concepts of the Frontier Mission Movement." *IJFM* 18, no. 2 (Summer 2001): 89–97. https://ijfm.org/PDFs_IJFM/18_2_PDFs/AJmajor.pdf.

Johnson, Alan. "Part III: Critical Analysis of the Missiology of the Frontier Mission Movement." *IJFM* 18, no. 3 (Fall 2001): 121–27. https://www.ijfm.org/PDFs_IJFM/18_3_PDFs/AJCriticalAnalysis.pdf.

Johnson, Alan. "Part IV: The Core Contributions of Frontier Mission Missiology." *IJFM* 18, no. 3 (Fall 2001): 129–31. https://www.ijfm.org/PDFs_IJFM/18_3_PDFs/AJCoreContributors.pdf.

Johnstone, Patrick. "People Groups: How Many Unreached?" *IJFM* 7, no. 2 (April 1992).

Joshua Project. "Why Include Professing Christians When Defining Unreached?" Accessed May 7, 2024. https://joshuaproject.net/resources/articles/why_include_adherents_when_defining_unreached.

McQuilkin, J. Robertson. "Assessing the Evangelistic Responsibility of the Church." Pasadena, CA: Ralph D. Winter Research Center and Archive, 1982.

Mott, John R. *Report of Commission I: Carrying the Gospel to All the Non-Christian World*. Edinburgh: Oliphant, Anderson, and Ferrier: 1910.

Wagner, C. Peter, and Edward R. Dayton. *Unreached Peoples '79: The Challenge of the Church's Unfinished Business*. Elgin, IL: David C. Cook Publishing Company, 1978.

Wagner, C. Peter, and Edward Dayton. *Unreached Peoples '81: The Challenge of the Church's Unfinished Business*. Elgin, IL: David C. Cook Publishing Company, 1981.

Wilson, Samuel. "SHARE (Systems, Hardware and Research for Evangelization): The Development of a Cooperative Information Network for World Evangelization." Ralph D. Winter Research Center and Archive, Pasadena, CA, 1980.

Winter, Ralph D. "Four Men, Three Eras." *Mission Frontiers* 19 (Nov 1997).

Winter, Ralph D. "Frontier Mission Perspectives." In *Seeds of Promise: World Consultation on Frontier Missions, Edinburgh '80*, edited by Allan Starling, 61. Pasadena, CA: William Carey Library, 1981.

Winter, Ralph D. *Penetrating the Last Frontiers*. Pasadena, CA: William Carey Library, 1978.

Winter, Ralph. "Report from Brazil: COMIBAM '87 The Meeting of the Century." *Mission Frontiers* (January 1988). Accessed July 2, 2020. http://www.missionfrontiers.org/oldsite/1988/01/j883.htm.

Winter, Ralph D. "The Concept of a Third Era in Missions." *EMQ* 17, no. 2 (April 1981).

Winter, Ralph D. "The New Macedonia: A Revolutionary New Era in Mission Begins." In *Perspectives on the World Christian Movement: A Reader*, edited by Ralph D. Winter and Steven C. Hawthorne, 353. Pasadena, CA: William Carey Library, 2009.

Winter, Ralph D. "Three Men, Three Eras: The Flow of Missions." *Mission Frontiers* 3, no. 2 (February 1981).

Winter, Ralph D. "Unreached Peoples: The Development of the Concept." In *Reaching the Unreached: The Old-New Challenge*, edited by Harvie M. Conn, 36–37. Phillipsburg, NJ: Presbyterian and Reformed Publishing Company, 1984.

Winter, Ralph D., and Bruce A. Koch. "Finishing the Task: The Unreached Peoples Challenge." In *Perspectives on the World Christian Movement*, 4th ed., edited by Ralph D. Winter and Steven C. Hawthorne, 536. Pasadena, CA: William Carey Library, 2009.

5
Foundations of Frontier Missiology
Core Understandings and Interrelated Concepts

Alan R. Johnson

Frontier missiology involves a complex of perspectives on the Bible, mission, history, culture, and the status of the Christian faith that together focus on the *telos* or end goal of God's mission in the world: A church among every tribe, language, people, and nation. This view of God's global purpose led to new understandings of "people groups" and the mission task. In this article, I explore some of the foundational ideas and core concepts put forward by one of the movement's primary spokesmen, Ralph D. Winter (1924–2009), founder of the U.S. Center for World Mission (now Frontier Ventures). Winter's original insights about people groups are part of a set of interconnected ideas that laid the foundation for what we now call "frontier missions."

Missiological Foundations

Winter's ten-year working relationship (1966–1976) with Donald McGavran at the School of World Mission (SWM) at Fuller Seminary exposed him to ideas that laid the groundwork for his key insights. He singles out four elements that he calls pure McGavran church growth thinking: (1) The sociological observation that, in terms of evangelism, cultural factors are more important than linguistic ones; (2) that there are settings where a "sphere" of people, such as a caste, can only be penetrated by a new form of the Christian faith; (3) that if in a conglomerate (mixed member) church, a person is present from a people segment that does not have the gospel, they can become a "bridge of God" to take the good news to their own people; and (4) that in this way the gospel can spread quickly among the same people and become a "people movement to Christ."[1]

Two of McGavran's ideas were particularly formative: (1) People need to receive the gospel in a culturally relevant form, and (2) persons who have come to faith elsewhere can serve as strategic "bridges of God" to take the gospel to their own people.

The Two Original Insights That Launched Frontier Missiology

Winter extended McGavran's insights by exploring the implications for non-Christians in a different people group or segment: What if there is not a culturally relevant version of faith available, nor a bridge person to share the gospel with them?

Winter's first big insight had to do with the significance of *barriers*. He "began to realize that if it is true that even minor cultural differences can separate people and keep them from going to the same congregation, etc., then this fact has horrendous implications for the existing mission movement."[2] His teaching on the expansion of the Christian faith showed that non-Christians in one segment of people did not automatically respond positively to the form of the Christian faith they were seeing in *other* people segments. This seemed

---
1 Winter, "Eleven Frontiers," 77.
2 Winter, 78.

true even when the two groups shared a common language. Furthermore, the same cultural differences that were a barrier for those "outside" a group to come to faith also hindered the Christians "inside" from "seeing" their non-Christian neighbors as people with whom they should be sharing the gospel.

Mission agencies inadvertently reinforced these barriers. Winter's historical lenses revealed that agencies operated with a faulty premise when it came to church planting: "They do not expect nor seek to have two or more different forms of Christianity; the form that develops in their first major beachhead [in a country] tends to be considered good enough for all the other groups."[3] The assumption that one cultural version of faith will naturally flow outward to other people segments turned out not to be true; thus, in evangelism and church planting, one cultural or "national" church "version" of the faith decidedly does not fit all.

The second insight grew from Winter's reflection on what happens when there is no bridge person present to carry the gospel to their own people.[4] McGavran felt that strategically the best investment of missionary effort was to work with groups where there were bridge people. Winter asked, "So what about the other groups for which there existed no bridge?"[5] He saw that the lack of a converted person from (or relevant fellowship within) the same cultural group meant there was *no near-neighbor witness* to share the gospel with their own people. Gospel penetration, by definition, would require *cross-cultural* effort. Putting these two insights together enabled Winter to see a world of peoples needing access to a culturally relevant version of the gospel. He came to the startling conclusion:

> statistically speaking, … from this perspective a very large proportion of world population is *sealed off*, as it were. … It meant that precisely those hermetically-sealed pockets of people around the world that had *not yet had any kind of a penetration* constituted by themselves *the major remaining frontier of Christian mission*.[6]

It is important to note that this "sealing off" from the gospel is social and cultural. This vision of the reality of the culturally shaped forms of faith, and the resulting need for gospel access in large "hidden" swaths of humanity, made true cross-cultural pioneer evangelism—not simply the diffusion of existing versions of faith—the "highest priority."

Core Understandings and Interrelated Concepts

The notion of "people groups" who need the gospel, however, cannot be understood in isolation. The people group concept is at the center of a *constellation of interrelated concepts* and understandings that serve to clarify these original insights. None of these concepts stand alone! They are useful for strategy development and best understood only in relationship to Winter's clear-sighted focus on gospel access.

Why is this important for our current understandings of peoples? Because too often Winter's critical insights have been lost in wrangling over notions of "peoples," "groupness," and "reached/unreached," and the various lists that attempt to document them. These concepts

---

3 Winter, 77–78.
4 Winter, 78.
5 Winter, 78.
6 Winter, 78 (emphasis added).

and understandings are human constructs that serve the larger vision of gospel access. What follows here is a brief look at the core understandings and concepts in frontier missiology and how they serve Winter's central point.

ACCESS: Christian world mission is about gospel access.
Winter's two original insights shifted the focus of missionary work from "individuals" who were not Christians to "peoples" without an indigenous Christian tradition among them. His preferred term to describe such groups was "hidden peoples," demarcated by "the absence of a church leaving people *unincorporable*."[7] If a culturally relevant church tradition was present allowing people to be *incorporated* into those churches, then near-neighbor, ordinary evangelism would do the job. For Winter, gospel access was more than just hearing, but the opportunity to become part of—incorporate into—a living fellowship. The kind of ecclesial embodiment he had in mind not only provided stability and durability but developed culturally appropriate forms that make people feel they "fit." In the absence of such a church movement, these peoples would not hear the gospel unless cross-cultural workers brought it to them. What set Winter apart was that he not only saw this as a remaining frontier of mission, he conceived of pioneer work as the fundamental missionary task, with the goal of bringing about an initial breakthrough—a "missiological breakthrough"—on which all other cross-cultural work builds.

PEOPLES: Frontier missions is about penetrating people groups.
The reality of culturally shaped forms of the faith means that one size does not fit all when it comes to evangelism. The history of Christian mission confirms that while some people will respond to a particular version of the faith, others will reject it. Frontier missiology takes us beyond a geographic view of mission, reaching individuals, and planting our preferred style of church. Rather, reminiscent of Paul in Romans 15, frontier missions is an "ambition" and call to relentlessly cross boundaries to penetrate segments of people who have no near-neighbor access to the gospel.

It is critical to understand that the concepts of "peopleness" and "groupness" in frontier missiology were developed from the perspective of evangelism and not anthropology. A "people group" was defined "*for evangelistic purposes*" as the largest possible group within which the gospel can spread as a (viable, indigenous) church-planting movement without encountering barriers of understanding or acceptance.[8] Winter was looking for the largest pockets of cohesiveness that could make up a "people segment" and felt free-flowing internal communication was the best indicator.[9] To express this idea, he coined the term "unimax people" as a "group *uni*fied in communication and the *max*imum size where gospel communication can proceed without encountering a barrier of acceptance or understanding."[10]

---

7   Winter, *Penetrating*, 40.
8   Winter and Koch (2002), "Finishing," 19.
9   Datema, "Defining Unreached," 55–56.
10 Winter, "Facing," 13.

BARRIERS: *Encountering barriers of understanding or acceptance signals the need to launch new pioneer church-planting efforts.*

The unimax concept meant that you could never fully know how many unreached groups there are because you need boots on the ground to encounter the barriers that indicate the need for a new cross-cultural church-planting effort. For Winter larger cuts of humanity like cultural blocs, affinity groups, socio-peoples, and ethnolinguistic groups were just ways of getting an initial baseline of areas of greatest need for gospel access.[11]

CULTURE: *Every cultural group must have a culturally relevant gospel message and church movement.*

Segments of people require cross-cultural workers to hear the gospel when there is no culturally relevant indigenous church movement among them to bear near-neighbor witness. Winter's E (evangelism) and P (people) scales highlight this need on two dimensions. The E-Scale compares the cultural distances the messenger needs to move in order to communicate the gospel with others, while the P-Scale compares the different cultural distances that potential converts need to move in order to join the nearest church. Scaled from zero to three, E3 means the evangelists are working in a culture very different than their own, which is a highly complex task. P3 means the only option for a new convert among this people would be a Christian movement that is vastly different culturally from them; thus, P3 peoples lack a culturally relevant indigenous Christian tradition among them. The reality of peoples who still lack gospel access means that E3 work among a P3 people remains a critical need. This complex labor to "pick the lock," as Winter was fond of saying, of a people segment in order to see a viable indigenous church movement started is not the work of amateurs on forays. It requires long-term workers with language and cultural competence.

CHURCH: *Breakthrough involves a viable, indigenous evangelizing church.*

Winter saw the initial goal as a "missiological breakthrough," resulting in the creation of a viable indigenous church. For Winter a viable church is where

> a true breakthrough has occurred when at least a minimal … yet sufficiently developed indigenous Christian tradition, is established that is considered capable of evangelizing its own people without E2 or E3 help. All it means is that the missiological breakthrough has been made.[12]

Missiological breakthrough represents a robust ecclesiology with the vision of a visible, living fellowship that endures across generations. *Viability* is not about size but the presence of the spiritual vibrancy that ensures ongoing replication so that the church survives on its own; it is *indigenous* in that it is rooted in local forms and not seen as foreign; and it is a *church-planting movement* because it continually produces intentional fellowships that can evangelize the rest of the people group.[13]

---

[11] Winter and Koch, 17.
[12] Winter, "Frontier Mission," 65–66.
[13] Winter and Koch (2009), "Finishing," 538.

MOVEMENTS: Breakthrough involves a Christward people movement.
For Winter a viable church was just a minimal goal.[14] Like McGavran he envisioned a flow of whole families embracing Christ, not just discrete individuals. Winter was exposed to movements in the thinking of McGavran but came to see them as having greater significance than just propagating the gospel. It is the flow of communication, what McGavran called "intimate social life within the boundaries of their own society," that plays a role in creating and sustaining a sense of "groupness." But it was the power of a culturally relevant gospel flowing through the channels of intimate social relations that allowed for movements; thus, movements, the embedded nature of our versions of faith, and the need for cultural relevance were closely connected for him.

Winter's familiarity with mission history enabled him to recognize that movements often take place beyond, or in spite of, missionary efforts, church/mission constraints and structures, and current Eastern or Western conceptions of what it means to be Christian.[15] He observed near the end of his career that many do not realize that missiological breakthrough

> almost always produces a church movement considerably different from what might be expected, just as Paul's work was very difficult to understand for Jewish believers in Christ. … *The rapid growth of our faith across the world is mostly of a movement of new indigenous forms of faith that are substantially different from that of the missionary.*[16]

In his subsequent writings Winter started to unpack the implications of this, showing how movements to Christ are radical, messy, and out of the box. Winter saw radical contextualization and the development of novel indigenized forms of "church," as a normal, even necessary, corollary of the God-driven expansion of the Christian movement into new frontiers.[17]

FOCUSED: The frontier missions task is a narrow focus that guides all expressions of cross-cultural ministry.
For Winter, planting the church among peoples where it does not exist was at the heart of the world Christian movement. At the same time, he also saw value in the broad cross-cultural activity that grows out of pioneer labor. However, all mission efforts must be aligned with that larger vision and passed on to the new church movement.

A primary focus on developing indigenous church-planting movements did not in his view "imply that any such church anywhere should be considered totally independent of the world family of Christians, nor that it cannot both minister through and profit from continued cross-cultural contacts and expatriate help."[18] For Winter *mission* differs from ordinary *evangelism*: the latter is "monocultural," whereas mission "is an activity involving the special problems of cross-cultural communication and contextualization."[19] Nevertheless, he

---

14 Winter, "Frontier Mission," 65–66.
15 I am grateful to Len Bartlotti, who worked with Winter at USCWM in the early 1980s, for this insight. Email communication to author, June 15, 2020.
16 Winter, "I Was Bombed," 160 (emphasis added).
17 Len Bartlotti, email communication to author, June 15, 2020.
18 Winter, "Frontier Mission," 65–66.
19 Winter, "From Mission to Evangelism," 156.

argued that a laser-like frontier focus does not devalue regular mission work with the existing church. In his view, "the mission that continues in evangelism and *allows and encourages an overseas church movement to become missionary* is doing a very strategic thing."[20]

For Winter, the four stages of mission activity—pioneer, paternal, partnership, and participation—each involved important work.[21] He was adamant that the most strategic thing in reaching the unreached is not mass redeployment of existing missionaries, despite accusations to the contrary that continue to this day,[22] but their *mobilization*. He wanted to see

> our existing missionaries (as well as those who join them), right where they are—wherever they are—catching a new vision. For what? A new perspective on whatever they are doing, making sure that prayed into and breathed into everything they do is *a new vision for the so-called younger churches to get involved in their own mission sending.*[23]

Note Winter's insistence that all stages of mission be *imbued* with vision and *impart* a vision for mission. The "continuing post-pioneer part of the picture is bright and shining and a blessed reality" when existing missionaries, anywhere and everywhere—and the churches they establish, teach, and serve—"get involved in their own mission sending."[24]

HOPE: *Mission to the unreached is rooted in the unchanging purpose and promise of God.*
Planting the church among peoples where there is no church is not some kind of missiological fad or innovation, but a firm hope. Winter's optimism and original insights into the "all peoples" vision were rooted in the heart of the living God as revealed in the Scriptures, as well as the outworking of that purpose in human history.

In 1980, Winter and his wife did a series in *Mission Frontiers* on missions in the Bible. His personal study led to the "radically new idea (to us) that the Great Commission was right there in Genesis 12."[25] This understanding led him "to rearrange my thought patterns to conform to the perspective of the Commissioning of Abraham in Genesis and to the Great Commission itself, which speaks of the discipling of peoples."[26] He saw throughout Scripture, from Genesis 12:1–3 to Revelation 5:9 and 7:9, God's purpose to be glorified among all the diversity of humanity. He came to see the Bible not as a "bundle of divergent, unrelated stories as taught in Sunday School," but as a single coherent drama of "the entrance of the Kingdom, the power and the glory of the living God in this enemy-occupied territory" where "we see the gradual but irresistible power of God reconquering and redeeming his fallen creation through the giving of His own Son."[27] Winter's faith, hope, and frontier missiology were grounded on God's "gradual but irresistible power."

Winter's knowledge of mission history made him both optimistic and realistic. His sense of the mission significance of Acts 1:8 was that bearing witness to Jesus necessitates *crossing*

---

20 Winter, 156 (emphasis added).
21 Winter, "Four Men," 256.
22 Carlson and Clark, "The 3 Words."
23 Winter, "Are 90% of Our Missionaries," 35 (emphasis added).
24 Winter, "The Role," 114.
25 Winter, "Twelve Frontiers," 29.
26 Winter, "Facing the Frontiers," 13.
27 Winter, "The Kingdom Strikes Back," 196

cultural boundaries to make disciples among the *ethne* (Matt 28:18–20). He recognized divine purpose behind the history of the Christian movement. Nevertheless, God's people have not always responded to his irrepressible call to mission. Our own sluggish generation could be passed by. But Winter saw how the Spirit repeatedly raised up people with vision to take the gospel to places and peoples where Christ was not yet known. The gospel breaks out and breaks through all barriers, even those within the church. He himself was one of those used by God to call the church to find and go to those without the saving message.

Conclusion

We are approaching fifty years since Winter's plenary on cross-cultural evangelism at the 1974 International Congress on World Evangelization rocked the missions world. He had the same facts in hand as many other people but saw them differently and was able to articulate them in a way that became a call to action for the church.

Ralph Winter's core insights and the concepts that arose from them generated a quantum shift in the way missions is envisioned. His clarification of the task around reaching peoples without access to the gospel had a prophetic impact on the church. We now know the names of places and peoples that have little or no access to the gospel, and we cannot be honest with ourselves that we are engaging *God's* mission unless we grapple with how we will respond to this reality.

Winter's original insights and core understandings and concepts remain relevant and powerful for missionary practice today. His original challenge to cross-cultural evangelism remains critical with 25 percent of the global population living in peoples who are 0.1 percent Christian or less. In a globalizing and urbanizing world of people on the move, where "missions" and "missionary" continue to be defined in terms of geography, travel, and activity, the call to cross-cultural outreach and culturally relevant forms of the faith are much-needed lenses to ensure all peoples have gospel access.

Bibliography

Carlson, Darren, and Elliot Clark. "The 3 Words That Changed Missions Strategy—and Why We Might Be Wrong." September 11, 2019. https://www.thegospelcoalition.org/Article /misleading-words-missions-strategy-unreached-people-groups.

Datema, Dave. "Defining Unreached: A Short History." *International Journal of Frontier Missiology* 33, no. 2 (2016): 45–71.

Winter, Ralph D. "Are 90% of Our Missionaries Serving in the Wrong Places?" *Mission Frontiers Bulletin* (November–December 1991): 34–35.

Winter, Ralph D. "Facing the Frontiers." *Mission Frontiers* (Oct–Nov 1982): 13.

Winter, Ralph D. "Four Men, Three Eras, Two Transitions: Modern Missions." In *Perspectives on the World Christian Movement: A Reader*, edited by Ralph D. Winter and Steven C. Hawthorne, 253–62. Pasadena: William Carey Library, 1999.

Winter, Ralph D. "From Mission to Evangelism to Mission." In *Frontiers in Mission: Discovering and Surmounting Barriers to the Missio Dei*, 155–57. Pasadena: William Carey International University Press, 2005.

Winter, Ralph D. "Frontier Mission Perspectives." In *Seeds of Promise: World Consultation on Frontier Missions, Edinburgh '80*, edited by Allan Starling, 45–99. Pasadena: William Carey Library, 1981.

Winter, Ralph D. "I Was Bombed by an Explosive Idea." In *Frontiers in Mission: Discovering and Surmounting Barriers to the Missio Dei*, 158–60. Pasadena: William Carey International University Press, 2005.

Winter, Ralph D. "The Kingdom Strikes Back: Ten Epochs of Redemptive History." In *Perspectives on the World Christian Movement: A Reader*, edited by Ralph D. Winter and Steven C. Hawthorne, 195–213. Pasadena: William Carey Library, 1999.

Winter, Ralph. "Part I: Eleven Frontiers of Perspective." *International Journal of Frontier Missions* 20, no. 3 (Fall 2003): 77–81.

Winter, Ralph D. *Penetrating the Last Frontiers*. Pasadena: William Carey Library, 1978.

Winter, Ralph D. "The Role of Western Missions in the 21st Century." In *Frontiers in Mission: Discovering and Surmounting Barriers to the Missio Dei*, 114–17. Pasadena: William Carey International University Press, 2005.

Winter, Ralph W. "Twelve Frontiers of Perspective." In *Frontiers in Mission: Discovering and Surmounting Barriers to the Missio Dei*, 28–39. Pasadena: William Carey International University Press, 2005.

Winter, Ralph D., and Bruce A. Koch. "Finishing the Task: The Unreached People Challenge." *International Journal of Frontier Missions* 19, no. 4 (Winter 2002): 15–25.

Winter, Ralph D., and Bruce A. Koch. "Finishing the Task: The Unreached Peoples Challenge." In *Perspectives on the World Christian Movement*, edited by Ralph D. Winter and Steven C. Hawthorne, 531–46. Pasadena: William Carey Library, 2009.

Reflection and Discussion
The Impetus for the Unreached Peoples Movement

1. What Scriptures most powerfully communicate to you God's heart and purposes for all nations?

2. What does it mean to "work backwards" from an "ends of the earth" mission goal and vision? How might this understanding impact your missions thinking, planning, prayer, priorities, and involvement?

3. List some of the "core concepts" of the people group approach.

4. What new understandings did you gain about these concepts and how they relate as a kind of "constellation" of concepts?

5. Why doesn't the gospel naturally cross people group barriers?

6. Do you agree that there should be an apostolic priority on unreached peoples? Explain.

7. Choose one Scripture to memorize this week.

Part 2
Impact of People Group Thinking on Agencies

Painful and Purposeful Adjustments

6
Run with the Vision

The Impact of the Unreached People Groups Concept on Students, Churches, and Sending Agencies

Greg Parsons

Prior to the first Lausanne Congress for World Evangelization in 1974, there was little awareness of unreached people groups (UPGs). As researchers began to get better information about the status of world evangelization, it became increasingly clear that, despite successes, there were gaps in mission efforts—especially within cultural blocs where the gospel had made little impact. Lausanne sought to address opposing calls for a "mission moratorium" by calling attention to the need to continue reaching out to the world with the gospel.

Ralph D. Winter's plenary challenge at Lausanne '74 was a clarion call to expand mission outreach. God used that presentation and a spirit of change on the hearts of leaders, young and old, to fuel what became a global movement to reach people groups without a viable church. The UPG vision and thinking impacted three groups: students, churches, and mission agencies.

Setting the Stage for a Movement

In the seventies, new, effective ways of digesting and disseminating up-to-date information on the world became more accessible. The MARC division of World Vision produced two series of books involving data sets, *Unreached Peoples of the World* and *Mission Handbook: North American Protestant Ministries Overseas.*[1] In 1976, the first edition of Patrick Johnstone's *Operation World* was published, and in 1982, David Barrett made available the *World Christian Encyclopedia*. Later, a group of creative data-focused mission leaders, fueled by a mostly young group of Caltech programmer-types, caught the unreached vision. Under the mature leadership and experience of Bob Waymire, they started Data Serve (later Global Mapping International) in 1986. The information infrastructure of the UPG movement was growing.

It was becoming clear that there were both successes and blind spots in the spread of the gospel. Leading up to Lausanne '74, Ralph Winter, with Donald McGavran and others, had spent eight years helping to train and learn from about one thousand field-experienced missionaries at Fuller Seminary's School of World Mission (now the Fuller School of Mission and Theology). He was also engaged with the burgeoning mission sending from Asia. In 1973, at the All Asia Missions Consultation, with only a few Westerners present, Winter presented "Two Structures of God's Redemptive Mission,"[2] which explains the now well-known distinction between mission (sodality) and church (modality) structures. At that same event,

---

[1] The first published survey of North American missions was in 1953. The Missions Advanced Research and Communication Center, or MARC, took over the publication of this book in 1973 from John R. Mott, who established Missionary Research Library. *The North American Mission Handbook* is now published by MissioNexus.org.

[2] Winter, "Two Structures," 122–39.

Winter also urged that many *more* missions be established in Asia.³ Mission structures, both Western and non-Western, would be essential and strategic in the developing UPG movement.

This fed into Winter's presentation in 1974: "The Highest Priority: Cross-Cultural Evangelism."⁴ In this presentation, as Lausanne recently posted, "Winter shared the concept of unreached people groups that significantly influenced evangelical mission energies ever since."⁵ "The massive need to take the gospel to unreached people groups, as presented by Winter and illustrated by [Donald] McGavran" is now recognized as one of three major emphases of Lausanne '74.⁶

In the fall of 1974, Ralph and his wife, Roberta, increasingly felt compelled to do something about this. In 1976, he left his tenured faculty position at Fuller and together they established the U.S. Center for World Mission (USCWM, now called Frontier Ventures.) Their clear and compelling vision: reaching the unreached. In 1979, that vision was distilled in the watchword: A Church for Every People by the Year 2000.⁷ For the vision of reaching unreached peoples to spread, the USCWM would have to be a "soapbox" galvanizing three groups: students, churches, and mission agencies.

Students

In the sixties and seventies, God seemed to be using general unrest among young people (reflected in the Jesus Movement and the burgeoning charismatic movement) to bring a spirit of change. Young people sought to "make a difference" with their lives.

Ralph Winter saw what was happening with these students and tried to engage them for the kingdom. He had attended every Urbana from the first in 1949 when he was in seminary. In 1970, only 8 percent signed the decision card, but at Urbana 1973, 28 percent signed, saying they were willing to become missionaries, should God direct. With that year's record audience of fourteen thousand, that meant almost four thousand young people had signed the cards.⁸ Winter got one of his many ideas and bounded into action. He contacted Urbana Director David Howard and convinced him to offer the students an intensive two-week course to help them go deeper with their commitments. Some six months later in the summer of 1974, students came to a precursor of what later became the "Perspectives on the World Christian Movement" course. Now well over 250,000 have taken the course globally.⁹

---

3 Chun, "All-Asia Mission," 7–8.

4 Winter, "Highest Priority," 213–41. In my thesis on Ralph Winter, I explain the insightful way the 1974 Lausanne Congress sought to engage delegates months before the meeting. The consultation provided for a unique, pre-conference global input, in that each plenary speaker submitted their paper six months ahead of time, and then based on that input, revised them for their presentation at Lausanne. Ralph Winter's presentation was completely different than what he first submitted.

5 "Remembering Dr. Ralph Winter."

6 In the lead-up to the third Lausanne Congress in Cape Town in 2010, Lausanne.org summarized three major outcomes from the 1974 meeting. The other two were the "Lausanne Covenant" and "the clear recognition and need for evangelicals to focus on social issues."

7 "Today's Crisis," 3–7. Much has been written about the value of this goal, what was achieved, and whether it caused a "letdown" when it was not completed. See www.missionfrontiers.org after the year 2000 for some of the follow-up evaluation, as well as *EMQ* and other sources during the early 2000s.

8 Parsons, *Ralph D. Winter*, 225.

9 Perspectives USA.

There were global gatherings focused on unreached peoples involving students and mission leadership. The USCWM helped organize the World Consultation on Frontier Missions (WCFM) in Edinburgh, Scotland in 1980 (E'80).[10] A significant and "novel addition" was a parallel "sister consultation" in Edinburgh, the International Student Consultation on Frontier Missions (ISCFM).[11] ISCFM was composed of 170 students from twenty-seven countries and grappled with the needs of unreached peoples as well as the challenge of mobilizing a new generation of student pioneer missionaries to hidden peoples.[12]

There were several outcomes of ISCFM. The students adopted the E'80 watchword ("A Church for Every People by the Year 2000") and produced and signed a consensus "pledge." This pledge represented a lifetime commitment to the cause of frontier missions, whether at home or abroad, and to spreading that vision:

> By the grace of God and for His glory, I commit my entire life to obeying His commission of Matthew 28:18–20 wherever and however He leads me, giving priority to the peoples currently beyond the reach of the gospel (Rom 15:20–21). I will also endeavor to impart this vision to others.

The ISCFM established a mechanism for ongoing "communication" of the frontier mission vision. Under the leadership of Brad Gill, the resulting *International Journal for Frontier Missions*,[13] launched in 1984, became the official journal of the new International Society for Frontier Missiology (ISFM). Soon, this was a vibrant network, meeting annually, including younger leaders, scholar-practitioners, mobilizers, and field workers. It has facilitated fresh thinking, prayer-focused research, theologizing, and praxis related to frontier missions.[14]

The challenge of mobilizing students was picked up by new initiatives like Caleb Project, founded by four Penn State University students who took the first extension "Perspectives" course in the early days of the USCWM. These passionate senders and goers embraced the challenge of mobilizing their generation of students, promoting the Edinburgh '80 ISCFM pledge—renaming it "The Caleb Pledge"—to make Christ known, "giving priority to peoples currently beyond the reach of the gospel," based on Romans 15:20–21.[15]

Many other tools, people, and ministries could be included here. In 1980, a student magazine was launched called *Today's Mission* (later renamed *World Christian Magazine*). Teams of students on the way to the field circulated among college and university campuses with a God-centered missions appeal to challenge students to follow them. Raising up young people with purpose and direction spread vision, not only on campuses, but also in churches, and helped redirect the energies of mission organizations to the unreached.

---

10 "Edinburgh 1980 Momentum Grows," 3; and Winter, "Edinburgh 1980 Reports," 1.

11 Information on ISCFM was provided by Len Bartlotti who attended Edinburgh 1980 and participated in both WCFM and ISCFM.

12 The latter goal was inspired in part by the Student Volunteer Movement, launched in 1886, which mobilized university students for the cause of world evangelization.

13 Now *International Journal of Frontier Missiology*.

14 Len Bartlotti, email communication to the author, June 2, 2020.

15 For background on Caleb Project, see *Mission Frontiers*, August 1988. Caleb Project and its companion ministries (e.g., the Perspectives-like text and course *Encountering the World of Islam*) are now associated with the agency Pioneers.

Churches

Winter knew that local churches were critical as the "home base" of the mission movement. Giving, awareness, prayer, mission education, and sending are grounded in the church. To reach unreached peoples, that home base would need renewing with frontier mission vision and biblical understandings of God's heart and purposes for all peoples. UPG thinking and vision began to impact churches, not only in North America, but in other parts of the world.

Unlike today, the idea and role of a mission "mobilizer" was not well understood. Winter was calling young people who joined him to raise a ministry support team and then stay in the United States to encourage others to go to UPGs. The reasoning behind it was simple: Why go alone when you can stay back and find others to go with you? One popular way of illustrating this was the notion of "waking sleeping firemen": If a person sees a burning building, he or she can choose either to get a bucket and try to put it out alone (meaning: go to the field directly) or go and wake up one hundred sleeping firemen for the task (meaning: take others with you to multiply the effort).

Effective mobilization requires ideas, resources, and examples to fuel prayer and action. In 1974, Winter helped former Xerox executive Don Hamilton establish a "professional network" for church missions committees called the Association of Church Missions Committees. ACMC was all about "churches helping churches" to plan, prioritize, and structure their mission efforts.

In 1979, the publication of *Mission Frontiers* magazine (*MF*) began as a "bullhorn" for these ideas. Mission leaders in local churches began to engage with key field issues in a new way. Agencies sought to lead the way while also keeping up with the students pushing to reach the unreached.

David Bryant, an effective student mobilizer with InterVarsity Missions, called people to gather in serious "concerts of prayer."[16] The USCWM produced the *Daily Prayer Guide* (later renamed *Global Prayer Digest*). It was modeled after Walk Thru the Bible's monthly resource, but with a prayer-focused "walk thru the world." It included specific unreached people groups for each day of the month. The goal was and is to "invade" people's minds, hearts, and devotional lives with prayer for the unreached. The thinking behind it: Only what one does daily will dominate one's life. It has been in continuous production since.[17]

People also needed to pray together in their churches, so the USCWM created the Frontier Fellowship. This would give an outlet for churches to reach specific people groups by encouraging both specific prayer for unreached peoples and collecting funds they could send to their denominational mission or preferred mission agency. The Presbyterian Frontier Fellowship (now www.frontierfellowship.com) raised millions of dollars from its churches for work among the unreached.

Other programs were designed to equip churches and spread the vision. *A Hidden Peoples Sunday* kit had sample sermon outlines and resources for churches to have a special Sunday emphasis. Other video and study resources for awareness and teaching were later "packaged" together into a "Year of Vision" mission renewal and education emphasis.

---

16 Bryant, "Concerts of Prayer," 6–11.
17 See www.globalprayerdigest.org (also available via mobile application) and www.joshuaproject.net.

In 1980, early USCWM Director of Mobilization Len Bartlotti proposed Adopt-A-People to enable churches to partner with agencies to "adopt" or focus on a particular people group for ongoing prayer, concern, and potential sending. The focus was not on "adopting" missionaries and workers, but on the specific unreached people group, with the long-term goal of a viable, indigenous church-planting movement among them. Today there are entire denominations, especially in Latin America and Asia, which have taken up this challenge, multiplying fervent intercession for specific UPG.[18] In the United States, denominations like the Evangelical Free Church, Foursquare, Presbyterian, Southern Baptist, Assemblies of God, and others have turned their attention and considerable resources—some quickly, others more slowly—toward UPGs and frontier missions.

Mission Agencies

Missiological discussions were already happening all over the world.[19] A number of agencies and denominational missions realized they needed to refocus their efforts on unreached peoples. They knew that the UPG vision would require (1) reaching into new cultures with the gospel, (2) crossing new barriers, and (3) recruiting new global workers. The early days of the UPG movement included much brainstorming and interaction at the USCWM, with conferences and meetings between people, church, and mission leaders from around the globe.

New sending organizations were started, such as Frontiers and Pioneers, with an exclusive or priority focus on pioneer church planting among Muslim, Hindu, Buddhist, or Tribal peoples. Other agencies looked to their roots and renewed their historical commitment to frontier work. The associations that brought together mission leaders from denominations and faith missions also turned their attention to UPG.

In 1980, *MF* included an article on the Foursquare denomination's plans "to establish mission coordinators at each local church and seek to reach 100 UPGs."[20] In an article for *Wherever* magazine, published by TEAM, Winter noted:

> All the major mission agencies are aware of the new era. The Sudan Interior Mission has a full-time man investigating new fields. The African Inland Mission is rapidly retooling. TEAM has been constantly reaching out to new fields. So has the Regions Beyond Missionary Union.[21]

In the mid-1980s, in a strategic move into the practical realm, the USCWM hosted summer training modules on reaching out to local Muslims. The Zwemer Institute, founded in 1979 and led by Don McCurry, brought together veteran missionaries and scholars for research, study, mobilization, and the training of multitudes of workers going into the Muslim world. After serving in diverse Islamic nations, some of these students are now themselves professors training another generation of young people.[22]

---

18 See the initial proposal in *Mission Frontiers* 2, no. 11 (1980). The AAP program became the Global Adopt A People Campaign (GAAPC), now based in Manila, Philippines, led by former USCWM staff member Phil Bogosian (globaladoptapeoplecampaign.org).

19 The largest-known school of missiology at the time was at the University of South Africa under David Bosch. Fuller's SWM was probably next in size and larger in influence in North American sending.

20 "NewsBriefs," 5.

21 Winter, "Some Unfinished Business," 1, 4, 6.

22 "1986 Summer Institutes," 12–13.

Non-Western sending agencies were also getting involved. The Latin world came on the global scene in 1987 with a gathering called COMIBAM[23] and with leaders like Luis Bush,[24] along with other international efforts.[25] In the Chinese world, Thomas Wang led the way, and in the late eighties both Wang and Bush helped to launch the AD2000 Movement, which mobilized globally and fulfilled its purpose up to its planned ending in the year 2001.[26] Winter estimated that 85 percent of the missionaries worked among groups already reached with the gospel. Only 15 percent served among the unreached.[27] So while evangelicals recognized they needed more missionaries, now there was pressure for them to more carefully consider where to send them.

As the UPG movement grew in influence, debates swirled around UPG thinking, theology, missiology, and praxis. The USCWM made a point never to push for the "redeployment" of missionaries from established fields to UPG as some did. They argued that an established missionary working in a reached group was in the best position to mobilize that "national" church for work among new UPG.[28] Still, some local churches began to question existing missionaries on long-established fields about their work. Over time, some workers were redeployed by their agencies; other ministries shifted or ended. In reaction, some ministries felt existing mission fields were being abandoned. The issues were discussed in several articles in EMQ during the eighties and nineties and more recently.[29]

Other objections were raised. Even as early as the '74 Lausanne event, there were those who felt that the focus on specific people groups created churches divided along ethnic lines. This debate circulates and has been argued from many angles on the pages of *EMQ*,[30] the *IJFM*, and other journals. Some argue that the church should be diverse. However, while this may appear ideal, it is hard to find models of "conglomerate" or multiethnic churches that are not dominated by one group or language—often English, or even Arabic (e.g., among Berbers in North Africa).[31] Others suggest that the Scriptures point to the beauty of different cultures expressing God's creativity and glory in new ways, and that "unifying" the church squelched that dimension. Another aspect of the debate over the unreached, focused on the lost among "reached" nations, arguing that these people should not be overlooked.[32]

---

23 There are now more than fifteen thousand missionaries from Latin America serving around the world; see Comibam.org.
24 Winter, "COMIBAM," 7–8.
25 Winter, "Explosion," 6–7; Dougherty, "Getting the Whole Story," 8–11; Winter, "Luis Bush," 1, 3, 5.
26 Bridges, "Meeting," 5.
27 The article by Johnson and Tieszen, "Personal Contact: The Sine Qua Non of Twenty-First Century Christian Mission," pointed out that this is an interesting, though not direct, parallel with their research that 86 percent of Muslims, Hindus, and Buddhists do not personally know a Christian of any kind.
28 Winter, "Planting of Younger Missions." Ralph Winter observed a blind spot of field missionaries: They did not establish younger missions on the field. Generally, well-established "mission field churches" were not sending out their own missionaries.
29 These critiques continue to be recycled even though Winter did not encourage redeployment or abandonment of existing fields. See Carlson and Clark, "The 3 Words," Newkirk, "Should Missionaries Focus," and others.
30 Hyatt, "From Homogeneous," 226–32.
31 Parsons, "Will the Earth Hear," 14–16.
32 Severn, "Some Thoughts," 412–19; Kendall, "Missions Should Not," 180–85.

In addition to the Lausanne Movement, groups, such as the World Evangelical Alliance,[33] have also furthered the collaboration, networking, and significant discussions on a range of church and mission issues. Non-Western-founded groups such as the Asian Missions Society[34] (founded in 1975) and the Asian Society of Missiology[35] (founded in 2003) have added their voices to the movement. More recently, a new US-based network called Alliance for the Unreached was established in 2015.[36] It is seeking to catalyze a movement that unites churches, organizations, and individuals around the cause of reaching every unreached people group on earth with the gospel of Jesus Christ.

Ironically, despite the continuing great "imbalance" in mission sending and funding, with the majority going to peoples and places with existing churches, there is still resistance by some to a focus on UPG. Recently, several organizations have refocused efforts on those UPG with less than 0.1 percent Christian of any kind and no movements to Jesus. They have been labeled "frontier people groups" and are considered high priority.[37] This suggests that UPG rethinking, discussion, and research should continue to help us grow in our understanding and effective field practice.

Conclusion

Growing out of Lausanne '74, a new vision of the unreached has impacted students, churches, and mission agencies right up to the present. The fruit of their labor can be seen in the advancement of new strategies, new sending, and new fellowships among formerly unreached peoples. We press on in prayer and service, seeking to reach those who are not yet reached, that they may be reconciled to God.

Bibliography

"1986 Summer Institutes at the U.S. Center for World Mission." *Mission Frontiers* 8, no. 3 (1986): 12–13.

Bridges, E. "The Meeting of the Century Is Announced." *Mission Frontiers* 10, no. 7 (1988): 5.

Bryant, D. "Concerts of Prayer: Waking Up for a New Mission Thrust." *Mission Frontiers* 5, no. 3 & 4 (1983): 6–11.

Carlson, Darren, and Elliot Clark. "The 3 Words That Changed Missions Strategy—and Why We Might Be Wrong." September 11, 2019. https://www.thegospelcoalition.org/article/misleading-words-missions-strategy-unreached-people-groups.

Chun, C. "The All-Asia Mission Consultation." MTh thesis, Fuller Theological Seminary, 1975.

Dougherty, D. "Getting the Whole Story: Researcher Releases Comprehensive Survey of Third World Missions Today." *Mission Frontiers* 5, no. 2 (1983): 8–11.

"Edinburgh 1980 E'80 Momentum Grows." *Mission Frontiers* 2, no. 4 (1980): 3.

Hyatt, E. "From Homogeneous to Heterogeneous Unit Principle." *Evangelical Missions Quarterly* 50, no. 2 (2014): 226–32.

---

33 See https://worldea.org/en/.
34 See http://www.asiamissions.net.
35 See http://www.asiamissions.net/partners/asian-society-of-missiology/.
36 See http://alliancefortheunreached.org.
37 For more information about frontier people groups, see joshuaproject.net/frontier to download a free prayer guide. For a simple animation of this concept, search YouTube for "frontier people groups." What this subgroup of the unreached peoples shows us is that the core of the remaining task is concentrated in South Asia.

International Congress on World Evangelization. *Unreached Peoples Directory*. Monrovia, CA: MARC/World Vision, 1974.

Johnson, T. M., and C. L. Tieszen. "Personal Contact: The Sine Qua Non of Twenty-First Century Christian Mission." *Evangelical Missions Quarterly* 43, no. 4 (2007): 494–501.

Kendall, G. "Missions Should Not Target the Unreached." *Evangelical Missions Quarterly* 35, no. 2 (1999): 180–85.

Newkirk, Mathew. "Should Missionaries Focus on Unreached People Groups? Yes." December 12, 2019. https://www.thegospelcoalition.org/article/missionaries-focus-unreached-people-groups.

"Newsbriefs: Foursquare Plans to Reach 100 Hidden People Groups." *Mission Frontiers* 2, no. 10 (1980): 5.

Parsons, G. *Ralph D. Winter: Early Life and Core Missiology*. Pasadena: WCIU Press, 2012.

Parsons, G. "Will the Earth Hear His Voice? Is Ralph D. Winter's Idea Still Valid?" *International Journal for Frontier Missiology* 32, no. 1 (2015): 5–18.

Perspectives USA. https://www.perspectives.org.

"Remembering Dr. Ralph Winter." Accessed on May 4, 2020. https://www.lausanne.org/tbd/lausanne-connecting-point/remembering-dr-ralph-winter.

Severn, F. M. "Some Thoughts on the Meaning of 'All Nations'." *Evangelical Missions Quarterly* 33, no. 4 (1997): 412–19.

"Today's Crisis, Tomorrow's Challenge." *Mission Frontiers* 1, no. 4 (1979): 3–7.

Winter, R. D. "COMIBAM '87 Missions Meeting of the Century." *Mission Frontiers* 10, no. 1 (1988): 7–8.

Winter, R. D. "Edinburgh 1980 Reports: World Consultation on Frontier Missions." *Mission Frontiers* 2, no. 12 (1980): 1.

Winter, R. D. "The Explosion of New Missions within the Non-Western World." *Mission Frontiers* 5, no. 1 (1983): 6–7.

Winter, R. D. "The Highest Priority: Cross-Cultural Evangelism." In *Let the Earth Hear His Voice*, edited by J. D. Douglas, 213–41. Minneapolis: World Wide Publications, 1975.

Winter, R. D. "Luis Bush, Latin America, and the End of History." *Mission Frontiers* 8, no. 3 (1986): 1, 3, 5.

Winter, R. D. "The Planting of Younger Missions." In *Church/Mission Tensions Today*, edited by C. P. Wagner. Chicago: Moody Press, 1972.

Winter, R. D. "Some Unfinished Business." *Mission Frontiers* 3, no. 5 (1981): 1, 4, 6.

Winter, R. D. "The Two Structures of God's Redemptive Mission." *Missiology* 2, no. 1 (1974): 122–39.

7

Re-envisioning the World

The Southern Baptist IMB Transition to People Groups

David Garrison and Zane Pratt

In 1980, the Southern Baptist Foreign Mission Board (FMB) was the largest denominational international mission board in the world. In many respects it was also a dinosaur.

At that time many denominations had subordinated their missionary deployments to the service of their overseas denomination in the form of fraternal work with national conventions. This subordination was a part of the emergence of new nations that accompanied the unraveling of Western colonial empires. As a nod to these newly independent nations, many Western denominations ceased sending missionaries unilaterally unless first requested by their new sister denominations overseas. While FMB missions followed this pattern in a few countries, most of its work retained a clear separation between FMB missions and the denominational organization with which they partnered.

When Keith Parks was elected president of the FMB that year, he inherited the legacy of a 135-year-old mission agency with 3,059 missionaries serving in a variety of cross-cultural ministries in ninety-four countries. Each country, or mission field, was represented by a country-focused mission, such as the Philippine Mission, the Kenya Mission, etc. (The only exception was the Brazil Baptist Mission, which was so large that it was subdivided into three missions: North Brazil, Equatorial Brazil, and South Brazil.) Around the FMB mission world, these mission stations met annually at which time its missionaries submitted their annual statistical reports and generated new personnel and budget requests back to the home office. These new missionaries continued to be deployed in response to requests from the FMB field missions. Priority was given to requests from existing mission stations rather than from the unreached, who, as one might expect, never requested a missionary.

The 1980 Foreign Mission Board was also deliberately isolated within the global mission enterprise. It was not a member of the Interdenominational Foreign Mission Association (IFMA), the Evangelical Foreign Mission Association (EFMA), or the Lausanne Congress, nor was its denomination a member of the ecumenical World Council of Churches or its subsidiary Commission on World Mission and Evangelism.

New Directions

Today the Foreign Mission Board has dissolved into history. Its legacy of ninety-four nation-based mission fields is a distant memory. In 1997, under the presidency of Jerry Rankin (1993–2010), the agency underwent a sweeping change that included a name change to the International Mission Board (IMB) in an initiative Rankin called "New Directions." The scope of the IMB's New Directions was described in a booklet titled *Something New under the Sun: New Directions at the International Mission Board*. The publication declared: "A third dynamic is shaping the new directions at the International Mission Board. It's a new focus. The focus is on people groups."[1]

Beginning with New Directions in 1997, 131 country-based mission stations were transformed into 303 *people- group and urban-focused teams* aimed at multiplying evangelism and discipleship that would lead to multiplying churches among the world's least reached people groups. Within a year, annual reports generated by field missions ballooned from roughly one hundred reports to more than three hundred reports reflecting the agency's missionary work among more focused people group strategies. Since that time, the number of IMB people group-focused mission teams has grown to 763.

While these seismic changes within the Southern Baptist global mission enterprise were identified with Jerry Rankin's 1997 New Directions initiative, their roots go back much further. To understand how and why the International Mission Board made such a dramatic transformation, we need to return to 1976 and Southern Baptists' embrace of a vision called "Bold Mission Thrust."

Bold Mission Thrust

In June 1976, the Southern Baptist Convention convened in Norfolk, Virginia, and adopted an ambitious vision: "That every man, woman, and child would have an opportunity to hear and respond to the gospel in their own language and culture by the year AD2000." While the vision statement had many subsidiary goals and progress markers, the die was cast that Southern Baptists would sharpen and refocus efforts to fulfill the goals of the Matthew 28 Great Commission to "make disciples of all nations, baptizing them in the name of the Father, the Son, and the Holy Spirit, and teaching them to obey everything I have commanded you."

With this denominational mandate, then FMB president Baker Cauthen (1954–1979) and subsequent president Keith Parks (1980–1992) pursued a course of increasing the number of missionaries and mission fields to accomplish the Bold Mission Thrust vision. That same vision soon revealed flaws in the current pattern of missionary deployment and engagement. Some of the older fields, such as Brazil, where Southern Baptists had been laboring since 1881, hosted the lion's share of personnel with 334 missionaries in 1985, while other countries with massive populations such as India, China, and the Soviet Union—representing 44 percent of the world's population—had either no FMB missionaries or only a handful of missionaries. Furthermore, the growing number of countries that were restricting or forbidding new missionary visas, a prerequisite for FMB missionary deployment, meant that Bold Mission Thrust was relegated to a rhetorical aspiration rather than an achievable reality.

Unseen by most Southern Baptists was the multiethnic complexity of people groups hidden within countries. Consequently, in many older fields, such as Nigeria where Southern Baptist missionaries had labored since 1850 and had seen a huge response from the Yoruba people, the mission had left untouched the nation's teeming millions of Muslim Fulani, Bambara, and Hausa people groups.

President Keith Parks brought new energies to the office of FMB president. Beginning in 1981, he directed the country-based mission fields under his administration to adopt

---

[1] IMB, "Something New under the Sun," 19.

vision statements that aligned with Bold Mission Thrust and then to detail priority goals and objectives that would lead to the fulfillment of their respective vision statement. In other words, the Philippine Baptist Mission would adopt a vision of "every man, woman, and child in the Philippines would get the opportunity to hear and respond to the gospel in their own language and culture by the year 2000." This strategic planning initiative forced missionaries to look beyond their legacy programs to the frontiers within their own country to ensure that the gospel reached "everyone."

David B. Barrett

Keith Parks took an important step in his pursuit of Bold Mission Thrust in 1985 when he invited Anglican Church Mission Society researcher Dr. David B. Barrett to relocate from Kenya to Richmond, Virginia, as a researcher and consultant to the Foreign Mission Board. Barrett had published his monumental *World Christian Encyclopedia* in 1982, establishing him as the world's leading authority on the status of global Christianity. Barrett brought to the FMB a window into the global status of Christianity and progress toward the Great Commission that exceeded the FMB's current research. The latter was largely derived from secular overviews filtered through the annual statistical reports received from existing FMB mission fields. Barrett had spent nearly twenty years building a database tracking the status of Christianity across thousands of denominations in 237 nations, and most importantly, tunneling down into more than fourteen thousand distinct ethnolinguistic people groups within those nations. Barrett's research would prove pivotal for the changes in the Southern Baptist mission enterprise in the years that followed.

While other missiologists, notably Ralph D. Winter, had highlighted the plight of the world's "hidden peoples," Barrett was the first to craft a global taxonomy of peoples based upon their language, religion, and ethnicity and then populate these sociological categories with data that included the status of evangelization among each of the ethnolinguistic communities. The FMB offered Barrett a more robust staff for managing the sprawling data sets. Within a year, the FMB was already responding to this new look at the world. Keith Parks created a new administrative assignment under the leadership of Dr. Lewis Myers to explore ways for Southern Baptists to go beyond traditional mission stations to take the gospel into previously unengaged peoples and countries. The new FMB department for what they termed "creative access" missions was called Cooperative Services International (CSI).

CSI intentionally eschewed the word "mission" from their nomenclature, and instead initially pursued the avenue of "tentmaking," i.e., missionaries taking secular postings in restricted-access countries. Teachers, agriculturalists, and others used secular visa platforms in countries such as China, Mongolia, and Vietnam (where Myers had served prior to the collapse of the South Vietnamese government). The people group focus was not yet explicit, but it was coming.

The Non-residential Missionary

In 1986, Barrett received a letter from Bill Smith, a furloughing FMB missionary from Thailand. Smith was seeking a Doctor of Ministry thesis topic and was directed to Barrett for suggestions. Barrett responded to Smith with the question, "Have you ever heard of the

Zhuang people?" Smith had not. Barrett went on to explain, "They are the largest people group in the world, some 12 million, who have no Scripture whatsoever in their own language." Smith was intrigued and took Barrett's small data set and turned it into a file folder with hundreds of pages of research on the Zhuang.

That same year, while speaking at a mission conference in Chicago, Barrett met and developed a friendship with Southern Baptist David Garrison who was pursuing his PhD at the University of Chicago. Barrett posed the same question regarding the Zhuang to Garrison. Conversations between the two led Barrett to extend an invitation to Garrison to join him in Richmond as a research associate, a position Garrison assumed in March 1987. Within the year, Garrison was introduced to Smith and his research, and the two collaborated to compose the first training manual for a new type of missionary that Barrett termed the "Non-residential Missionary."

A Non-residential Missionary (NRM)[2] was a full-time missionary assigned to a specific unreached people group with the aim of evangelizing that people group even though that missionary might not be able to secure a residential missionary visa. The first Non-residential Missionaries assigned by the Foreign Missionary Board were Bill and Susan Smith; their assignment was the Zhuang people of China.

Evangelizing a people group where one did not have missionary residence required the mobilization of numerous Great Commission partners: prayer supporters, Bible translators, media specialists, non-Western partners (who often did have access to the people group), and tentmaker (or creative access) missionaries. Within weeks, Smith had developed one hundred ministry options for engaging the Zhuang with the gospel, and the ministry was launched. It was the enormity of the challenge—"What's it going to take to reach 12 million people?"—that required Smith to develop collaborative partnerships with dozens of other agencies and individuals who came to be known as Great Commission Christians. Thus, interdenominational *collaboration* with translators, non-Western churches, radio broadcasters, prayer supporters, and others would become a core value of the new missionary paradigm from the beginning. For Southern Baptists a new missionary paradigm was born.

The following year, a second Non-residential Missionary couple, Mike and Kay Stroope, were assigned to engage Kurdish peoples from a nonresident base in Germany, where more than a million diaspora Kurdish immigrants lived as *Gastarbeiter* (immigrant workers). The following year, three more missionary units were deployed to the Kazakhs, Turkmen, and Azerbaijani peoples of the Soviet Union. That same year, Garrison was named director of the Non-residential Missionary program within the FMB's Cooperative Services International department. Over the next four years, the NRM program became the fastest-growing division of the Foreign Mission Board's work as scores of new NRMs were appointed to an equal number of previously unengaged people groups stretching from Mongolia and North Korea to North Africa and the Sahel of West Africa.

In 1988, Barrett was invited by Dr. Parks to address the FMB's Global Strategy Group, consisting of regional vice presidents covering the world, on the subject of "How are we doing in our pursuit of Bold Mission Thrust?" Barrett's address was complimentary, stating that few mission organizations had ever dedicated so many resources to fulfilling the Great

---

[2] "The Nonresidential Missionary" and later retitled "Strategy Coordinators."

Commission. However, they were doomed to fall short of the ambitious goal of Bold Mission Thrust. The reason, Barrett explained, was simple: the FMB was sending more and more missionaries, but these missionaries were going to the same fields (i.e., those countries that granted missionary visas). This flaw in the IMB's deployment paradigm meant the IMB was doomed to fall short of its goal of reaching every person with the gospel by AD2000.

Parks could see that the solution was to re-envision the world, not as country-based missions, but through the prism of ethnolinguistic people groups, each of whom deserved the right to receive the gospel in their own culture and language. Many of these ethnolinguistic people groups were, indeed, larger than the entire countries to which missionaries had been deployed for generations. This new perspective necessitated and accelerated the NRM paradigm of deploying to the world's least reached ethnolinguistic peoples, and the program grew accordingly. In 1990, at the request of World Vision's Mission Advanced Research and Communications (MARC) department, Garrison authored *The Nonresidential Missionary*, crystallizing the concept and adding weight to the new people group focus.

By 1992, the fastest-growing department of the Foreign Mission Board was CSI with its unreached people group-focused teams. Unsurprisingly, this imbalance toward frontier fields caused the organization to exhibit signs of strain. Voices from traditional mission fields expressed disquiet at what some perceived as an eclipsing of their role within the FMB as CSI's personnel count rose to numbers rivaling the FMB's other administrative regions.

That same year, Garrison was directed to produce an internal study of CSI and the NRM program to address some of the many questions and points of resistance that had been circulating within the agency. The results were an affirmation of the people group focus and a recommendation that CSI transition from what had been a pilot program into equal status with the other geographically defined regions of FMB administration. With this organizational evolution, David and Sonia Garrison transitioned to the field as Non-residential Missionaries to work with Libyan Arabs, and the FMB Board of Trustees elected NRM Mike Stroope to serve as area director for Cooperative Services International under the vice presidency of Lewis Myers.

Winds of Change

By 1992, denominational changes were underway across the Southern Baptist Convention. This led to the abrupt retirement of Parks and the election of new president Jerry Rankin who had previously been the area director for the Foreign Mission Board in South Asia and the Pacific. As an area director, Rankin had been a leading critic of CSI, opting instead for a harvest missiology that prioritized responsive fields over against what were perceived to be resistant people groups. As president of the IMB, however, Rankin's perspective shifted. Seeing for himself how what had been perceived to be resistant fields were showing remarkable responsiveness to the gospel, Rankin embraced the value of this new direction and became a champion of IMB efforts to reach unengaged people groups.

Meanwhile, the people group focus of CSI's Non-residential Missionaries grew exponentially under Mike Stroope's leadership (1992–1996), deploying hundreds of new short- and long-term personnel under this new missionary paradigm. Stories of breakthroughs and successful pioneer church planting among unreached people groups increasingly penetrated the consciousness of the Foreign Mission Board and the Southern Baptist Convention at large.

Challenges accompanied the foray into people groups. By 1996, Jerry Rankin found himself presiding over two organizations under one roof. There was legacy work in countries that had been underway for decades, and the new organization that was emerging under the CSI umbrella. An internal crisis was afoot.

In 1997, Rankin led a major reorganization of the Foreign Mission Board. Rebranding it as the International Mission Board, Rankin launched New Directions. CSI had outgrown its previous administrative confines and so was redistributed into five administrative regions.[3] Older regions, such as Western South America, Eastern South America, and Central America, were merged into a single administrative region. Rankin also led all of the IMB's missions to dissolve traditional country-based missions and adopt new people group- and urban-focused teams.

Organizational change is not without costs. David Barrett was released from his contract with the Foreign Mission Board shortly after Jerry Rankin became president in 1993. In 1997, Mike Stroope resigned from the International Mission Board and started a new agency called All Peoples. That same year, Garrison was invited back to Richmond's staff as associate vice president for global strategy. Two years later, he would write a fifty-seven-page booklet published by the IMB called *Church Planting Movements* that described how the initial efforts to evangelize unreached people groups had led to multiplying numbers of new disciples and churches in what had once been deemed resistant people groups.[4]

By 2000, the IMB was reporting 1,118 teams working among people groups, urban centers, and with denominations around the world. One of the IMB's regional vice presidents who had been with the agency for more than four decades observed: "IMB missionaries are now serving in more dangerous frontier places than at any time in our history."

Today that number has swollen further as the IMB has catalyzed global Great Commission partners to participate in God's work among people groups. The 2023 IMB Annual Statistical Report identified 6,275 people groups being engaged by Great Commission partners alone and a further 636 people groups being engaged by collaborative efforts between the IMB and its partner missionaries.

Conclusion

The International Mission Board's transition from country-based missions to people groups has not been a straight path, nor is it complete. It has, however, allowed Southern Baptists to participate in a global vision first commissioned by our Lord over two thousand years ago. Along the way, the effort has been challenged by tradition and competing interests. It has been scrutinized by trustees and fellow missionaries whose paradigms of what is possible have been challenged by God's remarkable faithfulness. As missionaries and mission leaders have stepped out in faith to obey the Great Commission even when it seemed impossible, we found God there, waiting for us to join him. As our Lord reminds us, "What is impossible with man is possible with God" (Luke 18:27 NIV).

---

3 The sprawling CSI area was divided into (1) East Asia, (2) SE Asia and Indo-Malaysia, (3) South and Central Asia, (4) North Africa and the Middle East, and (5) South and Central Asia, which were later divided into two distinct administrative regions.

4 The *Church Planting Movements* booklet found wide receptivity as it was subsequently translated into more than forty languages. The booklet was followed by the same author's *Church Planting Movements: How God Is Redeeming a Lost World* in 2004.

Bibliography

Barrett, David B., ed. *World Christian Encyclopedia*. Oxford: Oxford University Press, 1982.

Crawley, Winston. *Global Mission: An Interpretation of Southern Baptist Missions*. Richmond, VA: Foreign Mission Board, 1985.

Farah, Warrick. "The Genesis and Evolution of Church-Planting Movement Missiology." *Missiology: An International Review* 50, no. 4 (2022).

Garrison, David. *Church Planting Movements*. Richmond, VA: International Mission Board, 1999.

Garrison, David. *Church Planting Movements: How God Is Redeeming a Lost World*. Midlothian, VA: WIGTake Resources, 2004.

Garrison, David. *The Nonresidential Missionary*. Monrovia, CA: MARC, 1990.

International Mission Board. *Annual Statistical Report*. Accessed March 25, 2024. https://www.imb.org/research/annual-statistical-report/.

International Mission Board Office of Overseas Operations. *Something New under the Sun: New Directions at the International Mission Board*. Richmond, VA: IMB, 1999.

Robb, John D. *The Power of People Group Thinking*. Monrovia, CA: MARC, 1989.

8
Assemblies of God World Missions and the Unreached

Dick Brogden, Alan R. Johnson, and Leonard N. Bartlotti

Writing as participant observers, missionaries Brogden, Johnson, and Bartlotti chronicle the story of Assemblies of God World Missions (AGWM), the foreign missions division of the General Council of the Assemblies of God USA, in its engagement with the people group paradigm and unreached peoples priority over the past five decades. The story highlights theological, structural, organizational, and leadership challenges faced by a large mission sending agency grappling with missiological and ethnolinguistic realities. They trace the history of AGWM's interaction with the frontier mission movement and the factors that have led to purposeful organizational changes. Today the vision of church planting among unreached peoples not only guides more of what AGWM is doing but also influences new sending structures in the global AG fellowship. These reflections on painful and purposeful missional change provide important lessons for sending structures, new and established.

The story begins in 1914 with the founding of the Assemblies of God. In November of that year, this fledging movement committed themselves to God and to one another for "the greatest evangelization the world had ever seen." Cross-cultural evangelists were sent to pioneer in "neglected fields" and "regions beyond," not to assist existing works.

Gary McGee, Noel Perkins, and John Garlock, in their histories of Assemblies of God World Missions, chronicle some early decisions that reflect the belief that the Spirit's empowerment to take the gospel "to the ends of the earth" should be coupled with a practical realism (i.e., guidelines needed to safeguard that vision):

- In the 1915 council, they focused on evangelism "according to New Testament methods."[1]
- In 1917, a three-member committee consisting of two missionaries and a pastor was formed to suggest policy for the foreign mission work of the council. They laid down thirteen principles, including requiring two years of language study. The Executive Presbytery was tasked with surveying to determine where mission centers should be established and *where the need appeared greatest.*[2]
- At the 1919 council, a Foreign Mission Department was formed, and it was noted that schools should be established to train native workers. Disapproval was expressed of floating missionary efforts (i.e., aimless traveling rather than learning a language and settling down to do permanent missionary work).[3]

---

1 McGee, *This Gospel Shall Be*, 95.
2 Perkin and Garlock, *Our World Witness*, 41 (emphasis added).
3 Perkin and Garlock, 42.

- In 1920, a pastor was sent on a tour of mission stations in Japan, China, India, Egypt, and Palestine on behalf of the missionary department. He found duplication of effort—missionaries clumped in certain locations with vast areas needing evangelism, creating friction between local churches.[4]
- At the 1921 General Council in St. Louis, the Council outlined six key New Testament principles the Foreign Missions Department was to follow.[5] One was the establishment of "self-supporting, self-propagating, and self-governing native churches," while another stated, *"The Pauline example will be followed so far as possible, by seeking out neglected regions where the gospel has not yet been preached, lest we build upon another's foundation (Romans 15:20)."*[6]

These early AGWM missionaries had a profound confidence in the power of the Holy Spirit, the immeasurable support of praying saints, and the financial backing of their sending churches. What they did not have, in retrospect, was a game plan for what to do if their labors actually worked.

The Challenge of Success

The gospel did indeed "work" more than they had dared dream or imagine. Men and women in frontier contexts were saved and discipled, churches planted, and leaders trained. AGWM missionaries focused on biblical activities they saw modeled in the book of Acts. They summarized their methods as "Reaching" (evangelism); "Planting" (church planting and strengthening); "Training" (discipleship, training pastors and national leaders); and "Serving" (expressing the compassion of Jesus).

Using the not-so-secret sauce of indigenous church principles (the work of Venn, Anderson, Allen, Luce, Hodges, and others), by the 1930s AGWM began to see the formation of indigenous national churches. By the 1950s and 1960s Pentecostal churches multiplied throughout Latin America, Sub-Saharan Africa, and parts of Asia. AGWM was now deeply connected with national churches around the globe.

In effect, AGWM applied Ralph Winter's concepts of "missiological breakthrough" and "viable indigenous church" to indigenous national churches—not "people groups." That is, the aim was a breakthrough leading to an association of indigenous churches passionate about reaching "their own people," usually defined in terms of national (not ethnolinguistic) identity.

While in the early decades virtually everyone who went out was pioneering and planting, once that process began to bear fruit, it was natural to continue to send cross-cultural workers to strengthen that work. This ongoing work was called "partnership," an approach pioneered in AG missions by Morris Williams, field director for Africa. Left unanswered, however, were questions about how indigeneity, training, and partnership were connected to the unfinished task of world evangelization. No indigenous sending structures were established until much later. Ironically, the burdens of success began to erode the ability to move nimbly into peoples and places where there was no gospel and no church.

---

4 McGee, *Miracles, Missions and American*, 152–53.
5 McGee, 95.
6 McGee, *This Gospel Shall Be*, 96 (emphasis added).

Some leaders recognized the troublesome tension between pioneering and partnership. J. Phillip Hogan, executive director from 1959 to 1989, was deeply committed to the view that AGWM Pentecostal missionaries were to take the gospel to the world. In the 1960s Hogan thundered:

> Today, in some ecclesiastical circles, the missionary that is needed now, they say, is really a worker in some technical or pedagogical skills; and, really a helper to the indigenous church. Instead of being called a "missionary," he is called a "fraternal worker." This emphasis would put the Great Commission in storage while the church adopts a kind of "buddy" system, and the real heroes of the Cross are not men who confront heathen religions with the message of Calvary, but specialists who teach contour farming. The Assemblies of God does not believe this![7]

Clearly, Hogan's vision of global mission was framed in terms of taking the gospel where Christ was not known. Loren Triplett, who followed Hogan as executive director, felt the same tension between frontier evangelization and strengthening existing national movements. In one of his monthly letters to workers in the mid-1990s, Triplett quoted his predecessor Phil Hogan, who often said, "Let us not to measure ourselves by our successes, but by the unfinished task."

Nevertheless, AGWM's institutional energy began to lean naturally towards filling the slots to serve national church movements and their needs. The result was that by the 1980s the majority of AGWM cross-cultural workers were doing ministry in some kind of relationship with existing national churches.

Internal Tensions between Pentecostal Success and Missiological Realities

A significant internal tension for AGWM as a Pentecostal sending agency was clearly visible during the last two decades of Hogan's tenure as executive director.

As it became clear that Pentecostal missionary activity was having a global impact, doors opened for Hogan's involvement at meetings of the Evangelical Foreign Missions Association (EFMA) and Interdenominational Foreign Missions Association (IFMA). When facing outward to the evangelical world, Hogan was clear about his Pentecostal understanding of global mission as first and foremost a work of the Spirit. In 1970, he gave an address to the EFMA, saying:

> I have long since ceased to be interested in meetings where mission leaders are called together to a room filled with charts, maps, graphs, and statistics. All one needs to do to find plenteous harvest is simply to follow the leading of the Spirit. When one engages in this truth and begins to live by this principle, there will be communities, whole cities, whole nations, whole cultures, and whole segments of pagan religions that will suddenly be thrust open to the gospel witness.[8]

Hogan's stature among mission leaders is reflected by the fact that he was invited to be a responder to Ralph Winter's seminal plenary address on cross-cultural evangelism at Lausanne in 1974. His response to Winter is an instructive moment for AGWM's engagement with frontier missiology. Hogan was not dismissive of the concepts but, again, put the emphasis squarely on

---

[7] Klaus and Petersen, *Essential J. Philip Hogan*, 100.
[8] Wilson, *Strategy of the Spirit*, 136.

the work of the Spirit. He felt that his primary contribution in the response was to appeal to them to remember the sovereignty of the Holy Spirit and the truth of Acts 5:32. He noted, "We are witnessing worldwide an outpouring of the Spirit of God upon persons and places for which there is no human design and in which there is not one shred of human planning."[9]

Hogan acknowledged the challenge of cultural and sociological distance but looked to the Holy Spirit to break down these walls, ending his response with this challenge (contra Winter): "When the wind of God truly blows, E-3 evangelism becomes as easy and successful as E-1 or E-2, and perhaps one of the major concerns of this conference should be that we discover where God walks and get into stride with him in his march through time and eternity."[10]

Though Hogan foregrounded his Pentecostal identity and theology and claimed to be uninterested in strategy gatherings, his leadership of AGWM showed greater balance. Actually, he was interested and attentive to missiological developments.

Hogan's emphasis on the work of the Spirit did not suggest the passivity of just waiting for divine intervention. In the years following Lausanne, Hogan invited prominent voices like Winter and Art Glasser to lecture on unreached peoples at the AGWM Summer School of Mission for new workers and veterans, even though he did not embrace all their missiology. In a significant move, Hogan brought in Ed Nelson as Director of Foreign Missions Relations in the US, a former executive with the American Bible Society, who was a knowledgeable and enthusiastic supporter of frontier mission missiology.

It was through the friendship and counsel of Ed Nelson that Len Bartlotti, an Assemblies of God minister working with Winter at the U.S. Center for World Mission (USCWM) from 1979 to 1984, began to provide input to AGWM communications. Len had opportunities to interact with Hogan and AG, EFMA, and IFMA leaders about the needs of large unreached cultural blocs, especially in the Muslim world.

In his overview of the relationship of Pentecostal and charismatic Christianity to Islam, Bartlotti notes:

> Though Muslims were not a primary focus of early [AG] witness, a small number of Pentecostal missionaries pioneered in the Middle East (Palestine, Egypt, Syria, Lebanon, Persia), establishing schools and orphanages, distributing Gospel literature, visiting prisons, and bringing revival to traditional Christians. ... *In the fifty-year period after 1930, Pentecostals did very little about the Muslim world.*[11]

There were notable exceptions, including lauded pioneers like Calvin and Marian Olson (Bangladesh), David and Deborah Irwin (Egypt, Malawi), and Mark and Gladys Bliss (Liberia, Iran, Bangladesh).

> *However, most efforts were focused on non-Muslims and Christian-background believers. ... Like other missions, Pentecostals assumed that a revival among a Christian minority would lead to Muslim evangelization. The approach overlooked barriers of prejudice and culture, yielded meager results, and generally failed to produce indigenous Muslim-background churches.*[12]

---

9 Hogan, "Response to Dr. Ralph," 243.
10 Hogan, 245.
11 Bartlotti, "Islam," 265 (emphasis added).
12 Bartlotti, 265–66 (emphasis added).

At an EFMA meeting in the early 1980s, Greg Livingstone, the zealous executive director of North Africa Mission and (later) founder of Frontiers, pointed his finger in Len's chest and declared with an annoyance approaching vexation, "If you Pentecostals have so much power, why are there so few of you in the Muslim world?!"

Early Initiatives and Prophetic Voices

The unreached peoples movement began to surge among evangelicals following Ralph Winter's address at the 1974 Lausanne Congress and the founding of the USCWM in 1976. By the mid-1980s, a small but increasing number of AGWM workers and ministers were raising awareness about unreached peoples.

In 1984, missionary David Irwin, with a heart softened by his experience in the Middle East and encouraged by Ed Nelson, launched the AG's Center for Ministry to Muslims (CMM, now Global Initiative). CMM's premier effort was the Jumaa Prayer Network, a call to prayer and fasting every Friday at noon as Muslims head to the mosque to pray. Prayer literature and missions communications began tentative use of the terminology "unreached" and "people groups."

In 1983, Paul Yonggi Cho hosted his International Conference on Church Growth in Oslo, Norway, attended by thousands of Scandinavian and European pastors and leaders. Also in attendance was AGWM missionary John (and Lois) Bueno, founder of the twenty-two-thousand-member Centro Evangelistico church in El Salvador and area director for Central America (later to become AGWM executive director). Ralph Winter was invited to speak but sent Len Bartlotti in his place. In an environment enthusiastic about "church growth," Len taught frontier missions, entitling his workshop track "Church Growth Where There Is No Church." Only ten to twelve people attended—including John and Lois Bueno. Events foster the spread of ideas.

John Bueno invited Len to speak at a Central American missionary retreat in Costa Rica on the biblical mandate to reach all peoples. One of those attending was newly appointed Latin American AGWM missionary DeLonn Rance. Moved by the needs of unreached peoples, Len remembers DeLonn asking worriedly, "I'm teaching in the Bible school. If this is a priority, maybe I should go work with Muslims in North Africa?" "No, stay here!" Len replied. "Teach and help send Latino missionaries to unreached peoples." The Spirit led DeLonn to do exactly that; his mission mobilization in El Salvador and region-wide led to Latinos joining in the frontier task.

In 1985, Len and Debi Bartlotti felt a compelling call to leave Winter and the USCWM and go to the Muslim world. Influenced by J. Christy Wilson Jr. (Gordon-Conwell Theological Seminary), Don McCurry (founder of the Zwemer Institute), and Greg Livingstone (founder of Frontiers), and inspired by a small handful of contemporary AG pioneers among Muslims (David Irwin, Sobhi Malek, David Leatherberry, Paul Parks), they realized that the most strategic thing one can do is to obey. The Bartlottis joined David and Julie Leatherberry to pioneer among one of the largest Muslim people groups in Southwest Asia. Modeled in part on the Frontiers team approach, this was the first intentional AGWM church-planting (CP) team in the modern period.

Ed Nelson asked Len, before he left for the field, to coordinate a missions prayer room at the upcoming forty-first General Council in San Antonio, Texas. Bartlotti argued, "At a massive get together, nobody will show up in a prayer room unless we make it appealing." He proposed creating a media prayer experience that would be inspirational, educational, and attractive. Nelson was a door opener for influencers and ideas. At his urging, Hogan met personally with Len to hear his proposal, then gave Len $10,000 to make it happen.

The resultant "A Prayer Pilgrimage Through the Muslim World," written by Bartlotti and consulted with Hollywood designers, filled a room with a guided maze of colorful "prayer stations," with descriptions of Islamic regions, photos, prayers for Muslims, and the centerpiece—a massive, backlit map listing the names of every Muslim unreached people group. For over a decade, the AG's Center for Ministry to Muslims transported the display and other mission education resources to Christian colleges, churches, missions conventions, and District Council meetings across the US. The unreached peoples challenge was becoming visible.

Commissioned in 1984, Alan Johnson began his over three decades of pioneer work among unreached Buddhists in Thailand. Johnson's personal calling to missions came from reflecting over several years on Winter's original "pie chart" of unreached peoples and reading USCWM's *Mission Frontiers Bulletin*. Arriving in Thailand in 1986, he naively assumed that everyone inside AGWM thought this way. Strongly influenced by frontier missiology, friendships with like-minded AG thinkers like Bartlotti and Dick Brogden, and encouraged by a missiologically astute Asia Pacific field director, Bob Houlihan, Johnson went on to become a leading figure to contextualize and interpret Winter's UPG paradigm and challenge for AGWM and a global Pentecostal audience of national church leaders, field workers, and academics.

In the early 1990s a restructured team under Bartlotti's leadership joint-ventured with a German NGO team. In a field marked by political volatility and violence, a spiritual outpouring—timed sovereignly with the October 1993 "Pray through the Window" global prayer movement and the Toronto revival—led to unexpected, unprecedented fruitfulness. The hearts of urban Muslim refugees softened. The team model, grounded in daily worship, intercession, and the lordship of the Spirit, combined with compassionate service, cultural savvy, innovative outreach, and intentional discipleship, resulted in the formation of small fellowships.

Similarly, in this period missionary statesman John York, who worked in Nigeria and Malawi and had studied under Walter Kaiser (author of *Mission in the Old Testament: Israel as a Light to the Nations*), began to have an increasing impact in the AGWM environment. With his vocal passion for unreached peoples, John became known in Africa as the apostle of *missio Dei*. He was tireless in his teaching and preaching that not only workers, but also the emerging African churches, needed to make gospel access to unreached peoples a priority.

Despite advances in prayer, communication, and individual initiatives in the eighties and early nineties, there was no system-wide commitment to focus efforts and priorities upon peoples with little gospel access. "If the Spirit called" people to the unreached, that was fine.

The reality was that most AGWM personnel were working side by side with established national churches. Even in nation-states with numerous unreached peoples, missionaries tended to work with local churches that struggled to reach their own people and/or were not interested in those outside their own ethnic group. While this work was vibrant and the partnerships fruitful, AGWM was not purposefully fulfilling its original mandate towards the neglected regions beyond.

Missiological Issues and Institutional Concerns

The tensions seen with Phil Hogan between the sovereign work of the Spirit and the need for strategic missiological reflection were moderated in part by his relationships with leading evangelical mission thinkers. Hogan reminded them of the need for Spirit empowerment, but at the same time, he listened (more than he let on?) to their thinking on big issues like unreached peoples and gospel access.

With Hogan's retirement in 1989 and the loss of those relational connections, AGWM entered a reactive phase. The resistance was not so much against the concepts of frontier missiology, or the fact that a large bloc of humanity was unreached, but against high-powered missions marketing practices of the AD2000 Movement of the nineties and early 2000s.

Led by Global South leaders, the collaborative AD2000 and Beyond Movement gained steam under the banner of "a church for every people and the gospel for every person by the year 2000." Many AD2000 innovations (10/40 Window, databases tracking UPGs, etc.) were generated with a view to promotions and mobilization. The critique that labeled frontier missions a "managerial missiology" resonated with many in AGWM. One AG executive expressed concerns about what seemed to him "big talk and small action," ticking "boxes" of "adoptions of peoples" on a computer list, without making significant and verifiable progress on the ground. There seemed little room for the calling of the Spirit. Pressure to redeploy veterans with valuable experience and cultural insight, to start again in a new place, seemed unwise.

There were economic issues as well. When some US AG pastors learned of the needs of the unreached, they dropped support for missionaries to Europe or Latin America because they had the wrong address (not in the 10/40 Window), without consideration of the valued work they were doing. The Assemblies of God had a large mission force and considerable financial resources designated for Bible schools, literature, childcare, and other projects in Latin America. UPGs and the 10/40 Window were perceived as a threat. The snowballing of concerns eventually led to a policy for a time that, in official AGWM publications, the terminology of "unreached people groups" and "10/40 Window" were not allowed.

The alternative was also tried: When it was discovered that "unreached" was useful for raising money, attention, and personnel, some AG personnel started co-opting the terminology and bending its meaning so that what they were doing was "reaching the unreached." One issue of the AG missions magazine redefined "unreached people" so that nominal Christians and non-Christians who did not know Jesus were now "unreached," without reference to the original definition and related concepts of people group, incorporability, and barriers to gospel access. Mission education and maintaining conceptual clarity are critical because without it those encountering "barriers of understanding or acceptance" may be "hidden" by the "tall grass" of existing work, as Winter described it.

In addition to issues of economics, mission praxis, and promotions, institutional concerns were at odds with prioritizing the unreached. The emphasis on working with national churches created unexpected tensions: What does "national" or "indigenous" mean in a country with multiple people groups? Which AG church is national if there are multiple church movements with different languages, ethnicities, or religious backgrounds? Does partnership require working with the existing church even if they are not interested in missional outreach to unreached peoples within their nation-state?

Other structural issues involved the relationship between a nominally semiautonomous CP "team" and "team leader" (the Frontiers model) and the traditional "field fellowship" (semiautonomous individual workers in a country) under the authority of an "area director." Who makes the final decision on the makeup and direction of a team? Can a field fellowship vote down a team's focus and priorities? How does a CP team relate to traditional projects, funding, and relationships with the national church? These questions were unresolved and led to tensions.

Priorities were also unclear. In a meeting discussing the possibility of creating a new administrative region, Johnson brought up the idea of communicating to the US constituency that there is "one thing we do: Take the gospel where it is not present, with all other activities flowing from that and aiming towards that goal." The answer from an administrator was, "Because we don't just do one thing." The now broadened scope of AGWM missionaries working in and with national churches made any kind of prioritization a "splitting of the house," with potential to create confusion among the home-sending base.

Another concern was related to risk. The reality is that unreached peoples tend to be in locations that are unstable, with inhospitable climates, and insufficient health care and schooling, and are sometimes just hostile and dangerous. Dick Brogden was part of a conversation with two AGWM personnel regarding Somalia. When a field worker made a plea for deployment to Somalia, the leader responded, "Not on my watch. I am not going to be responsible for a missionary being killed in Mogadishu."

By the mid-nineties the rise of the information age and the internet allowed sometimes insular AG churches wider exposure to other views and initiatives in missions. More AG pastors had graduated from non-AG schools and seminaries; during their studies they encountered UPG thinking and advocates like John Piper and Ralph Winter, and books and resources like the "Perspectives on the World Christian Movement" course. Travel to the field for short-term visits also became more common.

Some thinking pastors observed that in most places where AGWM personnel worked there were plenty of churches of various denominations. In a broader cultural environment where, for many reasons, institutional trust was eroding, pastors began to question AGWM's strategy: Why is AGWM not more engaged with the unreached?

The Turning of the Tide

By the mid-nineties more personnel in Africa (Djibouti), Central Asia (Afghanistan, Pakistan), and Southeast Asia (Thailand) were focused on unreached people groups and mobilizing others. Some area directors (AD), mid-level leaders in AGWM, began to lift their voices as well. In meetings, conferences, symposiums, seminaries, schools, and seminars, ADs joined field workers to advocate for the needs of peoples outside the reach of existing church movements and traditional projects. Their voices were not always welcome, but the call at least was vocalized.

In 1992, Joseph Gordon started church planting among unreached peoples in northern India. The Holy Spirit then led him and his family to Laos, where they developed and led a team reaching the Laos majority. He then returned to India and was recently appointed regional director for AGWM's Eurasia region. For the past three decades, Gordon has been one of the most sought-after speakers in the AG movement and is an articulate and passionate voice beating the drum for the need to take the gospel to the unreached peoples of our world.

In the late 1990s, John York was part of an AGWM Commission on Strategy and Planning (CSP). One assignment of the commission was to craft a set of core values. Included was a milestone focal point—unreached peoples.

John York became a door opener for Alan Johnson, suggesting that he do a session on current missions issues, focusing on unreached peoples, at the summer 1999 candidate training program. With the encouragement of York and CSP, Johnson began writing out his thoughts on how to help a Pentecostal organization embrace frontier missiology, integrate it, and use it to renew core values in mission. These lectures were later published in the *International Journal of Frontier Missiology* (*IJFM*). For over twenty years, Alan had shared his burden to make unreached peoples a strategic priority in the Asia Pacific region; his mentoring and teaching now began to influence emerging leaders on the field and in the churches.

In 2004, DeLonn Rance from El Salvador joined the faculty of the Assemblies of God Theological Seminary (AGTS) in Springfield, Missouri. Rance helped launch a doctoral program in missiology in which unreached peoples figure prominently.

In 2006, Johnson was invited to serve for a year as the Hogan Chair of World Mission at AGTS. He further developed his thinking on the applicability of the Pauline model today and later published in the monograph *Apostolic Function in 21st Century Missions* (2009).

In this same period, Dick and Jennifer Brogden developed and led a church-planting (CP) team among a Muslim UPG in Sudan. In 1992, Dick was seconded to an interdenominational Pentecostal team led by an AG-credentialed minister in West Africa. This team's model was focused on teamwork, incarnational and simple living, language and cultural fluency, and biblically bounded contextualization. The Brogdens adopted a pioneer philosophy of missions and were given freedom by their area director to implement these explicit nonnegotiable principles in their work among Northern Sudanese Muslim Arabs.

The Brogdens' pioneer team in Sudan became both the trigger and model for a structural adjustment inside AGWM that made possible the purposeful focus on unreached peoples that many hoped and prayed for.

Convergence: Live Dead and the Priority of Unreached Peoples

No large-scale change in a mission organization has a singular catalyst. The previous sections highlighted multiple prophetic voices and practitioners who, through diverse means, were speaking into AGWM. The existing structure served a burgeoning movement of national churches. However, it was becoming clear that fresh vision and new structures were needed to seriously address the issue of gospel access for the unreached.

The critical structural and philosophical shift came with the founding of what came to be known as the "Live Dead" movement. Live Dead enabled AGWM to have a priority focus on unreached peoples while preserving its relationships with national churches and, in the process, invigorating the missions sending of those churches.

From 1996 to 2011, the Brogdens' work in Sudan utilized a "plug-and-play" model. That is, they actively recruited new team members and created ways for them to integrate immediately into local culture and ministry. This approach trained others for CP and led to multiplication; they grew into four teams by 2011.

In January 2011, Greg Beggs, area director for East Africa and sympathetic overseer of Brogdens' experimental model, asked the Regional Advisory Committee of East Africa to develop a training program for new missionaries that taught AGWM values. This process resulted in a reexamination of AGWM core values, including John York's regrettably dormant emphasis on unreached peoples. The resultant "Brackenhurst Manifesto" rearticulated the value of pioneering.

The impact of mid-level leaders who function as intraorganizational advocates cannot be underestimated. Beggs asked Dick Brogden to develop a way to renew pioneering efforts among the unreached peoples of East Africa, particularly the ones who live in resistant places (like Somalia). The idea was to take the Sudan model, with core values articulated in the Brackenhurst Manifesto, and franchise it across East Africa. Scott Hanson assisted with the strategic development of the proposal.

Charity Reeb, a marketing professional, was asked to help brand the new initiative. The Holy Spirit woke her up in the night with the name "Live Dead." This name was chosen so it would be clear from the beginning that reaching the unreached would be difficult, would require death to self, and would possibly lead to much suffering along the way.

From the beginning the Live Dead nonnegotiables included church planting, a focus on unreached peoples, and a commitment to work in teams. Over time, the twelve values of the Brackenhurst Manifesto were summarized and simplified into three: Abide (intimacy with Jesus), Apostle (take the gospel to the unreached), and Abandon (pay any price for the glory of God).

The expansion of unreached peoples work in AGWM through Live Dead represents the coming together of three critical vectors: a structural shift that allowed space for distinct CP teams; a vision shift toward UPGs that reinvigorated those working within national churches as well as those pioneering beyond; and importantly, a leadership shift that encouraged and facilitated these changes.

After 2011, regional directors (RD), who serve on the executive leadership team of AGWM, became major advocates, exhorting the mission and churches throughout the AG fellowship to move towards prioritization of the unreached. AD Greg Beggs became regional director of Africa and expanded Live Dead across Africa. In the Eurasia region, a vast area of forty-three countries stretching from North Africa and the Arab world to eastern Russia and southern Asia, RD Omar Bieler made Live Dead teams the fundamental working unit for the entire region. In China, RD Ron Maddux embraced the Live Dead structure to focus specifically on UPG minority groups in the mainland. AGWM missionaries working with Live Dead began to speak, write, and advocate in churches for more missionaries among unreached peoples. Mobilization surged.

Another critical leadership factor was executive director Greg Mundis (2011–2023). Mundis entered the role with a burden for peoples without gospel access, based on his own experience and research in Europe during his doctor of missiology studies. He began to raise his voice to support engaging the unreached; AGWM publications began to publicize the needs and opportunities. Other initiatives with a similar focus began to emerge.

Significantly, though started and stewarded by AGWM, Live Dead has intentionally partnered with "God's team"—workers from other organizations. More than thirty agencies are part of the Live Dead partnership and are equals in its vision and values. Around half of these partners are AG-sending structures, representing national churches around the world (Latin America, Europe, Africa, and Asia). In this way, Live Dead has influenced sister AG denominations globally. Other partners include evangelical sending agencies who recognize the value of collaboration or those without their own deploying opportunities.

By 2023, Live Dead workers comprised almost 30 percent of all AGWM missionaries sent from US churches. There are currently 770 Live Dead global workers (529 AGWM and 241 global partners), ninety Live Dead teams serving in 130 professional identities (BAM, etc.) across fifty-five countries, focused on pioneer disciple making among at least seventy-one Muslim, twelve Hindu, and seven Buddhist least reached peoples.

Lessons Learned along the Way

Since 2023, under the leadership of current executive director John Easter and his RD team, AGWM has re-prioritized preaching the gospel where Christ is not known and glorified. The mission statement has been rewritten: "We establish the church among all peoples, everywhere." AGWM has taken a painful and purposeful, Spirit-led journey back to where it started—a focus on the neglected peoples and places of the world. Some of the lessons learned from navigating this shift may be of help to other agencies, new and established:

- Missiological change in an organization requires multiple inputs along at least three primary vectors: biblical and missiological vision; structural channels for people to implement that vision; and leadership that clears the decks to pursue it. Changes over time lead to deeper rooting and a greater measure of ownership than if the change was a top-down decision only, or the dream of a single visionary individual.

- The shift in focus involved reframing apparent "innovation" as "realignment" with the original vision of the agency. Building on fruitful practices of the last one hundred years, the UPG challenge became a call to return to foundational understandings of the Bible, the compelling Spirit of mission, and founding AG vision of world evangelization.

- Change is difficult, whether personal or organizational. The journey has been painful at times. While some critique of the system and existing models was merited, zeal without compassion left some workers feeling undervalued. On their part, advocates encountered negative reactions, hostility, and broken relationships, or were marginalized and canceled. There was no natural forum or safe space for missiological discourse and debate. Acceptance or rejection depended on personalities, power, and regional variations in leadership style and approach.

- Leaders function as gatekeepers of ideas, information, resources, and access that affect organizational effectiveness. Leaders can control and limit conversations, decide to advance ideas, proposals, and practices, and assess who is "in" or "out." Ironically, in a Pentecostal organization, prophetic voices can be quenched. In the journey recounted above, other leaders welcomed innovation and opened doors. Without blaming anyone, we admit that the sobering result of a contested vision was twenty years of inadequate response to the desperate spiritual needs of millions of people in thousands of people groups who died without Christ.

- Organizations and churches must make room for and appreciate the value of "anointed mavericks." In the words of AG pastor and former district superintendent Bob Rhoden, mavericks "challenge the system by pushing the boundaries of change, but respect those in spiritual leadership ... focus more on vision and experiences than on policies and procedures ... seem to be more at risk because they are taking risks." He advises: "We need people who will challenge the system to help keep those in charge from merely rearranging their prejudices and calling it thinking."[13]

- The "all peoples" vision values every worker and ministry and all dimensions of the church's mission task. Mission and strategy issues can easily divide people if we give the impression that some work is more valuable and worthy of funding than others. There is no "A Team: we work with the unreached" and "B Team: we work with the church" in the missionary family. The reality is that the birth of new communities of faith leads inexorably to the need to strengthen, build up, and partner with those who come to faith. All the gifts are needed and must be aligned with the big task of seeing indigenous communities of faith established and growing within every tribe, language, people, and nation. Alignment with that vision will be the biggest ongoing challenge in the years ahead.

- A shift of focus to the unreached is impacting national church movements, leading to the emergence of new sending structures. Some workers are serving as mission mobilizers for national churches or as missionary educators who teach and develop curriculum focused on gospel access. Live Dead teams have also opened the door for partnerships, as national sending structures develop. At the global level, the World Assemblies of God Fellowship, a non-polity association comprising nearly seventy million Christians in over 150 national church movements, has a missions commission. Every AG national council is encouraged to develop its own appropriate sending structure and to prioritize peoples without gospel access.

- Mission education is essential for both field workers and leadership at all levels. New ideas can seem threatening to colleagues, leadership, and the status quo; they can be perceived as an attack on their personal significance and contribution to the mission. In retrospect, facilitating in-service mission education, along with better, more open, and safer dialogue between and among leaders and field workers, could have helped smooth the change process. Area and regional meetings that tended to focus on inspiration and fellowship could have benefited from a training and equipping track that upgraded missiological knowledge, understanding, and skills. Showing the resonance of an "all peoples" vision with the organization's founding purpose could have facilitated conceptual connections with AGWM's missiology and pneumatology, and perhaps paved the way for an easier, quicker transition.

---

13 Rhoden, "Hope."

- Revitalizing and educating local churches, the sending base of missions, is a critical part of the mission enterprise. In the past, organizations like AGWM did not consider local church mission education as part of its mandate. The second part of the triad "pray, give, go" tended to dominate: Annual "missions conventions" aimed to elicit "faith promise" pledges and congregations were extremely generous. Missionary speakers were and are the primary carriers of mission education in the AG. The downside is that in a forty-minute message or a five-minute "window on the world," a speaker must share their calling, needs of the country, and touching stories, all hung on a Bible story or few verses. Missing is any mechanism to connect the puzzle pieces into a big picture or to tell the grand story of a missionary God who from Genesis to Revelation and throughout history reveals his purpose to defeat evil and redeem a people from all peoples who will love, obey, and enjoy him forever. A compelling vision and understanding of where the church is, and where the peoples and places "where Christ is not known" are lacking and must be rebuilt.

The Glory of Jesus among All Peoples Everywhere

The recent history of Assemblies of God World Missions highlights the conceptual, missiological, structural, and leadership challenges faced by a large mission sending agency grappling with ethnolinguistic realities and organizational change. There have been bumps and bruises along the way, but it was a journey worth taking. Today the majority of newly appointed AGWM missionaries are commissioned to reach unreached people groups and/or to catalyze national church partners around the world to do so. The Pentecost paradigm is a proleptic picture of the final day toward which we labor—when people from all peoples, languages, tribes, and nations everywhere tell of the wonders of God and the glory of Jesus.

Bibliography

Bartlotti, Leonard N. "Islam, Relationship to." In *Encyclopedia of Pentecostal and Charismatic Christianity*, edited by Stanley M. Burgess, 264–69. New York: Routledge, 2006.

Hogan, J. Philip. "Response to Dr. Ralph Winter's Paper." In *Let the Earth Hear His Voice*, edited by J. D. Douglas, 242–45. Minneapolis, MN: World Wide Publications, 1975.

Klaus, Byron, and Douglas Petersen, eds. *The Essential J. Philip Hogan*. Vol. 1, *The J. Philip Hogan World Missions Series*. Springfield, MO: Assemblies of God Theological Seminary, 2006.

McGee, Gary B. *This Gospel Shall Be Preached*. Vol. 1, *A History and Theology of Assemblies of God Foreign Missions to 1959*. Springfield, MO: Gospel Publishing House, 1986.

McGee, Gary. *Miracles, Missions, and American Pentecostalism*. American Society of Missiology Series 45. Maryknoll, NY: Orbis, 2010.

Perkin, Noel, and John Garlock. *Our World Witness: A Survey of Assemblies of God Foreign Missions*. Springfield, MO: Gospel Publishing House, 1963.

Rhoden, Bob. "Hope for Anointed Mavericks." Accessed April 30, 2024. https://www.bobrhoden.com/hope-for-anointed-mavericks/.

Wilson, Everett A. *Strategy of the Spirit: J. Philip Hogan and the Growth of the Assemblies of God Worldwide 1960–1990*. Carlisle, Cumbria: Regnum Books International, 1997.

9
The Holy Vision Conceived in a Prayer Cave
The Korean Frontier Missions Movement

Jungkook Han and Mark Kim

Troubled by the lack of fruit in his ministry, Pastor Kim entered a prayer cave during the Korean winter of 1962. After completing his studies at Fuller Theological Seminary in the US and returning to Korea, Pastor Kim had founded the Korea Campus Crusade for Christ (KCCC). He was meeting with about twenty disciples. In the bitter minus-twenty-degree Celsius cold, he began to pray. At a time when the Korean church was still weak and missionary resources were scarce, he made the following Holy Spirit–inspired plea to God: "May hundreds of thousands of young people dream the dream of Jesus, see the vision of the salvation of mankind, holding the gospel in one hand and love in the other, traversing every corner of the globe, become a holy nation."

Twelve years later, KCCC Director Pastor Kim Jun-Kon (1925–2009),[1] alongside Dr. Bill Bright (1921–2003), hosted the Explo '74 conference in 1974. Tens of thousands of Koreans and nearly three thousand foreigners from eighty countries, along with 1.36 million believers worldwide, participated in the event.[2] The conference, which trained 300,000 in evangelism and discipleship,[3] led to an explosive growth of over 30 percent in the Korean Christian community and significant fruit in national evangelization. Importantly, the Explo '74 conference not only united churches but also served as a catalyst for the Korean church to embrace a vision for world missions.

In 1980, Pastor Kim Jun-Kon once again led a major conference. The World Evangelization Crusade (WEC) conference in Seoul, Korea, encouraged the Korean church, which had been focused largely on national evangelism, to participate in global missions. The Korean church had only sporadically sent missionaries to foreign countries such as Germany, Indonesia, and Guam. At that time, Korea was just emerging from the extreme poverty caused by the devastation of the Korean War in 1950. The idea of the Korean church serving the nations seemed almost unthinkable. It was during this period that the Korean church cried out to God to enable it to lead in global evangelization.

On the final night of WEC, a record-breaking crowd of 3 million people heard a declaration that committed the gathering to "place at God's disposal the resources of the church of Jesus Christ in Korea for world evangelization."[4] The Holy Spirit moved among the WEC attendees, and Pastor Kim called for 100,000 people to dedicate themselves to world missions by 1984—a thousand missionaries for every year of the Protestant mission effort in Korea. The conference

---

1 Also spelled Joon Gon Kim in various English references.
2 Plowman, "Explo '74."
3 "Cru Historical Fact Sheet."
4 Kennedy, "Troubled South Korea."

"publicly signaled" that the church in the Republic of Korea had "deliberately moved from being a missionary receiving church to a missionary sending one."[5]

The Beginning of the Unreached Peoples Movement

A distinctive feature of the Korean Protestant mission movement lies in its simultaneous focus on both unreached people groups (UPG) as well as general missionary efforts from its inception. Unlike other mission movements that evolved over time to strategically prioritize UPGs,[6] the Korean mission initiative placed a primary emphasis on reaching these groups from the very beginning. Data from the Korea Research Institute for Mission (KRIM), a professional institution for mission statistics, highlights this strategic focus: In 1982, the Korean church deployed 323 missionaries supported by forty-seven mission organizations. By 2002, these numbers had surged to 10,422 missionaries and 163 sending organizations.[7]

This remarkable growth in both missionaries and mission organizations can be attributed, somewhat paradoxically, to the focused commitment to ministering among unreached people groups. Some of the key elements that played a role in the emergence of the Korean frontier missions movement include the following:

1. *Introduction of the People Group Concept and Frontier Missions*

The Korean church has deep roots in Western theology. In fact, the mission movement developed by directly adopting Western missionary studies from the eighties and nineties. At a time when the term "mission" was still unfamiliar in the Korean church, missionary leaders like Bae Yun-ho, the editor and publisher of *Mission World* (the first mission magazine in Korea, now discontinued), and Moon Sang-cheol, the founder of KRIM, introduced Ralph Winter's concept of unreached peoples, and later the AD2000 Movement and the 10/40 Window.[8] While the Korean church shared the frontier vision of the Western church, translating terms like "unreached people group" and "adopt-a-people" into Korean was a significant challenge.[9]

2. *Cooperation among Mission Leaders, Organizations, and Churches*

Once a barren mission field, the Korean church began to create significant mission organizations through the cooperation and initiative of mission leaders. As college students emerged from the growing Korean church, Mission Korea encouraged them to dream of world missions. The first Mission Korea conference was in 1988 and every two years thereafter. Mission Korea was the most important student volunteer movement in Korean missions, with thousands of devoted students pledging their lives for world missions at each conference.

---

5 Kennedy.

6 See case studies in this volume by Garrison and Pratt on the Southern Baptist International Mission Board (IMB), and Brogden, Johnson, and Bartlotti on Assemblies of God World Missions (AGWM).

7 KRIM. "Current Status."

8 The 10/40 Window is "a rectangular geographic area that stretches from 10 [degrees north] to 40 [degrees north] latitude and from Morocco to Japan. The region encompasses much of North Africa, the Middle East, Central Asia, South Asia, East Asia, and Southeast Asia. The 10/40 Window is home to 83 percent of the world's remaining unreached people groups and over 90 percent of the world's remaining frontier people groups" (Pray 10/40, "10/40 Window").

9 Initially, for example, the term "adopt-a-people" caused many misunderstandings, with some missionaries interpreting it as adopting children from their mission fields as their own.

In the same way denominations, churches, and missionary organizations came together to form The Korea World Missions Association (KWMA).[10] This association of member organizations acted as a "control tower" to advise and steer the missions resources of the Korean church. KWMA led in the preparation of a master plan for Korean church missions, strategy research, resource allocation, mission field research, and missions administration.

Another groundbreaking moment for the unreached peoples movement was the establishment of Korea Adopt A People (KAAP).[11] This allowed the Korean church to approach missions strategically from the beginning. The first director, mission theologian Dr. Jeon Ho-jin, and missionary Han Jungkook, general secretary, served to oversee the entire ministry.

In the newly established Korean UPG movement, Pastor Han Jungkook played a very important role. He was instrumental in founding Mission Korea, KWMA, and KAAP, and from 2010 to 2017, served as the general secretary of KWMA, planning Target 2030 and effectively leading the Korean UPG movement.

Overall, zeal among mission leaders was high in this period. The aspiration to advance to the frontiers, rather than "building on someone else's foundation," is especially evident, for example, in the annual mission themes of Mission Korea. From the second conference in 1990 to the sixth in 1998, each conference theme emphasized the responsibility and challenge of the "unfinished task," the concept of UPG, frontier missions, and "unevangelized regions." As a result, the number of missionaries began to increase explosively from the late 1990s. Mission leaders and organizations made greater efforts to be more intentional in sending missionaries to UPGs.

3. *The Change in the Global Environment with the Opening of the Iron Curtain and Bamboo Curtain*

With the end of the Cold War and the fall of the Berlin Wall, the Soviet Union and China began to open, and many unreached peoples buried within the Communist bloc evolved into independent nations. These fields held excellent opportunities for dedicated Korean college students.

Notably, Koreans in the Soviet Union and ethnic Koreans in China, already assimilated into the local languages and cultures, provided support to Korean missionaries settling in these areas. Additionally, in Central Asia and Turkey, where Mongolian and Turkic peoples of the same Altaic language family are spread, Korean missionaries could quickly learn the languages. Koreans who were forcibly relocated or fled due to painful historical events in Korea provided a good platform for the Korean missionary community. This reminds us of Genesis 45:7: "But God sent me ahead of you to preserve for you a remnant on earth and to save your lives by a great deliverance." Ethnic Koreans in China, once unreached, became one of the fastest evangelized peoples. The assistance by ethnic Koreans enabled the gospel to be preached to many unreached peoples within China and the Soviet Union.

---

10 See kwma.org.

11 "The basic idea: get a church or other fellowship group, working in partnership with a mission agency, to 'adopt' one or more unreached peoples for long-term prayer, financial support, and/or personnel recruitment" (Dorr, "Adopt a People"). Under the leadership of Phil Bogosian, the concept and program expanded to become the Global Adopt A People Campaign (GAAPC), which facilitates breakthroughs among unreached peoples through targeted prayer campaigns (globaladoptapeoplecampaign.org); cf. Datema and Bartlotti, "The People Group Approach: A Historical Perspective," in this volume. Note that AAP focuses long-term prayer, support, and partnership on the *people group* rather than simply the missionary.

4. *The Freedom to Travel Abroad after the 1988 Seoul Olympics*

Meanwhile, having rapidly achieved economic growth since the 1970s, Korea hosted the Olympics in Seoul in 1988. This event served to erase negative perceptions about Korea's safety in the international community and showcase its developed status to the world. Simultaneously, from this point on, Korean citizens could freely travel abroad with a passport. While overseas mission work had been extremely limited due to the restrictions on traveling abroad, the liberalization of overseas travel after the 1988 Olympics led to an explosive development of short-term missions by the Korean church.

Other Driving Forces for the UPG Movement

Short-Term Missions

The growth of short-term missions (STM) trips was another factor driving the Korean frontier missions movement. Throughout the eighties, various conferences led to a pool of potential candidates dedicating themselves to missions. Eased overseas travel and increased income enabled them to visit other countries. This development came with challenges.

To Koreans who had just begun traveling overseas, all non-Korean ethnicities were perceived as UPGs. However, curiosity about the newly opened Communist bloc and guidance from mobilizers led many short termers to gravitate to unreached peoples in Mongolia, China, the former Soviet Union, and Eastern Europe.

Regions with populations of ethnic Koreans were particularly appealing for Koreans, especially those discouraged by the language barriers they faced. Initially, mission organizations provided brief training for their short-term trips. Gradually, many local churches began to organize their own short-term teams, and increasing numbers of believers joined missionary trips. The explosive growth in STM also led to criticism for misusing funds better invested in long-term missionaries and for treating missions as an excuse for overseas travel.

Many short termers went on to initiate prayer meetings for missions within their local churches or undertook missionary training before committing to long-term mission service. There are no exact statistics on STM transitioning to long term, though it is estimated that in the early nineties, over 50 percent of those who went on STM committed to long-term missions service or related activities within five years.

Missionary Training

Korean missionary candidates faced at least two major barriers, which some likened to an Achilles' heel. First, the perception among Christians was that missionaries required higher standards than pastors and must undergo theological education. Second, many believed that one must be proficient in English to train as a missionary and serve overseas.

Unfortunately, in the early nineties, only a handful of organizations in Korea were equipped with quality instructors and curriculum for missionary training. Those who could provide training were perceived as Western, which further deterred training. Theological schools were also slow to respond, as they struggled to keep up with the domestic demand for ministers. Education and training in frontier missiology were virtually nonexistent.

Indigenous organizations like InterCP International arose to meet the demand of young people wanting missionary training.[12] InterCP's "vision school" program runs once a week for eight to ten weeks and includes lectures, worship, prayer, small groups, and fellowship in each meeting. The program is designed to impart a vision for unreached peoples and share opportunities for short-term and tentmaker service. In the beginning there was no program for long-term candidates; this developed much later with a program focused on spirituality, character, mission strategy, understanding culture, spiritual warfare, language acquisition, and other practical subjects. The response to the training has been overwhelmingly positive. Moreover, the enthusiasm of those who have taken short-term trips or gone through the training has helped revitalize the vision of local churches.

Tentmaking Mission
Another important factor increasing momentum was the concept of "creative access" countries. The Korean church, which had previously sent missionaries to reached areas in Southeast Asia and Africa, recognized the need for new mission strategies to reach unreached people groups, especially those in the context of the former Communist bloc.

The rationale that non-ordained missionaries could be more effective in creative access areas led to the acceptance of "tentmaker" missionaries in the Korean mission community. Mission leaders from twenty-eight mission organizations mobilized doctors, businessmen, professors, and IT experts and launched the Korea Association of Tentmaking (KAT) in 1993. KAT not only provided theological support for the concept of professionals dedicating themselves as missionaries, but it also facilitated regular meetings to share information and discuss effective mission strategies in unreached areas.

Traditionally, the Korean church had resisted recognizing lay people as missionaries in contrast with ordained missionaries. This situation was reversed through the influence and support of Dr. Lee HyunMo, professor of missiology at the Korea Baptist Theological University and Seminary. Dr. Lee established an important theological foundation for the tentmaker movement. He stated, "If the universal priesthood of believers is biblical, then the concept of every believer being a missionary is also biblical."

Opposition against the UPG Movement

Although UPGs were an early part of Korean missions and were a feature of conferences like GCOWE '95 in Seoul, the movement faced significant opposition from those already on the mission field. Korean missionaries sent out in the 1980s were unfamiliar with the concept of unreached peoples. Some of the backlash was due to the perception that their roles and ministries were not adequately recognized in these new mission strategies.

First, there was resistance to the notion of reallocating missionaries. At the Lausanne Congress in 1974 (Lausanne) and 1989 (Manila), others in the global church, especially Westerners, had actively discussed the notion of reallocating missionaries from reached areas and prioritizing the

---

12 As of 2024, InterCP International has approximately seventeen hundred missionaries serving among more than fifty-five people groups in the 10/40 Window, including Turkey, the Caucasus, Central Asia, North India, Siberia-Mongolia, and other regions. Initially, InterCP was called Korea Tentmaking Mission and was later changed to Inter-coop; it is now known as InterCP.

deployment of new missionaries to UPGs. For example, in the 1990s, 254 Western missionaries were active in Korea. The Southern Baptist Convention of the USA took the drastic step of leaving only twenty missionaries in Korea and reallocating the rest. An American missionary reassigned to Central Asia recalled, "It was an exceedingly difficult command."

In a similar way in the early nineties, the Korean mission community also emphasized UPG missions and made efforts to reallocate Korean missionaries active among reached people groups in Kenya and the Philippines to areas with UPGs. However, these workers, many of whom were older, senior missionaries with established ministries, were deeply disappointed by the devaluation of their long-standing efforts.

Second, conflicts emerged between senior missionaries and new missionaries on the field. Short-term teams from Korea, though educated and motivated for frontier missions, found it easier to begin in reached areas with established missionary platforms than in uncertain, inaccessible UPG regions. The insistence, then, by these STM "newbies" that they should engage in UPG missions caused considerable discomfort among the established missionaries leading those fields. Additionally, visiting pastors from supporting churches began to ask, "What do you think about unreached peoples?" UPG mobilizers became the subject of much criticism at missionary conferences in Southeast Asia and East Africa.

Third, in unreached areas like Mongolia, both traditional, ordained missionaries as well as tentmakers were active. Korean ordained missionaries still perceived tentmakers as lower-level, incomplete workers, leading to conflict between the two groups. In one incident, a tentmaker baptized a newly converted Mongolian. When this was discovered, ordained missionaries called a council, arguing that tentmakers had no right to administer sacraments. Thus, non-ordained missionaries mobilized and sent for frontier mission work among unreached peoples were restricted to acting only as assistants to ordained missionaries. This led to further friction as some tentmakers responded by forming separate partnerships.

Fourth, the focus on the 10/40 Window (which encompassed the majority of the world's UPGs) as the primary and strategic locus of mission efforts caused strong backlash from Korean missionaries active in areas like Russia that were not geographically included in the 10/40 Window. Workers feared that as the frontier mission movement intensified, the Korean church would lose interest and not support their ministries.

Finally, there was a reaction against the unreached peoples and "Adopt A People" movements for overly narrowing the scope of mission objectives. Many Korean churches wanted to recognize the entire world, all countries, nations, and peoples, as the focus of missions. Suddenly narrowing this focus to a single people group felt like diminishing their church's role in global missions.

The Strategic Advance of the UPG Movement

With the rapid increase in the number of missionaries and the resulting boost in confidence, the Korean church embraced the "holy burden" of taking responsibility for one-tenth of the world's missionaries. This commitment at the GCOWE '97 conference in South Africa spurred efforts to improve both the quantity and quality of Korean missionaries. The Korean mission movement advanced in two directions.

First, in 2005, they established a master plan called "Target 2030" with goals to discover, train, and deploy 100,000 missionaries needed for global missions. This plan was based on an evaluation of Korean missions from 1980 to 2004, research on the number of missionaries needed worldwide over the next twenty-five years, and a calculation of the appropriate number of Korean missionaries that could be mobilized to five continents. Concurrently, under the auspices of the KWMA, the National Consultation on World Evangelization (NCOWE) was held in collaboration with Korean mission theologians, missionaries, leaders of mission organizations, and influential pastors. The resulting five-year mission plan included elements of strategy, mobilization, training, and administration.

As a result of these efforts, from 2006 to 2010, both denominational mission boards such as the Global Mission Society of the Presbyterian Church (GMS) and nondenominational agencies like the Global Missionary Fellowship (GMF),[13] InterCP International, and others sent out the largest number of Korean missionaries ever.

Importantly, this comprehensive mission strategy was focused primarily on the task of reaching the remaining unreached people groups. The "national [country] paradigm" shifted to an "ethnic paradigm."[14]

Church mobilization was also an important element in the strategic plan. Korean churches began to use the "people group adoption" strategy to participate in efforts to reach UPGs. Until then, missions in the local church was mostly limited to vague prayers and missionary support. However, the people group adoption strategy helped churches understand and be involved in the larger, complex process of reaching a specific people group.[15] The primary focus was on the mission—reaching peoples—rather than a missionary. Initially, Korea AAP prioritized 166 people groups for adoption. From 1993 to 1999, through this strategic approach, around three hundred people groups were "adopted" by denominations and local churches.

In addition, efforts were made to upgrade the short-term ministry of local churches. Previously limited to mission field visits, trips evolved into "mission field research." In this way, Korea Adopt A People was able to produce and distribute ethnic profiles of UPGs to increase awareness and prayer.

In a second major step forward, the Korean church began to conceive and promote its own mission theology and missiology and to develop Korean models to contribute to the world mission enterprise. One example was the "Comity, Adoption, Specialization" (CAS) strategy initially developed at the third NCOWE conference in 2000. The concepts of ethnic groups and affinity blocs, directly imported from Western missiology, felt alien to Koreans who had lived in a small territory as a single ethnic group for thousands of years. Instead, recognizing that "geographical regions" were a more understandable concept for Koreans, a strategy was devised to first "divide regions (Comity)," (i.e., "separate the world into 26 regional blocks," then

---

[13] GMF is an indigenous, interdenominational mission structure formed in the 1980s that brought together Global Bible Translators (GBT), OMF Korea, and the Global Missionary Training Center (GMTC) to collaborate with churches and agencies in sending cross-cultural Korean missionaries. See http://www.gmf.or.kr/pages/aboutGMF-1.

[14] KCM, "Report on the 2006 NCOWE IV."

[15] Unreached People Missions Alliance, "Korean Church's Unreached Peoples."

"subdivide the locations" into provinces, cities, and unreached people groups for adoption and specialized evangelization).[16]

Later, as migration and urban missions became key issues, the "C" in CAS was changed to represent "City." The CAS approach aimed to view mission fields from urban and ethnic perspectives, prioritize unreached areas for frontier work, and maximize missionary effectiveness through "specialization" in various mission functions.[17]

Organizations like the Unreached People Missions Alliance (UPMA) created "Frontier Mission Maps" that divided the world into twelve regions, with information on countries and unreached people groups within each region, and the corresponding index of persecution of Christians. These maps were provided to local churches and Korean missionaries nationwide.

In 2010, to commemorate the 125th anniversary of Korean Protestantism, the KWMA announced that, during its research on the relationship between Korean missiology and the mission DNA of Western churches, it had identified three distinct characteristics in the theology of Korean missions: (1) The Korean church pursued a theology of blessing in suffering (theology of suffering and blessing); (2) the Korean church was a transformative presence in times of crisis within Korean society (theology of crisis and transformation); and (3) the Korean church practiced a theology of national evangelization accompanied by global missions (theology of national evangelization and world mission).

The missiology of Korea has historically been rooted in the "Nevius Method." John Livingston Nevius, an influential American Presbyterian missionary, introduced his pioneering method for planting churches to the Korean church in 1890. His approach emphasized the importance of establishing self-propagating, self-governing, and self-supporting churches within the mission field. Nevius believed that missionaries should focus on training local leaders who would lead their congregations, fostering the autonomy of churches and the development of indigenous expressions of Christian faith and practice. His method deeply influenced the Korean church and subsequently the mission strategies of Korean missionaries.

Based on these theological foundations, the heart of Korean mission theology was identified as "dedication and passion." That is, at its core, Korean mission theology aimed to develop dedication and passion. With its short history of cross-cultural work and lack of a viable platform for frontier missions, Korean missions have been pioneered largely through the dedication and passion of missionaries. The Apostle Paul's admonition "suffer for the gospel" (2 Tim 1:8) has been a keyword in the theology of Korean missions.

---

16 For other details, see KCM, "Report on the 2006 NCOWE IV."

17 NCOWE constituted twenty-six "area specialization committees" in the Korean mission system to foster "specialized decision making and professionalism" and future cooperation. These twenty-six committees reveal something of the comprehensive vision and organizational mindset of Korean missions: Professional Mission Committee, UPG Mission Committee, Medical Mission Committee, Foreigner Mission Committee, MK Education Committee, Youth-Students Mission Committee, North Korea Mission Committee, China Mission Committee, Islam Bloc Mission Committee, Buddhist Bloc Mission Committee, Hindu Bloc Mission Committee, Catholic Bloc Mission Committee, Communist Bloc Mission Committee, Internet Mission Committee, Korean Diaspora Mission Committee, Christian Educator's Committee, NGO Mission Committee, Sports Mission Committee, Culture Mission Committee, Missionary Total Care Committee, Church Mission Promotion Committee, Missiology Committee, Mission Training-Education Committee, Mission Social Science Committee, Handicap Person Mission Committee, Children Mission Committee. See KCM, "Report on the 2006 NCOWE IV."

Crises and Challenges

The Korean frontier mission movement faced several crises, the most significant of which occurred in 2007. A twenty-three-member short-term mission team was kidnapped by the Taliban while traveling in Afghanistan. During their forty-day captivity, two members were martyred. After the South Korean government negotiated and paid a ransom to the Taliban, the other kidnapped individuals were gradually released.

This tragic incident had a significant adverse impact on Korean missions. The South Korean government banned travel to countries like Afghanistan, Iraq, Syria, Libya, Yemen, and Somalia. Long-term ministries were impaired as veteran Korean missionaries and tentmakers were called home by the government. Short-term missions by Protestants in dangerous regions faced nationwide criticism. Missions to Islamic regions, both short and long term, rapidly contracted.

A greater crisis emerged in the attitude of church and mission leaders addressing the issue. Many established churches strongly criticized evangelizing in dangerous unreached areas. Mission leaders and pastors failed to teach that suffering and persecution are natural when witnessing to the gospel.

An examination of the metrics of Korean missions reveals that, beginning in 2008, the number of missionaries and mission organizations stagnated. When the Korea Research Institute for Mission introduced stricter criteria for defining missionaries, this revealed an overall decline in the number of missionaries in 2020 from twenty-eight thousand to twenty-two thousand.

External factors, like the acceleration of migration, terrorist activities by Islamic extremists, and the COVID-19 pandemic, played a role. Mission leaders felt pressed to respond to immediate missional needs in Korea. More importantly, the leaders appointed later lacked field experience among unreached peoples, resulting in a lack of urgency to prioritize ministry to these groups. The KWMA, which had played a central role in the frontier mission movement, did not take leadership to chart the direction of missions after Target 2030.

Mission Korea, which had been at the heart of resource development for frontier missions, faced a similar situation. The united mission movement gradually lost its significance, and amidst the crisis, it reverted to mission activities centered around individual churches.

A greater challenge was a kind of psychological shrinkage. Due to population decline in Korean society and the drop in the Christian population, churches and organizations lacked the capacity to support existing mission activities, let alone expand into new frontier areas. The energy for pioneering new regions was absent. The interest of large churches, which in the early nineties had been actively adopting people groups and financially supporting frontier missions, shifted toward addressing problems facing Korean society rather than global missions. These factors, taken together, contributed to a significant loss of momentum in the Korean mission movement.

Prospects for the Future

Despite numerous challenges, Korean missions is poised to progress to the next stage. The experiences of the past forty years serve as a valuable foundation and suggest new directions for development. Churches are endeavoring to become more missional, with greater potential to mobilize mission resources. Many of the 1.3 million immigrants now living in Korea come from unreached people groups or from groups proximate to UPGs. About 7.3 million Koreans spread across 180 countries are potential partners and proximate church resources for evangelism among unreached people groups.

Recently, new mission organizations and churches emphasizing prayer, fasting, and traditional disciplines have emerged, creating transformative models to counter the secularization of society. With the advancement of social media, a younger generation, which easily communicates with Christians around the world, will collaborate more effortlessly with the global church than ever before.

Korean missions is distinguished by its pursuit of a theology of suffering and blessing, theology of crisis and transformation, and theology of national evangelization and world mission. At the heart of its theology and missiology is a DNA of dedication and spiritual passion—dedication to overcoming and transforming through crises, a belief that they will find a way through current challenges, a commitment to finish the task entrusted to the church, and a passion for God's glory over all peoples and nations.

Bibliography

Cru. "Cru Historical Fact Sheet." Accessed April 30, 2024. https://www.cru.org/us/en/about/cru-press/background/cru-historical-fact-sheet.html.

Dorr, Darrell Dorr. "Adopt A People! The Strategy for the 90's." *Mission Frontiers* (Jun–Oct, 1990). https://www.missionfrontiers.org/issue/article/adopt-a-people1.

KCM. "Report on the 2006 NCOWE IV Mission Strategy Conference." September 5, 2006. http://kcm.kr/mio_view.php?nid=26297?&page=12&kword=%25C&dt=1&ds=&dc=&dk=1&df=1&di=1&du=&dd=&de=&or=0.

Kennedy, Nell L. "Troubled South Korea Manages a Very Big Bash for Missions." Accessed April 30, 2024. https://www.christianitytoday.com/ct/1980/september-19/troubled-south-korea-manages-very-big-bash-for-missions.html.

KRIM. "Current Status of Korean Missions." Accessed April 30, 2024. https://krim.org/statisticsdata-2/?ckattempt=2.

Plowman, Edward E. "Explo '74: 'Christianizing' Korea." Accessed April 30, 2024. https://www.christianitytoday.com/ct/1974/september-13/explo-74-christianizing-korea.html.

Pray 10/40. "10/40 Window: The Ultimate Guide." Accessed April 30, 2024. https://pray1040.com/10-40-window/.

Unreached People Missions Alliance. "The Korean Church's Unreached Peoples Missions Examined through Adoption Missions to Unreached Peoples." *Web Journal* 2, no. 29 (2024). http://upma21.com/main/?p=7776.

10

Sub-Saharan Africa

Taking the Gospel to "Where the Smoke Is Seen"

Peter Oyugi with Mary Ho, Clara Litzsinger, and Zazá Lima

Peter Oyugi, a key leader in the Movement for African National Initiatives (MANI),[1] shares his perspective on frontier missions and unreached peoples in Africa. After introducing the spectacular growth of the church in Africa, Mary Ho and Clara Litzsinger (All Nations) and Zazá Lima (PMI) interview Peter to gain insight into the unique contributions and approaches of African cross-cultural missionaries, and what the global Christian movement can learn from African missions.

The Growth of Christianity in Africa

Africa has had a more enduring Christian history than Europe and North America.[2] Christianity on the continent hearkens back to the earliest church, when pilgrims from Egypt and Libya gathered with the nations at Pentecost.

Many of the prominent early church fathers, including Augustine and Tertullian, were of African descent. Contrary to common caricature, the birth of African Christianity predates and precedes colonialism by many centuries. In fact, Christianity has grown throughout the continent primarily as a grassroots African faith. Even during the height of European missions, Christianity spread through indigenous movements. Across the continent,

> the church has spread principally through lay activities … many without formal education … establishing preaching posts and communities of worship wherever they have been. After a century of missionary work on the continent, Africa's Christian leaders began decrying the fact that indigenous peoples bore the brunt of the Christian mission enterprise but they remained nameless, as unsung heroes, in a missionary historiography that placed the missionary at the centre of the story.[3]

Most of these unsung heroes were women. Esther Mombo maintains that "the church in Africa is largely composed of, and sustained by, women of unceasing devotions."[4] Global researcher Gina Zurlo goes so far as to confirm that the face of global Christianity is an African woman.[5]

---

[1] MANI (www.globalprn.com/m-a-n-i/) is "a network of networks" catalyzing African national initiatives; its purpose is to "affirm, motivate, mobilize, and network Christian leaders by inspiring them with the vision of reaching the unreached and least evangelized in Africa, and the wider world, through the communication of up to date research, reports, and models; consultations and prayer efforts focusing on the unfinished task."
[2] Asamoah-Gyadu, "Christianity in Sub-Saharan Africa," 20.
[3] Johnson and Zurlo, *World Christian Encyclopedia*, 20–21, 25–26.
[4] Mombo, "Mission and Evangelism," 383.
[5] Ho, "Growing Women Leaders."

Today, largely because of these unsung heroes, both men and women, Christianity is growing on the African continent at twice the pace of growth of global Christianity![6] The Christian population in Africa now leads the global church with over 667 million Christians in 2020, followed by Latin America (612 million) and Asia (379 million).[7] The majority of Christians in Africa is concentrated in Sub-Saharan Africa with more than 565 million adherents by 2015.[8] It is projected that Christianity will continue to grow the fastest in Africa: Nigeria and Democratic Republic of Congo (DRC) are respectively the fourth- and fifth-fastest-growing Christian countries in the world, with several other African countries not far behind.[9]

Sub-Saharan Africa is dominated by the three major religions of Christianity, Islam, and African traditional religions.[10] Although Christianity and Islam have been the fastest spreading religions on the continent, both are intermingled with folk practices from the African traditional religions.[11] Due to increasing conversions from African traditional religions and the high birth rates among Christians, it is projected that by 2050, Christianity may account for over three-fifths of the region's population.[12]

Africa was considered 77 percent evangelized as of 2020.[13] The continent still receives more missionaries (97,000) than sends missionaries (39,400) in 2020.[14] The largest African host nations are the DRC and South Africa, which rank as the world's fourth- and fifth-biggest receivers of long-term foreign missionaries.[15]

The Task Remaining

There is still a significant task remaining. According to Joshua Project, there are 3,745 people groups in Africa, of which 988 remain unreached, representing almost one-third of Africa's population.[16] Most of these peoples are in Sub-Saharan Africa, totaling 3,139 people groups, of which 658 are unreached people groups.

The increase of national Christian workers who serve cross-culturally in their own countries is a growing trend in African missions, totaling 1.87 million national workers as of 2020. In terms of missions to foreign lands, Nigeria ranks as the fifth-largest mission-sending country in the world.[17]

---

6 Johnson and Zurlo, World Christian Encyclopedia, 34.
7 Johnson and Zurlo, 4.
8 Zurlo, "Demographic Profile of Christianity," 4.
9 Johnson and Zurlo, World Christian Encyclopedia, 34.
10 Zurlo, "Demographic Profile of Christianity," 3.
11 Zurlo, 3.
12 Zurlo, 5. The largest Christian traditions in Sub-Saharan Africa are the Catholics (236 million by 2020), the Pentecostals/charismatics (230 million), and the evangelicals (162 million), according to Johnson and Zurlo, World Christian Encyclopedia, 9.
13 Johnson and Zurlo, 33.
14 Johnson and Zurlo, 32.
15 Johnson and Zurlo, 32.
16 Joshua Project (https://joshuaproject.net), March 2024.
17 Johnson and Zurlo, World Christian Encyclopedia, 32.

The Muslim-majority countries in Western Africa are the least evangelized countries in Sub-Saharan Africa and are the African region with the most UPGs. Even in Eastern African countries with the most Christians, there are a significant number of unreached people groups (UPGs) within them. In Sudan there are two hundred distinct ethnolinguistic groups, 169 of them unreached peoples, embracing over 45 million people and 95 percent of Sudan's population. The Chad-Sudan border has one of the greatest concentrations of unreached and unengaged peoples in the world.

Several of the world's one hundred largest unreached people groups are in Africa. These include the Algerians of Algeria; Arab of Morocco; Arab of Sudan; Arab of Tunisia; Bambara of Mali; the Yerwa Kanuri, Fulani, and Hausa peoples of Nigeria; Hausa of Niger; the Oromo Hararghe and Somali peoples of Ethiopia; and Somali of Somalia.[18]

Frontier Missions and Unreached Peoples in Africa

Q: *How have African churches and organizations responded to the people group paradigm and how have they embraced the challenge of unreached peoples?*

Peter: It is not well recorded, but African believers have been taking the gospel cross-culturally to unreached peoples for one hundred years. There were so many who embraced frontier missions over the last century that we will never get to know. The one thing they seem to have in common was their response to the Holy Spirit's prompting to take the gospel of Jesus Christ to neighboring villages and beyond. Most of these believers were nameless and underground. Many of them were women.

A lot of it was driven by the desire that, if they saw smoke in the horizon, it was a sign that there was some human life there. They would say to themselves, "We need to tell the gospel of Christ to those people where that smoke is seen."

This meant crossing several ridges and being in different ethnic groups. That's how Africa became the continent with the largest number of Christians.

The reason they remain nameless is mainly because, over the last two hundred years or so, we have often operated on a mission paradigm done from a place of power. In contrast, these African pioneers served from a place of weakness. While we tend to credit expatriate missionaries for the growth of Christianity in Africa, I am convinced that much of the fruit came because of Africans themselves taking the gospel to those who had not heard.

In the last forty to fifty years, new mission initiatives have come from student ministries in schools, colleges, and universities. Christian unions began to understand God's call to the nations through mission conventions like Commission (Kenya) and Witness (Nigeria). This stirred young Africans to engage cross-culturally. These students began to form indigenous mission agencies. The most notable were CAPRO[19] in Nigeria and Sheepfold in Kenya.

The churches in Africa have mostly focused on unreached people groups in Africa. More recently, the Movement for African National Initiative (MANI), which emerged from the

---

18 Joshua Project (https://joshuaproject.net), March 2024.
19 CAPRO is an acronym for Calvary Productions, the original name of Calvary Ministries, which started in 1975 as an outreach to unreached peoples of northern Nigeria and is now an international, nondenominational mission agency focused on UPGs in Africa and beyond. See https://capro.ng/index.php/about-us/.

AD2000 Movement and various other consultations, began to catalyze mission initiatives in churches across denominations. Agencies in many African countries began to reach ethnic communities within their national boundaries. MANI started to adopt specific people groups in the last twenty years, which greatly expanded the missionary efforts of African churches within the continent.

Q: *How many countries are in the MANI network?*

Peter: Though initiatives differ in each country, at least thirty countries are actively engaged in MANI. Some, like Ethiopia, have operated underground. We didn't know much of what was happening there until 2016. It was surprising to see how much the church has grown and has been reaching people in their country and surrounding nations. The East African revivals have been especially powerful and influential.

Most Africans do missions as a natural by-product of living out their faith. They don't think of it in a category like "we are doing cross-cultural missions." Missions has been organic and a spontaneous work of God. Today, countries like Nigeria, Ghana, Kenya, DRC, and Ethiopia are highly active missional countries.

Q: *It sounds like cross-cultural missions was birthed at a grassroots level, inspired by the Holy Spirit. How did they catch the vision for frontier missions?*

Peter: They read Scripture, prayed, and felt a call from God to take the gospel to where it has not been heard. Many of these places are very multiethnic. So when the gospel took root in one place within Africa, they would feel "we need to take the gospel to places where people have not heard." This involved crossing ethnic boundaries and learning new languages.

For example, when I was at a student prayer meeting in high school, a student prophesied that we were supposed to reach the Muslim world. We did not have missiological training. But from that time, I knew that God was speaking to me. There are many similar unwritten stories, past and present.

A well-known example is Apolo Kivebulaya from Uganda who served in the DRC in the 1890s. After he received Christ through missionaries, God moved his heart to take the gospel to different tribes, as they called them at his time. He did an amazing work in the DRC and churches multiplied over many decades. He was an indigenous person living out Christ in obedience. This is African frontier missions, characterized by individuals who somehow understand from Scripture a call to the nations.

Africans have always been taking the gospel to remote tribes and engaging in cross-cultural ministry. It is only more recently that there have been mission books, conferences, and conventions. It is only recently that the term "unreached people groups" filtered down into mission conferences. Africans who attended these conventions then became aware of the "people group" paradigm as we call it today.

Q: *Now that more Africans read mission literature and go to conferences, is there a more coordinated intentional strategy to reach the least reached?*

Peter: There has been a growing understanding over the last forty years that the gospel needs to reach those who haven't heard. Many countries, like Nigeria and Ghana, now have coordinated efforts. There are organized efforts to assign specific churches to go to specific people groups.

In 2001 at MANI, about three hundred leaders from fifty African countries made a commitment to be intentional in reaching the least reached. Western and southern African countries began to research, map, and identify people groups in their countries. In Africa, countries are in close geographical and cultural proximity. Urbanization has also meant that least reached peoples are very much within the neighborhood of existing churches.

However, many ethnic groups are much more complex than we knew. For example, we may aim at twenty-five people groups, but it turns out to be more than twenty-five because there are multiethnic groups, especially in places marginalized by the government.

CAPRO is the oldest cross-cultural mission agency in Africa working with least reached people groups. They list each people group by name and intentionally pray for every ethnic group in the world and for the president of every country. They have more than one thousand people in their daily prayer group, and they actively seek to move beyond African borders.

Here is a uniquely African angle: Many African churches aspire to extend their denominations across the world. They want to have a denominational presence in every part of the world. As they do that, it has a ripple effect on the African missionary effort. It is unconventional but powerful. For example, the Church of Pentecost of Ghana and the Redeemed Christian Church of God (mostly Nigerian) are now in more than 180 countries. They have a strong sense that God wants them to reach the world, including the Muslim countries in North Africa.

Although this approach has not always contextualized the gospel well, it has resulted in a Christian presence in new places and among least reached peoples. They are engaging with local communities and sharing the love of Christ. That is one way they are affecting the diaspora peoples. God is placing them there strategically.

Q: *In view of the wars, instability, and suffering in African countries like South Sudan and Mali, how is engaging suffering a part of the African calling and prayers? How is the Holy Spirit guiding you towards a place of grace for refugees?*

Peter: It is an important question because we need to recognize most of the African diaspora is within Africa itself. A lot of refugee movement and migration is within the continent.

Africa is a continent that has learned to live with pain and suffering. It has been on the receiving end of injustice. In such a place, suffering is seen as normal, not extraordinary. The church has been slower to see missional opportunities in the diaspora because their own people have so many day-to-day struggles. However, the church does provide hospitality, solace, and care to those who come as refugees and migrants. Maybe the African church could do better, but they may be at their capacity.

Colonization and slavery have been the main traumas in Africa that destroyed people's identity and created distrust of the West. This is a situation where we look to a new expression of the global church—churches in a better place to help and show compassion. Africa is down and depressed. A church anywhere with more "power" and resources can do something. Where African churches have grown stronger, they have started to act.

One thing I see very clearly is that modern African Christianity and mission are very holistic. There is a strong understanding that when I go into a community, I need to do something for the people's suffering. In the past, the missionary movements from the West established hospitals and schools. Western mission organizations today cannot simply come with the gospel and the Bible. Communities are asking, "How can we help these poorer unreached groups that don't have schools and hospitals?"

A big part of the African worldview is that a person is a whole person. Transformational discipleship has become very important to African churches and mission agencies. There has been a recognition that gospel outreach must be holistic and serve the needs of the community. Many times African missionaries go to people who are in a worse off situation than themselves. With limited resources, the African missionaries share what they can. First, they share their food. Then they focus on improving health and education, two important aspects of holistic or transformational discipleship.

Today, African workers often serve through their professions, sometimes through national service or partnering with NGOs (e.g., in Nigeria, Ghana, Uganda, and Kenya). They go as community health workers and teachers, choosing to live in least reached places to make disciples. Within the Sahel, we see fruitful disciple-making movements (DMM) ignited by professionals, traders, and entrepreneurs.

Q: *In MANI, how do you recognize and adjust to the ethnic and linguistic differences between peoples?*

Peter: Most Africans speak more than three or four languages and learn languages quickly. But cultures are very different. Sometimes, it is easier to take the gospel a few cultures away because the immediate neighbor may be a challenge. Sometimes, the tension and mistrust are too big with the people bordering you. So, you skip the immediate neighbor and go to the next.

You just go and learn the language as you go. There are no special programs for learning languages. Speaking the language builds a bridge. There is a realization that neighboring cultures in Africa can be totally opposite. In a sense, it is the beauty and blessing of Africa that they have learned to live with diversity. It is one of their strengths.

Q: *Africans seem naturally cross-cultural and relational. What are other strengths, innovative models, or unique elements of African frontier missions?*

Peter: Being relational is our strength. We have a great ability to be relational. It comes so naturally. We are generally interested in an individual's family. We also cherish community because people belong and find identity in communities. As we engage in cross-cultural mission, we aim to bring whole families to Christ. I think that reflects the heart of Christianity. We live among the people. We blend with the people.

The church in Africa also has spiritual vitality. Unfortunately, nowadays we tend to rely too much on education, methodologies, and trainings. Wholehearted dependence on God can slip away, and we risk losing it.

Using professionals, being traders or farmers, gives authenticity to African missions and allows us to be part of the community. Supported missionaries who don't seem to do work meaningful to the community raise a lot of questions. This makes African missionaries difficult to track: There are so many unique ways people are living out the gospel and making disciples! Of course, we also have indigenous African mission agencies built on Western models. But most of these still need a "side hustle" to be credible in a local community.

Another strength is that we have a great respect for people. We witness with dignity, respecting other people. That's why Africans prefer the term "least reached peoples" or "people with less access." We don't like the term "unreached" because who gave anyone the authority to call a people "unreached" if God may already be working there?

Q: *How do the concepts you have mentioned challenge the global Christian movement to reexamine how we view our own identity and how we view others?*

Peter: One thing we can learn from Africans is that when God calls us to cross-cultural mission, the underlying motivation is the love of Christ. When missionaries come from individualistic societies, the danger is that we don't listen to what God is already doing in a place or listen to the people we are trying to reach. Who defines who? Are we taking Jesus to others or is Jesus taking us to go to others?

We need a posture of humility. Many Africans who come from a place of weakness must put their confidence in Christ. In the last two hundred years, mission has often come from a place of power, but now we are seeing a growing number of missionaries coming from a place of lowness, which allows them to better understand and see people. Of course, we all have sinful natures and still make mistakes.

Q: *Western missions has an entire system of mobilization, support, training, sending, and member care. What does this look like in the African context?*

Peter: Training is growing. Mobilization is on the increase. We now have many indigenous mission agencies. In the last five to ten years, I have realized that the main challenge is the mobilization process, not recruitment. We need to help them understand God's mission, equip them as cross-cultural workers, and provide opportunities. One of the difficulties for African workers is that there are not many opportunities.

For example, I spoke at a mission conference in Kenya with forty-five hundred university students from many African countries. Over two thousand responded to the altar call and felt God was calling them to cross-cultural missions. Unfortunately, there is a sad disconnect between those people who sense God's call and the actual opportunities available. That is what we are trying to correct in mobilization. For a long time, people saw mobilization as a call to work with a church or mission organization. But the reality is that, because of the difficulties of finding support as a missionary, many will go out as professionals or tentmakers. They will even find work with foreign companies. And they will be planting churches as they go.

"Raising support" is still difficult because the majority of people have little disposable income. Local churches are not giving much to cross-cultural missions because of the mission model they observed over the decades. The biggest reason that churches are not giving is that there is a lack of vision to see Africa's responsibility in cross-cultural mission work. It is not that resources are lacking. Africa has a lot of resources.

There needs to be a paradigm shift for Africans who think missionaries must be Western. It is assumed that planting a local church is the church's end goal, but that cross-cultural missions should be done by Westerners. So, fixing this misunderstanding is the greatest paradigm shift needed.

Part of MANI's role is to change that way of thinking; missions is not about the color of your skin. If an African goes cross-culturally, most people think they are just a migrant worker, but if you're coming the other direction, you are a missionary. This is something we are trying to correct through training and building people's confidence. God calls us as Africans to take up our responsibility. I'm beginning to see churches and individuals taking financial responsibility to support missionary efforts.

Member care is the weakest link because it is closely tied to a lack of sufficient financial resources for workers. Sending, supporting, and member care are still poor because of a lack of resources. Cross-cultural workers have just enough to make ends meet. Travel within Africa is very expensive. People can't take a day off. All this adds to the stresses workers face. Not improving member care leads to attrition.

Whereas African missionaries have modeled sacrificial living, another transition needs to take place as people get older. People start off young and energetic, willing to make sacrifices. But as they grow older, they face school fees for children, health challenges, and retirement issues. There is a lot of disillusionment among those who have served on the field because we haven't had sufficient support structures.

Africans never would have gone if they didn't go by faith. The situation is improving among more indigenous African sending agencies. Still, most agencies will send you before you raise enough support. People have just gone by faith, trusting God will provide for them. And he usually does. But it doesn't always work out. This is where we are confronted by our lack of good member care.

The positive thing is that when you are going into local communities with a profession that people can see, they trust you. If you don't have a visible profession, people are suspicious. Therefore, professional jobs are helpful in the African contexts.

Q: *You have just explained some key challenges in mobilization, support, and member care. Do you have any warnings or cautions as you look to the future?*

Peter: We want to be aware of the dangers of repeating the same mistakes of the past and being stuck in an old paradigm. We face the tension between learning from the past and adapting to new contexts and prioritizing what God is saying and doing. We need to be aware of our preoccupation with preplanned human methods, priorities, and targets. We seem to want to do missions using the Western model without giving due attention to alternative structures.

The other issue is funding. The US dollar is still the driver of missions. To secure funding, we often compromise on how God is truly leading. We have failed to adopt a kingdom mindset where financial resources can be shared.

Q: *What do you think the rest of the global mission community can learn from African missions?*

Peter: I really hope that the rest of the mission community will accept that God is calling Africans alongside all the others. Most people agree and say "yes," but behind the scenes that is not always the case. To me, that would be the biggest breakthrough.

Another lesson is the way Africans so fervently pray. We have a deep spirituality, spiritual vitality, a high view of God, and a dependence on God, which are much needed in the mission world today. Some things can only be done through prayer, and all things should be done with prayer.

African workers are servant-hearted workers who discern the leading of the Holy Spirit. They are patient, humble, courageous, and resilient. They love and respect people and prioritize building relationships over meeting targets and producing numbers. This can frustrate people who are goal driven. But patience can be helpful in conflict situations because we prioritize people.

The fact that God is working through a continent that is low on many lists is a big plus. God is not dependent on our eloquence, powers, and opportunities. God can work through people that we dismiss when we first see them. Africans have a natural ability to go into places the gospel has yet to reach and where there is no sustainable church. That's one thing I really hope the rest of the world will celebrate. Africans are God's workforce to enter places where expatriate missionaries can't enter for various reasons.

I see promising breakthroughs as the youth become more engaged in missions. There is a growing missions interest in churches, and an intentional focus among newer mission agencies to go to least reached peoples and places.

Q: *There is a reason that God has enlarged the African church to be the largest in the world. He wants to mobilize his people.*

Peter: In 2011, MANI had a prophetic word to go to North Africa. But people ask me, "Aren't they racist towards Sub-Saharan Africans?" I answer, "Yes, they are. But that doesn't stop God from using Sub-Saharan Africans!" God does not always send us to people who will accept us. But if God is the one leading, they will accept us because we are coming in the name of the Lord!

Now is the time and season for African workers to lead the way, even to the hard places. Wherever we see "smoke in the horizon," there are people. As I said earlier, "We need to tell the gospel of Christ to those people where that smoke is seen."

Bibliography

Asamoah-Gyadu, J. Kwabena. "Christianity in Sub-Saharan Africa." In *Christianity in Sub-Saharan Africa*, edited by Kenneth R. Ross, J. Kwabena Asamoah-Gyadu, and Todd M. Johnson, 19–40. Peabody: Hendrickson Publishers, 2017.

Ho, Mary. "Growing Women Leaders from the Majority World." Lausanne Movement. October 2023. https://lausanne.org/content/lga/2023-11/growing-global-women-leaders-from-the-majority-world?utm_source=Lausanne+Movement+List&utm_campaign=2e74af1f1f-Lausanne_Global_Analysis-Sept2023&utm_medium=email&utm_term=0_602c1cb67d-2e74af1f1f-91897312.

Johnson, Todd, and Gina Zurlo. *World Christian Encyclopedia*. 3rd ed. Edinburgh: Edinburgh University Press, 2020.

Joshua Project. Accessed March 28, 2024. https://joshuaproject.net.

Mombo, Esther. "Mission and Evangelism." In *Christianity in Sub-Saharan Africa*, edited by Kenneth R. Ross, J. Kwabena Asamoah-Gyadu, and Todd M. Johnson, 376–85. Peabody: Hendrickson Publishers, 2017.

11
A Latin American Perspective on Unreached People Groups

Abraham Duran

The unreached people group paradigm was proposed by Ralph Winter at the 1974 Lausanne Congress. At the time, the World Council of Churches, responding to postcolonial perspectives, was questioning evangelistic international missions. Evangelical missions triumphantly envisioned "closure" as they got close to engaging all political nations. Ralph Winter opened the eyes of the evangelical church to see that about four-fifths of the world population was separated from the gospel and from the church due to linguistic and cultural barriers.

Today, sectors of the evangelical mission movement are questioning the validity of the unreached people group paradigm that became so important after that conference.[1] Peter T. Lee and James Sung-Hwan Park's "Beyond People Group Thinking: A Critical Reevaluation of Unreached People Groups" is just one article symptomatic of this reevaluation. Although they admit that this paradigm "revolutionized global mission by reorienting the focus of mission strategies from geographical nation-states to sociological groupings of 'people groups,'" they conclude that the UPG paradigm has "flawed theological, sociocultural, and missiological assumptions" and that it has "defective biblical and sociocultural foundations."[2]

Why Do Latin Americans Have Such a Passion for Least Reached People Groups?

Cristian Castro, the current executive director of the Iberoamerican Mission Cooperation (COMIBAM), shared with me how today, in contrast with his early missionary career, he often finds himself one of the few voices promoting unreached people groups in international mission circles while bewildered mission executives question his perspective. This is interesting since some of the earliest critics of this paradigm were Latin American missiologists. Samuel Escobar, for example, coined the phrase "managerial missiology" to criticize an approach to mission whose aim is, in his words, "to reduce Christian mission to a manageable enterprise."[3]

Most Latin American mission leaders would agree with Lee and Park in their criticism of the Homogeneous Unit Principle (HUP). An improper use of this perspective could "neglect biblical teachings regarding reconciliation and unity in diversity."[4] Most Latin American theologians and missiologists would agree with Padilla that:

---

1 Datema and Scribner, "40 Years of Unreached Peoples."
2 Lee and Park, "Beyond People Group Thinking," 212–25.
3 See Escobar, "A Movement Divided." Escobar did say, however, that if what he called "the managerial school" would accept "the need to enter in dialogue with theology and other missiologies, it could make its valuable contribution to mission in the third millennium." See also DeCarvalho, "What's Wrong with the Label."
4 Padilla, "Unity of the Church," 23–30.

the church not only grew, but it grew across social barriers. The New Testament contains no example of a local church with a membership that had been taken by the apostles from a single homogeneous unit, unless the term homogeneous unit means no more than a group of people with a common language. By contrast, it provides plenty of examples of how the barriers had been abolished in the new humanity.[5]

Whether or not the criticism is really directed to the principle[6] or to a misunderstanding of it, there is widespread condemnation of the principle for strong theological reasons.

So, why do many in the Iberoamerican movement still have such a passion for "unreached people groups"? Is it only the influence of American missiology? Despite unjustified caricatures, the Latin American church has proven itself adept in critical thinking and resilient against theological and missiological ideas from the West that may lack sufficient biblical support.[7] So why has the unreached people paradigm been adopted?

The Contextual Element: Indigenous Sociolinguistic People Groups

Latin America consists of thirty-three countries that were formed, in the words of Teresa Meade, through "the interaction, cross-fertilization, mutation, interpenetration, and reinvention of cultures from Europe, Asia, Africa and indigenous America."[8] It is undeniable that the Christian faith came to Latin America at the hands of European "discoverers" and "conquistadores" in the context of the Reconquista and the Inquisition. Religion was often used as an instrument to justify rape, assassination, plundering, and exploitation.[9] As Samuel Escobar has explained, it was often quite difficult to distinguish "between the cross and the sword."[10]

This does not mean that some Christians, such as Fray Antonio de Montesinos and Fray Bartolomé de las Casas, were not denouncing these grievances and advocating for the indigenous peoples. De las Casas was already thinking about evangelization in terms of people groups: "It was the will and work of Christ … that God's chosen should be called … from every race, every tribe, every language, every corner of the world. … The reason is, they are all human beings."[11]

However, even some of their efforts led to mixed results. De las Casas acquiesced to the idea of the importation of African slaves. It was not until the end of his life that he regretted his error, misleadingly affirming that he had "always held that they had been made slaves unjustly and tyrannically."[12]

Catholic missionaries often created successful small colonies where they concentrated indigenous peoples into Iberian-styled settlements with the purpose of developing indigenous leadership while instructing them in Catholicism and European language and customs.

---

5 Padilla, *Mission Between the Times*, 181.
6 See Datema and Scribner, "40 Years of Unreached Peoples"; and Carlson and Clark, "3 Words That Changed."
7 See, for example, Padilla, "Evangelism and the World." All Spanish and Portuguese translations are mine.
8 Meade, *History of Modern Latin America*.
9 Roberts, "Calls for Justice."
10 Escobar, *En Busca de Cristo*, location 83.
11 Burke and Humphrey, "New Black Legend."
12 Dubois, *The Negro*, 58.

Franciscan Friar Jacopo da Testera, writing to Emperor Charles V in 1532, described the linguistic challenges they were facing as a "wall" that separated the missionaries from the indigenous populations. Many of these missionaries were eager to learn the languages of the people they were trying to reach, but in general, they only translated portions of the Scriptures contained in primers and lectionaries; translation of the Bible had been banned by the Spanish Inquisition since the mid-sixteenth century.

Fortunately, some members of religious orders tried to make available larger sections of the Scriptures in indigenous languages. One of them, Juan de Zumarraga (1468–1548) was so enthusiastic about translating the Scripture that he came under suspicion by the Inquisition. Another Franciscan, Maturino Gilberti, published a book of Christian doctrine in Purepecha, a language of Michoacan, Mexico, that contained so much of the Gospels and Epistles that the book was banned by the Inquisition. A Dominican, Didacus de Santa Maria, seemed to have worked on a translation of the Epistles and Gospels into Nahuatl that was never published.[13]

With the independence of Latin American colonies and the subsequent abolition of the Catholic Inquisition, many Protestant missionaries arrived in Latin America. First came the Bible *colporteurs* (distributors). Paramount among them was the work of Scottish missionary James (Diego) Thomson (1788–1854). Thomson arrived in Argentina in 1818, only eight years after the beginning of Argentina's war of independence. He believed that mission efforts should have three components: the school society, the Bible society, and the missionary society. He did extraordinary work, distributing Scriptures in Argentina, Chile and Peru, Mexico, and the Caribbean. At the same time, he started and supported Bible translations into several languages, including Quechua, Aymará, and Nahuatl.

Many years later, in 1917, Cameron Townsend, an American colporteur, was distributing Bibles in Guatemala among the indigenous Kaqchikel people when a Kaqchikel man challenged him: "If your God is so smart, why doesn't he speak my language?" This confrontation led Townsend to learn and translate the New Testament into this language. He went on to found Wycliffe Bible Translators, an organization committed to translating the Bible into every language of the world. Based on his lifelong translation work, the Seventh InterAmerican Indian Congress in 1972 declared Townsend a "benefactor of the linguistically isolated populations in the Americas."[14]

Importantly, although mission history is often written from a Western perspective, most of these Bible translations were authored or coauthored by indigenous translators who were believers in Jesus. Indigenous Christians, burdened to share the gospel with others, learned the languages of other indigenous people groups.

Federico Bertuzzi, one of the most influential Latin American missiologists, wrote about how he met Huaorani believers at the World Evangelization Congress in Berlin in 1966 when he was only about seventeen years old. They transformed his life and his dedication to mission to the least reached.

---

13 Fisher, "Bible and Indigenous Language."
14 Townsend, "If Your God Is So Smart." Townsend of course was and is criticized by some for the religious and political aspects of his work.

He relates a conversation he had with a dear friend, a writer called Pablo Higuera. Higuera told him that his real nationality was not Argentinean or Bolivian, but Quechua Guarani. "The rest is an invention of the white colonizers who created frontiers."[15]

Given this background, it is not surprising that Latin Americans believe in crossing cultural and linguistic barriers to take the gospel to other people groups. I have a dear friend whose parents hosted the first Bible translators among his ethnic group. His uncle became the "first fruit" of a large Christward movement.

Christians in Brazil, in particular, faced the reality of many proximate indigenous populations that had no Scriptures in their language and no active testimony of the gospel. This led to an early consciousness of the need to cross cultural and linguistic barriers to share the gospel with all. Around 1925, Brazilian Zacarias Campelo, disconnected from any foreign mission, began working with the Krahô and Xerente communities, sharing the gospel and translating the Bible. In 1928 the first known Brazilian mission society was founded, the Missão Evangélica Caiuá.[16] By 1930, the Brazilian church was active reaching Japanese, Muslim, and Jewish immigrants.[17] The first association of indigenous churches, UNIEDAS, (União das Igrejas Evangélicas da América do Sul) was established in 1972; it formed the first mission society sending indigenous missionaries to other indigenous groups in Brazil.[18]

Notice that all this happened before the 1974 Lausanne Congress on World Evangelization. By 1991, the National Council of Evangelical Pastors and Leaders was born in Brazil, an indigenous group with the goal of ensuring that "the message of the gospel of the Lord Jesus be preached to the ethnicities that have not been reached."[19]

Second Element: The Influence of Lausanne and Mission Organizations

I am not suggesting, however, that Latin America was not influenced by the worldwide unreached peoples paradigm and the ideas developed by Ralph Winter and others. It certainly was. At the 1974 Lausanne Congress where Winter launched what became the unreached peoples movement, there were 219 participants from Latin America among the more than twenty-three hundred evangelical leaders from 150 countries.[20] All participants were encouraged to take the vision of reaching all people groups back to their countries. Many were also mobilized through the efforts of Operation Mobilization, Latin American Mission, the International Fellowship of Evangelical Students, OC, and others. What I am saying is that the Latin American church was permeable to these ideas because they resonated with what they already knew and practiced.

By 1975, Brazilian participants at the Lausanne conference had organized the first Latin American Missionary Congress in Curitiba with five hundred participants. The Congress affirmed that "the church is a missionary church or it is no church at all."[21]

---

15 Bertuzzi, *Encuentro Fraternidad Teologica*.
16 See https://caiua.org.br/historia/.
17 Smither, *Brazilian Evangelical Missions*.
18 Poquivi Terena, "História da Missão."
19 See https://www.conplei.org.br/institucional/quem-somos/.
20 See https://lausanne.org/gathering/lausanne-1974.
21 Smither, *Brazilian Evangelical Missions*.

Many missionaries had seen Latin America as just a mission field, barely able to contribute to the evangelization of the world beyond their own borders. J. Herbert Kane acknowledged: "In general, we need to admit that we did not establish missionary churches. ... Neither the indigenous churches nor the missionary agencies gave enough importance to ... the self-propagation of the Gospel."[22]

However, Luis Palau, an Argentinean called "Latin America's Billy Graham," had a different idea. Palau was growing in global influence and, since at least 1982, was encouraging Latin believers to see their potential as a global mission force. Several Argentinean pastors heeded the call, and on July 6, 1982, the World Mission Network (Red de Misiones Mundiales) was born.[23] Brazil had established a national mission movement five months before.

Hearing these developments, Argentinean Luis Bush, who had become CEO of Partners International, decided to research what was happening regarding missions. He noticed how the Holy Spirit was doing similar things throughout the whole continent. Bush and others decided that Latin American leaders needed to meet to discern what was the Lord saying to evangelical churches. This resulted in the first Iberoamerican Mission Congress (COMIBAM) in 1987.

During the Congress, Luis Bush gave voice to the conviction that was rising in many of the three thousand hearts present: "In 1916 Latin America was declared a missionary field; in 1987 Latin America declares itself a missionary body."[24] René Padilla agrees that COMIBAM's convocation was "undoubtedly wider and more ambitious than any previous effort."[25]

Since then, Iberoamerican churches have established at least four hundred interdenominational and denominational mission societies and have sent more than ten thousand cross-cultural mission workers around the world.[26] Brazil is now considered the second-largest mission force in the world![27] Although only a fraction of Latin American workers serves among least reached peoples, thousands of Latino missionaries and Christians have been among the first to take the gospel to many neglected groups and places.

This narrative makes clear how the unreached peoples paradigm was embraced by Latin American leaders and churches. However, there is a vital element that led to the Latin American church's acceptance of the UPG approach.

Third Element: A Scriptural Focus

According to theologian Rubem Alves, Latin American Protestantism "has given a central place to the reading and study of the Bible."[28] This is not surprising, since the Bible actually came before the arrival of Protestant missionaries.

---

22 Nelson, *Readings in Third World Missions*, 191.
23 Bertuzzi, *Los Inicios de Un Movimiento*.
24 Bush, "Luz Para Las Naciones."
25 Padilla, "La Misión Desde América Latina."
26 Escobar, "It's Your Turn," 23.
27 Zurlo, Johnson, and Crossing, "World Christianity and Mission 2020," 8–19.
28 Alves and Shaull, "Pietism in Brazil."

In such an environment, the unreached people paradigm was not received without a challenge. René Padilla, Samuel Escobar, and Orlando Costas were part of a small group of Latin American evangelical theologians who developed a form of Latin American evangelical contextual theology called integral mission theology. All were speakers at the 1974 Lausanne World Congress on World Evangelization and were known by the convener John Stott.[29] Padilla, Escobar, and Costas had an immense influence on the congress, reflected in the final version of the Lausanne Covenant, which affirms: "Although reconciliation with other people is not reconciliation with God, nor is social action evangelism, nor is political liberation salvation, nevertheless we affirm that evangelism and socio-political involvement are both part of our Christian duty."[30]

René Padilla, one of the first workers of the International Fellowship of Evangelical Students in Latin America, had obtained degrees in biblical studies from Wheaton College and Manchester University. Upon his return, however, he saw that he had not been trained to answer the questions that were being raised.[31] For Latin American evangelicals in a context of socioeconomic disparity, oppression, and injustice, Anselm's definition of theology as *fides quaerens intellectum* (faith seeking understanding) was not enough; it had to be, in the words of Míguez Bonino, "faith seeking effectiveness."[32]

The solution came through the work of roaming trainers for the evangelical student movement such as Ada Lum and Ruth Siemens who were equipping the students to use inductive Bible study techniques to analyze the Bible and to put it into practice.[33] Padilla encouraged evangelical students in Latin American universities to apply these methods to seek biblical answers to the challenges raised by Marxist and Maoist students.

What emerged was known as integral mission theology.[34] According to Padilla, its purpose was to recover the centrality of the Scriptures and develop a contextual theology that would combine solid evangelical doctrine, evangelistic zeal, and social responsibility.[35]

In the early years, there was a strong distrust between the group that promoted mission to unreached peoples and the one that promoted integral mission. The first was seen by the others as suspiciously close to American conservatives who had opposed integral theology. The latter was seen by the others as suspiciously close to ecumenicists and Protestant liberation theologians. At that time there was a global tension between two superpowers, and everything was interpreted through this lens.

At length, some Latin American theologians and missiologists who were involved in both movements saw the need to break these barriers and bring both movements closer. In April 1995, representatives of both movements met in Miami, Florida, to understand each other better and explore the possibility of cooperation.

---

29 McGilchrist, "The Kingdom of God."
30 Lausanne Movement, "The Lausanne Covenant."
31 Samuel Escobar, personal interview with the author, July 8, 2019.
32 Davies, *Faith Seeking Effectiveness*, 15.
33 Padilla DeBorst, "Integral Mission Formation," 52, 82.
34 Amorim, 'La Teologia de La Mision," 125.
35 Padilla, *Hacia Una Teología*, 4.

Soon COMIBAM leaders discovered that some integral mission theologians had been very interested in the obligation of the Latin American church to take the gospel to all peoples. Tito Paredes, for example, emphasized that the vision needed to be "the whole gospel for all peoples, from Latin America."[36] Integral mission theologians discovered that COMIBAM leaders were committed to the Lausanne Covenant and therefore to integral mission that combined proclamation of the gospel with social responsibility and activity. Valdir Steuernagel concluded:

> It seems essential to me that the two dimensions remain in tension, since if one or the other is isolated, we are going to impoverish the moment of God that we are living. Transcultural mission needs and lives from the Word and a mission theology and the practice of [integral] local mission, but a solid and good [integral] mission theology and a good local mission practice has to lead to a transcultural mission.[37]

After this meeting, of course, many differences remained between the groups. However, three things were clear from a consensual Latin American understanding of Scripture. First, the kingdom of God, coming through the birth, life, expiatory death, and resurrection of the Son of God and based on the totality of Scripture is the most useful paradigm to understand the mission of God and the mission of the church. Second, the mission of the church is not only the proclamation but the demonstration of the kingdom in good works. In the words of Orlando Costas, "to teach obedience to Jesus Christ in all things is the great challenge of world evangelization today."[38] Third, the mission of the church cannot be restricted to one language, one ethnicity, or one type of people.

Since this meeting in 1995, COMIBAM leaders such as Carlos Scott have emphasized the integrality of mission while integral mission theologians like Samuel Escobar and René Padilla joined the boards of COMIBAM member agencies such as PM Internacional or visited Latino workers working among least reached people groups in the Muslim world.[39]

Pentecostal pastor and missiologist Rodolfo Girón, who was the first president of the COMIBAM movement, summarized that "the purpose of God's blessings is for us to be a blessing, so that all peoples praise him and that all nations know about him."[40] René Padilla concurred, writing that "the church, in fulfillment of the promises of the Abrahamic covenant, inherits the blessing of being the chosen people of God and is called to be the means of blessing from God to all the families of the earth."[41]

Giron is part of the most influential segment of the Latin American evangelical church, Pentecostalism, which encompasses three of every four Latin American Protestants.[42] One of the largest Pentecostal denominations described their mission vision in these terms: "We give priority to the Great Commission the Lord left to his church before he ascended into heaven, which is to preach the gospel, make disciples, and testify of him, to every creature, in all nations, and to the ends of the earth. We focus the training of workers to this end."[43]

---

36 Bertuzzi, *Encuentro Fraternidad Teologica*.
37 Bertuzzi.
38 Costas, *Compromiso y Misión*, 24.
39 Giordano, *Peregrinaje en la Misión*. PMI was the first Latin American agency focused on the Muslim world.
40 Bertuzzi, Encuentro Fraternidad Teologica.
41 Padilla, "La Iglesia," 1382.
42 Pew (2014), 4.
43 Declaración de Valores Pentecostales. Asociación Teológica de America Latina de las Asambleas de Dios.

This theological perspective about the need to reach all ethnic groups is shared even by Latin American theologians who are not identified with conservative evangelicalism. Theologian José Míguez Bonino agreed that "the mission of the Church is to preach the Gospel to all nations, not only to all individuals, but to all nations."[44] And Emilio Castro affirmed that "to be able to witness, we must be there—that means within any geographical or social reality. There is still a need for Christians to cross geographical frontiers to the regions beyond, sharing the Gospel of the kingdom."[45] This remarkable consensus among Latin Americans is not due to naïveté, as it stands on very solid scholarship.

This leads to the fourth and final factor contributing to Latin America's engagement with the UPG paradigm: Latin American's own understanding of least reached people groups.

Fourth Element: A Latin American Understanding

Míguez Bonino believes that Luke's emphasis on "the universal reach of God's message ... is not the universality of assimilation but a universality that respects, affirms and protects the ethnic, cultural and linguistic spaces and validates them as equally loved by God."[46]

In 1992, FEDEMEC, a mission organization established by the Costa Rican Evangelical Alliance in 1986, hosted the Adopt-A-People Latin American consultation. At this consultation, the Latin American mission movement explicitly prioritized reaching the least reached peoples.[47]

Further advancement was led by COMIMEX (the Mexican Mission Cooperation, established in 1987). Through the leadership of Pastor Moisés Lopez, COMIMEX defined an ethnic group as "a group that has a common culture." Using this concept, COMIMEX's research department developed what is called the Morelia Scale.[48]

The Morelia Scale tries to describe how the gospel transforms a people group and classifies every sociolinguistic people group in seven stages:

- Stage 1: Without knowledge of the gospel.
- Stage 2: Sporadic knowledge. There has been some Christian testimony, but not sustained.
- Stage 3: Some converts. Some believers in the group who do not congregate regularly.
- Stage 4: Church in birth pains. There is a small group of believers who meet weekly.
- Stage 5: Growing church (numeric). The church has increased in number in the last year.
- Stage 6: Church in development (spiritual). The members are showing signs of transformation in their spiritual life.
- Stage 7: Mature church (in self-reproduction). The church complies with all of the above, governs itself, sustains itself, and reproduces itself.

The ethnic groups that are in stages one to three are considered "totally unreached" and require intentional cross-cultural effort to sow the gospel of Jesus Christ. Ethnic groups in

---

44 Campos, "Interview with Dr. José Míguez Bonino."
45 Castro, "Editorial," 120.
46 Miguez-Bonino, "Acts 2:1–42."
47 Bogossian, "The Meeting of the Century."
48 López, "Que Son Las Etnias."

stages four to six are still unreached but have growing churches that need to be supported from outside the ethnic group, so that they finish bringing the gospel to every person in the ethnic group. You need to "water" the seed with prayer and biblical teaching. Ethnic groups with a self-reproducing church movement in stage seven of the Morelia Scale are considered "reached." This is the time to "harvest" the seed to sow again in another group.[49]

Through the influence of COMIMEX leaders such as Moisés Lopez and David Markham in COMIBAM, this scale has become widely used. The narrative approach used in the scale (that describes how a people is reached) has resonated better with the Latin American church leadership than the statistical approach, perhaps because the numbers (5 percent of Christians and 2 percent of evangelicals) appear "somewhat arbitrary" as Joshua Project editors admit, even if based on psychological and sociological considerations.[50]

Latin American missiologist Pablo Deiros believes that "the *locus theologicus* and the *locus missiologicus* [place of authority of our theology and missiology] of our reflections should be placed in the future, and the *Sitz im Leben* [context, setting] which functions as our point of reference is a reality, which has not happened yet."[51] This means that we need to build our missiology from the future backwards, and the future that the Lord showed us which "has not happened yet" is "a great multitude that no one could number, from every nation, from all tribes and peoples and languages … crying out with a loud voice, 'Salvation belongs to our God who sits on the throne, and to the Lamb!'" (Rev 5:9 ESV). Deiros adds that "it is precisely the lordship of Christ that pushes the church to go to the whole world in its proclamation of the gospel."[52] Federico Bertuzzi agrees:

> In whatever way you want to count them, ethnographically, ethno-linguistically or sociologically, or however else you want to count them, the important concept that our Lord gives us here to understand is that all those groups in which humanity tends to divide themselves have to be reached by the preaching of the gospel of the Kingdom of God.[53]

Conclusion

In partnership with the global mission movement and younger churches springing to life everywhere, the Latin American mission movement has adopted as a key priority reaching all the least reached people groups with the good news of the kingdom of our Lord Jesus Christ. Mission must be biblical, culturally sensitive, incarnational (based on theology and the shared reality of the poor and powerless), evangelistic, holistic, in the power of the Holy Spirit, and in partnership with others. This holistic understanding of mission was not based on an uncritical acceptance of foreign missionary paradigms. Rather, it was shaped by contextual factors unique to the Latin American church and experience. These factors include an early consciousness of other ethnic groups with distinct cultures and languages, lack of a colonialist history, emphasis on a simple (but not simplistic) reading of the biblical text, evangelistic zeal, a habituation to seek supernatural assistance, and an eschatological perspective that sees

---

49 Lopez, "Lección 13."
50 See https://joshuaproject.net/help/definitions.
51 Deiros, "Eschatology and Mission."
52 Pablo A. Deiros, personal interview with author, July 2021.
53 Bertuzzi, *Federico Encuentro Fraternidad* (author's translation).

preaching the gospel to the nations as the goal that the Lord has set before the church. Despite resistance by some church leaders, this understanding permeates the membership of Latin American churches.

We are in a new day in missions. As Korean missiologist Chulho Han states:

> From the strategic perspective, the missions movement no longer follows the from-here-to-there pattern but it is a from-everywhere-to-everywhere movement going in all directions. At the same time, we must continue our effort to reach the unreached people groups that still remain.[54]

The Latin American mission movement would say, "Amen!"

Bibliography

Alves, Rubem, and Richard Shaull. "Pietism in Brazil." In *Religion in Latin America: A Documentary History*, edited by Lee M. Penyak and Walter J. Petry. Maryknoll, NY: Orbis Books, 2006.

Amorim, Joao Paulo Soares. "La Teologia de La Mision de C. René Padilla Frente a Las Críticas de José Míguez Bonino y Ricardo Gondim." South African Theological Seminary/Facultad Internacional de Estudios Teológicos, 2016.

Bertuzzi, Federico. *Encuentro Fraternidad Teologica Latinoamericana y COMIBAM Internacional.* Manuscript, 1995

Bertuzzi, Federico. *Los Inicios de Un Movimiento: Breve Reseña de Los Primeros Pasos de La Red Misiones Mundiales.* Self-published, 2007.

Bogosian, Phil. "The Meeting of the Century—Number Three." *Mission Frontiers* (1993). https://www.missionfrontiers.org/issue/article/the-meeting-of-the-century-number-three.

Browning, Webster E. "Joseph Lancaster, James Thomson and the Lancasterian System of Mutual Instruction, with Special Reference to Hispanic America." *The Hispanic American Historical Review* 4, no. 1 (February 1921): 49–98.

Burke, Janet, and Ted Humphrey. "The New Black Legend of Bartolomé de Las Casas." *Church Life Journal*, October 13, 2023. https://churchlifejournal.nd.edu/articles/the-new-black-legend-of-bartolome-de-las-casas/.

Bush, Luis. "Luz Para Las Naciones." In *COMIBAM 87: Luz Para Las Naciones*. Sao Paulo, 1987.

Campos, Bernardo. "Interview with Dr. José Míguez Bonino." *Instituto Iberoamericano de Ciencias y Humanidades*, February 7, 2021. https://www.inibercih.org/2021/02/07/entrevista-al-dr-jose-miguez-bonino/.

Carlson, Darren, and Elliot Clark. "The 3 Words That Changed Missions Strategy—and Why We Might Be Wrong." Gospel Coalition. September 11, 2019. https://www.thegospelcoalition.org/article/misleading-words-missions-strategy-unreached-people-groups/.

Castro. "Editorial." *International Review of Mission* 69, no. 274 (April 1980): 120.

Costas, Orlando. *Compromiso y Misión*. Editorial Caribe, 1979.

Datema, Dave, and Dan Scribner. "40 Years of Unreached Peoples Effort: Progress and Regress." *Mission Frontiers* (Nov/Dec 2016). https://missionfrontiers.org/issue/article/40-years-of-unreached-peoples-effort.

Davies, Paul John. *Faith Seeking Effectiveness: The Missionary Theology of José Miguez Bonino.* Zoetermeer: Boekencentrum, 2006.

DeCarvalho, Levi T. "What's Wrong with the Label 'Managerial Missiology.'" *IJMR* 18, no. 3 (Fall 2001). https://www.missionfrontiers.org/issue/article/whats-wrong-with-the-label-managerial-missiology.

---

54 Kim and Ma, *Korean Diaspora and Christian Mission*.

Deiros, Pablo Alberto. "Eschatology and Mission: A Latin American Perspective." https://www.gmanradio.org/2015/11/13/eschatology-and-mission-a-latin-american-perspective-pablo-deiros/.

Deiros, Pablo Alberto. *Protestantismo en América Latina: ayer, hoy y mañana. Un sello de Editorial Caribe*. Nashville, TN: Caribe, 1997.

Douglas, J. D., ed. *Let the Earth Hear His Voice*. World Wide Publications, 1975.

Dubois, W. E. B. *The Negro*, 1915.

Escobar, Samuel. "A Movement Divided: Three Approaches to World Evangelization Stand in Tension with One Another." *Transformation: An International Journal of Holistic Mission Studies* 8, no. 4 (Oct 1991). https://doi.org/10.1177/0265378891008004.

Escobar, J. Samuel. *En Busca de Cristo En America Latina*. Buenos Aires: Ediciones Kairos, 2012.

Escobar, J. Samuel. *In Search of Christ in Latin America: From Colonial Image to Liberating Saviour*. Carlisle: Langham Global Library, 2019.

Escobar, Samuel. "It's Your Turn, Young Ones." In *The Reshaping of Mission in Latin America*, edited by Miguel Alvarez, 23. Oxford: Regnum Books, 2015. https://digitalshowcase.oru.edu/re2010series/34.

Fisher, Linford D. "The Bible and Indigenous Language Translations in the Americas." In *The Oxford Handbook of the Bible in America*, edited by Paul C. Gutjahr. Oxford: Oxford University Press, 2018. https://doi.org/10.1093/oxfordhb/9780190258849.013.31.

Giordano, Christian. *Peregrinaje en la Misión*. PM Internacional, 2009.

Hunt, Robert A. "The History of the Lausanne Movement 1974–2010." *International Bulletin of Mission Research* 35, no. 2 (2011).

"Instructions to Commander Nicolás de Ovando, Third Governor of Hispaniola, from King Ferdinand and Queen Isabella of Spain." In *New Iberian World: A Documentary History of the Discovery and Settlement of Latin America to the Early 17th Century. Vol. 2, The Caribbean*, edited by John H. Parry and Robert G. Keith. Translation revised in 2018 by Anthony Stevens, with the assistance of Dr. Carmen del Camino Martinez and Dr. Reyes Rojas Garcia. New York: Times Books, 1984. https://wams.nyhistory.org/wp-content/uploads/2019/01/instructions-for-comendador-ovando.pdf.

Kim, S. Hun, and Wansuk Ma, eds. *Korean Diaspora and Christian Mission*. Minneapolis, MN: Fortress Press, 2011.

Kirkpatrick, David C. "C. Rene Padilla and the Origins of Integral Mission in Post-War Latin America." *Journal of Ecclesiastical History* 67, no. 2 (April 2016): 351–71.

Lane, A. N. S. "Anselm." In *New Dictionary of Theology: Historical and Systematic*, edited by Martin Davie, Tim Grass, Stephen R. Holmes, John C. McDowell, and T. A Noble, 37–39. Downers Grove, IL: IVP Academic, 2016.

Lausanne Movement. "The Lausanne Covenant." Accessed May 14, 2024. https://www.lausanne.org/content/covenant/lausanne-covenant.

Lee, Peter T., and James Sung-Hwan Park. "Beyond People Group Thinking: A Critical Reevaluation of Unreached People Groups." *Missiology* 46, no. 3 (2018): 212–25.

Lopez, Moisés. "Lección 13—Que Son Las Etnias No Alcanzadas y Por Que Subsisten." *Misiones Transculturales*, August 31, 2018. https://misionestransculturales.org/leccion-13-que-son-las-etnias-no-alcanzadas-y-por-que-subsisten/.

López, Moisés. "Que Son Las Etnias No Alcanzadas y Por Qué Subsisten." *Misiones Transculturales*, November 28, 2009. https://misionestransculturales.org/que-es-un-grupo-etnico-no-alcanzado-y-porque/.

Mackay, John. *The Other Spanish Christ: A Study in the Spiritual History of Spain and South America*. Eugene, OR: Wipf and Stock, 1933.

McGilchrist, Donald. "The Kingdom of God." Navigators History (blog) 2017. https://navhistory.org/category/worldwide-partnership/.

Meade, Teresa A. *A History of Modern Latin America: 1800 to the Present*. 2nd ed. Malden, MA: Wiley-Blackwell, 2016.

Miguez-Bonino, José. "Acts 2:1–42 A Latin American Perspective." In *Return to Babel: Global Perspectives on the Bible*, edited by Priscilla Pope-Levison and John R. Levison, 13–16. Louisville, KY: Westminster John Knox Press, 1999.

Nelson, Martin L., ed. *Readings in Third World Missions*. Pasadena, CA: William Carey Library, 1978.

Padilla, René. "Evangelism and the World." Lausanne Movement. July 25, 1974. https://lausanne.org/content/evangelism-and-the-world.

Padilla, C. René. *Hacia Una Teología Evangélica Latinoamericana: Ensayos en Honor de Pedro Savage*. Miami, FL: Editorial Caribe, 1984.

Padilla, René. "La Iglesia." In *Comentario Bíblico Contemporáneo: Estudio de toda la Biblia desde América Latina*, edited by C. René Padilla, Milton Acosta, and Rosalee Velloso, 1382. Buenos Aires, Argentina: Ediciones Certeza Unida, 2019.

Padilla, C. René. "La Misión Desde América Latina." *Revista Iglesia y Misión* (blog), accessed June 5, 2021. http://www.kairos.org.ar/index.php?option=com_content&view=article&id=1337&catid=90%3Aarticulos-de-la-revista-iglesia-y-mision&Itemid=157.

Padilla, C. René. "La Teoria de La Liberación: Una Evaluación Crítica." *Revista Iglesia y Mision* no. 2 (1982).

Padilla, C. René. *Mission between the Times: Essays on the Kingdom*. Carlisle: Langham Global Library, 2010.

Padilla, René. "The Unity of the Church and the Homogeneous Unit Principle." *International Bulletin of Mission Research* 6 (1981): 23–30.

Padilla DeBorst, Ruth. "Integral Mission Formation in Abya Yala (Latin America): A Study of the Centro de Studios Teológicos Interdisciplinarios (1982–2002) and Radical Evangélicos." 2016.

Pew Research Center. "Religion in Latin America: Widespread Change in a Historically Catholic Region." November 13, 2014. https://www.pewresearch.org/religion/wp-content/uploads/sites/7/2014/11/Religion-in-Latin-America-11-12-PM-full-PDF.pdf.

Poquivi Terena, Ricardo. "História da Missão entre os Povos Indígenas no Brasil." *Conplei*, February 12, 2010. https://www.conplei.org.br/historia-da-missao-entre-os-povos-indigenas-no-brasil/.

Roberts, Daniel. "Calls for Justice in the New World: The Prophetic Life of Bartolomé de Las Casas in the Spanish Colonization of the Americas." History of Christianity II Paper, Whitworth University, 2018. https://digitalcommons.whitworth.edu/th314h/18.

Salinas, J. Daniel. *Taking Up the Mantle: Latin American Evangelical Theology in the 20th Century*. Carlisle: Langham Global Library, 2017.

Schilling, Annegreth. "Between Context and Conflict: the 'Boom' of Latin American Protestantism in the Ecumenical Movement (1955–75)." *Journal of Global History* 13, no. 2 (2018): 274–93.

Smither, Edward L. *Brazilian Evangelical Missions among Arabs: History, Culture, Practice, and Theology*. Eugene, OR: Wipf and Stock, 2012.

Stern, S. "Paradigms of Conquest: History, Historiography, and Politics." *Journal of Latin American Studies* 24, no. 1 (1992): 1–34.

Synan, Vinson. *El Siglo del Espiritu Santo: cien años de renuevo pentecostal y carismático*. Buenos Aires, Argentina: Editorial Peniel, 2006.

Topf, Daniel. "Fundamentalism, Marginalization, and Eschatology." *Spiritus* 5, no. 1 (2020): 99–119.

Townsend, Cameron. "If Your God Is So Smart, Why Can't He Speak My Language?" *Mission Frontiers* (June 1982). https://www.missionfrontiers.org/issue/article/if-your-god-is-so-smart-why-cant-he-speak-my-language.

Zurlo, Gina, Todd Johnson, and Peter Crossing. "World Christianity and Mission 2020: Ongoing Shift to the Global South." *International Bulletin of Mission Research* 44, no. 1 (January 2020): 8–19.

Reflection and Discussion

The Impact of People Group Thinking on Agencies

1. Compare (what's similar) and contrast (what's different) in the transitions of the IMB and AGWM toward unreached people.

2. What did you learn about the organizational barriers—structural, conceptual, theological, leadership, financial, marketing, personal, and relational—that can affect missional change, innovation, and outreach to the least reached? What barriers do you recognize in your church or organization?

3. Compare (what's similar) and contrast (what's different) the development of the Korean, Saharan African, and Latin American frontier mission movements.

4. What are some lessons the global church can learn from their experiences and journeys?

5. How would you describe the relationship between integral (holistic) missions and frontier (unreached peoples) missions? In what way are they complementary? What are some benefits and liabilities?

6. Write a brief prayer for our brothers and sisters and partners in the Great Commission.

Part 3

Impact of People Group Thinking on Field Workers

Voices from the Field

12

Voices of Pioneer Workers on the Challenge of "People Groups"

Various Authors from Central Asia, South Asia, India, Pakistan, Transnational, Middle East, Turkey, Eurasia, Horn of Africa, and Southeast Asia

Over eight hundred field workers among unreached peoples were invited to submit brief case studies on the challenge of "people group" thinking in their context. They were asked about ways their field experience has led them to "rethink" people group concepts and approaches. The following notes from the field offer a glimpse into ministry among unreached peoples. These voices provide insights that take us from missiological theory to the challenges and ambiguities of frontier mission practice. Many of the issues explored in other articles are illustrated here, including disjunctions between lists, databases, categories, and field realities; migration, urbanization, and social change; power dynamics; language and ethnic identity; multiethnicity; diaspora and transnational networks; hybrid and multiple identities; and implications for evangelism and church planting. The reports have been edited for clarity and length, and locations and authors' names veiled for security.

Central Asia
Anthony Roberts

As our agency's first team in this restrictive Central Asian country, we chose the largest people group listed as unreached: the "Ghairat." This gave us focus and was useful in recruiting a team. However, what seemed simple quickly became complicated. Once on the field we soon ran into internal and external challenges related to using the people group approach as a church-planting strategy.

To begin with, we faced opposition from foreign coworkers who saw our people group approach as divisive and discriminatory against other ethnicities. In our country context, ethnic identity had been used by warlords to factionalize and discriminate against other groups. Using ethnic identifiers had immediate political implications.

We adapted by avoiding the use of people group terms and not giving preference to Ghairat in our local relationships. We did this by learning both official languages even as we moved into a predominantly Ghairat area. We also decided to share good news and disciple whomever God brought to us. Ironically as I look back, we discipled far more people from other ethnicities than from among our adopted people group.

The external challenges to our people group approach came as we interacted with those who we thought were Ghairat, but who in fact had a muddled ethnic and linguistic background. They did not neatly fit into the ethnic box we found so useful in recruiting. The people had intermarried with other ethnic groups. Traditional Ghairat ways were diluted. They spoke a yet unnumbered variety of dialects (some mutually unintelligible). Others spoke several languages even at home (e.g., the trade language with their mother and Ghairati with their father.) Many could not speak or read their traditional tongue. Some, though not ethnically Ghairat, had been living so long in their area that they acted just like the majority around them.

Cities were particularly confusing. Higher levels of education, in contrast to rural areas, made ethnic identity less important. Yet even if their practices and values reflected urban lifestyles, Ghairat still claimed to be Ghairat. In some situations, ethnic status still had advantages (e.g., legitimizing an acquired position of power, or appealing to ethnic ties for political or military support). How utterly frustrating it was to try to answer: "Who is a real 'Ghairat' and how much does it matter?"

As I reread Romans 15:20–21, I saw Paul focused "where Christ was not known"; it was a geographic or "place" indicator not based on ethnicity, religion, social standing, gender, or nationality. Similarly, he did not gather the church into segments based on ethnic or socio-economic factors. The simplicity of the gospel encourages a common sense of identity in Christ. Distinctions of culture were secondary to the unity of the body.

Why aim for a monoethnic church when there was no church of any kind in the area? A local proverb says, "There are five brothers (fingers/thumb), but not all are the same (equal)." There is a cultural recognition that everyone is different, yet they can be unified. In a country torn apart by decades of interethnic strife and ethnonationalism, I choose not to tie the gospel to ethnic separatism. I sought to establish urban fellowships based on common identity with Christ, rather than on ethnic or religious factors that reflect the subtle but pernicious divisions around us.

South Asia
Tom Tonges

A large church in the Midwest of the US decided to find an unreached Muslim people group and reach them. They were assisted by a mission organization with a similar focus. They prayed over the list for Bangladesh for one year and then sent a high-level group to scout out this Muslim unreached people group (MUPG) to make a plan to reach them. The group included the lead pastor, an associate pastor, missions chairman, an elder or two, and a couple of women in leadership.

The head of the mission organization had led other such trips and did so for this one also. He knew me from years before and emailed me about this trip telling me that this church had selected the "Ansari Muslims" of Bangladesh. I wrote back telling him that I doubted they would find such a group. There were supposedly twenty thousand in my area, but I knew that "Ansari" was a title, not a specific people group. The church leaders came to a city where there were supposed to be over one hundred thousand Ansari Muslims. There they managed to locate some kingdom workers who told them the same thing I had said—there was no such MUPG in their city or region.

The so-called Ansari Muslims are part of the larger Bengali Muslim people group and are not a distinct group. Ansari, in the Bangladesh context, is a title, not a group specifier. Very frustrated and sad, the church group left after four days.

Happily, that is not the end of the story. My friend called and asked if they could visit us. During that visit, the group fell in love with our people group (which is still not listed!), adopted it, and have seconded a couple to our team.

This example seems to reflect a larger issue affecting UPG lists for South Asia. For example, in the Greater Bengal, there are massive groups of Bengali and Bengali-related speakers both in India and Bangladesh. "Sheikh" is listed as the predominant group; however, "sheikh" is simply a title and has nothing to do with a group in which the gospel could flow. I cannot venture a guess as to how someone listed this title as a group. The lists in no way reflect the reality on the ground. I have discussed this with those in charge of the lists, but it is mostly ignored.

South Asia
Jack Smith

In obedience we went to vast South Asia to work among Muslims some years ago. For a few years, we learned language and culture and gained some experience. We were trying to figure out where we fit. Then we received a clear call to a specific region. Initially, I looked on the people group lists but found that Muslims of South Asia were divided into categories that made no sense to a person on the ground. In fact, we made several important discoveries.

First, after two years in the city, I discovered that this region had its own language, which was not the national language. Before moving to this city, my team had all learned the national language well. I had a professional position as a consultant, and the senior staff were cordial to me. They spoke to me in English. The staff, like all educated people, spoke the national language excellently, but to exclude me from their conversation they spoke in their "heart language." I have since learned that this is how people groups with a strong ethnic identity treat outsiders. Speaking someone's heart language makes an enormous difference so our team set out to learn it.

Second, in South Asia, the easiest way to define a people group might be by intermarriage: If families normally marry in and out of that group, it is not a distinct people group. In our region, there is a distinct disdain for outsiders largely coinciding with language. In addition, a given language is divided into Muslim and Hindu groupings, and there is virtually no intermarriage between them. There are also fewer barriers between the extremely wealthy, the very poor, and the middle class. The few Christians in the area are not even originally from this region, nor from Muslim backgrounds.

When I think of the "great multitude" before the throne from "every ethnos" (Rev 7:9), I see a gap—an empty place for millions from our previously unengaged, but still unreached Muslim people group. As yet we are nowhere near the full number; there is a great deal of space for more.

South Asia: Rohingya
Harry Wilson

For decades, the Rohingya have faced tensions and discrimination at the hands of the Burmese government. In 1982, the Burmese government issued a new citizenship law that recognized 135 "indigenous ethnic groups" but defined citizenship in a way that excluded the Rohingya. For the past forty years, the oppression in Myanmar has led to a steady stream of Rohingya fleeing their homeland. The downward spiral of discrimination and violence culminated in brutal military campaigns; the worst of which triggered the exodus of about 1 million people to neighboring Bangladesh in 2017.

What does it mean to be Rohingya? The definition of Rohingya ethnicity differs widely. Some people define it along religious lines, saying every Rohingya is Muslim. Others consider language the decisive factor, meaning everyone who speaks the same language is Rohingya, whether Muslim, Buddhist, or Christian. Still others define it according to region of origin (i.e., Northern Arakan). Ethnic identity markers are contested.

God first stirred our hearts for the Rohingya through the entry in *Operation World* around 1990. When we moved to Myanmar in 1997, we quickly discovered a more complex ethnic situation than was listed or than we imagined. Numbers, definitions, names, and boundaries appear very debatable.

Today Rohingya are spread over more than twenty countries; only 20 percent of the overall population remainss in Myanmar. The diaspora situation over two generations has drastically diversified the identity of the people group. Now we are working in Bangladesh among the refugees, which brings additional challenges. While it was easy to differentiate the Rohingya from other groups in Myanmar, in Bangladesh they blend into the host community much more in terms of language, features, and religion.

Our approach towards disciple making has evolved according to the context of our ministry and changing dynamics overall. Locally, we are praying and working towards Discovery Bible Study (DBS) groups within the camp, apart from the local host community. At the same time, we are actively involved in an international network that helps coordinate the work among Rohingya worldwide; so we are indirectly helping work among them in many contexts. The unifying factor is work among Rohingya wherever they are found.

India
George Lewis

In my early years in India, we had discovered E. Stanley Jones's contextualized approach called the "satsang" or "fellowship of truth." This is a Hindu cultural tradition of people sitting together to discuss spiritual truth. We started to hold these in our region. I am a professional and quickly became aware that many less educated people in the region did not speak the national language (Hindi), which I had spent years learning. They spoke Bundelkhandi, a non-written language with different grammar and some different vocabulary. I had begun to learn it to manage to talk to some of my clients.

The satsangs that we held were well attended, mostly because there was nothing else to do. Generally, the children made a lot of noise, and the people did not pay much attention to what was being said. In one village we had a good relationship because our healthcare team went there weekly, so they were open to having a satsang. It was the same story: noisy children and no one paying attention. We happened to invite a man from a neighboring city to lead it. He was speaking to the people in nice Hindi, as we did in all the satsangs to that point, until in one moment he mistakenly slipped into his mother tongue Bundelkhandi. That changed everything! The crowd of people told the children to stop throwing dirt and shut up. They threatened to beat them if they did not. They told the speaker to stop speaking Hindi and to speak to them in Bundelkhandi. He did, and the conversation really took off. They even took over our harmonium and sang some of their songs. It became a real fellowship of truth just because we presented it in their heart language. We never did it in Hindi again.

India: Delhi
Ed Alansky

The "people group" we work with is really a religious-linguistic group: Urdu-speaking Muslims in the Delhi area. We have not felt that we have the luxury of singling out people groups based on other traditional methods of identifying people groups in India (such as caste). Most of the Urdu speakers in Delhi are first- or second-generation immigrants to the area, and all the Urdu-speaking Muslim people groups tend to live on top of each other, while their kinship and ethnic ties tend to be to other parts of India, especially villages. Though they share a language and religion, neighbors will often not interact much or know each other well.

People will rarely bring us into their networks of relationships because the people they trust do not live locally. On the other hand, from our perspective, since Muslims are a minority—even in many "Muslim" neighborhoods—we cannot afford to be choosey about those with whom we relate.

There are clearly significant cultural differences and a strong sense of identity within and between the groups. For example, one time some Urdu-speaking Muslim men who work at the same company began discussing the differences in how their respective castes relate to their relatives. I was surprised to learn that not only did they have vastly different norms for relating, but that each man was largely unaware of the practices of the other group.

Has urbanization affected the way people relate to each other and see their identity? Definitely, but the traditional people group "core" still seems to be the dominant reality. Marriages, for example, are still overwhelmingly conducted within caste. I have yet to observe the gospel moving between people groups via other affinities, such as shared interests. In my limited experience, there is little trust within non-kinship affinity groups. People rarely know each other well and are unwilling to be vulnerable in such groups. Generally, in India occupations are tied up tightly with caste, and therefore do not represent an alternative to people groups.

In reaction to this situation, we find ourselves forced to work almost exclusively with individual nuclear and extended families within various Urdu-speaking people groups. Admittedly, this feels less effective than focusing on a specific group if that was an option. Because we have yet to see the gospel move beyond families that live together, it remains an open question as to what degree that movement will occur within traditional people groups versus other affinity groups.

Based on my experience, I would say that urbanization has increased the challenge of starting movements by isolating individuals and nuclear family units from their wider relationships of trust without replacing those relationships with new relationships of trust. Surrounded by more people than ever, people seem to be increasingly alone.

Therefore, it seems plausible that despite our best efforts to adapt and capitalize, urbanization represents, for the present, a net challenge to mission movements regardless of our paradigm of "people group" or identity. Even as we seek to adapt in the face of new challenges, we need to be careful not to hastily blame "people group" paradigms when the challenge might really be social fragmentation itself. Phenomena such as multiple identities, multiethnic churches, and urban networks are, in my view, symptoms of that fragmentation, rather than promising alternatives to people groups.

We have been pursuing social media outreach for less than a year. So far, we have seen no confirmed success but believe that we have much to learn and that there is much sowing potential in social media. One advantage of social media in this age of urbanization is that it allows us to sow across extensive rural areas. Social media may allow us to have the advantage of reaching large populations like those present in cities while avoiding the problem of urban social fragmentation.

Pakistan
B. M.

Over the past ten years in Pakistan, we have been hoping, praying, and pleading with people to come and help us. Sadly, some potential workers who come with fixed "people group" thinking leave disappointed by realities on the ground. Here are a few of the lessons we have learned.

First, the way outsiders define people groups does not always match how local people define themselves. Locals have expressed dislike for our focus on specific ethnic groups. For example, I have met many urbanites, especially so-called "Mohajirs" (Urdu-speaking migrants who settled after the 1947 partition of British India), who define themselves as "Karachiites" or even just "Pakistanis." This is especially true for the younger (second or third) generation who were born and raised in Karachi. At times, people are very reluctant to share with me what their "people group" is. They still have pride in their ancestry and family traditions, but it is not such an important factor.

From 2011 to 2013, when ethnic violence and religiously motivated target killings in Karachi were at a height, I met many Karachiites who downplayed their ethnic background. They instead wanted to focus on unity, not differences, of the commonality of all being Pakistanis (or Karachiites).

Second, we need to embrace multilingualism. Traditionally it has been said you can best reach people if you learn their heart language. Use of other languages was discouraged. Among urban populations, this is no longer true. I know several Pashto and Hindko families. Though their parents and older relatives speak it in the home, the younger generation born and raised in Karachi have minimal comprehension and do not speak either language. Among their own age group (e.g., siblings, cousins) they speak Urdu. Culturally they consider themselves Pashtun, but Urdu is their mother tongue and language of literacy.

An Afghan Hazara friend in her mid-twenties speaks Hazargi or Farsi in her home with the family. Her closest friends, however, are from Hunza, Gilgit, and Skardu in northern Pakistan. When I visited her home, there were six different language/people groups represented. Most of the time we used Urdu as the common language, occasionally switching to English (used in schools and workplaces). Throughout the evening they switched back and forth between five different languages. Despite their different backgrounds, they appreciated the fact that they could all sit together and be friends. Note: They are all Agha Khani (Ismaili) Muslims, a sect of Shia Islam. This was the defining, common factor, not the language or ethnic background.

Third, over the years I have met a significant number of families who are "mixed" and consider themselves a part of various groups. This mixing through marriage and/or living in close proximity suggests the need for a multi people group approach. At a recent wedding, I was told that part of the family is Pashtun, part Punjabi, and part Mohajir—all through marriage. When asked what people group they considered themselves to be part of, they said all of them. Being part of the same family, rather than identifying with the same people group, seemed more important. Several families I know from the northwest provincial capital of Peshawar (population of 2 million) are mixed Hindko and Pashtun and speak both languages fluently. In the city of Quetta in Baluchistan, I have several friends where Hazara and Pashtun are married. In Karachi (population of 16 million), several of my Pashtun friends live in communities that are quite mixed, with a high proportion speaking Balochi and Pashto. A Pashto cleaning lady, with little education, spends most of her time with her Balochi neighbors; her Pashtun relatives are married to Balochi.

In all these cases, they have lived together in the same neighborhoods for decades. All of them originally come from villages far away; they have a chance to visit their "home" town once or twice in ten years. They all consider Karachi to be more their home than their original "village." Their deep relational bonds are the most important factor for them.

Eurasia
Dan Nilsen

Our area is home to at least thirty-four distinct ethnic groups (up to fifty if linguistic subgroups are included) in an overall population of about 3 million. Thus, we have done a lot of thinking and "rethinking" about people groups. When I arrived on the field twenty-five years ago, our team did not have a specific UPG focus, which made sense given the ethnic mix in our growing city of over 1 million residents. About 40 percent of the country still lives in rural villages and towns.

One of the requirements for launching a new team was to target a particular UPG, so I chose a UPG with a few workers whose homeland was in the south. However, I realized there were other factors to consider besides the UPG's "reachedness." First, I had to gain residency and have a viable role. Both required an urban platform and fluency in the trade language. Further, in the multiethnic world of our city, where few members of that UPG lived, it was unrealistic to focus exclusively on them. Prioritizing fluency in the trade language would not only allow us to communicate with all people groups but also have implications for the home fellowships we believed would emerge.

A survey by local social scientists revealed that people of this republic have a hybrid and multiple identity. Some ethnic groups identify primarily by ethnicity and language. Others place national or district identity first, then their ethnic group. Within the republic, ethnicities compete for access to governmental posts to improve their clan's financial interests and increase its political influence. Outside the country, in another cosmopolitan city or wherever they are a minority, they stick together—no matter their ethnicity—as citizens of their republic. In an ethnically diverse place like our republic, we should allow the UPG focus to be taken up after the preliminary steps are accomplished. These include fluency in the bridge language that facilitates a broad range of friendships, a credible vocation, and spiritual conversations.

Disciples, too, must learn the kingdom value of passing on truths to others, whether they are of the same people group or not. It would not make sense to push language homogeneity in house fellowships unless the members were all of one ethnic clan. This could occur in urban settings but is likely to be futile. The younger generation growing up in the city often have parents of mixed ethnicity and do not know their parent's heart language well enough. Moreover, even if both parents are of one people group, they tend to use the trade language in the home and do not pass on their heart tongue to the children.

Thus, Bible studies or house fellowships envisioned would include a mix of common and mother tongue language use and rely on Scriptures in both languages. Even in rural communities, people prefer to read in the trade language and listen to audio Scriptures in their heart language. Invitations to more ethnically homogeneous rural communities would be a next step. So, in an ethnically diverse region like ours, engaging and catalyzing disciple-making movements among UPGs is a multilingual, multiyear, multistage process.

Eurasia: "Alpania"
Will Kershon

When we arrived in the Republic of "Alpania," I had the multicolored map of neatly numbered blobs emblazoned in my mind (and soon taped to my wall). The over thirty-six peoples of Alpania were cleanly organized as distinct language groups and clustered in their own mountain valleys. Extensive research and surveying undergirded the colorful blobs. They remain a critical organizing tool for educating outsiders and mobilizing prayer. We hoped God might lead us to the smallest groups in the highest mountains.

But how useful would the map be in our ministry on the ground? In the capital city where we live, language and ethnic divisions blur and sometimes go into hiding. In the first place, everyone speaks the dominant "language of wider communication" (LWC). It is the language of government and business. Yet relational networks of the largest language groups (e.g., workers in the bazaar or shop owners on a street) may speak a local language when together. I found at one gas station a cluster of men aged twenty to seventy working; they were all from a language group numbering fewer than seven thousand in total. Even though they did not all speak their own language, something kept them bound together.

Links to the mountains remain strong. Networks of ethnicity, language, and kinship act as conduits of social capital. Yet for the socially ascendant, a mountain identity may register zero or even negative. In the big city the LWC gets the job done. Everyone I have met identifies with an ancestral village, but some have never even been there. In the city, marriages are often mixed between ethnicities; it is unclear to me how families choose which lineage determines primary identity, or if a primary identity even exists.

The following anecdote illustrates these dynamics. A would-be tour guide invited a mixed group of locals and foreigners to his village for the weekend. When I received my invite, my eyes shone: The destination was a remote mountain region home to the "Akhush," an unengaged Muslim subgroup of a large language bloc we will call "Ukhmar." But it is confusing: Some speakers consider Akhush a unique language; others lump it with the Ukhmar. Linguists have shown it as distinct—thus, the blob on my map. But what do locals say?

As we approached his home perched atop a precipitous mountain slope, our host's prattle glittered with pride for everything from towers to trees to the tarmac we drove on. Deep in the valley, a stone's throw away, lay the village Akhush. So I asked our host about the village and the language. My questions failed to register. He called it all by the larger group name.

That evening, to my delight, musicians came to play, and I asked if they knew any specific Akhush songs. I was met with blank stares. The only thing my host said about that village was that it once was the regional capital. Now it has a population of fifty.

Instead, what I came to learn over the weekend was how proud he and his family were of their region—a federal geographical division not based on ethnicity or language. The republic's former president had hailed from that region and had brought it much honor. He brought in paved roads and rebuilt old towers. He even built a volleyball court on the cusp of a thousand-foot drop in our host's village. A handwoven carpet picturing this man seated at his desk and surrounded by telephones hung on our host's wall. Such was their sense of pride.

Thus, the ethnolinguistic division attested by the data made little apparent difference for the locals I met. The town bearing the dialect's name was a passing thought and mere blip on the road. Instead, they identified with the honor and wealth of the region. Could it be that this draws direct lines between them "in the sticks" and the power centers of the capital? Most notably to me, the musicians played no local songs.

If I were to draw a preliminary hypothesis, I would hazard that the locals' strongest sense of group connectivity is regional, not centered on a sublanguage. This may not be true of other groups whose languages are their primary markers. But here, even with a distinct language, the regional identity is foregrounded over the sublanguage.

What does this mean for gospel communicators? It may signal that already developed language products (Bibles, disciple-making tools, video, audio recordings) and witness from a larger language group can connect with subgroups and thus have an expanded reach. The risk is that those who are monolingual could be further marginalized. Workers are still needed among them. This will likely need to be sorted out on the ground through relationships. My takeaway is that "the research is made for man, not man for the research." That is, let us do all the research we can but be ready to flow with what the locals tell us is important to them.

Middle East: Refugees
Scott Pearson

I am a worker in the Middle East who has hung in there for between twenty-five and thirty years. We work in a small city that has undergone radical changes over the last ten years. The population has more than doubled due to the influx of refugees. Around 85 percent of these refugees are from three large cities in a neighboring country. The vast majority are lower middle-class people with working/trade backgrounds (e.g., construction workers, drivers, government clerks). Most have only a sixth-grade education and can only barely read and write.

Many are only nominally Muslim. I sometimes will start to talk about a prophet, and they will respond, "Moses who?" Most fast and pray on Fridays; they may observe a couple of prayer times during the day, but not all five.

We have focused on the refugee people group around us. I also share a lot with local nationals, although we have seen less fruit there. Due to urbanization, war, and people seeking refuge, there has been a lot of intergroup mixing. That said, marriages are arranged in the traditional way, preferably with a cousin or second cousin, someone from their city of origin, or at least a Sunni Muslim. I know five to seven families where a local man married a woman from the refugee community, but all but one of these women were from an area closest to this country.

While some Muslim-background believers have joined local churches, I try to encourage believers to share with others in their networks. We think that groups comprised of like-minded, similar culture, similar education, and similar age people will stick together better.

How have my views changed? Most of the last nine years I have been in the context described above, focused on one people group. The previous seven years I lived in a larger, more cosmopolitan city in a neighboring country. There our friendship networks spanned Muslims from a variety of backgrounds, both Sunni and Shi'ite. I have been more fruitful in this setting, partly because our current city is smaller and because we are more focused on one group.

Horn of Africa: Somali
Stefan Harth

When God called me to serve the Somali people, I had no idea how complicated that could be. On the People Groups website (peoplegroups.org), the Somali people are divided into fifteen different "people groups," eight of which are considered unengaged. Joshua Project listed even more "people groups" at a total of twenty-four, with fourteen designated "frontier peoples." Yet when I ask my Somali friends, they assure me that they are all one!

How did we end up with fifteen to twenty-four different Somali "people groups?" Simple: The logic of our current people group model dictates that we differentiate people by country. In other words, the Somali of Ethiopia are a different people group than the Somali of Kenya, just because they live in a different country. Of course, there are good reasons to develop separate engagement strategies for different countries, but does that mean we have to subdivide the people with whom we are engaging as well?

In the 1980s, significant Somali communities lived in five different countries: Somalia, Kenya, Ethiopia, Djibouti, and Yemen. Since the civil war in the 1990s, Somali refugees have spread all over the world, apparently creating new "people groups" whenever they cross a border. Today Somalis communities can be found in many countries, way more than the fifteen or twenty-four listed by the above databases. To make matters worse, these communities are not static but continue to move. In the urban center where I live, I can meet Somalis from Somalia, Kenya, Ethiopia, the United States, Australia, and Europe on any given day. Does that mean I am effectively engaging a half dozen unengaged people groups? Or do they all become "Somalis in Kenya" once they leave the airplane?

Most Somalis belong to one of the many clans that make up Somali society, and most clans have dedicated online groups and forums to mobilize people in times of crisis. These online groups connect clan members across dozens of countries, enabling rapid flow of information and resources across the world. Instead of dividing the Somali people by country of residence, should we perhaps divide them into transnational clans?

We need to think of alternatives to the spatially bound people groups. Many Somali clans have been transnational for a long time, spanning several different countries within the Horn of Africa, connected through social and relational networks beyond borders and across the world. If we define UPGs mainly based on social pathways that allow for the flow of the gospel, then it makes more sense to focus on social networks across countries, rather than a composite network comprised of a people group in one country.

Horn of Africa: Somali Bantu
Andreas Wagner

"Why is it that the Somali Bantu refugees I'm talking to are not receiving any help from your NGO?" I asked a social worker of a local refugee aid organization. She used the same explanation I had heard from other organizations: "We are advertising our services through the refugee leaders. If the Somali Bantus are not organized, if they don't have a leader, then they might not know about us." This approach saved NGO resources and allowed for more community ownership.

Note that the categorization of local "tribal" groups, formerly in the hands of the colonial powers, is now perpetuated by aid organizations! In both cases, the allocation of resources and services is contingent on clearly defined social groups among the beneficiaries. Also, in both cases, people who do not "fit" into the social categories used by those in power are disadvantaged. People without clear community structures do not have access.

The Somali Bantu are a very interesting example of these power dynamics. Up until the early 1990s, they simply did not exist as an ethnic group. The people who now make up the "Somali Bantu" formed small communities scattered across southern Somalia. Some were integrated into Somali clans (usually facing discrimination as second-class members), while others formed their own distinct groups. They did not have a common origin or language. The only thing these people had in common was the racial status forced upon them by Somali society. As members of these racial minorities fled Somalia in the early years of the civil war, UN officials and other aid workers noticed the similarities in their situation and started calling them "Somali Bantu." As a label, it signified vulnerability and oppression, but it was also the only non-derogatory name available for these people, and so it stuck.

Today, there are between seven hundred thousand and 1.5 million Somali Bantu, even though the term itself is contested within the community. They do not fit into the Somali clan system, and the different groupings speak their own distinct dialect of one of the Somali minority languages. The awareness of a common status in Somalia, the shared experience of flight and resettlement, and the pragmatic need to "fit" in a category in order to access resources have created a new ethnic group.

The Somali Bantu have been the focus of a number of academic studies, and the construction of their ethnicity has been marveled at by social scientists. But even these studies portray the Somali Bantus as a unique and clearly defined group, which they are not. Interacting with different members of the Somali Bantu community, I have come to observe social, cultural, and linguistic differences within the community. Clearly, being Somali Bantu comes on a spectrum, with a clear core and a fuzzy periphery. (In my interviews with members from different social categories, they all agree that they are one larger community and claim to intermarry, while acknowledging internal differences and differing degrees of acceptance of the "Somali Bantu" label.)

The people group list for Somalia is based primarily on linguistic criteria and a secular linguistic study from the 1980s. Consequently, when we arrived on the field, we based our original vision and strategy on linguistic criteria, assuming this would be the most important barrier to the gospel within southern Somalia. But my research in the following years revealed that many social and even family networks cross these linguistic lines. I would now argue that the most significant barrier in Somalia is racial, not linguistic.

While churches and groups in the United States are ministering to their diaspora Somali Bantu neighbors (over fifty thousand), the international mission agencies seem largely oblivious to all these developments. The data on southern Somalia that informed the Registry of Peoples was collected in in the 1980s, before the creation of the Somali Bantu ethnicity. Since then, there have been very few attempts by mission agencies to engage Somali Bantus, partly because this group is hard to identify and access, and partly because they do not show up in certain databases. (The Somali Bantu are listed on Joshua Project website, but not on the IMB's peoplegroups.org used by many mission organizations.)

The social worker I mentioned at the beginning of this case study had a simple solution: "They need to organize themselves. They need to appoint leaders and approach us." Within our current paradigm, she is right. People like the Somali Bantu will be systematically overlooked unless they can fit into a neat "people group" category.

What does this mean for church? As long as one is considered ethnic Somali, one can find one's place within the Somali church. But Somali Bantus are not accepted as equals even among believers, and they generally do not fellowship together. Because of this, we see the greatest need for a separate ministry effort within the Somali context among the Somali Bantu. Apparently, nobody will pray for them, recruit workers to send to them, or develop a strategy to serve them, unless we have given them a label and added some nice numbers.

Turkey
K. M.

After decades of living in Turkish society, we have come to the realization that family or community is the basic core group and the lowest common denominator for disciple making movements. If our thinking is to be transformational, we must look beyond individuals to the larger family.

Rapid urbanization is a reality of our world in Turkey. When we arrived, the population was sixty percent rural, forty percent urban. Now those numbers are reversed. However, merely moving locations does not change the culture of a rural person. The underlying values are still there, now carried into an urban setting. If you scratch a little, you will see there is something else beneath the veneer of modernism. Looks can be deceiving, so a cross-cultural worker must be adept at perceiving differences in group identity.

For us identifying a "people group" in the larger sense is merely a place to start. The idea of "groupness" must be refined down to the level of a specific community or larger extended family network. The beliefs, values, and practices of that "mini-people group" will determine how they themselves create boundaries for an independent identity. Their own self-determination of "groupness" must be understood and honored for a gospel movement to take root.

Southeast Asia
L. A. M.

The "Bridge" people are originally from an island near Java. Today, only half of the people group live on the island; the rest have emigrated to other parts of Indonesia and abroad. They tend to be very religious and proud of their ethnic identity.

We work in a major city where the Bridge people make up about ten percent of the population. Since our people group is a minority here, we have chosen to have more of a city focus, so are willing to find and follow up with "people of peace" from other UPGs. I still go out of my way to make sure I am with members of this community about sixty percent of my outreach time. Those I am interacting with are tightly knit with their own people and have only a few close friendships with Javanese or other peoples.

I believe that the classic people group approach is the most appropriate approach to reach the Bridge people here. However, since our context is urban, we have more of a "dragnet" approach. We are willing to reach all ethnic people groups (using the DMM model), depending on how the person of peace defines their oikos (household/network). We encourage the person of peace to open their oikos to everyone, but to define it in a way that includes their own people. The missing step for teams engaging the Bridge people is that they aren't going deep in their vernacular language and culture.

Transnational: Deobandi Movement
Louise C. Wood

As we rethink people groups, we need to recognize that there are other important groupings and identities that go beyond location or ethnicity. One example is the transnational Deobandi movement within Islam, with whom I have had contact both in South Asia and Europe.

The Deobandi madrassa movement began in 1866 in north India and rapidly spread by encouraging graduates to start new madrassas and teach local communities the Deobandi brand of Sunni Islam. Deobandi Islam emphasizes a "back to basics" version of Islam that models Mohammad in everything, including wearing the style of clothes Mohammad wore and cleaning teeth with a twig as Mohammad did. Deobandis are very cautious of "innovations" or adopting common practices of the wider society (such as watching TV or listening to music), preferring to stay unnoticed and distinct. What distinguishes Deobandis is their capacity to maintain a distinct identity and this very traditional version of Islam within a larger non-Muslim society. They began in India where Muslims are a minority among a majority Hindu society, and as they establish new mosques and madrassas in the West, they teach others how to maintain Muslim practice in that context. They consider themselves less as a distinct movement than as the genuine Muslims among the less pure Islamic community; a Deobandi Muslim would not feel comfortable visiting a non-Deobandi mosque.

The Deobandi movement is distinguished by a standard curriculum in all locations, covered by every leader during their training, although each madrassa may apply the teaching to their specific location. For example, some offer comprehensive lists of acceptable foods among the local cuisine, moon sightings (for feast days), or how to respond to local holidays. They may teach in the local language rather than the traditional Urdu or Arabic. Just as significantly, a book for women (Heavenly Ornaments) has rules and guidance for family life. Deobandi women are often given this book at their wedding, and they will study it deeply throughout their lives. This foundation of religious teaching and common understanding of home and family life produces a shared Deobandi identity and view of life as well.

Deobandi madrassas have advanced what has been called "a revival from below." This "bottom-up reform" is largely invisible compared to the top-down reforms propagated by the Islamist political groups. There are currently about one hundred thousand Deobandi madrassas (religious schools) on at least four continents. These madrassas not only train new mosques leaders, but also function as places of spiritual guidance, education, and identity for the local Muslim community.

A significant number of the Sunni population of Pakistan, India, Bangladesh, Afghanistan, and Iran identify with Deobandi Islam. Beyond South Asia the movement is growing among Muslim minority populations, particularly in South Africa, the United Kingdom, Canada, United States, and Trinidad and Tobago. Historically, this was associated with the South Asian diaspora. However, current students may identify more with the host (diaspora) country where they were born than with the country their grandparents emigrated from. New adherents may not have a South Asian background at all.

Globally, Deobandi madrassas are both connected and independent. In some countries they are affiliated with political or extremist groups, but in most locations, they do not engage with wider society except to invite new members to join. They are not the majority in any one country or people group, and they often stay unseen from the outside. It is difficult to get a clear number for each country due to the lack of research; in India, it is estimated to be about forty million, and in Pakistan a similar number.

What will it take to reach such a group? Approaches must be rooted in local communities while finding ways to influence a highly connected transnational network. The Deobandi represent an identifiable "people group" that transcends boundaries and countries and provides a sense of group identity not based on ethnolinguistic criteria.

Reflection and Discussion

The Impact of People Group Thinking on Field Workers

1. Which case study stood out to you and/or touched your heart?

2. What are some of the challenges workers faced using the people group approach as a church-planting strategy?

3. Describe some of the cultural and contextual "realities" that led workers to "rethink" and modify their understanding of their people group.

4. How did this affect their approach to disciple making and conception of what a movement of disciples and churches might look like?

5. What are some cautions that both senders and goers need to keep in mind as they engage a "people group"?

6. Based on the narratives, what words would you use to describe the lives and characters of these field workers?

7. Choose one case study to reread. Pray for the worker and the people group they have dedicated their life to reaching with the gospel.

8. Go to JoshuaProject.net and choose one unreached people group to pray for today.

Part 4

Impact of People Group Thinking on Local Churches

Mobilizing for Strategic Engagement

13

The Local Church and Adopt A People

PCC

PCC is a nondenominational, evangelical, Reformed-leaning church. It was planted in 1983 by a nearby church with roots in the Christian and Missionary Alliance, which means missions was in our DNA from the start. Unfortunately, we followed our mother church into a "mile-wide, inch-deep" and missionary-centric missions strategy.

By 1990, we realized we needed a focus for our global passion. Three things influenced us to place unreached people groups (UPGs) at the center of our missions goals and strategy: (1) our lead pastor who studied under Harvie Conn (a professor with UPG experience and passion) at Westminster Seminary in the early eighties; (2) home visits in the mid-1980s with two field workers (who were good friends of the pastor), working with UPGs in Central Asia and East Asia; and (3) the "Perspectives on the World Christian Movement" course in the mid-nineties. It was the course that pushed us over the edge. We realized that the real culprit, the source of "the great imbalance" problem of worker allocation (over 85 percent work among Christians, not unreached peoples) was the local church, not missionaries or their sending agencies.

The first unreached people group we adopted in 1996 was an animist minority that we referred to as "East Asia."[1] We sent youth groups to help with English camps, which provided access via bike tours to remote villages. Professionals in medicine, higher education, and business, as well as nonprofessionals in construction and conversational English, were recruited for trips and provided training to local people. Over the years, over fifty teens and twenty-five adults have had in-country experience serving among this UPG. Pastors know the spiritual vitality that this type of personal engagement brings to the life of a church, and this is what we experienced.

While the country recently closed to Americans (sending our three long-term workers home), our people group focus (versus missionary/worker focus) means that our commitment to reaching this UPG has not changed. Instead, we are working to restructure our means of engagement. It is likely that we will rely more heavily on non-Western workers with whom we have a relationship. We will also increase our efforts to find and engage members of our people group who live in diaspora or immigrant communities.

Our second people group adoption involved the "Silk Road People" (SRP) of Central Asia. This engagement began to unfold in 1982 when our pastor and his wife befriended a couple from the mother church doing educational and medical work among the SRP in Central Asia. While the couple was on home leave, they reported to the church and were sent out again with prayer.

---
[1] For security purposes, in our communications we use pseudonyms or regional terms rather than the names of specific countries or people groups.

In 1999, our congregation formed a task force to explore the possibility of adopting a Muslim UPG. Over the course of a year, unreached people groups in Kenya, Turkey, UAE, Pakistan, Greece, and Afghanistan were identified using research provided by the Joshua Project and sending agencies. Our selection criteria included (a) missionaries with whom our church had or could establish and maintain; (b) contact through personal visits at least every few years; (c) philosophy of ministry and theological compatibility; (d) some degree of personal chemistry; (e) access whereby people from the church could use their gifts and talents to augment long-term work; and importantly; and (f) partnership with workers who are focused on the eventual establishment of multiplying indigenous churches.

In 2000, the church sent the lead pastor and his wife to spend a week in each of the areas identified. They got to know the workers (if not previously known), saw their work, and sought guidance as to whether a fit was likely.

Upon their return they reported to the task force, and after significant discussion and prayer, a recommendation was made to the missions committee and then to the board of elders that the Silk Road People of Central Asia (SRP) would be our focus. A "Central Asia Task Force" (CAT) was established, and a strategy was developed together with our SRP field partners.

Over the next twenty-four years, the church has engaged with SRP and supported long-term disciple making in multiple ways by sending: interns to learn language, culture, and apologetics; a physician to set up a virtual training program for doctors in an urban hospital; six home group leaders to train men whom the workers believed had potential to become small group leaders; educators who engaged with the SRP diaspora in the Arab Gulf region; and pastors to encourage workers and new believers. As with our first people group adoption, these trips, along with home visits from the workers, have kept the fires burning.

Because adopting a people group is primarily focused on the people group, not the workers, let alone workers only from our church, we have developed dozens of relationships with SRP workers from other organizations. Our church actively participates in the annual PAN conference, which brings together a network of field workers, pastors and church leaders, support ministries (translation, literature, media), interns, aspiring workers, member care personnel, and intercessors—all focused on this one large unreached people group, the Silk Road People.

The church adopted a third UPG in 2005, the Aweer people of coastal Kenya, in partnership with a church in Nairobi. The benefits of church-to-church partnership have been significant. I mention this because it rounds out our current UPG commitments to unreached peoples. Each UPG receives quarterly prayer in a worship service, priority allocation of short-term trips each summer, and every three years, special focus in one weeklong conference.

Another helpful feature has been mission education. The course "Perspectives on the World Christian Movement," which we have hosted four times, has been a positive influence on the church. Over two hundred of our people have taken the course.

But perhaps the single most significant element of the strategy has been the "First Sunday Prayer" time, held monthly on Sunday mornings. We share recent updates and virtual or live reports and discuss "complex issues" (e.g., polygamy, spousal abuse, the insider movement, the Son of God translation controversy, local believers wrestling with staying or leaving an oppressive context). This has added an important element to the prayer times by engaging the minds of our predominantly college-educated congregation.

14

An Ecosystem for Sending

Austin Stone and the 100 UPG Cooperative

Todd Engstrom

Since its founding in 2002, The Austin Stone Community Church (one church composed of six congregations) has been zealous for reaching the nations. In 2009, we developed a measurable vision for sending one hundred goers to unreached people groups (UPGs) called the "100 People Network." In 2014, we sent our one-hundredth goer and began to pray and consider the next phase.

We had a lot to learn in our early years, but we began with a sincere conviction about the strategic priority of the unreached. Initially, we built our strategy on preexisting mission relationships. It was mostly a "who do you know that we can partner with" strategy. This led to tension with national partners because we were not thoughtful about our convictions or strategy. Without debriefing and informed insight, we unintentionally created enduring partnerships with ministries misaligned with our UPG vision. In our sending, we discovered that, alongside preaching, experiential learning and missions knowledge were crucial to form the convictions and experience needed. We praise God for several sending agencies that extended grace to us and served as guides while we learned these lessons.

From 2014 to 2016, our vision grew to see one hundred churches reproducing to the fourth generation. God answered that prayer by birthing a church-planting movement in South Asia.

In 2017, the Lord gave us a vision to catalyze church-planting movements (CPMs) among one hundred unreached peoples. With our agency partners and field team leaders, we have so far identified church-planting movements that have emerged among twenty-seven UPGs globally. We continue to work toward the goal of one hundred.

One of the enduring lessons we have learned is that it takes both committed senders as well as goers to accomplish a dynamic global vision. Since 2011, the generous senders in our church have invested more than $23.5 million in global missions infrastructure and initiatives. Approximately 11 percent of our total annual budget goes to missions, and approximately 80 percent of global missions funding is directed specifically to frontier missions among unreached people groups. We currently support over 140 long-term goers who work on field teams in partnership with mission agencies. A culture of sending has infused our congregations.

We take collaboration seriously. In 2017, we developed the "100 UPG Cooperative," a partnership of churches, ministries, and leaders that aims to accelerate the fulfillment of the Great Commission by catalyzing church-planting movements among one hundred unreached people groups (100upg.org). The cooperative functions as a "global ecosystem" of churches, mission agencies, and leaders to recruit, train, send, and support workers in pursuit of our shared vision.

We take training for cross-cultural work seriously. At a minimum, a candidate spends almost twelve months in disciple-making communities that participate in cross-cultural evangelism and discipleship among internationals in our city. Through extensive training in church planting and movement principles, and ongoing peer and mentor coaching, candidates are equipped for perseverance and fruitfulness in long-term ministry. Candidates also identify a cross-cultural team with a sending agency and take at least one vision trip to that field of service.

Due to the size of our network, we have an international field office dedicated to goer oversight. Field office staff provide support in doctrine and moral discipline issues and collaborate in care, coaching, and crisis management.

Like any partnership, there have been opportunities for collaboration and varied challenges. Even like-minded churches with virtually identical doctrinal beliefs differ in culture and expectations. Building an international cooperative requires humility and dexterity to appreciate multiple contexts and balance small team dynamics with large-scale organizational desires. Though the work can be challenging, we believe the Lord will bless these efforts and that we will see a great harvest.

15
Robust Commitment

The Well

Pastor C. C.

The Well Community Church was planted in late 2000 in urban Portland, Oregon. Membership is approximately 150 adults, and a weekly attendance of 140 to 175 people. Primarily an Anglo congregation, with some ethnic diversity, The Well is nondenominational, theologically Reformed, continuationist, and complementarian in its convictions. Due to its nondenominational and urban community church roots, The Well is an eclectic mix of believers from a wide spectrum of theological backgrounds.

The church sent its first worker (this author) to work among Muslims in 2002. Since then, a significant number of workers have launched from The Well relative to the size of the congregation. Currently, there are fourteen households serving as workers (representing forty-three adults and children), the majority of whom are serving among peoples considered unreached by missiological definition.

How and why did The Well develop such a robust commitment to sending to unreached peoples? The primary reasons are essentially "two sides of the same coin": God's word and God's Spirit. First is the regular, consistent, methodical exposition of the Bible. World mission is everywhere in the Scriptures, and a steady diet of the Bible has established global mission as a normative endeavor for the church and every faithful Christian. Second, the Spirit of God has been at work among us. The leadership of The Well is acutely aware of its weakness and what we lack. The sovereign Holy Spirit has breathed life into our congregation to enable us to send from within.

Two additional factors have contributed to a strong UPG sending emphasis. The first is a robust commitment by the church leadership to global mission. For example, one of the pastors/elders is the director of an agency based in Southeast Asia. Another of the pastors/elders served with OM in London and North Africa. A strong, visible commitment by senior leadership to global missions has set the course of the church's vision to include the unreached as a primary emphasis.

Second, the leadership's deep commitment to global missions is shared by church members, many of whom are serving or have served cross-culturally. For example, one couple serves in mobilization with Frontiers. Another couple serves as Bible translators in the Sahel. Yet another couple leads an organization that works among marginalized communities in East Africa. Our partnerships with sending agencies have helped to maximize our impact. What is communicated from the leadership is modeled in the congregation, thus creating what might be called a "360-degree" commitment to the evangelization of all peoples.

The barriers and obstacles we encounter to sending to unreached peoples are not unlike those experienced by other churches. There can be a tendency to focus on what is nearby and regularly seen, causing the Christian to forget about the peoples and places of the world that are far away and unseen. In a similar vein is the inclination to prioritize local needs, providing a justification for neglecting world mission and Christ's commission to disciple "all nations." There is also a temptation to focus on numbers and quick, quantifiable results, leading some to draw back from ministry among peoples who require slow, sacrificial gospel witness that may take many years.

Added to this is the emotional toll: disillusionment, discouragement, the sacrifice of saying repeated goodbyes to cherished friends now "going," and spending money globally that could be spent locally or internally for the church. However, in our experience, when Christ and his gospel as revealed in the Scriptures are the church's primary focus and purpose, these barriers need not hold us back from "setting apart" and "sending off" more people called to the nations (cf. Acts 13:3–4).

We continue to engage in practices that, when combined, have helped to develop a mission culture and to build vision toward unreached peoples. Pastoral prayers before the sermon often highlight global needs and the need for more workers to be sent. Worker interviews happen regularly during Sunday gatherings, normalizing career missions as a vocation to be pursued. An annual all-night prayer meeting has helped catalyze people and interest. Small groups that emphasize and pray for missions have provided a regular space in the church calendar for people to hear about and grow in mission awareness. Finally, congregational initiatives to send church-based teams have united the church around a common missional goal.

We are a small urban church with a big God. By grace, the leadership and church have been willing to release and send out, with tearful goodbyes and robust faith in God's word and Spirit, significant numbers from our congregation for the sake of God's glory among all peoples and nations.

16
The Sending Process

Canyon Hills Community Church

Global Outreach of Canyon Hills Community Church exists to make more and better disciples of Jesus Christ by planting churches among unreached peoples of South Asia and Japan. This specific vision was catalyzed by our encounter with the people groups God brought near to us in Bothell, Washington. As we researched the community demographics surrounding our church, we developed a strategy that prioritized these near-neighbor peoples, as well as the two global regions and eight countries they represented.

Mobilization and training are vital in a sending church. We believe that creating a "sending pipeline" that leads to long-term cross-cultural service and faithfulness is one of our primary responsibilities as a local church. We take our role and the sending process seriously.

Canyon Hills hosts *monthly prayer meetings* during which we focus on the needs of our global partners and pray for gospel advance in the challenging contexts of Japan and South Asia. Each year our *Global Encounter Trips* (short-term trips) enable over two hundred people to experience life with our global partners. We hope that seeds planted here will lead to a long-term vision for the nations.

Each quarter Global Outreach hosts a half-day training called *R3ACH*. The "3" emphasizes the 3 billion people who live in over seven thousand unreached people groups (UPGs) lacking an adequate witness of the gospel. Trained facilitators teach on the majority religions within our strategy area, help trainees understand cultures, and provide practical tools for engaging these peoples.

Each spring and fall Canyon Hills offers a *ten-week disciple-making training program* that helps participants discover God's heart for all peoples. We explore team life, evangelism, and an ambassadorial lifestyle that equips members to multiply and make more disciples.

Our twelve-to-eighteen-month *sending pipeline*, required for all aspiring global partners, helps them discern their readiness and possible future roles. These *mid-term global partners* spend a summer, semester, or up to two years overseas, sharing the gospel in a cross-cultural context. We also have a *church-based residency ministry*, which allows aspiring global partners to further develop character and leadership skills and engage in ministry, working together with Global Outreach to help mobilize Canyon Hills church.

Member care of workers is a huge value and a critical lifeline of support between the sending church and global partner. We have *lay-led member care teams* who are in consistent communication with global partners; they recognize celebrations like anniversaries and birthdays and meet with global partners monthly to pray. Caring for global partners is equally important at each stage—before they launch, once they land, and after they return home. The church hosts an annual *GO Week*, and every three years, we highly encourage all global partners to return for GO Week and for our triennial workers retreat called *The Grove*. During this time, we take the adults away for five days and pour love, care, and encouragement into them.

Global Outreach is currently making intentional efforts to resource and equip other ministries within Canyon Hills, helping to *integrate Great Commission vision and conviction*. This is especially critical for our Life Group ministry, which we view as the lifeblood of the church. We are witnessing momentum as more missional communities develop that are committed to evangelism, multiplication, and the work of ministry.

The Global Outreach advance team serves alongside both Global Outreach pastors as they keep global convictions a priority, present aspiring global partners to the elders, and make financial decisions. The financial commitment to global partners is determined by their individual vision and strategy and the alignment with the overall vision of Global Outreach.

Currently, we are launching individuals and families to join existing cross-cultural teams. However, in the future we look forward to launching our first *church-based teams*—team leaders and team members envisioned, recruited, equipped, and sent from our congregation in partnership with an agency. Although many aspiring global partners like the vision of church-based teams, most want to gain field experience before pursuing team leadership.

Persuaded that the local church is central in God's plan for kingdom expansion, we aspire to be a "sending church" and embrace the carefully worded definition offered by the Upstream Collective:

> A Sending Church is a local community of Christ-followers who have made a covenant together to be prayerful, deliberate, and proactive in developing, commissioning, and sending their own members both locally and globally, often in partnership with other churches or agencies, and continuing to encourage, support, and advocate for them while making disciples cross-culturally and upon their return.[1]

Our God is a sending God. His church is a sent people. Together we affirm our identity and pledge to fulfill our calling to make disciples of all peoples and nations.

Bibliography

Bradley, Zach. *The Sending Church Defined*. Louisville, KY: The Upstream Collective, 2015.

---

1 Bradley, *Sending Church Defined*.

17

Sowing Broadly Together

Swedish Pentecostal Churches

Bo Lundin, Hans Olofsson, and O. K.

Based on Acts 13:2–3, the Swedish Pentecostal churches have always believed that local churches are the primary platform responsible for international mission. Although there are joint initiatives and formed organizations like IBRA (media ministry) and PMU (humanitarian aid agency), the local church bears the main responsibility. At the founding of one of our earliest churches, one of the first decisions in the constitutional meeting was to send out a missionary. As the same church prepared to construct a new building, it first decided to send out another missionary.

Since its beginning, the Swedish Pentecostal Church has primarily focused on African and Latin American countries. That focus gradually changed. Today there is greater focus on countries in the Central Asia, South Asia, and Asia Pacific regions, along with an increased awareness of least reached people groups.

The values of collaboration and cooperation characterize the relationships between Swedish local churches. Given their joint focus on certain areas, they connect with each other for strategic discussions and prayer. In this way, macro decisions regarding initiatives and financial support are grounded in the decisions of individual local churches within the larger constellation.

One significant example of collaboration is the radio ministry IBRA and its gospel broadcast to one of the largest language groups in Central Asia. Beginning in the seventies a local church in Sweden sent a missionary to the region. His main commission was social development, but he also recognized the great need to share the gospel in the restricted-access country. He contacted a colleague in a neighboring country, and with the help of IBRA and national believers, they began to produce radio programs in the language of a large Muslim unreached people group. The first program aired in 1973. In the early years the response was very low. They faced many obstacles, such as the creation of culturally relevant content, the development of solid follow-up procedures, security, etc. Still, the programs continued to air and sow the seed of the gospel.

Over the years IBRA developed partnerships with other organizations. The programs were refined for relevancy towards cultural and spiritual needs and issues (e.g., drug addiction, women, family, conflict, and reconciliation) and styles of communication (e.g., music, radio drama). Trained native speakers provide sensitive follow-up, answer questions, engage in Discovery Bible Studies, encourage, comfort, and pray for the needs of listeners. Staff also network with workers on the ground. Today through its partnership, IBRA broadcasts forty-five minutes daily in that language on both shortwave and medium wave.

In 2021, when many field workers were forced to leave the region, Swedish leaders shared a vision with local churches: "This is not a time for pulling back. We need a gospel surge to meet the people's spiritual needs and provide a message of hope." Local churches responded. Broadcast times were doubled. Local churches increased efforts to reach out to immigrants and asylum seekers around them. Churches stayed engaged through regular prayer meetings, reports, and conferences. In addition, a group of churches embraced plans to launch new programming in the language of a neighboring Muslim people group. Those programs began airing in 2023.

As turmoil and instability in the region increased, response to the programs also increased. Thousands of calls were received in 2023. Here are some follow-up notes from a recent conversation with a listener:

> About fifteen to twenty people are listening together, especially the dramas. Listening for the last two to three weeks. His wife is blind but well connected with other women in the village. She wants to start a group among women to learn from the radio and she needs some guidance about this.

The response from the other Muslim people group in the region is encouraging. In the first year that the programs have aired, more than one thousand individuals called in for prayer or with questions. This represents thousands of other listeners and households.

This entire initiative is made possible through the prayers and support of ten local churches in Sweden and Norway. For over fifty years, local churches have sown in faith. In Scripture Jesus teaches the power of "sowing broadly" the seed of the gospel. As we do our part, God does his part.

> This is what the kingdom of God is like. A man scatters seed on the ground. Night and day, whether he sleeps or gets up, the seed sprouts and grows, though he does not know how. All by itself the soil produces grain—first the stalk, then the head, then the full kernel in the head. As soon as the grain is ripe, he puts the sickle to it, because the harvest has come. (Mark 4:26–29 NIV)

18

Where Mountains Inspire Poets

Oitava Church, Brazil

Célia Margareth Oliveira Laranjo and Luís Fernando Nacif

As a church we recognize our identity in Christ as a community that blesses and is blessed. We believe we are invited to join a movement of divine generosity to proclaim and incarnate the love, justice, and hope of God in this world.

Otiava Church (The Eighth Presbyterian Church) is located in Belo Horizonte, Minas Gerais, in the southeast of Brazil—a place where glorious mountains inspire poets and God inspires mission. We are a congregation of approximately nine thousand members with a shared vision of being a biblical church that is culturally aware, hospitable, present in the community, and a partner in world evangelization. To realize this vision, our church has launched ministries of teaching, evangelism, social work, and cross-cultural mission, led by committed pastors, elders, and members, along with outside partners in God's mission.

We understand our calling, in obedience to the Great Commission, to enlighten Brazil and other nations through the proclamation of the gospel of Jesus Christ. We prioritize minority peoples and unreached groups in hard and difficult-to-reach contexts.

We are a church devoted to prayer and intercession, committed to the development of gifts, talents, and financial resources to see Jesus made known and glorified throughout all the earth. We recognize our weakness and deep dependence on God. We are conscious that our life on earth is not evaluated by our strategic, technological, or organizational capacity, but by how we love God and one another and serve together in unity through diversity.

To fulfill Christ's global mandate, we work both inside and outside of Brazil alongside churches, agencies, and mission organizations. We partner with those who recognize Jesus Christ as their only Lord and Savior, acknowledge the authority of the Holy Scriptures, are firmly planted in values of the kingdom of God, and are dedicated to seeing people and communities transformed by the power of the Holy Spirit. Oitava Church seeks to understand its community and fulfill its calling to incarnational mission.

We try to cultivate and grow in the fundamental values of partnership and cooperation in mission. With this in view, we created the Congress of Pastors and Leaders (CPL), a network of support and encouragement for pastors and leaders across Brazil. CPL hosts an annual event that gathers approximately five hundred participants from different Brazilian denominations and other countries. Speakers with years of field experience and deep theological and missiological knowledge help mobilize, support, and challenge leaders to live lives coherent with the gospel. Leaders are encouraged to impact regions of the world with a gospel that transforms all spheres of life.

Since its founding in 1969, Oitava Church has nurtured a commitment to mobilization and generous partnership in preaching the gospel. Today, we support thirty missionary families on four continents, in addition to mission trips, local mobilization, and support efforts in education, health, and theological and missiological development.

Oitava believes that "the remaining task" begins and ends in the local church. We are conscious that God's mission requires involvement and collaboration with the indigenous peoples. We teach that the church must step out of a posture of colonizing and instead promote deep, dignifying, and respectful relationships.

To reach that goal, our church joins hands with mission agencies. We recognize the unique roles of missionaries, churches, and agencies, and the need for mutual agreement and genuine collaboration. Projects, dreams, and feelings are shared openly so that we can meet goals that glorify God.

We try to maintain good communication with our missionaries, sharing our own difficulties and listening to the struggles they face on the field so that each partner can provide support and help to those on the frontlines. We also commit to participate in every step of preparation for a missionary's return. Our biggest challenge has been communication with missionaries located in closed or restricted-access countries because we want to respect and be sensitive to their sometimes dangerous contexts. Oitava equips and invests in each missionary candidate who is a member of the church—from their initial calling to their departure. We encourage theological and missiological study, with special emphasis on each candidate's respective project and area of calling.

As a church, Oitava takes initiative to care for and support its leadership, members, and missionaries. We do not regard our workers as heroes or as victims, and in our member care approach we emphasize values of integrity, transparency, and self-care with dignity. To minimize the disconnect between field workers and the congregation, we try to create discrete ways and spaces for the church to hear and relate with our missionaries.

Our desire is to continue to hear God's voice and to learn obedience and commitment to his mission. Our passion is to advance his kingdom in places where Christ has yet to be preached. With joy and gratitude, we celebrate the grace of collaboration with others in God's mission.

19

Everyone Leaves, Everyone Is Sent Onward

Koinonia International Church, Middle East

Brian McSwain

The magnitude of sharing the good news of Jesus globally can feel daunting. "Making disciples of all nations" includes 8 billion people in 195 countries. The beauty of international cities like Dubai is that God brings the nations to us for a short season of time, then unleashes people back to their home countries carrying the message of Jesus.

More people than ever in recorded history are moving outside of their home countries into global cities. In 2020, the United Nations estimated the total number of migrants, "people on the move," and expatriates "residing in a country other than their country of birth" reached over 281 million; others estimate upwards of 350 million.[1] Female migrants constituted 48 percent of the total.[2] Spanning a range of categories, the term "international migrant" includes migrant workers, international students, humanitarian migrants, and people who move abroad for lifestyle, work, or family reunification reasons.[3] If all migrants were crammed into one country, it would be the third- or fourth-largest population on the planet (just between the US and Indonesia)!

Ministry to migrants, therefore, is key to reaching the world and spreading the gospel to unreached people groups (UPGs). Due to technology and ease of travel, migrants maintain close connections with family and friends, send money back home, and remain engaged in the cultural life of the country of origin.[4] The ebb and flow of people includes money, resources, and new ideas, like the gospel!

Like many international churches in key global cities, Koinonia International Church exists to reach out to migrants. Expatriates make up roughly 90 percent of the total population of the United Arab Emirates. That's not a typo—nine out of ten people in the United Arab Emirates are from another country. Strategically placed at a crossroads of travel and business between the Western and Islamic worlds, the United Arab Emirates has wisely embraced migrants from all over the world.

Due to the high population of migrants, Koinonia International Church constantly explores intercultural understanding and tools for intercultural ministry. We have over one hundred different nationalities in our church, and we long for even greater diversity. We want all people to see God's multifaceted beauty in the nations he has brought to us, through multiculturally enriched preaching, leadership, Bible study, worship, and pathways to spiritual growth.

---

1 United Nations, "International Migration."
2 United Nations.
3 MPI, "Top Statistics."
4 MPI.

Sometimes "making disciples who make disciples" can seem complicated, but this model is simple: Displaced and disconnected migrants find a home and connection in the church and ultimately, connect with Jesus. Few people stay in the UAE forever. So we are passionate about equipping our people with the knowledge, vision, and practical skills to make intercultural disciples—and to take that good news back to their home countries, or to the next country they will call "home."

Everyone leaves, so we lead with the end in mind. One of the challenges of any international church is the high turnover of people. The volunteers, leaders, staff, the "movers and shakers"—all have a short "shelf-life" in one church. This transience can seem negative and discouraging—because "everyone went away." But we can also view it as a huge positive: This is God's way of reaching UPGs represented here in UAE and those beyond throughout the world! Instead of thinking "everyone went away," our mentality is "everyone is sent onward!"

When people leave our city, they land at the airport terminal of their next assignment. Our goal is that they are fully equipped to share the good news when they arrive. For some departing expats, this means they go to another country where they will need to learn a new language, culture, and effective techniques to share the gospel. Others leave and return to their home countries, carrying the good news of Jesus with them; they can be competent gospel heralds in their mother tongue and culture. Still others leave our city and church to return to lands less tolerant of the gospel, among peoples and places many of us will never see, but that Jesus can transform with his good news.

One man we call "David" left his home country in search of a better life in the Middle East. When he arrived, he and his family found life both challenging and empty. They had achieved the dream of expat living in one of the world's elite cities, but they were not content. David searched for answers to his deep questions and soul longings. The only answers that resonated with him were the answers of Jesus. He put his trust in Jesus and found deep satisfaction as he grew in God's family. David learned not just about Jesus, but also about the rich tapestry of the global, international family of God. He grew in his love for God and appreciation for his grace. David taught his wife and children the truths of God, and his family thrived!

In less than a year, David lost his job and had to move back to his passport country. He wrestled with what this would mean for his family and their newfound faith in a land not tolerant of his way of life. David knew he would face dire consequences. He prayed and sought God's wisdom. David was reminded of God's heart for the nations, his desire to spread the good news, and the "sent" nature of his people. With zeal and purpose, David relocated his family to their home country. In just a few weeks, as David shared the gospel, God brought more children into his family. In less than twelve months, a man named "David" migrated in search of a better life but discovered God's path to eternal life, a path that led back to his homeland with a message that would lead still others to discover the way, the truth, and the life!

Bibliography

Migration Policy Institute. "Top Statistics on Global Migration and Migrants." Last updated July 21, 2022. https://www.migrationpolicy.org/article/top-statistics-global-migration-migrants#Size%20and%20Share.

United Nations. "International Migration." Accessed May 7, 2024. https://www.un.org/en/global-issues/migration.

20

The Role of Existing Churches in an African Movement

Aychi B. R.[1]

Existing local churches play a vital role in this disciple-making movement. From the beginning of our ministry, we underlined this principle: whatever ministry we do, we make sure the church will be actively involved in kingdom ministry. Sometimes people think, "If a new church is not traditional, it won't be accepted by existing churches." I believe the key is relationship. We approach church leaders at whatever level they are on and share the bigger vision: the Great Commission. That's more than the local church, more than their neighborhood, more than their immediate context. If we share with love, relationship, and sincere motive of kingdom expression, we have found that churches will listen.

In one area, we currently have formal partnerships with 108 totally indigenous groups. Some are local churches, and some are indigenous ministries.

At the start, we approach them through informal conversation. We talk about the task God has given in the Great Commission, which leads us to formal discussion with the one responsible in the church. If they are open, we set up a training for initial exposure, which lasts two to five days. We strongly encourage them to invite the right people. We aim for about 20 percent of attendees to be people in leadership and about 80 percent practitioners. The proportion is important; we do not want to train just church leaders or just practitioners. Church leaders tend to be busy and even though they have a good heart, they do not always have time to implement what they learn; that is where the training of practitioners helps. Practitioners (i.e., field leaders or church planters) may find implementation difficult without the input from the decision makers (the church leaders), so training them together is vital.

We focus first on heart issues. We talk about the Great Commission, the unfinished task, and the challenge. Then we talk about opportunities and how we can fulfill the Great Commission. That is where the disciple-making movement strategy comes in. The final question is: "What are we going to do about this together?"

Whenever we do a training, we commit to follow-up and involve the decision makers in the development. One training event with a church is not the end. We want to walk with them on a journey. Our motto is: "Ignite, accelerate, and sustain disciple making movements." We do not stop at just igniting—we work for accelerating and sustaining.

We have a strategic coordinator and grassroots coordinators doing follow-up after trainings. At the end of each training, an action plan is laid out. A copy is given to each person who received the training and a copy to the church, as well as a copy for our ministry. The plan includes the name and phone number of the church's contact person. Our leaders

---

[1] Aychi B. R (pseudonym) is a movement leader in Africa who has been involved in cross-cultural ministry for the past twenty-four years. His passion is to see disciple-making movements ignited, accelerated, and sustained among unreached groups in Africa and beyond.

then follow up by phone—both individually with those who have taken the training and with the church's contact person. After three months, we make a formal call to follow up and learn what is happening in relation to the plan they made.

We then continue communication with those going forward in the ministry. We make sure to cultivate those relationships and provide the needed training, mentoring, and coaching. We link them with other field workers in that area, so they have a network to encourage them. Then we watch for workers who show significant potential to become a strategic coordinator for their area.

As people begin to implement, their reports from the field must pass through their church. The church must stand with it and verify what is happening. We do not want to go around the local church. We want the church involved with the ministry. That gives the church a sense of ownership and helps the relationships to grow stronger.

We always make sure to update church leaders on the progress being made. Some unreached groups being reached are quite sensitive. In those cases, the church may not need or want to be directly involved in progress with that movement. But the church will be aware of and pray for the ministry and help in appropriate ways. They also allow the new churches being planted to worship in ways that fit the new believers' cultural context and feel appropriate to the new believers.

In this process, we do not try to change the ministry patterns of the existing churches, which would just make them feel threatened. The existing church can go on as it is. Our mission priority is to reach the unreached. The paradigm shift we aim for relates to the unreached. So we challenge, train, and equip the church to reach the unreached. We communicate clearly that the church's normal patterns will not effectively engage unreached people groups. We want them to have a movement mentality and attitude towards the unreached people groups.

Sometimes that new mentality ends up coming back and transforming the whole church. Some of the church leaders also become practitioners and become movement leaders. So the paradigm sometimes impacts the local churches directly. That is just a byproduct, not our goal.

Partnering with existing churches is a critical element that has helped us accelerate the disciple-making movement. We all came from those churches, and our goal is to impact other churches and start new churches. We praise God that he is present and working in and through existing churches to bring movements of brand new churches planting churches among the unreached.

Reflection and Discussion
The Impact of People Group Thinking on Local Churches

1. What local church case study stood out to you?

2. Compare (what's similar) and contrast (what's different) the way these churches responded to the challenge of reaching unreached peoples.

3. How and why did these leaders make UPGs a priority in the life and mission of their local church?

4. How would you evaluate your church's awareness, response, and engagement with unreached and unengaged peoples?

5. What did you learn about partnership and collaboration between local churches and mission agencies? What is the distinctive role and value of each in God's redemptive plan?

6. List some lessons you learned about mobilizing the local church for strategic engagement. What is the role of leadership, mission education, prayer, training, collaboration, and other factors?

7. With whom will you share what are learning? List two or three action steps to increase your church's strategic engagement with least reached peoples.

8. Check out the "Resources" in Appendix 3. Click on the QR codes to visit websites and download videos and other resources for prayer, learning, and mobilization.

Part 5

International Multiplication

Polycentric Pioneers and Collaboration

21
Iberoamerican Missionary Partnership

The Journey of COMIBAM

Cristian Castro, Zazá Lima, and Allan Matamoros

COMIBAM was born in the aftermath of the first Ibero-American Mission Congress in São Paulo, Brazil, in 1987. This pivotal gathering brought together over thirty-two hundred delegates who collectively affirmed a transformative vision: "Ibero-America is no longer just a mission field, but also a mission force." Emerging from this significant event, COMIBAM—the Iberoamerican Missionary Partnership—began leading the Spanish- and Portuguese speaking world in prayer, dialogue, and mobilization towards God's mission.

Unlike traditional sending agencies or associations of mission agencies, COMIBAM does not claim to represent the entirety of Iberoamerican mission endeavors. Instead, it serves as a platform for dialogue and collaboration, committed to engaging churches, mission agencies, Christian organizations, and training centers in God's mission. There is a special focus on reaching the less reached people at the frontiers of his mission. This commitment includes sharing God's news with a respectful attitude that affirms and recognizes the dignity of each person and community.

As COMIBAM approaches its fortieth anniversary, we reflect on a journey in missions characterized by significant challenges but propelled by an unwavering passion for God and his kingdom. In this brief paper, we share insights from our experiences and some lessons we have learned.

Learning Resilience: Recognizing Our Vulnerabilities

Our journey has been marked by significant challenges and hardships. The Latin American missions movement experienced a "semiofficial" birth during the tumultuous 1980s—a decade characterized by civil unrest and economic difficulty across the region. This era marked a painful transition for many countries, moving from military dictatorships to more democratic regimes amid successive economic shocks. Even today, many of these nations remain fragile democracies with vulnerable economies.

In these challenging times, COMIBAM emerged. It partnered with Latin American churches even as it forged relationships with national and international networks. This collaboration underscored COMIBAM's role in blessing the nations. The Latin American missions movement thrives on the courage and persistence of those willing to serve their Lord despite tears and suffering, yet always with hope and celebration. Resilience in the face of adversity is a testament to the steadfast desire of Latin American believers to fulfill the Great Commission through both words and deeds globally. This dynamic embodies the paradox of an apostolic faith: "sorrowful, yet always rejoicing; poor, yet making many rich; having nothing, yet possessing everything" (2 Cor 6:10).

Learning from Growth: Fostering Collaboration

COMIBAM has grown into the largest umbrella network across Iberoamerica for cross-cultural missions, with a primary focus on unreached people groups. Despite adversities, evangelical growth has been remarkable across much of the hemisphere. COMIBAM has expanded through intentional dialogue, collaboration, and robust connections among churches and leaders, leading to the development of publications, training programs, forums, and member care consultations.

However, this growth has not been without challenges and temptations. Some churches and denominations appear tempted to build their own "empires" rather than focusing on the kingdom of God. Institutional growth is prioritized over collaboration with other agencies and believers in the regions where missionaries are sent. Additionally, there is the "Constantinian temptation"—the pursuit of luxurious buildings and political power, which often steers the mission away from its core objectives.[1] In some countries, these approaches have led to polarization and strained relationships, jeopardizing collaborative efforts to fulfill the Great Commission.

God's mission challenges us to overcome our "Towers of Babel." COMIBAM is committed to fostering simplicity, reciprocity, and hospitality at shared tables while embracing the risks associated with being sojourners together. COMIBAM seeks to be a beacon of unity in our diversity, steadfastly displaying values of the kingdom of God.

Learning from Our Roots: A Holistic Gospel

The roots of COMIBAM lie in both the integral mission movement and the frontier mission movement. When COMIBAM was founded, the concept of holistic missions was gaining significant traction within the Latin world. Emphasizing the comprehensive nature of the gospel through both proclamation and demonstration, this movement rapidly expanded in influence across many countries on our continent. "Holistic" or "integral" mission champions values such as justice, reconciliation, peace, and stewardship of creation—core aspects of our obedience to God and ethics that align with both the great commandment and the Great Commission. The profound impact of this movement reminds us of the broader implications of our mission and inspires us to strive for peace and justice in all our work, even in the most remote parts of the world.

At the same time, numerous voices emerged that challenged us to share the gospel to "the ends of the earth." Latin American churches began to prioritize unreached places where Jesus has not yet been announced, regardless of the risks and costs involved.

This is a tension in our ongoing journey, marked by healthy and often spirited debates among Latin American missiologists. Some express concerns that an excessive focus on social action might overshadow the core message of Jesus as Lord and Savior. Others are exploring ways to articulate the gospel through both words and deeds.

In this process, Latin Americans have discovered that our deep-rooted love for extended family, community life, friendships, and shared vulnerability have been invaluable gifts from God and bridges to peoples. These elements of an incarnational life, combined with

---
1 Freston, "Universal Church of the Kingdom of God," 33–65.

disconnection from global political agendas, have enriched our presence in the communities we serve worldwide. Our spiritual and transformational journey seeks to uphold kingdom values of humility and integrity amidst political polarization and social fragmentation.

Another COMIBAM goal is to cultivate a culture of prayerful reflection concerning the temptations of power, relevance, and pride, creating spaces where pastors, missionaries, and leaders can enhance their spiritual lives through repentance, humility, and mutual accountability. Servant leadership is nurtured through encounters, consultations, and training spaces. This transformational journey helps develop ministries rooted in community, dialogue, prayer, and reflection.

Kingdom values, however, are challenged by other influences. These include the pervasive effect of prosperity theology within many of our churches, along with risks associated with pride and managerial theologies. Triumphalist rhetoric and antagonistic attitudes toward non-Christians also undermine the principles of service and sacrifice required by our commitment to the Great Commission.

Learning to Contextualize: Affirming Our Shared Dignity

Our deep belief in the gospel's transformative power fuels our cross-cultural missionary efforts to reach the unreached. We endeavor to bear witness among diverse religious communities, including Muslims, Buddhists, Hindus, and others, with the goal of making disciples in Jesus's name. This involves a conscientious effort to contextualize the gospel, respecting the dignity of local peoples, cultures, and worldviews. While we challenge aspects of worldviews that conflict with the gospel, cross-cultural encounters also compel us to reflect critically on our own perspectives.

This area of ministry is an ongoing learning process. In Latin America, pluralism involves a spectrum of Christian denominations under the diminishing influence of the Roman Catholic Church. The challenges are different in contexts of religious pluralism and increasingly secularized environments. Workers are learning how to minister respectfully, drawing insights from our European counterparts who have navigated similar challenges.

COMIBAM encourages Iberoamerican mission agencies and workers to engage in equitable and respectful collaboration with local church expressions in various contexts. Where no established church exists, we support the foundational work of planting new churches, partnered where possible with Iberoamerican workers.

Learning from Diversity: Affirming Our Identity

As we participate in *missio Dei*, we are learning that this is God's mission, not ours. COMIBAM recognizes that his church is a global body that extends far beyond our understanding. Reaching the unreached necessitates a collective, mutual, humble, and collaborative effort from the entire church everywhere. This sense of unity, spirituality, and shared purpose inspires us to continue our work with joy and confidence in the almighty God who oversees the mission.

The diversity of Latin nations and cultures, each marked by distinct Spanish and Portuguese influences, has deeply enriched our identity. This rich legacy and historical context present COMIBAM with the challenge of creating leadership opportunities for younger Christians. Embracing new voices and vocations requires missiological reflection and an incarnational approach. This requires learning from one another, actively listening to diverse contexts and realities, and manifesting God's presence up to the very frontiers of his mission.

The Latin missions movement is committed to advancing collaboration with approximately 500,000 local churches and the wider body of over 100 million evangelicals. Already, an estimated thirty thousand cross-cultural workers are actively serving and proclaiming the gospel both locally and internationally.

Importantly, a network of twenty-five national missionary cooperation movements has emerged across the hemisphere. These national groups within COMIBAM (called CMNs) form the tangible backbone of the movement and foster mutual learning and a spirit of collaboration that drives mission forward.

Learning from People around Our Tables

Recognizing the broad scope of the Latin American missions movement, we have developed a variety of tools and micro-networks within each CMN (Cooperative Mission Network). These resources are designed to foster prayer, training, youth involvement, and active engagement with churches. Individuals from across Latin America are either embarking on or advancing their vocational journeys at universities, Bible seminaries, and missionary centers. Our efforts extend beyond local communities to include relationships with regional and national initiatives, and supporting the churches in areas that surround unreached populations.

Samuel Escobar has highlighted a significant yet often overlooked mission force: the millions of Latin American Christian migrants dispersed globally.[2] These individuals, some of whom are refugees and others who have moved for educational or economic reasons, carry with them a passion for the Lord and a readiness to serve. Remarkably, some, through their professional connections, manage to enter countries that are typically closed to Christian missions. The ongoing challenge is to effectively connect this potential mission force with local believers in their new countries and integrate them into what God is already doing there.

Learning and Sharing: Innovation, Complexity, and Diversity

In response to the diverse and complex landscape of Latin America, COMIBAM has designed its structure to facilitate and enhance adaptable missionary capacity. This approach aligns with the region's polyphonic, polyrhythmic, and heterogeneous realities.

The organization is divided into four key departments—mobilization, training, sending, and fields. Each department is further subdivided into specialized areas such as women in mission, new generations, reaching specific ethnicities, collaboration, intercession, and missiological reflection. This structures ongoing research and the development of methodologies that promote careful listening and discernment.

A main goal is to increase the effective participation of local churches in God's global mission. This involves raising the number of committed churches, active pastors, and missionaries dispatched from the continent to share the gospel across the globe. Churches in the region are learning how to provide better support and care for their missionaries, and to accept suffering and martyrdom as aspects of the missionary vocation and identification with Jesus.

---

2 Escobar, "Migration," 17–28.

COMIBAM is also creating a body of knowledge that can be shared with others in the global mission movement. This involves documenting, systematizing, and sharing missiological knowledge refined through field experience, including case studies that highlight breakthroughs in the field. An overly triumphalist tone is avoided, in favor of a narrative that celebrates progress and encourages effective learning and collaboration. This approach not only enhances COMIBAM's own missiological practices but enriches the global mission movement.

Looking Forward

Looking back on its forty-year journey, COMIBAM celebrates the commitment of Latin American churches and the faithfulness of Spirit-empowered Latin missionaries. However, the vision extends beyond these historical milestones.

The challenge today is to deepen our understanding and to step outside our comfort zones—to listen attentively to our Lord Jesus and to each other, discern the times, and love the nations. Our initial, natural enthusiasm, bursting with youthful vigor, has matured and evolved into a more realistic blend of joy and suffering, both at home and globally. Recognizing our fragility yet fortified by divine grace, we aspire to the example of the incarnate Lord Jesus. With the Apostle Paul, "We have this treasure in jars of clay to show that this all-surpassing power is from God and not from us. We are hard pressed on every side, but not crushed; perplexed, but not in despair" (2 Cor 4:7–8 NIV).

COMIBAM is driven to spread the saving gospel of Jesus to the ends of the earth. We aspire to see the gospel transform lives, societies, relationships, families, and communities and address situations of injustice. Our mission DNA—sharing the whole gospel to the whole person—guides our involvement in the Great Commission and our journey with Jesus to "the ends of the earth."

Bibliography

Escobar, S. "Migration: Avenue and Challenge to Mission." *Missiology* 31, no. 1 (2003): 17–28.

Freston, P. "The Universal Church of the Kingdom of God: A Brazilian Church Finds Success in Southern Africa." *Journal of Religion in Africa* 35, no. 1 (2005): 33–65.

22
Sub-Saharan Africa

The Sahel

John Becker

The Sahel region of Africa encompasses 90 million people in 354 Muslim unreached people groups. Spanning the area from Senegal, Mauritania, and Mali, through Burkina Faso, Niger, Chad, and Sudan, to Ethiopia and Eritrea, between the Sahara to the north and tropics to the south, this region has been a zone of conflict for decades. Jihadist insurgencies, counterinsurgencies, and political instability, matched with economic decline, crime, and violence, have increased the rate of displacement and migration.[1]

One region in the Sahel is currently considered the world's largest and worst humanitarian crisis. Over 25 million people need humanitarian assistance, and more than 10 million have been displaced. Tragically, this escalation follows decades of genocidal atrocities against specific populations in the country's western and southern regions.[2] Although the national church has suffered immense persecution, it remains resilient and committed to seeing its broken nation transformed by the gospel.[3]

Alignment around a Shared Vision

In 2014, a shared vision led several national leaders to unite with international friends to form a coalition. This motivated several courageous indigenous leaders to return to their native homelands after living years as displaced refugees. The agreed-on priority focus was reaching the multiplicity of tribes in the mountainous region in the south.

The leaders asked a series of questions: What current challenges and strategic opportunities to multiply disciples do we face in our nation? What can we do together that cannot be done by any of our organizations independently? What collective resources could we bring to the table and leverage for greater gospel advance?

The coalition was based on five building blocks:

- Aligned vision: agreement on direction, focus, and measurable results, and a clear, compelling, contagious vision
- Trusted relationships: based on shared values, a servant mindset, authenticity, and accountability

---

1 Council of Foreign Relations, "Violent Extremism in the Sahel." See maps in Appendix 2.
2 Sources: UNCHR IDP-DTM/IOMs and Refugees; https://operationbrokensilence.org/.
3 Open Doors, "World Watch List 2024." Ranked eighth on "The World Watch List" on Open Doors's annual ranking of the fifty countries where Christians face the most extreme persecution.

- Complementary contributions: offering one another unique skills, resources, and time, with unselfish humility
- Commitment to action: proactive leadership engagement and participation
- Common practices: defined roles, processes, and responsibilities, prayer, communication, reports, and evaluation

Peoples, Priorities, and Prayer

The coalition's focus area is sixty-one thousand square miles, roughly the size of the US state of Georgia, with fourteen major administrative centers. The population ranges from 2 to 3 million, not counting the recently returned internally displaced people (IDP) reported to number around 400,000. The area contains a few thousand unmarked villages and forty major towns.

Between eighty-seven and ninety-six distinct people groups inhabit the area. Twenty-three peoples have existing churches, a few of them with large numbers of believers. There are three local Bible colleges training local leaders for the ministry.

Our coalition rallied around a holistic approach with four strategic priorities or "pillars": gospel engagement of the unreached, relief, capacity building, and education. During our second annual consultation, we met in a large refugee camp on the border. During our week of meetings, five simple church buildings were burned down by radical fundamentalists within the camp. But more surprising than the proximity of the persecution was the response of our local brothers and sisters. Instead of bitterness and anger towards the perpetrators, there was a greater resolve to let their light shine—not only where the church was already present, but among the remaining least reached peoples and places in their beloved mountainous homeland.

As we began to work together, we increased our prayer together. Norman Johnson, coalition member and founder of a national prayer mobilization network, initiated a weekly three-hour Friday virtual prayer gathering. For the past three years, Friday prayer has become the highlight of coalition members. Twice each year we also have three days of prayer and fasting. The result was growing unity, Spirit-led strategies, and a miraculous move of God.

Collaboration to Engage

Over the last decades, people group data from the region has swirled in confusing crosscurrents. War, lack of infrastructure, and poor communication have all played a role in the resulting fuzzy picture. In response, the coalition initiated a systematic survey of every county and subcounty. Despite the initial lack of accurate data, coalition partners collaboratively hosted awareness workshops and disciple multiplication training.

Through the Global Alliance for Church Multiplication (GACX), alliance member organizations, such as Africa Inland Mission, The Timothy Initiative (TTI), and Christ Commission Fellowship (CCF), caught a vision for the region. Trainers came from as far away as the Philippines. The organizations implemented MC2 training, a biblical disciple-making and church-planting movement (DMM/CPM) process developed by Cru that is centered on multiplying disciples.

Jim Welchel, MC2 trainer and mission pastor of CCF, reflected:

> One of the cool things that the coalition has done is help us highlight other organizations interested in doing DMM training in the area. When we work together, rather than in competition, we are more fruitful, and there is unity. We pray together, work together, are on the same team, and all do this for the kingdom.

The result? By coordinating efforts and facilitating cooperation rather than competition, coalition partners have made disciples among over sixty different tribes, including eleven previously unengaged unreached people groups (UUPG). More than fifteen hundred small groups and house churches have been birthed.

Incredibly, unlike many other Muslim-dominated areas, the local autonomous government has welcomed Christian missions. Several Muslim villages in the focus area have expressly welcomed us: "Come live among us. Plant a church here."

Survey Teams Confirm Data and Clarify the Task

In November 2023, led by Nathan Coles and Yassir Hussain, partners from the Greater Nuba ACTSion Coalition (GNAC) trained a team of ten experienced field workers around the four priorities (gospel, relief, education, capacity building). After the training, they were outfitted with motorbikes, tents, fuel, and paperwork and sent out.

In each county and subcounty, survey teams met with top officials to review preliminary data; this helped us understand which people groups lived in which subcounty. For each unique people group with no record of gospel engagement, the survey team gathered with the tribe's paramount chief and tribal elders for an in-depth interview. In this way, the survey team was able to confirm or revise the data, determining if the people group names on the draft list were a unique tribe or clan. They also confirmed gospel engagement.

By year's end, under very difficult conditions, they had completed three rounds of field work. The complete reports submitted confirmed that fifty-three tribes are unengaged unreached people groups (UUPGs). These are people groups with no known churches, no known missions working amongst them, and most with no known believers.[4] The coalition's approach underscores the value of rigorous, grassroots, field-based research.

Scripture Engagement, Mobilization, and Sending

The survey also resulted in an unprecedented multilingual Scripture engagement strategy led by Harvest Mission Ethiopia. In 2023, Executive Director Zetseat Fekadu mobilized five of the major Bible translation ministries to partner with national believers for the advancement of Bible translation, Jesus Film and Scripture engagement, and language development for a region that has as many as 199 language variants. Strategies such as oral Bible translation (OBT) and Multiplying Hope trauma healing groups are being deployed with incredible success. In fact, during one trauma healing OBT training with five language groups, the soldiers providing

---

4 The UUPG survey has confirmed thirty-eight tribes believed to be UUPGs. Of these, thirty-one groups are new to the IMB database at peoplegroups.org. IMB has been helpful in confirming these new groups and adding them to their database. There are still an additional twenty-two tribes believed to be UUPGs, but they have not yet been surveyed. We are thankful to IMB and Joshua Project for their readiness to respond to the field survey.

security for the groups pleaded with the trainers, "You must do this trauma healing with us! We are all traumatized and we need this!"

The coalition's aim is to see every UUPG in the country successfully engaged with the gospel through what we call Transformational Community Development (i.e., holistic, integral strategies that bring transformation). We want to see the gospel finally come to every UUPG, a church established in every village within that tribe, and those who believe growing to maturity in Christ.

To this end the National Missionary Training Center (NMTC) has been established, along with a national missionary field support structure. By mid-November 2023, the national council of churches had cast the UUPG vision to dozens of area churches and denominations from nearby already reached tribes. Men and women who caught the vision arrived. A week later, the NMTC opened with seventeen new candidates, and three months of intense training commenced.

Training is divided into Bible training for worldview transformation, DMM ministry skills, Kingdom Business livelihood training,[5] and ADAPT community agricultural training.[6] The NMTC team is comprised of experienced missionaries and skilled trainers from various African and international mission organizations that are coalition members.

Together, coalition partners are dedicated to trusting God with everything needed to begin to engage every UUPG. Entry strategies will vary according to need and effectiveness. National missionaries are expected to live with the focus people group. Kingdom Business, a micro-business agricultural-based model, has worked effectively in this area, and this will be the initial entry strategy. Other options will be explored depending on the needs of the area, the receptivity of the tribe, and the ability of the national missionaries to gain access.

Expanding to Other Regions

In one of the most conflicted regions in the world, despite protracted conflict, poverty, and instability, God is at work. Ten years of interagency collaboration between local and international member ministries has not only catalyzed fruitful gospel advance among unengaged peoples but has also stirred a commitment to expand to other regions in the nation with significant unreached populations.

Bibliography

Council of Foreign Relations Center for Preventive Action. "Violent Extremism in the Sahel." Updated February 14, 2024. https://www.cfr.org/global-conflict-tracker/conflict/violent-extremism-sahel.

Open Doors. "World Watch List 2024." Accessed April 30, 2024. https://www.opendoors.org/en-US/persecution/countries/.

---

5 Kingdom Business training is a process created by Activate Global and coached by 3P Ministries members.
6 ADAPT stands for Agriculture Development Aquaculture Production for Transformation.

23
"Lord, Stir Us Up!"

The Acceleration of the Nigerian Missions Movement

Mike Adegbile and Adeoluwa Olanrewaju

The motivation behind the formation of the Nigeria Evangelical Missions Association (NEMA), the umbrella body of the Nigeria Missions Movement, can be summed up in the words of Steve Moore, former president and CEO of Missio Nexus, "The Great Commission is too big for anyone to accomplish alone and too important not to try to do together."

Beginnings

The association was formed in 1982 at a time when only a few church denominations in Nigeria had mission structures and there were less than ten indigenous mission organizations. A few visionary young leaders saw the need for the Nigerian churches to work collaboratively to help fulfill the biblical mandate to take the gospel to all the world's unreached peoples. They came together and formed an organization with the vision statement: "To see a completed Great Commission through the active involvement of the Nigerian Church and Missions Movement in all the unreached nations of the world."

From the outset, the association was committed to collaborative efforts focused on the Great Commission. Worthy of mention among their initiatives is the research effort to identify the unreached peoples of Nigeria. The first attempt at this was published in 1985. It identified eighty-two Nigerian unreached and unengaged peoples and helped the NEMA leaders focus on strategic mapping to reach these groups. NEMA also organized nationwide meetings, such as Mission Awareness Conferences and Go Festivals (GoFest), which helped mobilize the workforce for mission agencies. The 1998 GoFest had about ten thousand participants, mostly students and young people, and many of the current Nigerian missionaries are products of these mobilization campaigns.

The Searchlight Project and Vision 5015

NEMA's research efforts advanced into what was called The Searchlight Project, the next step toward ensuring that all the unreached and unengaged groups in Nigeria were not only identified but also engaged. In 2005, this effort assumed a new aspect in response to worldwide attention to the 10/40 Window. NEMA leaders called for a solemn assembly where they reflected and challenged one another on the role that the missions movement in the Nigerian church needed to play in engaging the 10/40 Window. This culminated in Vision 5015. The goal of Vision 5015 was to mobilize at least fifty thousand partners from the Nigerian church and to send and support at least fifteen thousand workers to thirty-four mostly Islamic countries, beginning in north Nigeria to the gateway to North Africa (Sahel) and farther on into North Africa (Maghreb), the Horn of Africa, the Arabian Peninsula, and Jerusalem neighborhood within fifteen years. The leading strategy in achieving this vision was to catalyze collaboration among the Nigerian mission senders and receivers in the target countries.

Seeing clearly that their lofty vision could only be achieved through collaborative efforts, NEMA leaders concentrated on identifying opportunities for cooperation, in addition to aggressive mobilization and training. In 2020, when the Vision 5015 initiative was evaluated, four thousand missionaries were deployed to thirty-one of the thirty-four countries. This was short of the target but a significant achievement and strong evidence of the possibilities of pushing the frontiers through collaboration. The Vision 5015 initiative has now been rebranded Vision 5015 Plus, and NEMA is building on its past successes to fully achieve its original goal.

Tackling the Remaining Task in Nigeria

As work on the Vision 5015 project continued, it dawned on those of us involved that there were still pressing needs on the home front. Despite previous efforts, there were still unreached and unengaged peoples in Nigeria. We felt a burden to be good stewards of the huge investment the Lord had made in this country of 55 million evangelicals. Surely the Nigerian church had sufficient resources to ensure that no people group was left unengaged. While continuing to pursue the Vision 5015 project, we called for a meeting of Nigerian missions organizations to determine the scope of the remaining task in-country and the best ways to address it. We worked together to evaluate local and global data sources and authenticated the data by visiting the identified unengaged and unreached peoples.

At the same time, the leadership of NEMA began to visit churches, church leaders, and mission organizations who had the capacity or potential capacity to take up the task of engaging the unengaged peoples in Nigeria. It did not matter to us whether these groups were officially registered members of the association; our intention was not to imprint our "brand" on the initiative but to share our vision and to inspire others to take up the grand task to which God was calling us.

These visits made clear that we needed to call for a national strategy consultation, which we did in 2017. It was tagged "Go North" because all remaining unengaged and unreached peoples of Nigeria were in the northern part of the country. While NEMA is strategically headquartered in the north, the Nigerian church's presence was far greater in the south. The Go North Consultation was therefore held in Lagos in southwest Nigeria and coincidently (or perhaps providentially) near the town of Badagry, the entry point of the first attempt to reach the country by evangelical Thomas Birch Freeman in 1842.

Over five hundred church and mission leaders attended the consultation. Speakers included frontline missionaries from the Arab Maghreb region in northwestern Africa. The research report on the state of the Nigerian harvest was presented, as well as the capability of the Nigerian church to respond to the remaining task.

We had approached this crucial meeting trusting in the Lord to "stir us up" in the spirit of Haggai 1:14 (NIV), "So the LORD stirred up … the spirit of the whole remnant of the people. They came and began to work on the house of the LORD Almighty, their God." And this is exactly what happened! By the end of the consultation, the common question on the hearts and lips of participants was: "What shall we then do?"

In February 2018, a follow-up consultation was held in the northern part of the country. The primary goal of the meeting was to secure engagement for the seven remaining unengaged peoples in Nigeria. Mission leaders in attendance were challenged to adopt the unengaged groups and, in one sitting, the engagements were secured. Follow-ups were also planned to ensure that the commitments were translated into action.

The Outcome

The Ural[1] in north-central Nigeria were adopted by a mission group that had been working nearby but was unaware that the Ural were unengaged. Another denominational group had established a church in the traditional headquarters of the Ural but had not made a deliberate effort to engage them. This church was happy to join forces with the adopting mission group. Interestingly, a Bible translation and Scripture engagement organization heard about this effort and asked how they could take part in the work. What a joy it was to have three organizations working together to reach a previously unengaged people group.

The Ploawa groups in north-central and northwest Nigeria are largely Muslim. They had been unengaged until a mission agency adopted them and deployed a missionary couple to work among them. Ploawa is one of the most difficult places in the world for Christian outreach, and it became apparent that an access ministry was needed to build relationships within the community. NEMA engaged to explore the possibilities of language preservation and oral Bible translation. This approach has been successful. The Christian workers are well accepted, and secret disciples are being multiplied.

The Rumage live in northeast Nigeria. One of the NEMA mission agencies adopted them and deployed a missionary couple who learned of a church-based mission nearby. After the couple shared their purpose in coming to the area, they began to work with the mission, such that their converts were received into the church. In 2019, a student and youth mission-focused organization sent more than one hundred young people on a monthlong, short-term outreach among the Rumage. The young women taught the women and young girls how to make home care supplies (e.g., soap, cream, perfumes, air fresheners, etc.). The young men went to farm with the Rumage men, exposing them to modern farm techniques such as composting. The Lord blessed the youthful energy, zeal, and creativity of these young people. A good number of the Rumage made decisions for the Lord and became part of the local church.

The Wudai live in a totally closed area in the extreme northeast of Nigeria. Their language is almost extinct. A mission agency responded to the call to adopt them and deployed a missionary to the area. The agency did not have adequate resources to send or sustain the missionary on the field. A nearby church mission team aided him, and another mission support group placed him on a stipend and began visiting him regularly. Three organizations brought together by NEMA helped kick off the engagement by organizing a medical outreach among the Wudai. The resident missionary was trained in a common business in the area—fish smoking and selling—and he was equipped with the resources to open two locally cooled shops. Christians trained in disciple making manned the shops and used them as access ministry platforms. The results have been encouraging.

---

1 The people group names are pseudonyms due to the sensitivity of the specialized work among them and for the security of current workers.

The Sabi live in north-central Nigeria. A church-based mission group committed to adopting them but failed to follow through. NEMA therefore encouraged another church-based group working nearby to adopt the Sabi, and they responded positively. Their resident missionary was given training in disciple-making movement (DMM), and he reports that the training made the work easier as ordinary believers from other people groups were excited to reach the Sabi.

The unreached Dugo are in northeast Nigeria. One of the prominent NEMA member agencies committed to engage them, but just before moving in, they received the good news that a leading church group in the region had deployed a missionary to the Dugo. This was the same situation with the Gwarya in north-central Nigeria.

Within eleven months of the 2017 Go North Consultation, all identified unengaged groups were engaged. While continuing to monitor progress among these groups, NEMA has begun a new campaign called "No Place Left." Its goal is to reach the seventy-three unreached peoples identified in the 2017 collaborative research survey. Our December 2023 research update shows that forty-three unreached and least evangelized peoples remain in Nigeria.

The association continues to challenge its member agencies on the need for unrelenting engagement. NEMA also carries out periodic training and mobilization campaigns, raising resources and connecting member agencies to support groups who are providing either resources or access ministry opportunities.

In the last four years, NEMA has stepped up its commitment to Bible translation and Scripture engagement. Nigeria initially ranked third among countries with Scripture needs. NEMA is currently working through its agencies and, in collaboration with Bible translation support groups, on translations into twenty-seven languages, mostly among unreached and gospel-needy groups. Another ten language groups are in the pipeline for Bible translation projects in 2024. Many of these groups have been inaccessible by the traditional forms of missional engagement. The way to these groups is paved by Bible translation, Scripture engagement, language development, and especially collaboration between mission organizations willing to work among the people as well as translate the Bible.

Lessons Learned

Mission work is most effective when it is approached collaboratively. The body of Christ may appear fragmented, but fragmentation can be overcome when the work is approached in the spirit of Christian love. NEMA's success proves that this is not wishful thinking. Going solo is an unnatural, unbiblical approach that makes our God-given task harder to accomplish.

Vision casting can be a catalyst for effective collaboration. For this to happen, people need inspiration with a vision to accomplish something tangible and worth pursuing. We need a kingdom-sized vision convincing enough to inspire diverse groups with different priorities. Without such a vision, collaboration becomes burdensome and befuddling. In the Nigerian mission experience, the vision that has united disparate groups is the goal of counting down to zero the number of unreached and unengaged peoples as well as ensuring that no place, person, or language is left out.

Facilitating collaboration requires honesty, sincerity, and transparency. There must be no attempt to deceive or manipulate people or organizations to achieve personal interests. Trust must be built around the pursuit of a common goal.

Missional collaboration requires information to be shared and secured. Information is necessary for effective decision-making and must not be hoarded within collaborating structures. At the same time, when considering the dissemination of information outside those structures, discretion and discernment are needed as many of the remaining unreached peoples are in security risk locations.

To be effective, collaboration must occur in an open atmosphere. Everyone and every group have a share in the work and of the harvest, each according to their capacity, gifting, and specialization. Collaboration must be approached in such a way that everyone is excited to make their contributions in strategic ways.

Collaboration must be for the glory of God. Former US President Harry Truman famously said, "It's amazing what you can accomplish if you don't care who gets the credit." This must be true of collaborative mission work. Whether the collaboration is between local or international partners, God must receive all the glory. Many are wary of collaborating because they feel they would become subservient in the process. The idea of the bigger partner or donor taking the credit or lording it over smaller partners must be discarded. The only ambition of our hearts must be for God to be glorified.

Conclusion

Collaboration for NEMA, as a national mission network, is not just a slogan. It is a key strategy for affirming our submission to the Lord of the harvest and how he wants the Great Commission to be completed. This approach has helped to reduce duplication of effort, maximize the deployment and usage of available resources, and effectively utilize the contributions of different groups toward meeting a common challenge. The Nigerian church and its mission movement is an emerging mission force that has been hugely blessed with potential, resources, specialties, and ingenuity that can accelerate the completion of the Great Commission. The harmonization of these advantages towards our common pursuit is key. We must keep learning, trusting, and working together. This is the blessing that the Nigeria Evangelical Missions Association has been and will continue to be to the Nigeria Missions Movement.

24
When Collaboration Blooms

Reaching India's Muslims

Martin Hall

It started with fasting and fellowship, feasting and friendship. The year was 2003. Seven leaders from five different mission organizations asked God how we could see Revelation 5:9 fulfilled. They asked the Lord, "How could we set aside competition in place of collaboration to see an effective church-planting movement started among every Muslim people group?" By God's grace, collaboration increased, and by 2007, seventy-eight mission organizations came together to ask God for wisdom in starting movements among the Muslim unreached. We began to pool our data and identify the scope of the work before us.

Having established a platform for collaboration, we began tracking which Muslim people groups (MPGs) were unengaged (no one working among them) and under-engaged (insufficient cross-cultural workers among them), and those that had no church and no in-culture witness. Three major "clusters" emerged that encompassed the majority of all unreached Muslim people groups (MUPGs): North India, Sudan and Chad, and Indonesia. Starting church-planting movements would require focused efforts on these three regions. The Vision 5:9 (V59) network decided to hold assemblies in each of the three cluster regions.

In 2007, OM had small indigenous teams focused on church planting among MUPGs in two of these clusters. I will focus here on the North India cluster and how we built a partnership so that India's Muslims might worship alongside us at the throne of the Lamb.

Collaboration Begins

In 2009, I took the train to Bangalore where the V59 network assembled. We had sought to include local Indian mission agencies focused on sharing with their Muslim neighbors and invited as many as we could find. Twelve organizations joined us at the assembly. Unfortunately, however, none of the Indian missions were willing to share their work or their vision! All those present refused, expressing their suspicion of the others.

My friend and I decided to begin sharing. We openly presented the work of our ninety-eight church planters focused on Muslims. My friend talked about their work and fruitfulness.

Suddenly, the other leaders became willing to stand and present on the work of their organizations. Everyone became excited about the potential of partnership, and we formed a small leadership team for V59 India.

Collaboration Grows

However, in 2011, when V59 gathered in Indonesia, we realized that little collaboration had taken place over the last three years. On the penultimate day of this assembly, Brother Biswajit came and informed me that I was to host an early breakfast meeting for the Indian mission leaders. He said, "We need an outsider, an honest broker, to help us come together."

By the end of breakfast, the Indian leaders decided that a "launch consultation" was needed. This was to be the first all Indian Muslim missions conference. But there was much debate over who would be the speaker (i.e., the main "attraction"). We were at an impasse. Then someone suggested George Verwer (founder of OM), and everyone enthusiastically agreed. They settled on a date and venue and told me to "tell George to come in February next year."

Since being deported from India years prior, George had only been back to India once, so it was with some misgiving that I called him and relayed the request. I was speechless at his reply. "I haven't told anyone, but in a prayer time last month, I decided to be in North India in February next year. I want to celebrate the anniversary of our first outreach in India, a team led by Greg Livingstone amongst the Muslims of Delhi," he said.

So it was that in Lucknow in February 2012, the Vision 5.9 India partnership launched. One hundred twenty Indian church planters and missions leaders working among Muslims met to begin exploring what they could do together that they could never do apart.

They asked for my input, so I attended their leadership gatherings. But I insisted that I sit outside the table, joining only when they reached an impasse and wanted an "outside" perspective. What they built needed to be completely Indian, not an Indian veneer on a Western model. Their first two attempts based on hierarchical leadership models failed. They asked for our input. The leaders then decided to appoint people to a variety of roles within the network based on their skills and capacity. A chairperson was appointed who had proven track record of partnership and leadership of an indigenous mission movement. The Lucknow meeting was a tipping point for the Indian V59 network.

Collaboration Blooms

Another memory imprinted in my mind is from my arrival at the 2017 India Missions Association (IMA) in Calcutta. I watched seven Indian mission leaders greet each other with great excitement—what a contrast from their earlier distrust! Leaders who had viewed each other as competitors now met as partners in a common task. They saw the value of collaboration.

The leaders came together in Calcutta to host seventy denominational leaders from across India. The topic was "reaching neighbors." The head of India Methodist mission, the superintendent of Assemblies of God for Hyderabad, an ACI bishop, and other influential leaders attended. Acting alone, none of the small Indian Muslim-focused missions could have called such a meeting, but together and in their partnership with the IMA, they saw something happen.

From my perspective, the meetings were vibrant, but long and a little chaotic. However, I have never been to a more effective missions conference. The head of the Methodist church mission spontaneously led in a call for corporate repentance for neglecting to take the gospel to India's Muslims. Another leader arranged a conference for five hundred of his pastors for "envisioning and equipping." For another three hours, leaders shared testimonies about their "paradigm shifts" regarding the least reached. They made pledges. Tangible planning took place. It was effective chaos.

Nurturing Collaboration

Since 2017, Vision 5:9 India has become a strong missions movement. What lessons can we learn from their journey about collaboration in taking the gospel to the least reached peoples?

First, networks need to be indigenous. Outsiders can have a valuable coaching role, but if we intentionally or unintentionally insist on imposing "outsider," far-culture strategies and methodologies, the local networks will not flourish. Second, networks thrive and collaboration flows where friendships form and relationships grow. Third, failure is sometimes necessary for success, so perseverance is crucial. There will be occasions when we accidentally create barriers to collaboration by failing to recognize our own cultural and denominational bias or when rivalries and past hurts go unresolved and unforgiven. Fourth, collaboration requires true humility in which we focus on others more than ourselves. Finally, expect to be amazed at the blessings our Trinitarian God pours out when we work together to see his kingdom come.

25
Facing Roadblocks on the Indian Road

A Closer Look

Sushil Tyagi

There are many reasons that South Asia, India in particular, is called "the final frontier of missions." The dizzying cultural diversity, hundreds of languages and dialects, castes, clans, races, and religions, all contribute to the challenge of missions there. Sadly, differences and divisions have dominated the Indian missions movement and denominations.

Pride creates roadblocks to collaboration. Collaboration begins at the point where we see that the kingdom of God is much larger than our egos, personal beliefs, and cultural superiority. Jesus is our example; he gave up his superiority and showed great humility on earth, even willing to meet with a Samaritan woman at the well. We need to have the mindset of Jesus. In the process of establishing partnerships in India, it has been important to identify the roadblocks and hindrances we face in reaching the least reached with the gospel.

Recognizing the Immensity of the Task

Collaboration requires a recognition of the immensity of the task to reach the least reached. An African proverb says, "If you want to go fast, go alone. If you want to go far, go together." We cannot do it alone—we must go far. Some decades ago, when I was a young person, I led a team to share the good news in North India. We visited villages and towns without any Christian witnesses. We were driven by passion, but quickly realized we needed help! We invited a local Cru team to join us. With our local knowledge, we prepared them to show the Jesus Film in the village's language. We then introduced the seekers to known local believers for follow-up, linking them with Scripture-producing organizations to receive materials for discipleship. Through this early experience of interorganizational collaboration, we were able to build trust within the community, which led to a huge increase in the effectiveness of our ministries.

Roadblocks

In early 2000, only a handful of national workers were engaged in reaching unengaged, unreached Muslim people groups in India. This was due to several factors: First, there was a lack of trust between the national agencies; second, a lack of knowledge on unreached Muslim people groups; third, in the absence of fellowship across mission organizations and denominations, we lacked training and tools; and finally, attitudes of cultural and social superiority, regionalism, and a fear of losing both donors and workers prevented partnerships from forming. Satan had blinded our eyes to see the greater task we would accomplish if we could put our differences aside and serve together.

After attending Vision 5:9 Network assemblies (between 2007–2012) and closely observing the trends, it was evident that things must change, and roadblocks must be removed. But how?

The Road to Collaboration

It has been said, "If you want to move the mountain, start by clearing stones." We started by holding small awareness gatherings. Regional gatherings helped build trust and relationships between individuals, agencies, and churches. Many were excited to share their stories of what the Lord was doing in different places and through different ministries. From these stories, we identified what worked and what did not, and began to see the recurring principles and patterns that lead to success (what have been called "fruitful practices"). The trust-building environment led to greater openness and honesty between agencies and individuals, each of which was struggling with effectiveness in reaching the unreached. Regional cooperation groups began to meet for fellowship and to share information about the people groups living in the area they served.

Collaboration Step-by-Step

Regional gatherings paved the way for workers to meet together for prayer and to share information. This made it easier for those producing resources to distribute them and have direct interaction with field workers. Feedback led to revised, more effective materials and the identification of gaps between the available resources and the needs of the field. Regional groups worked together to provide translators for audio and printed resources. These collaborative efforts resulted in the growth of each ministry. On the last day of one such regional gathering, a senior couple hugged me and cried saying, "We have never seen so many Muslim-background believers together in our lifetime. Thank you for providing us with this opportunity."

At these gatherings, regional leaders were encouraged to share their wisdom by hosting seminars for missions mobilization at local churches. Local churches, professionals, and even mission agencies caught the vision to prioritize the unreached peoples living in their area. Those interested were then equipped with the necessary training before they began their outreach.

A Long Way to Go, Together

After seven years of these Vision 5:9 gatherings, awareness seminars, fellowship meetings, and trainings, we finally trusted each other enough to move to the next level: financial partnership in various ministries and projects. These efforts provided a morale boost and encouragement, and in the following seven years have led to a 100 percent increase in national workers within India.

Looking back, this fourteen-year journey has been pivotal. In these years, we learned step-by-step how to overcome roadblocks to collaboration. By God's grace, we have grown in our "partnership in the gospel" (Phil 1:5), mutually giving and receiving in relationships of increasing trust and support, that those who have not heard may hear and obey him. We still have a long way to go, but we are going together.

26
From Research to Movement

Partnership in Southeast Asia

Yahya Ilyas

In our large Southeast Asian country, two factors played a vital role in launching the frontier missions movement among unreached peoples in this majority-Muslim nation. First, for over three decades, our nation has had a massive, cross-denominational prayer movement. This national prayer movement nurtured unity among the body of Christ and fostered ministry among the unreached people groups (UPGs). This prayer movement also brought a realization that we cannot separate societal transformation from spiritual transformation among the diverse ethnolinguistic groups in our nation.

A second critical factor was the Lausanne II Congress in Manila in 1989, which called the church to reach out to unreached people groups. Thomas Wang's description of the people group strategy and the importance of research, along with the Manila Manifesto published at the end of the Congress, helped inspire research efforts focused on unreached people groups within our country.

As a result, in 1991, several international mission agencies and local mission practitioners began research on neglected peoples in our nation. To lay a foundation, those involved agreed to define an unreached people group as having less than 1 percent of the population who believe in Christ. Also, research was limited at that time to people groups having a population greater than ten thousand people.

The results were staggering. The initial research determined that our nation encompassed 132 UPGs in twenty-three clusters. Seventy-four percent of the national population were within those UPGs. Among those groups, only about 0.04 percent of the population confessed faith in Christ.

From Research to Missions Movement

The research results were published in a booklet designed to mobilize local churches across the country to pray for the UPGs of this land. In 1996, a major missions event near the capital, the Caring Love Consultation, introduced the concept of UPGs to local churches and ministries and mobilized prayer for them. The conference was attended by 420 people from forty-six denominations and ministry institutions, as well as international mission agencies.

In subsequent years, similar conferences were held, with more participants and denominations. The fourth national consultation, held in 2000, had 750 attending, including members from ninety-three denominations. Meanwhile, initiatives emerged to adopt these UPGs, beginning with prayer and continuing toward on-the-ground ministry among them. To accomplish this, our national network initiated five efforts.

The first was to form regional networks in major cities of the country. These cross-denominational regional networks functioned to generate UPG mission awareness among churches in those regions. The regional networks now conduct regional consultations and missions mobilizer training. Those who complete training are expected to mobilize their respective churches for involvement in reaching the unreached.

The second effort was the preparation of training materials about outreach to UPGs. Our national network produced three such courses: "Blessed to Be a Blessing" (a contextual "Perspectives" family course), "Business as Mission," and "Professionals as Mission." These courses, held in local churches, increase awareness of UPG work and the potential for various roles in outreach.

The third effort was student mobilization—building mission awareness among students through missions conferences. As these university students complete their education, they can play a key role in the marketplace. We believe missions awareness among Christian students can have a major impact on missions work in the future.

The fourth effort has been to rally prayer movements for UPG work. This task force mobilizes prayer specifically for missions, collaborating with the Children's Prayer Network, Women's Prayer Network, and City Prayer Network.

The fifth effort has been to continuously update research on the status of UPGs in this country. In 1996, when the results of our research began to be disseminated, only twenty-one of the 127 UPGs in our country (with greater than ten thousand population) had Great Commission workers serving among them. By 2011, 105 of those 127 UPGs were engaged by workers and teams.

The years since then have brought encouraging developments; still, a huge task remains. On one hand, an increased number of least reached people groups are gaining access to the gospel. On the other hand, twenty-two of the 127 UPGs still remain unengaged. Therefore, one of our primary efforts is to continue mobilizing ministry among our country's remaining unengaged people groups.

Lessons Learned

We praise God for the important lessons he has taught us about UPG ministry in this large Southeast Asian country:

- The importance of *prayer* movements nationwide. The advance of UPG ministry across our nation cannot be separated from the development of an integrated, cross-denominational prayer movement here.

- The importance of involving the *church* in missionary work. Local churches in our nation have significant resources. Increased missions awareness among them can increase active involvement in completing the Great Commission.

- The importance of healthy *cooperation* among mission agencies and churches. We have experienced effective cooperation and partnership among diverse groups within Christ's body. This partnership has enabled us to build missions awareness, conduct research, develop service strategies, provide member care, and encourage contextual Bible translation—all of which have contributed to advances in taking the news of Christ's kingdom to our nation's unreached peoples.

27
Diaspora Peoples in Europe

Simon Lunt

The continent of Europe continues to draw significant numbers of refugees and migrants. As of January 2023, 27.3 million people (6.1 percent) of the 448.8 million people living in the European Union (EU) were non-EU citizens. Many of these "peoples on the move" come from Muslim-majority homelands and represent unreached people groups. How the church and mission agencies respond and the ways we collaborate will have a major bearing on the effectiveness of our outreach as the hands and feet of Christ.

The Hidden Faces of Europe

Diaspora peoples come to Europe from all over the world for a variety of reasons. Some are "push" factors and others "pull" factors including:

- Feelings of desperation due to famine, war, oppression, injustice
- Seeking asylum and fear from terrorists
- Economic hardships at home
- The hope of finding a better life in Europe
- Desire for employment or education
- Need for money to send back home to help family and relatives

In recent years Europe has experienced a record influx of asylum seekers fleeing conflicts in Syria and other predominantly Muslim countries. This wave of Muslim migrants has prompted debate about immigration and security policies in numerous countries. It has also raised questions about the current and future number and status of Muslims in Europe. According to the Pew Research Center, Muslims are expected to make up 8 percent of Europe's population by 2030.[1] Migration and demographics are primary factors. Muslims are much younger and have more children than other Europeans; 50 percent are under the age of thirty, compared with 32 percent of non-Muslims in Europe.[2]

Engaging the Muslim Diaspora

Across Europe, mission agencies and churches are responding in many different ways to this opportunity to engage. The Welcome Churches initiative in the UK is a large network of over fourteen hundred churches committed to welcoming refugees through a range of projects serving the different needs of refugees, asylum seekers, and migrants. "Christians are called to love and welcome the stranger, whatever their cultural background. Every church has theprivilege and opportunity to welcome and care for refugees and asylum seekers in some way."[3]

---

[1] Pew Research Center, "Future of the Global Muslim Population."
[2] Pew Research Center, "5 Facts about the Muslim Population in Europe."
[3] Welcome Churches, "Vision and Values."

Mahabba, another initiative birthed in the UK, is a relational network of Christians "giving people of Muslim heritage the opportunity to find and follow Jesus." Local groups across the country have been set up for prayer and to equip Christians to reach out. Mahabba groups have been initiated in other European countries. Their vision is "to see ministry among people of Muslim heritage as a normal part of church life."[4]

Collaboration

Over 150 Christian organizations across Europe are working specifically with Muslim outreach. In recent years several networks in Europe have emerged, convening gatherings aimed at helping workers more effectively engage Muslims on European soil. For example, Hope for Europe (2010), the European Leadership Forum (2011-2015), the European Evangelical Alliance (EEA), and European Evangelical Missionary Alliance (EEMA) (2016), and in southern Europe, Blue Med (annually) have encouraged workers to express Christ's love and compassion to Muslims.

Complementing these efforts is the Vision 5:9 network. In 2003, five mission organizations met together to wait on God and to explore how partnering together might help advance the kingdom among all Muslim peoples everywhere. The network they founded, now involving over 180 Western and Majority World organizations, draws its name and aim from Revelation 5:9, the eschatological scene of worship from persons from "every tribe and language and people and nation."

In 2012, Vision 5:9 brought together immigrant and international ministry decision makers in Europe to crowdsource the challenge of Europe's remaining unengaged Muslim people groups. This Diaspora Peoples in Europe (DPE) Consultation is now the European regional expression of the Vision 5:9 network. Ongoing consultations have been held in a number of European countries, including the Netherlands, Spain, Germany, Greece, and Turkey. The most recent consultations convened in Paris, France (2022), and Malaga, Spain (2023).

Collaboration has been a central focus of DPE since its beginnings. The current DPE Steering Team includes eleven members representing eight countries from four continents. "Collaboration" was also the theme of the most recent DPE consultation in Malaga, Spain. Keynote speaker Rosalyn van Baaren from OM addressed the subject based on a course she helped develop to equip teams for more effective collaboration.

Outcomes

A summary of outcomes from recent consultations highlights the benefits of such gatherings:

- A viable and visible demonstration of fellowship and unity. Workers from various cultural, organizational, and denominational backgrounds met in a show of unity with the goal of sharing Christ with Muslims in Europe.
- Networking with ministries across Europe, building relationships, and strengthening connections.

---

4 Mahabba, "About Mahabba."

- Sharing ideas, concepts, and methods. Concepts highlighted included consistency, availability, and character as key drivers for effective, fruitful discipleship that goes beyond the impartation of knowledge.
- Inspiration through stories of hope and transformation from Muslim-background believers (MBBs).
- Understanding the need to find ways to integrate MBBs more effectively into the DPE network.

Three Tangible Models of Collaboration

Collaboration between mission agencies, churches, and organizations must be embodied in tangible ways. Here are three examples of effective collaboration among the diaspora peoples of Europe.

Diez 10:42, Málaga, Spain

The former chair for DPE, the late Laura Eller of One Challenge, served in Spain and helped establish Diez 10:42 (or Ten 42). Eller was moved by the plight of refugees entering Spain. Diez 10:42 takes its name from Matthew 10:42: "If anyone gives even a cup of cold water to one of these little ones who is my disciple, truly I tell you, that person will certainly not lose their reward." The multiorganizational ministry initiative she initiated is designed to be a place for immigrants, refugees, and others new to Spain to find friends, gain skills, and receive practical help to integrate into their new communities. Through language classes, job training, activities for parents, exercise, art, and other programs, refugees and migrants develop a greater sense of personal dignity and value in their new home.

Collaboration thrives through inspirational servant leaders like Laura (later OC's first female European area director) who help expand opportunities, explore strategic initiatives, and draw others into Spirit-led community. The future of Vision 5:9 and DPE collaboration, and multiagency projects like Diez 10:42, depends on leaders who in like manner display a warm heart, enthusiastic vision, and epic hospitality to impact the lives of the most vulnerable refugees throughout Europe.

The Lighthouse, Woking, United Kingdom

Erik and Rebecca Jesperson founded and direct The Lighthouse in Woking, a city of 100,000 people southwest of London. In 2021, 24.2 percent of the population were non-UK born; 8.6 percent of Woking residents were born in the Middle East and Asia; 8.3 percent were born in the European Union; and 3.7 percent were born in Africa.[5]

In partnership with many local organizations, churches, groups, and individuals, The Lighthouse currently runs twenty different projects with three hundred volunteers and staff in three different sites.[6] The foundation for their ministry is prayer, not only for their current projects but also for work the whole community of Woking. Psalm 34:8 proclaims, "Taste and see that the Lord is good." As a ministry, The Lighthouse paradigm is for people to come and experience a tangible sense of peace, joy, and hope.

---

5   UK Census 2021 (https://www.ons.gov.uk/census).
6   The information that follows is based on a livestream interview with Erik and Rebecca Jesperson, DPE 2023, Spain.

Shared vision and values are key to the ongoing development of collaborative work. Volunteers go through an induction program that unpacks the meaning of fifteen different values, including dignity, respect, compassion, honesty, authenticity, and love of God. Volunteers completing the induction process are given role descriptions with clear expectations related to their work and relationships with project leaders.

Some Lighthouse projects provide for practical needs (e.g., food bank, clothing bank, and children's equipment). Other projects are based in the community (e.g., storytelling workshops, cooking classes, and community lunches). There are groups that focus on mental health and on the vulnerable; coaching to prepare people to find employment; and efforts to serve a variety of age groups (e.g., youth group, citizens group). The Lighthouse also regularly leads Bible studies, the evangelistic Alpha Course, and prayer groups.

With every new project, a foundation of prayer and new champions are needed to take it forward, providing new opportunities for collaboration. Erik and Rebecca use a metaphor to describe the reason so many people have become involved: "If you plant a beautiful tree, it just seems to draw interest and attention."

Humanitarian Initiative Bridges, Athens, Greece

In 2013, Ilias and Voula say that they "read the 'signs of the times' and got prepared to receive the huge wave of refugees fleeing the Syrian War." There are now over seventy thousand displaced people in Greece. They founded Humanitarian Initiative Bridges "for such a time as this."[7]

Humanitarian Initiative Bridges offers services in Arabic, Kurdish, and Farsi languages to displaced individuals and families. They create "bridges" with other NGOs, agencies, the asylum offices, the Greek Ministry, individuals, local communities, churches, and professionals. The goal is to bring together different stakeholders to speak on behalf of the voiceless and to support their human rights. They raise awareness on local and international levels regarding the issues facing displaced persons and the rights of refugees.

Using a holistic approach, Humanitarian Initiative Bridges seeks to address the spectrum of needs of displaced individuals who arrive in Greece, including physical, psychological, social, and spiritual, in order to serve them adequately and to help them integrate. Along with legal information, access to the asylum office, counseling, social services, and the distribution of goods, Bridges is passionate that refugees leave having experienced that their lives are precious and that they can start a new life from the beginning.

Bibliography

Humanitarian Initiative Bridges. "About Bridges." Accessed May 13, 2024. https://www.bridges.org.gr/who-we-are.

Mahabba Network. "About Mahabba." Accessed May 13, 2024. https://www.mahabbanetwork.com/about-mahabba.

Pew Research Center. "Future of the Global Muslim Population: Region: Europe." January 27, 2011. http://www.pewresearch.org/religion/2011/01/27/future-of-the-global-muslim-population-regional-europe/.

Pew Research Center. "5 Facts about the Muslim Population in Europe." November 29, 2017. https://www.pewresearch.org/short-reads/2017/11/29/5-facts-about-the-muslim-population-in-europe/.

Welcome Churches. "Vision and Values." Accessed on May 13, 2024. https://welcomechurches.org/team#vision.

---

7 Humanitarian Initiative Bridges, "About Bridges."

28
Networking Networks

Ryan Emis and Allan Matamoros

"How good and pleasant it is when God's people live together in unity!" David opened Psalm 133:1 with these words, and they are still applicable and truthful.

Today, more and more church and mission networks are finding creative ways to work together to take the gospel to the ends of the earth. Existing networks are joining together into thousands of larger ones to collaborate for the sake of the gospel more effectively.

In many ways this is not a new development, as church and mission leaders have been coming together since the first century. Consider, for example, the Jerusalem Council in Acts 15. Church leaders came together to seek consensus on how the Scriptures should inform an important matter. They discussed the related issues and the right way forward and then acted together. This is the foundation for how mission networks continue to this day. Working together is crucial for their success.

When we look back over the last one hundred years and see the massive growth of the church all over the world, it is not surprising to see an accompanying increase in local and indigenous-led mission structures and networks. This is a wonderful development as the national churches need to share in the joy of the global mission. The full participation of these national groups requires an increase in multinational mission structures as well as networks that facilitate communication, collaboration, and understanding.

Many "networks of networks" have now been established, such as the World Evangelical Alliance (WEA), Lausanne Movement, Global Church Planting Network (GCPN), Global Alliance for Church Multiplication (GACX), Vision 5:9, and many others. These "umbrella" networks help bring focus and clarity to the work for many dozens of smaller networks that share a common goal and vision. These networks commonly have multinational leadership teams to ensure that there is not only cultural diversity but also cultural understanding of the various strategies employed.

Many regional networks like COMIBAM (Latin America), AIM, and the Korean Mission Association (KMA) serve in their respective geographical regions, and there is a growing movement known as South-to-South connections. During the last few years, the Korean, Latino, and Indian movements have been gathering to stimulate connections and synergy between them as Global South initiatives.

There are many advantages to networking mission groups that share the burden to see a "church for every people." For example, sharing information about the current needs in a region can help leaders consider if the Bible is available in the local languages and if there are human resources on the ground or nearby that can help with church-planting efforts or other ministry-related activities. If a mission structure is considering sending teams to work with a specific people group, the network can inform them if there are already churches engaging there. Some organizations are tracking people group engagement and making this data available so that other mission structures can consider where to send new teams. All this communication can help reduce redundancy so that mission structures can be better stewards of the resources God has provided.

Many mission networks recently came together in Batam, Indonesia, to consider how networks can "collaborate to saturate." Participants discussed and collected best practices with a desire for mission groups in every nation to consider collaborative strategies for disciple making and saturation church planting. Each global region was encouraged to develop a model for a contextual, effective, and practical roundtable meeting so that more leaders in their home contexts could participate. Going forward, the leaders of the newly formed "Colloborate to Saturate" (CS2) umbrella networks are committed to working together and sharing information so that all the networks are kept informed and collaborating effectively.

Mission networks will continue to play an important role in bringing global leaders and practitioners together. The value these networks provide is vital: They provide the global church a seat at the table and also serve as the kitchen where meals are made. The task to take the gospel to all nations is for the global church, and everyone has a part to play. Let us pray with the Lord Jesus in John 17:22–23 (NIV) that these network expressions reflect his desire "that they may be one as we are one—I in them and you in me—so that they may be brought to complete unity. Then the world will know that you sent me and have loved them even as you have loved me."

Reflection and Discussion

International Multiplication

1. Which regional case study stood out to you? Touched your heart? Challenged your thinking?

2. What were some common "lessons learned" about collaboration by these regional leaders, churches, ministries, and networks?

3. As you reflect on these narratives, what are some of the "people problems" we encounter as we pursue collaboration and partnership in mission? How might we begin to overcome these roadblocks in our hearts and relationships?

4. What are some of the advantages of collaboration and networks in reaching the remaining unreached peoples?

5. What possibilities for collaboration (between churches, ministries, sending agencies, networks) could you envision in your church or ministry context?

6. What steps can you take to put a greater priority on unreached peoples?

Part 6
Issues Affecting Progress

Challenges, Changes, and Trends

29
Fog in the Pews

Factors behind the Fading Vision for Unreached Peoples

R. W. Lewis

Throughout Protestant mission history, a small minority has felt called to prioritize people groups "where Christ has not been named"—variously called "unoccupied fields," "regions beyond," and "unreached people groups." God raises up these people to ensure that his promise to Abraham is fulfilled and all the "families of the earth" partake in the blessing of knowing God through Jesus Christ. Simultaneously, Satan opposes the advance of God's kingdom by sowing confusion, fear, and apathy.

For the last two hundred years, the Protestant frontier mission thrust has depended on a clear grasp of the remaining task through data and field-informed discussion of various "means" to send witnesses and communicate meaningfully. Fervor for the frontiers fades whenever it appears that the pioneering job is done. Today the global church's passion and commitment to reach all "unreached people groups" is fading again—although 25 percent of the world population still live in people groups with few, if any, believers and no viable, indigenous movements to Christ. Why?

This chapter focuses on two areas: (1) factors clouding understanding of the remaining task—confusing terminology, conflicting databases, and overwhelming numbers, and (2) factors impacting commitment to frontier missions, such as changing global realities and perceived colonial bias of people group terminology, partnership versus pioneering missions, and the shift toward short-term mission experiences. The huge problems of rising uncertainty about the universal need for Christ and the power of the gospel will be largely left for others to unpack.

Reached versus Unreached: How Confusing Terms Obscure the Task

The terms "reached" and "unreached" have been confusing and often misused from the beginning. In the 1970s some argued that the presence of churches in nearly every country meant the missionary task was over, though much evangelism remained to be done by the local church in those countries. However, Dr. Ralph Winter's research revealed that roughly seventeen thousand people groups (containing nearly 60 percent of the world's population) had virtually no access to the gospel—isolated from existing churches by language and cultural identity.

Winter called these overlooked people groups "the final frontier" and sparked new efforts among these "Hidden Peoples." He excluded nominally Christian people groups with Bibles in their own languages, churches, priests, etc. He reasoned that historically revivals and reforms often take place in such groups without any "outside" or cross-cultural missionary help. He also excluded people groups where indigenous movements to Christ were already underway, not because they no longer needed any help, but because the pioneering frontier mission breakthrough had already been accomplished, making cross-cultural mission work less necessary.

By the 1980s, people groups with successful gospel progress became known as "reached" people groups. Conversely, those groups with no indigenous community of believing Christians were called "unreached people groups" (UPGs). For consistency in gathering data, a threshold of "2 percent or more evangelical" was agreed on for "reached people groups." And this seemed a reasonable way to measure whether the cross-cultural breakthrough of the gospel had been accomplished. Even if all the missionaries left, two hundred evangelicals in a people group of ten thousand (or twenty thousand evangelicals in a group of 1 million) should be able to finish reaching the rest of their own group.

The frontier mission goal was to extend cross-cultural outreach into people groups where there was *not yet* a breakthrough of indigenous faith. But the goal subtly shifted when the terms "reached" and "unreached" peoples replaced "hidden peoples."

Problems Arising from "Reached," "Unreached," and the 2 Percent Cutoff

Two Different Meanings

"Reached" was already in use for individuals who had accepted the gospel and "unreached" for all "unsaved" individuals. At the 2019 Evangelical Missiological Society conference, one plenary speaker urged against focusing on UPGs, saying that there are unreached people all around us, even in our own churches. The 250-plus mission professors seemed to agree, so, even after forty years of discussion about UPGs, they were still confusing unsaved people (unreached individuals that the local church can evangelize) with unreached people groups (ethnolinguistic people groups that require cross-cultural pioneering mission effort).

"Reached" Caused Pushback

People resisted calling a people group "reached," even where indigenous movements were strong and self-sustaining, while the vast majority (up to 98 percent) were still not saved. In response the Joshua Project website published four stages of "reached people groups": "minimally reached," "superficially reached," "partially reached," and "significantly reached." These categories emphasized the needs remaining among reached groups, inadvertently diluting the focus on "hidden peoples" where as yet no work at all had started. Forty years later, thirty times as many cross-cultural missionaries still go to "reached people groups" as go to "unreached people groups." However, having 2 percent of a people group committed Christians (two thousand baptized believers in a group of 100,000, or one out of every fifty people) is actually high enough for them to reach out to the rest of their people group in an indigenous way, even without outside help.

Databases Became All-Inclusive and Overwhelming

The databases were pushed to fairly show the needs of all people groups, rather than listing only those people groups beyond the reach of existing missions and churches. And the databases went even further, adding on tiny diaspora or special interest groups like blind or deaf people. The resulting ever-expanding list of "unreached people groups" became overwhelming, and new laborers lacked strategic guidance regarding where to go.

"Unengaged Unreached" (UUPGs) Initiatives Focused on Effort Rather than Results
By drawing attention to "unengaged" UPGs with no witnesses,[1] Finishing the Task (FTT) successfully focused on a reduced number of people groups and revitalized a vision for frontier work. However, FTT deleted from their "unengaged" list large people groups with no gospel breakthrough once they confirmed even a couple of long-term witnesses were in place—even in a massive people group with millions of people.[2] In so doing, FTT unwittingly skewed attention toward increasingly tiny people groups. This threshold of no witnesses dropped out too many fields where pioneering work was still badly needed.

The 2 Percent Evangelical Cutoff Was Too High to Identify Fields That Still Needed Pioneer Work
One veteran church movement planter estimated his large people group no longer needed pioneering missionaries long before it reached 0.5 percent evangelicals (fifty evangelicals in a town of ten thousand). Once such a movement starts, the work of outsiders shifts from pioneering to partnership with nationals in evangelism. Many UPGs have achieved strong, "self-sustaining indigenous movements to Christ" long before reaching 2 percent evangelical. These groups no longer need pioneering work even though they may still be included on UPG lists because of the percentage criteria. Further analysis has revealed that a better cutoff for identifying frontier groups where pioneering work is needed is less than one out of one thousand (0.1 percent) identifying with Jesus.

The "Evangelical" and "Unreached" Definitions Caused Divergence in Databases
Dissonance resulted in disillusionment as charts, graphs, and lists disagreed with each other due to differing interpretations of the criteria. For example, in the fall of 2019, a prayer guide for Latin America was published with a graph showing 550 million "unreached people" (meaning "unsaved persons") out of a total population of over 604 million.[3] Yet, the same agency's UPG database listed only 7 million people in "Unreached People Groups" in Latin America, and the Joshua Project database listed only 700,000. Why was there such disparity using the same "2 percent evangelical" criteria? It had to do with who was counted as an "evangelical" or "born again." Some organizations included all believers who studied the Bible and spread their faith as "evangelicals"—including charismatics and other renewal movements in older denominations, such as Reformation Protestants with infant baptism. Others did not. Nominal Christians were also in different categories.

Counting "Unsaved" Nominally Christian Groups as "Unreached" Peoples Gave False Impressions and Also Caused a Split between Databases
Ralph Winter originally did not count nominal Christians as having no access to the gospel because they had had centuries of mission work and Bible exposure. Controversy arose about whether "unsaved" nominal Christians are as "unreached" as Muslims, Hindus, etc. Agreeing with Winter, the Joshua Project excluded people groups as "unreached" with more than 5 percent self-identifying as Christians.

---

1 The global network FTT (finishingthetask.com), now led by Pastor Rick Warren of Saddleback Church (CA), hosts an annual conference for church and mission leaders.
2 Other mission leaders pushed back and called for focus on large groups they considered "under-engaged."
3 IMB, "Prayer Points."

However, the International Mission Board (IMB)[4] decided not to distinguish between nominal Christians and older denominations (including Reformed Protestant denominations) and people of other religions or atheists—with significant consequences. For example, at one point the IMB website listed the "Scottish" people group as the largest "engaged but unreached" people group in the world because Scottish Presbyterians were not considered "evangelicals" (in the Anabaptist sense), though Scottish Presbyterian missionaries had long been major players in world evangelization. As a result, many groups identified as UPGs on the IMB database were listed as "reached" on the Joshua Project database. Unfortunately, churches did not realize how these decisions affected the IMB data representations, so they were left with grossly false impressions, such as "Europe is as unreached as India."

For Renewed Vision, Churches Need Simplicity, Clarity, and Hope
Most of the confusion involved in the above points cannot be clarified by doubling down on the original definition because there are inherent problems in the terms and percentages themselves. To help solve this problem, a subset of UPGs that fits the original definition of groups with no indigenous self-sustaining movement to Christ was culled out of the Joshua Project UPG list in 2018. To emphasize the ongoing need for "frontier" or "pioneer" mission work, they were called "frontier people groups" (FPGs). This simple act revealed amazing things: Huge progress has been made in the last fifty years, but also the remaining task is simpler than expected:[5]

- 40 percent of the global UPG population appears to have self-sustaining movements to Christ underway.
- 60 percent of the remaining UPG population has no visible progress toward indigenous faith (FPGs).
- 25 percent of the entire world's population is in this subset of UPGs called FPGs.
- 51 percent of the population of these FPGs is in India; over 70 percent is in South Asia.
- 97 percent of the global FPG population is either Muslim (56 percent) or Hindu (41 percent).
- 44 percent of FPG population is in just thirty-seven people groups over 10 million in population.
- Roughly 80 percent of the FPG population is in less than three hundred groups larger than one million; these nearly three hundred groups contain 20 percent of the world's population![6]

It is encouraging to many, especially in the Global South, to understand that focusing on just the three hundred largest frontier people groups could impact nearly 80 percent of the global population still needing pioneer work.

---

4 IMB is part of the Southern Baptist Convention, the largest Protestant denomination in the United States, and has a significant commitment to frontier mission (www.imb.org).
5 The figures are provided by Joshua Project and the various maps and charts linked there. For a fuller discussion of frontier people groups, see *Mission Frontiers* (Nov–Dec 2018) and Lewis, "Clarifying."
6 These FPGs are shown on a sortable map and list at Joshuaproject.net/frontier/interactive.

Globalization versus People Groups: How a Rising Global Culture Obscures People Group Realities

Monocultural but multiethnic megachurches in large cities give the impression that identifying "people groups" is no longer important.

"People group barriers" are sometimes presented as not just a thing of the past, but also as evidence of residual racism and colonial "ethnic" constructs. Increasingly, some church planters are encouraged to disregard and even discourage people group identity, terminology, and loyalties. They do not realize that promoting indigenous churches for all people groups actually celebrates their diversity of language and culture, valuing each people group as unique before God. The danger in "multiethnic" churches is that the dominant culture usually eclipses all other languages and cultures, giving a mere illusion of diversity, while actually undermining ethnic identities and diversity.

For example, Delhi, a city of some 25 million people, has perhaps a dozen multiethnic megachurches. Audiences have Asian-looking people from Northeast India, dark-skinned people from South India, and a smattering of North Indian natives and expats from other countries. Services are in English, the mother tongue of none, and worship teams sing Western songs projected on large screens. These churches are frequently lauded for bringing the ethnic diversity of God's people under one roof.

But the popularity of "melting pot" urban churches among Western-educated "global nomads" obscures the people group loyalties of the vast majority of modern city dwellers. Worshipers in those contexts are often urban transplants without their own local ethnic community. These are essentially churches of immigrants, often from "reached" people groups, who already have movements to Christ in other parts of India or in other countries.

As a result, Delhi's "multiethnic" churches have not started movements in Delhi or beyond among the hundreds of sects or ethnicities of Muslims, Hindus, Sikhs, and Jains with centuries-old roots in North India. Nor are they greatly impacting the large diaspora communities in Delhi of Nepalis, Bengalis, Afghans, etc., whose ethnic loyalties, languages, and culture are zealously preserved.

Similarly, even in the West, most urban churches barely engage the unchurched people of their same culture, much less large ethnic groups with different languages and cultures. Occasionally a few people from unreached people groups break with their community to join such multiethnic churches. However, churches usually need specialized cross-cultural training to equip these Westernized believers extracted from UPGs to start gatherings in their own languages, instead of merely the trade language they have grown accustomed to using in worship.

People group lists cannot capture the cacophony of cultures in most major cities of the world—nor should they. UPG databases should not aim to describe all people groups most accurately, but to clarify and direct the global church to send witnesses to those without any movements to Christ. People group affinities resemble Venn diagrams more than discrete circles. Such affinities are not static and are largely self-defined. Some people align more with religious than ethnic group identity, like the Tablighi Jamaat (Society of Preachers), a swiftly growing one-hundred-year-old Indian Sunni Muslim reform movement which has reached 80 million, spanning one hundred countries and many people groups. This Sunni movement does not appear on any UPG list but would be a great movement to introduce to Jesus.

Planting monocultural multiethnic churches is unlikely to significantly advance the gospel into the least reached people groups. Even in cities we must seek out those highly defined groups who eschew such conglomerate churches. People group lists are therefore still crucial, despite their limitations. Indigenous movements among minorities are still a priority worth highlighting.

Partnership versus Pioneering:
How Success in Pioneering Shifts Emphasis to Partnering

When churches or agencies prioritize partnering with national churches and believers, fields with no believers are inadvertently excluded.

In history, whenever significant progress was made in winning a people group to Christ, the focus shifted to partnering rather than pioneering. It is happening again. However valuable the partnership stage, the continuing needs of remaining pioneering fields should not be obscured.

When pioneers are successful, they tend to remain and build on the foundation they helped lay in partnership with their new disciples. Their recruiting then draws new workers to where breakthroughs are already happening but usually neglects people groups where there are no workers.

As a result of advocacy for unreached people groups over the last five decades, many peoples in the 1977 "final frontiers" list are now in the "reached" category, most notably the Han Chinese. However, fewer than 4 percent of global missionaries work among UPGs, where 60 percent of the world's nonbelievers live, including the 1 percent that work with the 25 percent of the world's population that is in the UPG subset of frontier people groups.[7]

Popularity for partnering with existing believers is resurgent. We need to avoid bypassing the national workers in reached groups—as well as those in the 40 percent of remaining UPGs with communities of indigenous believers. When evangelism by national believers becomes self-sustaining and widespread, then pioneering work by cross-cultural workers (from other people groups) is no longer necessary. Wherever indigenous believers exist, partnering with them to spark and lead movements among their own people group is preferable.

However, partnering is impossible where there are no indigenous communities of believers. Sixty percent of remaining UPGs have no sign of gospel progress. These least-reached UPGs, the frontier people groups, count for 25 percent of the global population (nearly 2 billion people). Distinct training in pioneering is needed to successfully plant an indigenous movement to Christ in a people group with no preexisting indigenous community of believers accepted by the rest of their people group. Winning the first community of believers to Christ while guiding them to stay one with their people is the most difficult stage of pioneering, followed by effectively training a handful of believers to spark an indigenous movement among their own unreached people group.[8] We must find believers with genuine callings from God for pioneering ministry, and we must commission them and work and learn humbly alongside them.

---

7 Joshua Project, "Frontier."

8 Some try to skip this stage by sending inexperienced workers to train believers from nearby "reached" people groups to do pioneering cross-cultural witness, which the former have never done on their own. This historically fails due to barriers of mutual prejudice.

Short-Term versus Long-Term:
How Short-Term Missions Neglect Least Reached People Groups

When churches or agencies prioritize sending short-term teams, fields with no believers are bypassed again.

The recent boom of short-term mission trips—which Barna more accurately labels "service trips" or "adventure trips"[9]—absorbs church and "missions" funds without producing movements in areas with little gospel access and no national believers. Short-termers who are not preparing for long-term service inevitably help existing missionaries or partner with national believers because they lack language or cultural knowledge. According to one recent study of the few who continue to long-term service, 48 percent return to where they previously served short term—virtually always to a "reached" people group.[10]

Short-term teams rarely go into dangerous areas, or to people groups with no believers, although some have distributed literature in these areas or helped during disasters. Around 2 million Americans go on short-term mission trips each year, many on second or third trips.[11] These droves represent substantial financial, health, and leadership costs with little more outcome than positive effects on themselves, and virtually no increase in long-term workers, especially for UPG areas. These trips may also do more harm than good to the receivers. Short-term missions have been portrayed idealistically as "locking hands with our brothers and sisters around the world." Concurrently, however, they put significant burdens on receiving churches, especially poor ones with unpaid leaders and few resources to care for a group of vulnerable foreigners. Meanwhile, efforts to reach unreached people groups are defunded or never even considered.

Losing Sight of the Frontier Task
Because of Loss of Faith in the Gospel

This chapter has assumed a common goal: taking the blessing of the gospel to "all the families of the nations" (Pss 22:27; 96:7)—the good news of freedom from sin and death, and eternal life with God through Jesus. Obviously, vision for unreached peoples is also fading for an even more serious reason than those given above: creeping universalism or secularism impacting every area of Western culture. Additionally, concerns for justice, poverty, and well-being (which have always rightly accompanied mission movements), have, for some, become of singular importance. However, historically, initiatives that do not bring people to Christ evidence little lasting change. Finally, belief in hell has faded, and it is assumed that everyone is going to heaven, especially those aborted; death is the end of life and eternal life is an illusion. People who have abandoned hope in Christ will have no life-giving message to share and no urgency to share it.

---

9   Barna, "Despite Benefits."
10   Pettengill, "Short-Term."
11   Barna, "Despite Benefits."

Conclusion

Throughout history, God has burdened specific people with a passion to reach those who have no chance of learning about Jesus: the Apostle Paul, Saint Patrick, Loyola, William Carey, Hudson Taylor, etc. In every case, they spread their own vision and concern by pleading the cause of peoples without hope and encouraging others to join the effort. The consistent pattern for two thousand years has been to identify peoples and places without the good news and to send witnesses to live among them and reach them.

The latest such wave has been the fifty-year push to send witnesses to the unreached people groups. It has grown increasingly complicated to figure out where the neglected peoples are, as the gospel spreads to more places and a rising number of "global nomads" obscures ethnic realities. Until very recently there has been no distinction between the 40 percent of the remaining UPGs that now have a community of indigenous believers among them and the 60 percent that still need pioneering work; thus, the need for pioneer work has been largely overlooked. Short-term visits to believers overseas have replaced a determination to send long-term witnesses to peoples with no believers, and no viable, indigenous church movement.

Simplicity and *clarity* and bringing *hope* are the keys to revisioning the global church about the world's peoples with no progress of the gospel—the frontier people groups. It is not necessary to engage every small group or to constantly nuance our people group lists to reach each one of these peoples. Movements tend to flow from larger influential groups to smaller related groups. Indigenous movements to Christ could impact vast populations "where Christ has not been named" if the global church will focus primarily and urgently on the largest least reached UPGs, namely the nearly three hundred largest frontier people groups—with a combined population of 1.6 billion, 20 percent of the world's population!

Bibliography

Barna Group. "Despite Benefits, Few Americans Have Experience Short-Term Mission Trips." October 6, 2008. http://www.barna.com/research/despite-benefits-few-americans-have-experienced-short-term-mission-trips/.

IMB. "Prayer Points: A Praying People Impacting a Lost World." October 2019. http://www.imb.org/wp-content/uploads/2020/03/Oct19_PrayerPoints_WEB3.pdf.

Joshua Project. "Frontier People Groups." Accessed April 13, 2024. http://joshuaproject.net/assets/media/handouts/frontier-peoples-overview.pdf.

Lewis, R. W. "Clarifying the Remaining Frontier Mission Task." *International Journal of Frontier Missions* 35, no. 4 (October–December 2018): 154–68. http://www.ijfm.org/PDFs_IJFM/35_4_PDFs/IJFM_35_4-Lewis.pdf.

Pettengill, Mike. "Do Short-Term Mission Trips Produce Long-Term Missionaries?" May 8, 2016. http://www.theaquilareport.com/do-short-term-mission-trips-produce-long-term-missionaries/.

30
Rethinking the People Groups Concept

Globalization, Urbanization, and Migration

Minh Ha Nguyen[1]

The pile of shoes, mostly sandals, grows at the front door. Rich smells of turmeric, cumin, and curry waft from the apartment. Slowly, people crowd into the circle on the floor—first six, then ten, then fifteen. An older woman adjusts the flowing scarf that she wears over her long tunic, typical of South Asian dress. Toddlers, bangles dangling from their wrists, weave happily between people willing to entertain them with pens and cell phones. It's time for church. But this is not South Asia—it is Richmond, Virginia.

Three Megatrends Impacting the Christian Mission

Globalization, the growth of cities, and the global movement of people are interrelated processes that have deeply transformed the contemporary social, economic, cultural, and political landscape as well as the way Christian mission understands peoples and carries out the task among all peoples and places. More than 1 billion people are on the move with estimates between 85 percent and 95 percent ending up in cities.[2] This means one of every seven persons on the planet is a migrant, a phenomenon that simultaneously benefits and exacerbates cities and societies around the world. Yet little research has been done to assess the impact of these mega trends on the people groups concept. This article, therefore, seeks to show how globalization, urbanization, and migration (hereafter GUM) stretch the understanding of peoples and unreached people groups and impact Christian mission and frontier missiology.

Mega trends like GUM are not isolated issues. Weaving these processes into one thread is a daunting task, to say the least. This article will focus only on a few aspects of GUM that relate to our understanding of people groups. In dense, diverse urban contexts, core people group dynamics have increasingly been challenged by postmodern, multicultural, and complex societies. These include the concepts of homogeneity (where people share common characteristics that separate them from other groups), ethnolinguistic consolidation (where language and ethnicity are the determining characteristics of people groups), and intercultural delimitation (where thick boundaries are emphasized between people groups). The migrations of peoples worldwide into cities demand that Christian mission seeks new epistemological frameworks for seeing, understanding, and making disciples among all peoples and places.

---

[1] Our colleague Ming Ha Nguyen passed away in a tragic accident July 2024.
[2] United Nations, *World Migration Report*, 19.

Peoples on the Move

Migration and urbanization have accelerated to such a degree that it has become a cliché to mention that more than half (55 percent) of the world's population now live in cities. More than 2.5 billion will join their ranks by 2050, increasing the world's urban population to over two-thirds (68 percent).[3] Keep in mind that in 1950, when the people groups concept and homogeneous unit principle were being formed, the urban population was less than one-third (30 percent).

There are 272 million living outside their home country, representing about 3 percent of the world's population.[4] Some Gallup polls show these numbers could be higher, as more than 750 million worldwide would migrate internationally if they could.[5] Global migration also includes an estimated 800 million internal migrants moving from the rural areas to cities. India and China account for the largest shares of internal migration, with 325 million and 221 million, respectively. Importantly, the data shows that international and internal migrations are connected: Internal migration leads to international migration, and vice versa.[6] Taken together, there are over 1 billion migrants in the world today.

Globalizing Cultures

Globalization refers to the "widening, deepening and worldwide interconnectedness of all aspects of contemporary social life."[7] Globalization is also simultaneously a political and technological process.[8] While there are anti-globalization trends like nationalism and rejection of Western liberal democracy, technological globalization has enabled widespread communication, travel, and access to education. The growth of "transnational networks" has exposed the limitations of state control. Remittances, relationships, innovation, and entertainment flow through the internet and cable television across permeable borders. This technological process has led to the emergence of new cultural groupings that span traditional ethnic, linguistic, and geographic boundaries.

Four examples of global cultural groups are worth mentioning. First is the "Davos culture," an elite group of 40 million highly educated people who operate in the rarefied domains of international finance, media, and diplomacy sharing common beliefs about individualism, democracy, and market economics, who follow a lifestyle that is instantly identifiable anywhere in the world and who feel more comfortable in each other's presence than they do among their less sophisticated compatriots.[9] Second is the international "faculty club," an international network of academics who share similar values, attitudes, and research goals and who wield tremendous influence through their association with educational institutions worldwide with certain success in promoting feminism, environmentalism, and human rights

---

3 United Nations, *World Urbanization Prospect*.
4 United Nations, *World Migration Report*.
5 Gallup, "More Than 750 Million Worldwide."
6 Skeldon, "International Migration," 1–10.
7 Held et al., *Global Transformations*, 1.
8 Czaika and de Haas, "Globalization of Migration," 284.
9 Berger and Huntington, *Many Globalizations*.

as global issues.[10] Third is the nongovernmental organizations advocating a view of global culture based not on the "replication of uniformity" but on the "organization of diversity" seeking to preserve cultural traditions in the developing world.[11] A final example is the transnational workers, the English-speaking professionals such as software engineers and internet entrepreneurs of Silicon Valley, California, who trace their origins to South Asia but who live and work elsewhere and whose social world includes multiple home bases and a unique network of individuals and opportunities.[12]

These examples point out that, while globalization has sought to homogenize the globe into a single world order and culture, it paradoxically led to a plethora of other highly influential subcultures, networks, and tribes segregating along social, economic, and cultural boundaries. Some of them prioritize education or lifestyle above ethnic and linguistic identities; their members choose to associate with like-minded others with whom they do not even share the same mother tongue or cultural heritage. They come together to form diverse networks often under the umbrella of a dominant language such as the English language and a dominant culture such as the Western culture. Others morph into multilingual and hybrid groups striving to maintain multiple identities in an "in-between" way of life; they are more than the culture they left behind but not assimilated to the culture of destination.

One thing is clear: GUM processes open the door to new ways of forming communities, networks, and affinity groups. This does not mean that ethnolinguistic people groups are no longer relevant. It does mean that peoples have more choices to come together. It also means that there are more bridges and far-reaching ties for the preaching of the gospel of the kingdom.

Cities and Peoples

GUM's transformative effect on peoples is magnified in the cities. The influential Danish urban designer Jan Gehl states, "First we shape the cities—then they shape us."[13] While rural areas tend to have a conserving effect on the culture, in the cities GUM processes radically change who people are and how they see themselves.[14] According to Edward Glaeser, a Harvard professor of economics and urban studies, we cannot understand the demand for cities unless we understand how cities change people's lives.[15] It is therefore important to understand how GUM processes are taking place and to appreciate the transformative effect of cities on peoples and unreached people groups.

A hundred years ago, Émile Durkheim, the father of modern sociology, developed the concept of "social facts" in order to scientifically study the impact of society on the individuals taken as a group living in a geographical location. Durkheim posited that social facts are elements of collective life that exist independently of and can exert an influence on the individual. They are collective, stable, external to the individuals, and coercive to them. They are external and not individual characteristics. Individuals cannot choose whether they

---

10 Berger and Huntington.
11 Hannerz, *Transnational Connections*, 101.
12 Appadurai, *Modernity at Large*.
13 Gehl, *Cities for People*.
14 Tönnies, *Community and Society*.
15 Glaeser, *Cities for People*.

have the effect or not. Social facts are coercive, meaning they impact everyone residing in that context. They are collective, meaning they apply to everybody. They are things, meaning they can be measured with empirical data. One of Durkheim's key findings was the positive difference suicide rate between the Protestants and Catholics as well as between soldiers and civilians.[16] Max Weber's "disenchantment" effect of modernity on society is another example of social fact.[17]

If Durkheim and Weber are correct, it is in the city that the dynamics of GUM are most noticeable and have far-reaching impact on the people group understanding. People prefer contact with others from the same group, but they also prefer contact with others from different groups to no contact at all.[18] Social facts influence peoples in the city by exposing them to diverse cultures and ways of life, showing weakness in their worldview, and pointing them to the strength in others. The city's population density provides the critical mass needed for people to come together and the freedom to do so.

Social Facts of Urban Life

There are at least four examples that illustrate how GUM processes are magnified in urban contexts leading to new group formation and changing the ways we see and disciple peoples in today's world.

First is the formation of urban tribes. Urban tribes are emotional or affectual communities defined by shared interests and lifestyles. Like the tribes of the Amazon, these urban tribes band together in the concrete jungles of contemporary megacities to define meaning and share life.[19] Examples include micro-groups of punks, bikers, hipsters, and other sexual orientation types.[20] They are typically between the ages of twenty-five and forty-five. They prefer the urban lifestyle, which offers an alternative to traditional family structures.[21] There is a Christian version of urban tribes, too, called the "Benedict Option," where busy, young, urban professionals come together to create community in a monastic fashion.[22]

A second example of group formation in urban contexts is global tribes. While urban tribes emphasize affectual characteristics, global tribes focus on economic, cultural, and ethnic preservation. In his book *Tribes: How Race, Religion and Identity Determine Success in the New Global Economy*, the world-renown urbanist Joel Kotkin mentions five examples of global tribes: the Chinese, Japanese, British, Indians, and Jews. These groups have in common a strong diaspora presence that contributed significantly to the formation and growth of global cities such as London, New York, Singapore, and Hong Kong.[23]

---

16 Durkheim, *Suicide*.
17 Weber, *Sociology*.
18 Blau, *Crossing Social*.
19 Maffesoli, *Le Temps*.
20 Kwak et al., "From Bikers to Surfers." Because urban tribes are groups of people who have similar visual appearances, personal style, and ideals, and because these groups are also very active on social media platforms, uploading over 300 million photos a day to Facebook alone, scientists in the fields of AI and machine learning are developing algorithms to capture the features that distinguish each subculture and classify them into an urban tribes database.
21 Watters, *Urban Tribes*.
22 The main proponent of the "Benedict Option" is Rod Dreher. See Libresco, *Building the Benedict*.
23 Kotkin, *Tribes*.

A third example of urban group dynamics is hybridization, also known as creolization, a phenomenon where languages and cultures collide to give birth to new ones. Cultures are not homogenous islands but are often characterized by multiple identities that overlap with one another.[24] This is most accentuated in the cities, where cultures become less homogenous and where people jump over the porous boundaries from one culture to another.[25]

"Ethnoburb" formation is the final example. Ethnoburbs are suburban ethnic clusters of residential areas and business districts in large metropolitan areas. They are multiethnic communities in which one ethnic minority group has a significant concentration but does not comprise a majority. In ethnoburbs minority groups are able to maintain their ethnic identity. Ethnoburbs are some of the most dynamic and highly diverse places in gateway cities. It is in these ethnoburbs that transnational connections and relationships are most often formed.[26]

GUM are human, transformative, and coercive realities that the global church needs to learn to manage in order to reach people in the twenty-first century. In urban contexts ethnicity and languages still play critical roles; however, large cities provide peoples the freedom and critical mass to form new groups along occupation, institutional affiliation, or common interest characteristics. Furthermore, cultural hybridity and interdependency between the groups lead to new multiethnic and interethnic communities. All cases point to a complex system of group formation that requires new ways of seeing, understanding, and reaching peoples. Christian mission in urban contexts necessitates multiple models including monoethnic,[27] multiethnic,[28] or interethnic[29] church planting, as well as other strategies that do not follow ethnic or linguistic boundaries.

Rethinking People Groups Concept

In rethinking the people group concept and the impact of GUM on the understanding of peoples and unreached people groups, the global church must consider that ethnicities and languages are not the only ways through which people come together. Global flows connect

---

24 Barth, *Ethnic Groups*, 11.

25 Welsch, "Transculturality."

26 Li, *Ethnoburb*, 171.

27 In the monoethnic model, the worship service is conducted in the language most familiar to the ethnic group. For the majority group in the country, the language would be the national language; for all other international groups, however, the language would be the one they speak in their homes. Often, there is very little interaction among them even when they worship within the same city. But the strength of the monoethnic church is in its homogeneity, thus making it difficult or nearly impossible for it to transform.

28 In the multiethnic model, the worship service is done in the national language. Those who advocate this model see it as the New Testament pattern that expresses the unity that joins differing ethnic groups together. There is a desire to reach the different ethnic groups in the city and bring them together into one church. The multiethnic model's insistence, however, on using the national language makes it less effective in reaching first-generation immigrants who often are the most responsive to the gospel. In some cases, the strong dominance of the majority ethnic group in leadership, worship, and outreach preferences prevents the assimilation of other minority groups into the church. Another challenge of multiethnic church is the use of the national language. This monolingual requirement means that to become a Christian, one must first learn the national language and adopt certain cultures and customs of the host country. The most significant challenge of multiethnic churches, however, is the absence of indigenous worship and leadership. Because it is multiethnic, each joining group must give up something to prevent the church from breaking apart. The natural tendency, and least resistant mode, is that people like to be with those who are like them. They like to form enclaves and live in enclaves.

29 See an example of interethnic church planting at the end of the chapter.

peoples with multiple and far-reaching ties in a worldwide network that could provide new bridges and shorter paths for the spread of the gospel. Furthermore, cities attract peoples seeking new opportunities to improve their lives; these include members of many unengaged and unreached people groups from restricted places. Finally, cities are bedrocks of ideas and innovations. As disciples are made in the cities, they have the potential to become influential spreaders of the good news in circles different than their own.[30] These are some of the reasons that make the cities centers of frontier missions.

The central aim of this chapter has been to discuss some of the problems and impacts of GUM on the understanding of peoples and unreached people groups and to suggest a solution for the Christian mission. GUM processes have not only created new groupings of people beyond the ethnolinguistic boundaries but also new ways for peoples to come together in hybridizations and ethnoburbs. Furthermore, GUM processes highlight the potential for gospel movements among the global communities with significant linkages in the city and around the world.

The solution does not appear to lie in expanding the current people groups database into an ever-increasing listing of hundreds of thousands or even millions of entries. But nor are the answers to be found in abandoning the current listings themselves on the grounds that they have lost their shine and are no longer attractive—some things could be right and valuable regardless of the attraction they project.

The suggested way forward is the development of a missiological research framework that provides new data and models for seeing and understanding peoples, cities, and migration flows. The Shalom City Index™ (SCI) and its databases could provide such a framework.[31] On the one hand, SCI provides the theological and missiological framework that centers on shalom as the comprehensive, cohesive, and complex adaptive system for understanding the preaching of the gospel of the kingdom among all peoples and places. On the other hand, SCI provides two new databases on global cities and diasporas that will supplement the current people groups database. The SCI framework is the author's self-reflection on the seven-year period of interethnic church planting that led to the formation of the International Community Church, a house church network in Richmond, Virginia.

An Example of Interethnic Church Planting

The South Asian church mentioned at the beginning of this chapter is one of the thirty house groups that formed the International Community Church (ICC)—a house church network that connects affinities, peoples, and languages groups from Nepal, Burma, Cambodia, Vietnam, Central Asia, Africa, South America, and other places. House groups meet weekly in various locations throughout the city. They all come together once a month for worship celebration, fellowship, and leadership formation. In the homes, the groups gather weekly along their specific boundary, be it linguistic, social, or cultural affinity. Each group decides the language of worship, evangelism, and mission strategies that are most effective and contextual to their community. In the monthly gatherings for celebration, groups take turns

---

30 Granovetter, "The Strength," 1360–80.

31 The limitations of this article prevent the precise and detailed description of the Shalom City Index, but it is a major part of the author's PhD dissertation that is in progress. See www.shalom.city.

to conduct the worship service, preach the word, and lead one another in praying for all other ethnic groups in the city that do not have a church yet.

ICC is a response to the challenges of both monoethnic and multiethnic church-planting models. On the one hand, the monoethnic model, while reaching people in the heart language and worldview, offers very little interaction with other groups in the city. Furthermore, this model runs into difficulty with retaining the second or third generation that do not speak the language of their parents. On the other hand, the multiethnic model, while effective in bringing multiple groups together, faces challenges of its own. First, the insistence on using the national language would not only rule out the first generation of immigrants but also project the expectation that to become Christian one must learn the language and adopt the culture of the host country. Second, the dominance of the majority group in leadership and worship would treat the minority groups as second-class citizens. Finally, the absence of indigenous leadership and worship would lead to some form of "extractionism." To join the multiethnic church, each group must give up something in order to prevent the church from breaking apart.

The interethnic model is simple but effective in meeting both the monoethnic and multiethnic needs. Home groups, as the smallest local church unit found in the Scriptures, are easy to start and multiply with the development of lay leaders. ICC is small enough to reach all peoples in Richmond yet large enough to celebrate and multiply reaching the urban tribes, subcultural groups, and global cities networks.

Bibliography

Appadurai, A. *Modernity at Large: Cultural Dimensions of Globalization.* Minneapolis: University of Minnesota Press, 1996.

Barth, Roland. *Ethnic Groups and Boundaries: The Social Organization of Culture Difference.* Long Grove, IL: Waveland Press, 1969.

Berger, Peter, and Samuel Huntington, eds. *Many Globalizations: Cultural Diversity in the Contemporary World.* Oxford: Oxford University Press, 2002.

Blau, Peter. *Crossing Social Circles.* Orlando: Academic Press, 1984.

Czaika, Mathias, and Hein de Haas. "The Globalization of Migration: Has the World Become More Migratory?" *International Migration Review* 48, no. 2 (2015): 283–323.

Durkheim, Émile. *Suicide: A Study in Sociology.* New York: Free Press, 1966.

Esiova, Neli, Anita Pugliese, and Julie Ray. "More Than 750 Million Worldwide Would Migrate If They Could." December 10, 2018. https://news.gallup.com/poll/245255/750-million-worldwide-migrate.aspx.

Gehl, Jan. *Cities for People.* Washington, DC: Island Press, 2010.

Glaeser, Edward. *Cities, Agglomeration, and Spatial Equilibrium.* Oxford: Oxford University Press, 2008.

Granovetter, Mark. "The Strength of Weak Ties." *American Journal of Sociology* 78, no. 6 (1973): 1360–80.

Hannerz, Ulf. *Transnational Connections: Culture, People, Places.* London: Routledge, 1996.

Held, D., A. McGrew, D. Goldblatt, and J. Perraton. *Global Transformations: Politics, Economics, and Culture.* Cambridge: Polity, 1999.

Kotkin, Joel. *Tribes: How Race, Religion, and Identity Determine Success in the New Global Economy*. New York: Random House, 1993.

Kwak, Iljung S., Ana C. Murillo, Peter N. Belhumeur, David Kriegman, and Serge Belongie. "From Bikers to Surfers: Visual Recognition of Urban Tribes." Accessed April 17, 2024. https://vision.cornell.edu/se3/wp-content/uploads/2014/09/utribes_bmvc13_final.pdf.

Li, Wei. *Ethnoburb: The New Ethnic Community in Urban America*. Honolulu: University of Hawai'i Press, 2012.

Libresco, Leah. *Building the Benedict Option: A Guide to Gathering Two or Three in His Name*. San Francisco: Ignatius Press, 2018.

Maffesoli, Michel. *Le Temps des Tribus*. Paris: Merridiens Klincksieck, 1988.

Skeldon, Ronald. "International Migration, Internal Migration, Mobility, and Urbanization: Toward More Integrated Approaches." *Migration Research Series* 53 (2018): 1–10.

Tönnies, Ferdinand. *Community and Society*. Mineola, NY: Dover Publication, 2002.

United Nations Department of Economic and Social Affairs. *World Urbanization Prospect: The 2018 Revisions*. New York: United Nations, 2019.

United Nations International Organization for Migration. *World Migration Report*. Geneva: UN Migration, 2020.

Watters, Ethan. *Urban Tribes: Are Friends the New Family?* New York: Bloomsbury, 2003.

Weber, Max. *The Sociology of Religions*. London: Methuen, 1971.

Welsch, Wolfgang. "Transculturality—The Puzzling Form of Cultures Today." In *Spaces of Culture: City, Nation, World*, edited by Mile Featherstone and Scott Lash. London: Sage, 1999.

31

Ferment in the Church

Missions in the Fourth Era

Alan McMahan

In 1955, Donald McGavran's book *The Bridges of God* launched the field of modern missiology, and it shook the evangelical world with its conclusions on the validity of people movements occurring in northern India. Evangelistic fruit was showing up where many were not expecting it. The cognitive dissonance the book engendered led to a new way of thinking about the harvest, eventually giving rise to church growth and the frontier missions movements with its emphasis on reaching unreached peoples. Today a new set of factors converge to once again shake our understanding of how God is redeeming the lost peoples of the earth.

We live in unprecedented times. Never in the history of the world have we seen so much upheaval and opportunity among the world's peoples that causes us to reconsider our missionary paradigms, definitions, and strategies. In the accounting of the advance of modern missions, we may be at the threshold of the fourth era.[1]

Three Major Trends

Three major factors are manifesting themselves in ways we could have not imagined. They are converging to create a unique opportunity in human history that can influence the completion of the task of global evangelization. The three factors are urbanization, migration, and globalization.

Urbanization

In the 1930s, less than 30 percent of the world's population lived in cities. By the year 2050, that number will hit 70 percent in the developing world and 90 percent in the developed world, doubling the global urban population to a total of 6.4 billion people.[2] That is equivalent to adding a city the size of Los Angeles each week to the world's urban population.[3] In 1997, David Barrett reported that 127,000 non-Christian urban dwellers were being added daily—a number that is undoubtedly much higher now.[4] Most of these are represented by the urban poor located in the world's megacities with minimal Christian impact.

Migration

The peoples of the earth are moving away from their homelands at rates higher than ever seen before. In 2019, more than 272 million people[5] crossed international boundaries in search of a

---

1 Winter, "Three Mission Eras," 263–78.
2 United Nations, *World Urbanization Prospects*, 1.
3 Prince Charles, address to the World Urban Forum, February 13, 2018.
4 Barrett, "Annual Statistical Table," 24–25.
5 World Economic Forum, "Global Migration."

better life.[6] When this number is added to the number of those migrating within their country of origin, the total is close to 1 billion people, or one-seventh of the world's population.[7] They move for many reasons: economic or educational opportunities, war, natural catastrophes, family reunification, governmental initiatives, etc. But they move in hope of a better life. These conditions create new receptivity and a mixing of the world's peoples that realign traditional beliefs, patterns of living, and social norms.

Globalization
Thanks to dramatic improvements in transportation, communication, and technology—coupled with the exercise of free enterprise—ideas, products, and services are moving at lightning speed across international boundaries. The results are numerous, from a homogenization of ideas and trends, the emergence of never-before-seen affiliations and innovations, and the rise of a global youth culture in which a young person in Jakarta, Indonesia, may have more in common with the youth of Los Angeles than they do with their own parents.[8]

The convergence of these three factors in the world's urban contexts interact with and amplify each other to create an environment where the laws of strange physics dominate. Three metaphors of the city will illustrate.

The city functions as a "black hole" in that the bigger a city is, the greater is its gravitational attraction; the city sucks in everything around it to fuel its need for food, water, and natural resources. As the city increasingly pulls, its population density increases, driving up costs and competition for scarce resources, distorting even the rules for social engagement and human interaction.

Second, the larger the city is, the more intense its subcultures become that may orbit around a culture of origin, lifestyle preference, or hobby. Lovers of poisonous snakes can form a club because in the city they can find enough others who will join them. People who were rejected by small-town friends because of their sexual preferences can now align with like-minded others to carry out political or social action initiatives to force change in the larger society. At the same time, the city is characterized by enormous diversity and heterogeneity. Here, in this high-density environment, some find themselves pressed together where they can no longer avoid each other. Cultures that are dramatically different are placed in proximity. In this way the city functions as a "supercollider," where particles of different types are smashed together at high speed and yield strange new elements to those observing it.

Third the city functions as a "culture-making engine" leading many to an exploration of new ideas, recombinations, and new collaborations (even marriages!) that are not subject to censure by the elders and the former traditions. It is not surprising that most new ideas, trends, fashions, and music emanate from great urban centers, which are then transmitted to the rest of the world.

General Implications

The results of these interacting forces generate some interesting findings for reaching UPGs that demand the development of a new toolkit for missionaries today.

---

6 This is a number higher than the population of Indonesia, the fourth most populated nation on earth.
7 United Nations, "Cross-National Comparisons."
8 At least this may be true in terms of aspirational identity as opposed to the identity of origin.

First, our understanding of people groups must move beyond static, monocultural, geographically and linguistically based definitions. In the hybridity characteristic of the city, hyphenated subcultures are rapidly emerging and the aspirational identity of many urban dwellers centers around values and characteristics that differ from their identity of origin. The "glue" that binds urban dwellers together may relate more to age, education, socio-economic status, music, occupation, a hobby, or a common dream of the future than it does to language, religion, or a common homeland. Today it is often true that young people may marry someone outside their cultural or religious group, move to a context foreign to both, and build their lives together in that third-culture environment. What culture will their kids form their identity around? What people group are they a part of now? These hybridized population segments become key bridge people to cross-cultural divides and overcome traditional patterns of resistance.

Second, urban environments function to break down societal control as traditionally practiced in the homeland of a people. In the city one becomes anonymous within a block or two from where they live. Informal controls over deviant behavior, usually manifested in the form of gossip, become ineffective in a world of strangers. Urban migrants, then, find a new freedom to explore beyond the permitted constraints of their worldview. A new receptivity emerges that more freely experiments with new ideas, patterns of living, and affinity groups. This new freedom is simultaneously terrifying and exhilarating, and it may lead to either good or bad choices, but it is quite different from the traditional life in the homeland.

Consider the young Muslim women in Jakarta who live in traditional families but work in the commercial or corporate centers of the city. They depart for work wearing the traditional Muslim clothing expected by the elders that covers them completely, but on the bus that traditional clothing is removed to reveal smart, Western business attire underneath. At work they associate with their Chinese Indonesian colleagues who invite them to a lunchtime worship service at a local Christian fellowship nearby, where they hear the gospel and meet more Christian friends. At night they return home on the bus, putting on the Muslim dress they removed earlier, return to their traditional families, and resume the identity they had before they left. At some point, if they do find Christ, they will be forced to make a choice about which faith they will follow. Perhaps this occurs when they get married or start to raise children, but never before did they have such a direct exposure to this life-changing message of salvation. Such scenarios are not at all uncommon in the city.

Third, ministries that seek to penetrate a UPG by going to the homeland of the people and using highly contextualized forms valued mostly by the older generation are still important and should be continued, but they may face more resistance and see slower results than what might be possible in the city. I have ministry colleagues who have worked in highly contextualized ways for two or three decades in the homeland of a UPG and by God's grace have raised up a few Christian fellowships of Jesus followers. Their commitment and persistence are commendable and inspiring. I have also visited megachurches[9] in nearby

---

9 Some of these megachurches were running 5,000 or 10,000 or 40,000 or even over 120,000 attendees in weekend services. Though the core constituencies were often made of displaced Christian migrants from other areas or hyphenated peoples, such as Chinese Indonesians, there were, nevertheless, many representatives from UPGs in the area.

urban centers where one would expect to find no such UPG people, but they, on the contrary, have in some cases hundreds, or even thousands, of converts from UPGs from areas where my other colleagues worked.

Even more shocking is that many of these megachurches used worship forms that were obviously not contextualized as they sang Hillsong music in English accompanied by large jumbotrons, laser lights, and smoke machines. These contexts which looked and sounded like what I would expect to see in Los Angeles or New York were effective in bringing a new, younger generation to Christ. In these uncontextualized, Western forms of ministry, UPG peoples were coming to Christ. In 1955, when Donald McGavran wrote *The Bridges of God*, his observations indicated fruit was being produced in unexpected places. That is what we see now too.

Furthermore, these same patterns that I observed in Indonesia were also apparent in Singapore, Kuala Lumpur, Bangalore, Chennai, Hong Kong, Manila, London, New York, Los Angeles, and to a much lesser extent in Beijing and Moscow, where I conducted similar research. Indeed, it is predictable that among the urban migrants coming into cities, the larger the city, the more pronounced the patterns; we see members of UPGs from throughout the surrounding regions who are becoming more receptive and have hope for a new life. In some cases it is possible to find Christian believers who are among members of multiple UPGs living together in the same apartment complex. The population density and geographical proximity to one another increase the likelihood the gospel can "hop" across cultural boundaries that previously would have prevented communication and effective evangelization.

Implications for Missions

The implications for missions are numerous. First, we need to develop the ability to see pockets of receptivity wherever they occur, even if they do not show up in the expected places. Since urbanites may affiliate with others based on factors other than language, culture, and place of origin, we need to become good at "glue-sniffing" to find what holds them together, then follow the trail to see where it leads. That may mean we need to develop more sophisticated tools to define and track UPG streams. Maybe the affiliations are forming through social media such as Facebook, Instagram, or others. Receptivity may occur in unpredicted spaces and times. Our definitions and anthropological and ministry tools may be good at examining "detailed complexity" (looking at all the cultural patterns and attributes of a people) but fail at understanding "dynamic complexity" to understand how people's identities shift and receptivity rises and falls at different phases of migration and in the presence of certain stimuli.

Second, better communication and cooperation need to occur between personnel deployed in the homeland of UPGs and those engaged in ministry in pluralistic migrant destinations. Migration is seldom a one-way flow. More typically, people are engaged in a circular migration pattern as they visit their parents in the homeland bringing with them the rewards purchased by their "high paying" jobs in the city, only to return to the city again and continue their status-building, wealth-generating careers. With these visits, they also bring new ideas, new perspectives, new values, even their new faith.

To prepare UPG converts in the urban contexts to "take the gospel home," urban churches need to be equipped with the vision and the tools to identify, equip, mobilize, and problem solve with new UPG-background believers so they can be effective upon their return home.

How many times do young people return home wearing the clothing style of the city only to face the scorn of their parents? Sensitivity training is needed to help the new convert talk about their faith in loving and winsome ways to the skeptics at home. Christian workers also need to cooperate with each other in the homeland and the city as much as possible to conserve the fruit of these interactions.

Third, it is important to plant multiethnic churches in the city where the dominance of the largest ethnic groups within the congregation is diminished and space is created for minority voices.[10] Research on multiethnic churches indicates that the hardest minority group to add to the congregation is the second one because it tends to stand in sharp contrast or in polarity to the largest ethnic group. If the contract can be negotiated between these two groups, then adding a second or third minority group is much less difficult.

As a church becomes more variegated and diverse, adding other minority voices becomes easier, and space is created for even more people who do not fit any of the identified groups to join. Such is the case with congregations in Indonesia that might be dominantly composed of Chinese Indonesians. The larger the church becomes and the more diverse it is, the easier it is for members of UPGs to anonymously explore the claims of the faith without being discovered. Church-planting efforts that are multiethnic match the city's diversity and are more contextualized to that pluralistic context.

Fourth, we need to consider the possibility that contextualization may not match what we have been trained to see. Many would dismiss Western-style worship services and megachurch models as having nothing of value for reaching UPGs. It does not fit our paradigm of frontier missiology. Yet, if it is understood what the rising generations of urban nomads are looking for, some of these forms might be worth considering as a first level of engagement. If these young urban migrants first adopt new Western or K-pop forms, there will need to be study on how this is eventually engrafted back to the identity of origin lest it be discarded for being foreign and alien. Perhaps this is a level of self-theologizing with which the indigenous church will need to grapple.

Finally, we need to refine the toolkit for equipping the next generation of missionaries and cross-cultural workers. Our methods of equipping too often assume our workers will work in monocultural environments focused on a single UPG. Instead, we need to equip some to work in environments of high diversity, high density, and rapid change. We need to pay close attention to the people who are shifting between cultures and recognize that they may be able to operate in two environments. These migrants may be the honeybees that will pollinate the flowers of new advancement of the gospel.

---

10 For a complete explanation of these concepts, see Gary L. McIntosh and Alan McMahan, *Being the Church in a Multi-Ethnic Community* (Fishers, IN: Wesleyan Publishers, 2012).

Conclusion

Doing missions in the fourth era marked by urbanization, migration, and globalization will require recognizing the forces quickly changing our ministry context. These forces are redefining the pathways people follow as they come to Christ, as well as the cultural frame they will prioritize in their choices and values. Will it be their culture of origin or their culture of aspiration that leads to greater receptivity? How will God use these changing conditions to take the gospel to the last UPG? What new toolkit does the next generation of missionaries need to be successful? What strategies will yield the most fruit? These are questions that urgently need to be addressed as we rethink our people group missiology.

Bibliography

Barrett, David. "Annual Statistical Table on Global Mission: 1997." *International Bulletin of Mission Research* 21, no. 1 (January 1997): 24–25.

United Nations Department of Economic and Social Affairs. *Cross-National Comparisons of Internal Migration: An Update on Global Patterns and Trends.* Accessed on August 1, 2020. http://www.un.org/en/development/desa/population/publications/pdf/technical/TP2013-1.pdf.

United Nations Department of Economic and Social Affairs. "World Urbanization Prospects, The 2018 Revision." Accessed May 16, 2024. https://population.un.org/wup/Publications/Files/WUP2018-Report.pdf

Winter, Ralph D. "Three Mission Eras and the Loss and Recovery of Kingdom Mission, 1800–2000." In *Perspectives on the World Christian Movement: A Reader*, edited by Ralph D. Winter and Steven C. Hawthorne, 263–78. Pasadena: William Carey Library, 2009.

World Economic Forum. "Global Migration, by the Numbers: Who Migrates, Where They Go and Why." January 10, 2020. https://www.weforum.org/agenda/2020/01/iom-global-migration-report-international-migrants-2020/.

32
Unleashing Next Gen Pioneers

Clara Litzsinger and Lisa Pak

In today's globalized world we have more opportunities to share the good news of Jesus with others than any generation before us. Beyond digital innovation, a generational shift is happening. This shift finds expression in our cultural conversations, the circumvention of the traditional, and the human desire to pursue one's passions. In an unsettled world, younger leaders can draw on their innate insight into their generation's ambitions and dissatisfactions even as they pursue being equipped with the missional skills and the resilience needed to navigate the challenges of serving among neglected peoples.

A God of Generations

The God of Abraham is the God of generations. He will always reserve a faithful remnant for himself. This paper will explore some of the characteristics of today's younger generations and their potential for mission mobilization and service among the least reached peoples. Many in this generation are open to cultural exchange, flexible in their thinking, creative, and adaptable. We can be confident that God is raising up those who will "serve the purposes of God in [their] own generation" (Acts 13:36).

Above my desk, I (Clara) have two of my baby photos: in one I am sitting on my mom's shoulders and in the other I am standing on my father's lap. My parents' support—the wisdom and experience of those who have walked with God ahead of me—provided me with a foundation that anchors me to a spiritual heritage and compels me to press on.

Every generation exhibits certain generational characteristics. For example, Gen Z (born 1996–2010) stands out because they are digital natives, emphasize personalization, possess a high cultural intelligence (CQ), and desire to be accepted for what makes them unique. These traits can be considered strengths as we collaborate to take the gospel to unreached places. Kingdom work will move forward if spiritual mothers and fathers invite, and even urge, the rising generations to stand on their shoulders, encouraging and unleashing them to use their unique characteristics for the mission Christ gave us.

Generational Differences as Missional Strengths

A Faithful Remnant
True followers of Jesus have always been a minority. Jesus taught, "But the gateway to life is very narrow and the road is difficult, and only a few ever find it" (Matt 7:14 NLT). Even among the Baby Boomers, only 10 percent hold a biblical worldview. Gen Z stats are lower—an estimated 4 percent of this generation hold a biblical worldview; the estimate is 6 percent for Millennials. The likelihood of a Gen Z holding any religious faith varies greatly by country. For example, the Varkey Foundation found that 77 percent of African youth thought their

religion was very important to their lives, while 61 percent of Japanese youth said religion was not important to them.[11] While these statistics may be disheartening, they reveal that despite extreme cultural hostility in some places, young believers are standing firm in their faith. They are not an apathetic generation. In fact, some suggest that Gen Z missionaries "will likely be a strong, resilient, and committed remnant."[12] They are worth investing in.

Digital Natives

Our lives are lived in and through technology, and we are flooded with information. With a foot in both the analog and digital worlds, Millennials (born 1980–1995) were greatly shaped by technology, but to a lesser extent than subsequent generations. Gen Z grew up as digital natives, with instantaneous access to the world around them. Gen Alpha (born 2010–2024) are practically born with a phone in their hands. How can we empower these generations to be willing and effective witnesses to the least and the last in this digital era?

Younger generations have a large capacity to take in information at a rapid pace and through various mediums. Millennials and Gen Z are constantly exposed to volumes of information that previous generations could only imagine in the form of library stacks, and they can access all of it through handheld mobile devices. They are the most connected generation that has ever lived. The digital world has shaped and taught them to explore and circumvent traditional pathways in virtually every field. Millennials are well known as entrepreneurs, and Gen Z has perfected the craft of fashioning online careers. The potential impact of equipping, empowering, and unleashing a generation of digital natives for the Great Commission is far-reaching.

Robotics, ChatGPT, 3D printing, AI, and even Bitcoin can be used for missions.[13] In an interview, mobilizers and founders of the NextGen Movement, Jim and Sterling O'Neill, said that since there are still many remaining unreached people groups (UPGs), both older and younger leaders are asking, "What barriers hinder gospel movements within UPGs and what innovations [can bring] breakthrough?"[14] Further developments in AI can help local churches quickly translate the Bible and discipleship resources for their unreached neighbors, and new digital platforms can connect first-time Muslim-background believers with a much-needed spiritual community.[15] Maybe augmented reality will soon allow goers to experience life on the mission field before they arrive![16]

The absolute pervasiveness of technology, however, its rapid development, and our societal dependence on it have markedly affected those born in the last few decades. Access to unquantifiable amounts of information is overwhelming and confusing when it comes to discerning truth and deciding one's life trajectory.[17] The vast amount of digital experiences

---

11 For more global statistics on Gen Z trends, see the 2017 Varkey Foundation's report "Generation Z: Global Citizenship Survey."
12 Erlacher and White, *Mobilizing Gen Z*, 16.
13 Frontier Ventures uses Bitcoin for missions.
14 Jim and Sterling O'Neill, Zoom interview, April 2024.
15 All Nations International is developing an app for the Muslim diaspora in Europe.
16 For more examples of how technology is being used to further missions, see *EMQ* 59, no. 3 (2023).
17 For more on this topic, see dcdx's report "From Digital Natives to Digital Captives: How the Internet Changed Gen Z" at https://dcdx.co/digital-captives.

absorbed by these generations through platforms like TikTok, Netflix, or YouTube "is capable of having a greater effect on their values, convictions, and well-being than institutions like school, church, and family."[18] Therefore, as we empower digital natives for missions we need to remember two things: First, "if you don't exist online, you don't exist to a young adult considering missions," and second, relational discipleship rooted in a study of Scripture is vital.[19]

Personalization

One of the fundamental values of younger generations is personalization in all things, something reflected in the world around us. We choose our car interiors, customize our Starbucks orders, and pick our favorite clothing and décor from millions of options. While Western societies are known for their individualism, globally many in Gen Z have more opportunities to live a personalized lifestyle than their previous generations.

If personalization is a core value, how can we celebrate uniqueness as we vision cast and equip them to go to the least and the last? As a starting point, consider asking the following questions:

- **Who** has God *uniquely* made you to be?
- **What** strengths and spiritual gifts do you *feel* God has given you?
- **Where** do you think Jesus is *inviting* you to invest in his kingdom?
- **When** did you *learn* about God's heart to see every people before his throne?
- **Why** is it important that you *participate* in the great commandment?
- **How** can you share your *experience* of Jesus with those around you?[20]

Youth today can feel insignificant within a world of over 8 billion people. These kinds of questions help young Jesus followers reflect and engage with missions in a way that honors the uniqueness of who God made them to be (Ps 139:14). Simply put, mobilizers will be most successful when they can help individuals discover their role in the Great Commission; "56% of potential Gen Z missionary candidates listed 'how helpful I think I could be' as a reason that would increase their interest in going to another country as a missionary."[21] Many in this generation are wired to jump in and help when "who I am" and "what I have to offer" are valued and can make a difference. When given the opportunity, young people are just as eager as previous generations to participate in the great commandment (love your neighbor). They want to be a part of taking care of the poor, widowed, and orphaned with the talents they have to offer.

Relational Evangelism and Personal Spirituality

There are many "traditional" ministry methods that younger Christians dislike, which can lead mobilizers to misinterpret an aversion to methodology as a lack of commitment to the mission. The reality is that, in some contexts, methodologies that have worked in the past may not feel authentic to a generation that values personalization, desires to respect others' beliefs, and wants to build authentic relationships. As Erlacher and White state, "While

---

18 Erlacher and White, *Mobilizing Gen Z*, 52.
19 Erlacher and White, 111.
20 Italicized words are ones that we think will especially draw in those from younger generations.
21 Erlacher and White, *Mobilizing Gen Z*, 119.

evangelism efforts commonly taught or accepted in missions contexts often require young people to act incongruently with their generation's cultural norms, 'relational evangelism' bridges many of these concerns."[22] In the West, door-to-door evangelism is a distressing thought to many young Jesus followers, as the idea of attempting to shift the eternal destiny of a stranger through the course of an afternoon feels not only uncomfortable to them but disrespectful.

Furthermore, young believers today either grew up in a postmodern society or have been influenced by postmodernism and prioritize personal experiences and encounters. It also means that there is skepticism over the accuracy of rigid interpretations gained from the exegesis methodology. This is not a denial of divine inspiration or the authority of Scripture but rather questions that passages have single interpretations. Chong Kim, a goer and a spiritual leader in this generation, explains it well: "The fact that there are differences alone does not and should not divide the people of God, regardless of religious and cultural background.. … The refusal to recognize and celebrate the differences betrays the very reading and hermeneutical reflection of Scripture."[23] This is why methods such as Discovery Bible Study (DBS), which is commonly used in missions, is well received by younger Christians as it makes space for individuals to encounter God in a personal way that honors who they are.

I (Clara) believe that Kim speaks to our generation when he says

> The divine original blessing extends to all humanity and the single greatest pursuit of all life is to discover and live out the original blessing and design by being us which means accepting how God created each of us. Furthermore, the process of how each human being bears and stewards the blessing is to walk on a uniquely distinct path culminating in an incredible array of diversity of such expressions. All bear the image and likeness of God and what I do bear is also unrepeatably and uniquely mine.[24]

God has blessed each of us to bear his image and live out, discover, and create as part of this image bearing, and this gives every person permission to embrace their unique life experiences.

"Co-Finder" of The Table Collective refers to this type of spirituality paradigm as "mutualism." He explains, "There is, then, objective truth, indeed Truth. However, it is also true that there are many ways of experiencing that Truth, and of describing the experience."[25] He continues by saying that in religion, mutualism is an active process of giving, receiving, and correcting each other as we acknowledge that each of us is made in God's image. It is honoring other cultures for what we can sincerely learn from them, not just learning to contextualize and communicate our gospel message better.[26] This type of spiritual perspective outlined by Kim and Caldwell speaks to this generation's longing to share to the truth of Jesus while creating room for those they share with to be contributors, even teachers, within the discipleship process.

---

22 Erlacher and White, 75.
23 Kim, "Human and Spiritual," 36.
24 Kim, 34.
25 Caldwell, "Mutualism," 94.
26 Caldwell, 99.

Cultural Intelligence

Another strength of Millennials, Gen Z, and Gen Alpha is their tendency to grow up with great cultural intelligence (CQ). In many countries, no other generation has been as ethnically and culturally diverse as Gen Alpha, a trend that is projected to continue. In America, for example, as of 2021, The Brookings Institution reports Boomers grew up in a nation that was 72 percent Caucasian, whereas Gen Alpha was born into an America with only 49 percent Caucasians. While ethnic diversity does not equate to cultural intelligence, the concepts are related, and the observable global trend reported in 2019 by the Pew Research Center is towards ethnic diversity within nations. In 2017, global research done by the Varkey Foundation on Gen Z found that "most young people are tolerant and know people from other religions; just under two-thirds state that they have close friends who belong to religions different to their own." Younger leaders are well positioned to bring together the cultural and ethnic diversity of the global church because of the exponential increase in migration, developments in travel, and innovations in technology. Youth today are more open to cultural exchange, more nomadic, and curious for lived experiences.

Many agree that CQ is an invaluable skill when mobilizing people to go to UPGs. However, mentors may have to encourage their disciples to "unplug" in order to tap into their CQ potential. The loneliness, anxiety, and culture stress (shock) can trigger young people to shut down and rely on technology to insulate themselves from the challenge. The O'Neills describe a cross-cultural worker's lack of ability to disconnect as a hindrance to "one of the most important ingredients in cross-cultural work: the ability to express dependence on your host culture." In these instances, having a mentor to travel with them geographically, culturally, and spiritually empowers these young leaders to step into their potential. Another advantage of globalization is that mentors can be from anywhere in the world. In fact, "young Western missionaries will benefit from the mentorship of leaders from the Global South, who can offer perspectives and insights that may not be present in a post-Christian Western context."[27]

Discipleship by Spiritual Mothers and Fathers

A significant factor in raising up the young generation to be missionally minded is the intentional presence of spiritual mothers and fathers, mentors, who will invite young people to co-labor alongside them and help them to understand and discern how Jesus is calling them to follow, serve, and lead.

Biological parents have an irreplaceable role in the spiritual growth of their children. Jim and Sterling O'Neill observe, "There is something to be said profoundly for the emotional, psychological development of human beings in God's plan through mom and dad."

However, the O'Neills warns that "it's really hard to quantify the emotional impact that a dysfunctional home life has on the career of a missionary. It really manifests when you go cross-culturally." There are burdens, along with the blessings, passed down generationally that must be healed before we send people into missions, especially to difficult places and to UPGs where spiritual warfare usually intensifies. To prepare future missionaries for these challenges, a sending organization or church can provide pre-field debriefing and a support system where

---

27 Erlacher and White, *Mobilizing Gen Z*, 142.

coworkers, pastors, congregations, and leaders commit to being with them for the long haul. Over the last twenty years, the O'Neills have observed the encouraging upsurge of sending organizations providing greater member care, but they wondered how many receive the same level of care once they are on the field. In addition to pastoral care, young believers interested in long-term missions also need a rooted understanding of their identity in Christ.[28] Senders can help reaffirm their identity as the beloved of God, empowered by the Holy Spirit, and Jesus's witnesses to the ends of the earth (Col 3:12; Acts 1:8).

Each generation needs to know that as followers of Christ, they, too, are the recipients of the promises of the Great Commission and that they are neither excluded from the blessings and privilege of obeying Jesus's mandate (Matt 28:18–20) nor are they free of the cost of following him (Luke 9:23).

Here we'll suggest a few discipleship methodologies that have proven effective, edifying, and fruitful amongst the younger generations.

Relationship over Resources

First, the focus of discipleship should be an authentic, personal relationship, where giving advice and equipping comes later in the journey as life stories and passions are shared. Ironically, as Gen Z (globally) spends more time online, they feel more disconnected, lonely, and depressed. A Barna poll states, "Gen Z values connection over content and presence over program."[29] Despite the ability to connect over digital platforms, nothing beats in-person connection. Today's youth are capable of looking up any logistical details online—and most of them prefer self-learning.[30] Gone are the days where most young people will feel called to missions through a brochure, training, webinar, or any nonpersonal encounter. The O'Neills, who act as spiritual parents and friends to younger generations globally, emphasized the importance of relational discipleship:

> What's needed is a discipleship that utilizes relational language and not technical language. We want to talk about it in terms of fathers and mothers in the faith, big brothers and big sisters ... as friends. We believe the disposition of friendship transcends generations, transcends culture. We need to listen to the next generation and hear their hearts. We find where they are at and come alongside of them.

Through their time discipling multiple generations of youth from different nations, they have seen that a lack of relational discipleship can hinder the success of cross-cultural missionaries. If one's own spiritual model did not take the time to listen to their thoughts and struggles, and to ask questions, then likely they will lack these skills when discipling others. As the O'Neills state, "They will not know how to come alongside a host culture ... if their models have told them what they need to believe instead of drawing it out of them and validating their unfinished and raw thoughts."

Young people are looking for mentors to share their testimonies of who God is to them, all that God has done through their lives, and the wisdom gleaned from experience and past

---

28 The O'Neills.
29 Erlacher and White, *Mobilizing Gen Z*, 93.
30 Erlacher and White, 97.

mistakes. For all the connectedness of the digital age, our rising generations are looking for leaders who will do life with them.

Shared Spaces

If authentic relationships are key to discipling young people, then we also need to "create shared spaces to listen and learn together."[31] Different generations always have contested priorities and passions. Millennials and Gen Z are highly compelled by social justice, racial and gender equality, and reconciliation through missions. When we create shared spaces, we can steward and apply past missional knowledge while being open to new approaches and methodologies of next generation leaders.

In 2003, the O'Neills started the NextGen Movement to create shared spaces for co-learning. I (Clara) had the privilege to attend a NextGen gathering, and it was a very diverse space both generationally and ethnically. The presence of the global church in this space appealed to me because of the opportunity to experience different parts of the body of Christ. To those looking to mobilize the younger generations, consider creating these shared spaces where young believers can be co-learners with other believers, older and younger, from different parts of the world, with different experiences yet all following Jesus, and with a heart for missions.[32]

Missiological Interpretation and Biblical Literacy

It is vital that discipleship is rooted in Scripture. The O'Neills encourage leaders to "teach [young people] to see the Scriptures missiologically." There is no replacing biblical literacy, and "Perspectives on the World Christian Movement" and similar courses give young people an opportunity to dive deep into the missiological reading of Scripture in a co-learning shared space. Moreover, biblical understanding should deepen through mentoring relationships.

The Role of Churches

The local church also plays an important role. Congregations ought to be multigenerational, including young generations as active members who also give, pray, learn, and go.

To this end, the church can also create shared spaces by prioritizing relationships over program and actively teaching young people how to read the Bible missiologically. Let's not underestimate either their interest or ability to grasp godly principles and cultivate their minds and hearts for missions.

In the O'Neills' extensive experience, the local church can best prepare youth to consider long-term ministry to UPGs by preaching a comprehensive ministering of Scripture and by providing ministry opportunities and purpose-filled cross-cultural experiences as part of their discipleship. Missionaries can regularly be invited to speak and engage with the church in a meaningful way. The testimonies of missionaries and mobilizers remind the local church of its calling and God's faithfulness to equip us for Christ's mission.

---

31 The O'Neills.

32 To connect with the NextGen movement and join in the conversation with young leaders, visit https://www.nextgenleader.net/blog-2/.

Passing the Torch

As the world continues to accelerate, I (Lisa) believe there are always new opportunities for Christian leaders to mobilize God's next generation. Our young people don't exist to keep the legacy of our mission projects alive by adopting our strategies. They are the strategy. They are new good news messengers who will be figuring out what outfits them best to "run with perseverance the race marked out" for them (Heb 12:1b). For all the resources and experience that we have currently accumulated, with all that the Lord has blessed us, we can be stepping stones—leveraging all that we have so that we can continue the momentum of Jesus's kingdom work and set up the next generation to lead the global church into the twenty-second century. To do this, we must not only think about passing the torch but actually pass it, trusting that God will weave his good plan and purpose seamlessly into the next generation.

Passing the torch means actively engaging our young people to learn, be trained, get experience, make mistakes, and join in co-creating missional strategies in a world of constant change. It means supporting them and bringing them along to journey with you in the prime of your leadership influence so that they can experience what living missionally for Christ looks like. It also means modeling for them how gospel "runners" have their gaze set on "Jesus, the pioneer and perfecter of faith" (Heb 12:2a). This means allowing them to make mistakes without judgment but rather with the view that together we are always co-learning. We will be successful in mobilizing not only the next generation, but every generation, if our focus is on building this foundation of spiritual parenthood for Jesus's daughters and sons, the selfless giving of our attention, of our encouragement, and of our friendship to the next generation. No generation has a monopoly over the Holy Spirit, and the Great Commission is not a single generational mandate. We do this together or it remains undone. And when we participate in lifting up the next generation for missions, when we let them stand on our shoulders, it should bring us great joy.

Bibliography

Caldwell, Kevin. "Mutualism, the Image of God, and Missiological Implications." *ASFM Generational Frontiers in Mission for the Remaining Task in Frontier Mission* no. 19 (October 2023): 34–100.

Erlacher, Jolene, and Katy White. *Mobilizing Gen Z: Challenges and Opportunities for the Global Age of Missions*. Littleton, CO: William Carey Publishing, 2022.

Kim, Chong H. "Human and Spiritual Journey as Subjective, Personal, and Experiential." *ASFM Generational Frontiers in Mission for the Remaining Task in Frontier Mission* no. 19 (October 2023): 34–100.

O'Neill, Sterling, and Jim O'Neill. "Next Generation Leaders." Accessed April 18, 2024. www.nextgenleader.net.

33
The Making of Lists

Dan Scribner

In the Gospel of Matthew, Jesus's last words to his disciples were "therefore go and make disciples of all the nations." This mandate raises at least two questions: Who are the nations of the world, and which ones have few, if any, disciples? Since the 1970s, various efforts have been made to answer these questions.

A Brief History of Global People Group Lists

Dr. Ralph Winter gave his landmark unreached peoples presentation at Lausanne '74. No comprehensive global people group list existed at the time. In the late seventies and early eighties, the Missions Advanced Research and Communications Center (MARC) division of World Vision, headed by Ed Dayton, began publishing annual Unreached Peoples Directories. These were partial lists of unreached ethnolinguistic people groups. *Operation World*, while focusing primarily on political countries, also began including some people group information in the editions starting in the 1980s.

The foundation of global ethnolinguistic people groups lists is the language research of the Summer Institute of Linguistics (SIL) over the last eighty years presented in the *Ethnologue*,[1] a catalog of the world's languages.

Three comprehensive global people group lists exist today. These lists have distinct definitions, sources, criteria, audiences, and philosophies as outlined in Table 2.

The initial effort to produce a comprehensive global people group list was in 1982 with the first edition of the *World Christian Encyclopedia* (WCE), edited by Dr. David Barrett. This list continues to be updated and available through the Center for the Study of Global Christianity's *World Christian Database* (WCD).

A second global people group list, the Integrated Strategic Planning Database (ISPD), later renamed the Church Planting Progress Indicators (CPPI) database, was started in 1991 by the International Mission Board (IMB) SBC. The purpose was to track IMB church-planting activity among people groups. While the ISPD/CPPI had its roots in WCD data, it has been extensively modified by IMB field staff over the last three decades.

A third global people group list, Joshua Project, was birthed in 1995 and owes much of its genesis to Patrick Johnstone. Joshua Project is also indebted to OMID research for South Asia, Asia Harvest research for China and the Buddhist world, IPN research for Southeast Asia and Indonesia, in addition to numerous other national people group researchers, mission agencies, and on-site missionaries.

---
1 See https://www.ethnologue.com/.

Table 2: A Comparison of the Three Global People Group Lists

	World Christian Database	CPPI (IMB)	Joshua Project
People Definition	Globally ethnolinguistic only	Outside South Asia ethnolinguistic South Asia mixture of language and caste	Outside South Asia ethnolinguistic South Asia by caste, religion, and language
Start Date	1982	1991	1995
Unreached Definition	Less than 50 percent evangelical	Less than 2 percent Evangelical	Less than 2 percent evangelical and less than 5 percent Christian adherents
Unreached Measures	Exposure	Response	Response
Sources	Census and academic reports[1] Denominational reports Ethnologue	IMB field staff Ethnologue	Census and academic reports Regional and national researchers Networks, individuals, other data sets Ethnologue
Audience	Secular media, academia	IMB field staff and leadership	Global missions community
Philosophy	Adds groups when documented in published research	Adds groups once verified by field staff	Assumes worst case, adds all potential groups, removes if verified as not existing or extinct

Why Three Global People Lists?

Different perspectives on the same situation are a healthy thing. Looking at a picture from several angles often yields greater appreciation. Using different definitions and criteria can help clarify a task and highlight areas needing further research. People group database compilers are confronted by questions such as, Is language always the primary definer of a people group? Should caste be considered when defining a people group? Should Christian adherents be considered when setting the criteria for unreached? Should unreached be defined by exposure or response to the gospel? What are acceptable sources for input and edits? The three global people group lists answer these questions differently and thus provide different but valuable perspectives.

---

1 Includes sources such as national government census, UN, CIA database, and other state/government-generated data.

Segmentation within People Group Lists

Segmentation can be described as levels of detail or refinement. For example, the animal kingdom is segmented into a hierarchy of phylum, class, order, family, genus, and species with each level more and more specific. In a similar way, people group lists have traditionally had various levels of segmentation. These segmentation levels create a hierarchy moving from very broad, general classification (level A) to increasing detail and specificity (level E).

Different methods of segmenting people group lists have been suggested. Three of the most common approaches to segmentation are the columns in Table 2.

Levels A, B, and C would be considered traditional people group categories and lend themselves to global lists. However, levels D and E are not tracked in existing lists. These two levels are not necessarily smaller types of segmentation but rather a reconfiguration with multiple, mixed, or hybrid identities.

There is growing interest in greater detail, particularly among on-site workers seeking relevancy for local church planting. The interest in moving to segmentation levels D and E and greater detail does not preclude the importance of people group lists at segmentation levels A, B, and C. Levels A, B, and C serve as entry points for focusing on people groups. However, this desire for greater detail is pressing the limits of current people group lists.

Table 3: Comparing People Segmentation Levels

Segmentation Level	Dayton / Wilson (1984)[1]	Winter / Koch (Perspectives)[2]	Johnstone Joshua Project[3]
A		Major Cultural Blocs—broad categories of people groups, defined by religious-cultural spheres, strategic significance is global overview.	Affinity Bloc—All people groups, who either live in a particular region or have similar cultural roots. Peoples are broadly grouped into blocs with affinities based on language, culture, religion, politics. In nearly every bloc there are widely dissimilar and unrelated linguistic minorities, but often there is one particular culture that is dominant.
B			People Cluster—Within each Affinity Bloc are a number of more closely related peoples which, for strategic purposes, may be clustered together. These relationships are often based on a common identity of language and name but sometimes on the basis of culture, religion, economy, or dominance of one group over another.
C	Primary—ethnolinguistic preference which defines a person's identity and indicates one's primary loyalty	Ethnolinguistic Peoples—often a cluster of unimax groups, defined by linguistic, ethnic and political boundaries, strategic significance is mobilization and strategy.	People Group—"A significantly large group of individuals who perceive themselves to have a common affinity for one another because of their shared language, religion, ethnicity, residence, class or caste, situation, etc., or combinations of these. For evangelization purposes, a people group is the largest group within which the gospel can spread as a church planting movement without encountering barriers of understanding or acceptance." (1982 Consensus)

---

1 Dayton and Wilson, "Unreached Peoples '84."
2 Winter and Koch, "Finishing the Task."
3 See Joshua Project, Definitions.

Segmentation Level	Dayton / Wilson (1984)[4]	Winter / Koch (Perspectives)[5]	Johnstone Joshua Project[6]
D	Secondary—a sociological grouping which is to some degree subject to personal choice and allows for considerable mobility. Regional and generational groups, caste and class divisions are representative.	Unimax Peoples—networks of families with a shared identity, defined by social and cultural prejudices, discovered onsite, strategic significance is church planting.	Subgroups—a segment of a people group that may or may not need a unique church planting effort. In many cases, subgroups will require separate church planting efforts. In other cases, reaching the parent people group may reach the subgroups. In these cases, the gospel will likely flow between subgroups without encountering significant barriers of understanding or acceptance. Determined by onsite workers and research.
E	Tertiary—casual associations of people which are usually temporary and the result of circumstances rather than personal choice such as high-rise dwellers, drug addicts, occupational groupings and professionals	Socio Peoples—an association of peers, defined by activities or interests, discovered onsite, strategic significance is small group evangelism.	

Granularity and Complexity

Another term for segmentation is granularity. Granularity is the level of detail and refinement of data. Increasing granularity can be pictured as moving from boulders to large stones to fist-size rocks to pebbles to sand. People group lists generally track groups at the country and language (i.e., level C "fist-size rocks"). Greater granularity would mean tracking by province or district, subgroup, and/or dialect (i.e., level D "pebbles"). For example, current lists have an entry "Pashtun of India" while a more granular list might have "Yusafzai Pashtun practicing Barelvi Sunni Islam speaking Urdu in Farrukhabad district of Uttar Pradesh, India" as a distinct entry. Further refinement by occupation, shared interests, skills, education, networks, and/or social status would create lists at level E "sand."

Figure 7 illustrates the relationship between people group list granularity and complexity. The graph is divided into the segmentation levels in Table 3. Very general uses are suggested for each section. The numbers in parenthesis are counts from the Joshua Project list as of May 2020. Groups to the left of the dotted line would be considered traditional people groups and groups to the right would be considered dynamic groupings. Table 4 compares traditional people groups and dynamic groupings.

---

4 Dayton and Wilson, "Unreached Peoples '84."
5 Winter and Koch, "Finishing the Task."
6 See Joshua Project, Definitions.

Table 4: Comparing Traditional and Dynamic Groupings

Traditional People Groups	Dynamic Groupings
Barriers are based on fairly well defined linguistic, ethnic, political, religious, or historical boundaries.	Barriers based on almost any kind of "glue" (e.g., occupation, hobbies, interests, social networks, relationships, economic status, affinity groups, etc.)
Permanent, durable, fixed	Temporary, fluid, changing
Individuals are only in one group and stay in that group for a lifetime.	Individuals can be and are most likely in several groups at the same time.
Have served segmentation levels A, B, and C reasonably well for the last forty plus years	Not addressed by current people group lists
While imperfect, it is possible to catalog globally as demonstrated by WCD, IMB, and Joshua Project people group lists.	Unrealistic and impossible to catalog globally. Lists may be feasible by on-site workers and researchers on a very local level.

Consider the Fulani of Central Africa. Moving from left to right across Figure 7, the Fulani can be viewed as a single People Cluster[7] (level B "large stones"). This level does not distinguish specific Fulani people groups and combines 40 million individuals into one category. Typically, this is the level of granularity that the secular media and general missions education material use. To protect believers, movements to Jesus among the Fulani are reported at this broader segmentation level. However, a church adopting a people group for prayer and engagement needs greater detail and a smaller size group to focus on. The church would likely adopt a specific Fulani people group such as the Fulani, Pulaar in Senegal[8] (level C "fist-size rocks"). As workers began on-site ministry, they might focus on the Toucouleur dialect-speaking, millennial age, healthcare professional Pulaar Fulanis living in Matam, Senegal. This would be a hybrid grouping (level E "sand"). The glue that holds such a hybrid group together goes beyond ethnicity and language.

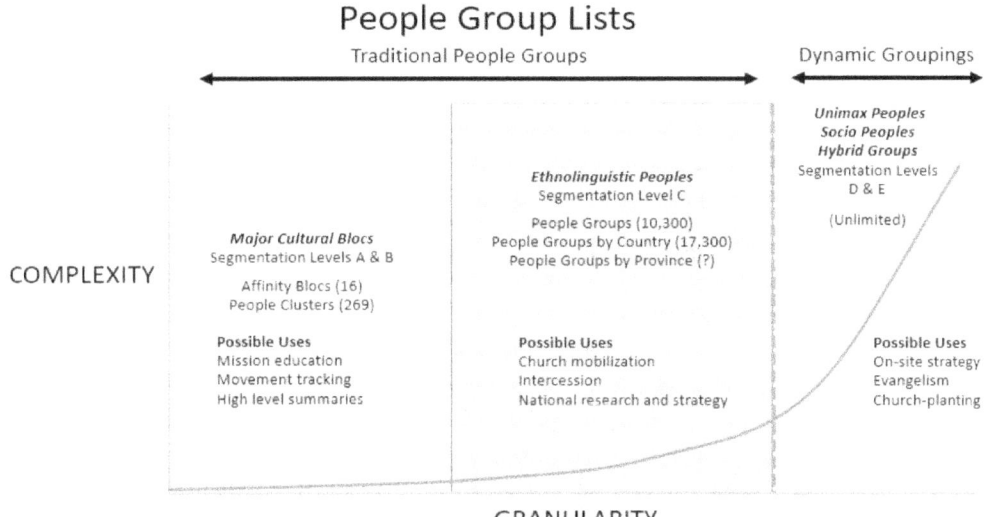

Figure 7: Granularity Versus Complexity in People Group Lists

---

7 See https://joshuaproject.net/clusters/173.
8 See https://joshuaproject.net/people_groups/15622/SG.

People Group List Challenges

As the Fulani example illustrates, a great deal is being asked of current people group databases. One size does not fit all; in fact, one size may end up confusing all. People group list challenges include a variety of potential uses, a wide spectrum of audiences, and significant security risks.

Variety of Uses

The uses mentioned in Figure 7 are very general and are simply suggestions. The main point is that people group lists are used in numerous ways ranging from challenging new believers to the big picture of the Great Commission to a local church mission committee selecting a specific people group for adoption to on-site workers identifying a strategic focus to maximize the spread of the gospel.

Spectrum of Audiences

Each end user has different interests and needs. Pastors giving an annual missions sermon may be looking for simple, high-level summaries. An intercessor might want a descriptive people profile. Mission leaders want detailed data to make deployment decisions. Traditional people profiles and lists have probably proven more useful to mobilizers than to on-site workers. The breadth of potential audiences for people groups lists is problematic. Current lists attempt to serve all audiences but may not be optimized for any of them.

Security Risks

The more information included in a list (i.e., the more "pebbles" and "sand" presented), the greater the security risks in sensitive areas. This often prohibits publishing lists. For example, reporting too detailed information on Christward movements among the Fulani below the level B "large stone" could jeopardize growth and endanger lives.

Changing Barriers

From a church planting perspective people groups boundaries are defined by barriers to the spread of the gospel. Whichever barriers are highest defines the extent of a people group. Changing barriers are causing an expansion from what might be called *traditional* people groups to what might be termed *dynamic* or *hybrid* groupings. Table 33.3 compares these perspectives.

Traditional Boundaries Are Changing

The forces of language consolidation, urbanization, globalization, and migration are blurring the boundaries of traditional ethnolinguistic people groups. Existing people group identities are being mixed and recombined, and new hybrid identities are being created. For example, language consolidation is reducing the language barrier that traditionally has defined many people groups. Speakers of smaller languages are rapidly learning one or more global languages, usually for education and job opportunities. These are often languages widely used on the internet. New mobile devices are allowing on-the-fly, real-time translation. A rise in linguistic nationalism is also occurring which results in people groups being merged together through administrative governmental pressure. At the same time, some people groups are dividing over a desire to preserve language and its cultural contexts. Few boundaries are truly rigid; the edges have fluidity.

Urbanization and migration are reducing ethnicity barriers. Groupings of individuals in cities are being driven increasingly by occupation, shared interests, skills, education, networks, social status, and activities rather than by ethnic background. Globalization is reducing the ethnic as well as religious barriers. An interconnected world allows exposure to and opportunity to explore different worldviews, values, and religions. Globalization allows connections and relationships with other like-minded individuals around the world, rather than only those in one's immediate physical area. Efforts like SpaceX's Starlink project to bring internet to rural communities are accelerating globalization.

New Groupings Are Emerging

These forces are changing the barriers to the spread of the gospel and impacting how the *ethne* of the world are defined from a church planting perspective. Growing reports of movements to Jesus crossing traditional people group boundaries demonstrates a shift in how the gospel flows. For example, it has been suggested that Gen-Z youth of Riyadh have more in common with the youth of Chicago than with their own parents. That might be an exaggeration, but it makes a useful point. Youth in many cases are not identifying as strongly with their traditional people group, based on ethnicity and language, as they are with others in their age group and social experience.

For on-site workers, other ways of grouping are becoming more useful and needed than groupings by ethnicity and language. The closer lists get to social and ethnic realities on the ground, the more needed and useful are other ways of grouping. For example, classifying Saudi Arabian Gen-Z youth in a database using traditional people group definitions could potentially obscure their preferred identity for church planting purposes and limit reaching them with the gospel. Identifying Saudi Gen-Z youth as a unique dynamic grouping might accelerate the flow of the gospel along relational and common interest pathways.

Complementary Perspectives

Traditional people group lists are still important and useful but need periodic "rethinking." Lists help to outline the unfinished task of the Great Commission and provide church leaders and mobilizers with motivating benchmarks. At the same time, new perspectives and dynamics are bringing other groupings into focus. The glue that binds these new groupings together may not be language or ethnicity, but occupation, education, shared interests, social networks, generational issues, and worldviews. These dynamic groupings will be increasingly strategic and effective pathways for the spread of the gospel. Both the traditional and dynamic perspectives of people groups are useful and should not be viewed as old versus new, but as complementary.

Conclusions

- People group thinking is not going away. Traditional people group lists are still very applicable in parts of South Asia dominated by the formal and informal caste system, in tribal settings, and in rural areas. This includes much of Africa and Asia, where the great majority of unreached people groups reside.

- At the same time, the forces of language consolidation, urbanization, globalization, and migration are creating new social dynamics and changing both the barriers and boundaries by which some groups are defined.
- These hybrid, transnational, and other groupings must be considered for evangelistic purposes, disciple making, and church planting movements.
- Global people group lists, as currently structured, do not support dynamic groupings (i.e., to the right of the dotted line in Figure 7).
- Thus, new ways of listing and tracking dynamic groupings on a local level are needed to advance the initiatives of on-site workers.

Bibliography

Dayton and Wilson, "Unreached Peoples '84," cited by Dave Datema in "People Group Paradigm in 2020" webinar.

Winter, Ralph D. and Bruce A. Koch. "Finishing the Task: The Unreached Peoples Challenge." International Journal of Frontier Missions, 19, no. 4 (Winter 2002): 15–25.

Reflection and Discussion
Issues Affecting Progress

1. What are some reasons for "fog in the pews" about the vision for unreached peoples and the priority of finishing the task? How would you describe the "fog" in your church?

2. What is one astonishing fact or figure you learned about unreached people?.

3. What percentage of your church's missions budget goes to "regular missions" (where the church is) and what percentage goes to "frontier missions" among unreached peoples (where the church isn't)?

4. Ask God to lead your church or ministry in "adopting" an unreached, unengaged, or frontier people group. List some first steps you can take to learn more.

5. Explore JoshuaProject.net, read about UPGs in a country in the Muslim, Hindu, or Buddhist world, and choose one unreached, unengaged, or frontier people group for prayer.

6. What ethnicities or people groups do you see represented in your city, school, workplace, or context? Pray especially for people who migrated (for work, study, or other reasons) from peoples or countries in the largely unreached Muslim, Hindu, or Buddhist cultural spheres.

Part 7

Imagining Fulfillment

Purpose and Promise of People Vision

34
A Church for Every People

A Retrospect on Mapping Peoples

Brad Gill

In the 1970s, when my wife and I determined we would pursue ministry among Muslims, I remember needing a map. I was not lost, really, but I needed orientation. The mapping of "unreached peoples" had gained some momentum, and we used it to explore the labyrinth of Muslim peoples. I recall highlighting the Muslim Hui of China, the Kurds of the Middle East, and the Berbers of North Africa.

It was then that the watchword "A Church for Every People" arose and gave impetus and force to mission among unreached peoples. After four decades, the watchword appears to have lost its edge in the American evangelical public. Let me bracket the concept of church, setting it aside for now, and focus on the concept of peoples. As a disclaimer, I was quite invested in this idea of peoples—of unreached peoples. I studied under Donald McGavran at Fuller Seminary's School of World Mission and benefited greatly from the anthropology of Paul Hiebert and Charles Kraft. They effectively hammered at my American evangelical individualism and reshaped my understanding of receptivity among sociocultural groups. But I also married into Ralph Winter's family, and his statistical anthropology would map for me a global ethnoscape of peoples. My wife and I actually sat with McGavran and Winter when the concept of unreached peoples coalesced into this watchword. To say the least, we were a bit entangled in the assumptions and inclinations behind this missiology of people groups.

We would soon find out, as they say, that "the map is not the territory."[1]

The complexities of "a church for every people" would mushroom for a younger generation sent to these fields. The evidence of new movements over the arc of forty years is impressive—even unprecedented—and more often confirms the presence of those "bridges of God" that McGavran claimed would transmit the gospel throughout a people. On the other hand, any rough, superficial mapping of people groups had to gain social and anthropological maturation. The temptation has more recently been to discard such a crude mapping of ethnolinguistic peoples. From my experience, I would contend it provided an excellent orientation for ministry.

Re-mapping the Territory: A Field Odyssey

I arrived in the North African country of Morocco, where quite an auspicious league of anthropologists had already done field research. They included Clifford Geertz and Ernst Gellner, both theoretical leaders in their respective schools of thought. For all the rank atheism

---
1 Farnam Street, "Map."

of modern anthropology, I am greatly indebted to the men and women who began to map out the territory for me. Early French ethnography had divided Arab and Berber in a colonial effort to control that historic Muslim kingdom. While there was substantial social reality to those ethnic distinctions, the reigning king was attempting to assimilate these peoples in an effort to modernize his country.

My wife and I were the first American family to settle into our Atlas Mountain town. In the early 1980s, there was an opportunity to establish a small business that introduced me into the town's commercial life. Historically, that town had been the nexus of a large confederation of tribes. Their powerful chief had led a heroic tribal resistance against French colonization in the early twentieth century. But when his sons later flipped their support to the French, the monarchy of Morocco had to carefully negotiate this wily region when it established its independence from the French. This was a Berber town that was navigating its way into a modernizing Arab world.

The watchword "A Church for This People" provided a basic map for our purposes in this small urbanizing peasant town. I recall the day down in the center of that market town when I happened upon an old building with the words *Dyur Shiukh* inscribed on the entry way: "The Houses of the Sheikhs." This was the original small parliament of their tribal confederation. Looking around there was no immediate indication of that sociological reality. This peasant society appeared to be well on the way to developing a more urban civic government, and the reality of "peoples" or "tribes" seemed to be dissipating. T. E. Lawrence once said that Arabs did not believe in institutions, only individuals, and I wondered if it was true of these Berbers as well.

The local contours of "peoplehood"—that sense of collective social inclusion—only gradually emerged. I can best describe it through different episodes in my relationship with two men who became my dear friends. Abdurahman (Abbas) and Abdulaziz (Aziz) lived in the same town and spoke the same dialect of Berber from that region, but their lives pointed in two very different directions. Those distinct orientations distinguished them socially, culturally, and territorially. Their lives helped my rudimentary attempts to map Berber culture and eventually to settle on a social watershed that was potentially relevant for any future turning to Christ.

Admittedly, that town forty years later has yet to see a movement to Christ of any significant form. There are encouraging indications of a turning to Christ in the region, especially with new forms of social media. But one of those who had begun to follow Jesus was my friend Aziz. His life helped me appreciate the texture of Berberness in our region.

Aziz's faith had led him out of town, down to the big city where he was able to assimilate into a small but diverse group of Moroccan believers. That is where I first met him, when I was visiting the senior foreigner who was discipling Aziz. I recall this expatriate's blunt response when Aziz introduced himself as a Berber from our mountain town, interjecting, "They're all the same, Arab and Berber." Morocco certainly gives that impression, but I could tell Aziz had more on his mind. A few months later, he visited us up in his hometown. He became a friend who helped us understand the hidden Berberness of this urbanizing region.

He took us up the road to another town where he had relatives. Sitting on the floor, eating, I watched the sudden transformation of my friend. He became animated and appeared to be experiencing some kind of psychological release. He pulled out the *bendir* (large, round, handheld drum) and began to lead a round of traditional Berber songs. The whole environment changed. Gone was his formal and stiff social comportment of the city. He was back home. He was where he belonged.

A year or so later, he visited and asked us a dangerous question, one that would not find a sympathetic ear in his fellowship in the big city. "Would it be all right to marry a girl from my Berber town, even though she is not a Christian?" It seems he had chatted on the bus with a nice girl from town on one of his visits. He could tell she had a sweet spirit and might be open to Christ. Hmmm. Aziz was not getting any younger, and he wanted to marry someone from his home, a Berber who spoke his language. Well, his mind was pretty made up, the marriage happened, and it led to her coming to faith, to children, and to a wonderful life together. Marriage is so often the bottom line of identity.

I was tempted to feel Aziz's decisions were confirming the validity of ethnic identity for communicating Christ into this bilingual, bicultural mountain region. But towns are complex, which became vividly clear when I introduced Aziz to another younger Berber believer in town. As we sat together that day, I was surprised by the social distancing, the formality, and the absence of any personal affinity. Christian reality had hit a wall. In the days that followed I learned that I was witnessing a severe socioeconomic cleavage. Aziz was from a family who had served as privileged serfs on the great landholdings of aristocracy (the oppressor), while my other friend was from a squatter family struggling to make it on the edge of town (the oppressed). So much for a wonderfully homogenous people. The urban realities of megacities were already manifesting in this modest-sized mountain city. An ethnic map is not the actual territory.

This ethnic reality was made even clearer when I got to know yet another friend, Abbas. He was from a small oasis on the other side of the mountains, where the Sahara begins to stretch south into Africa. That is the opposite direction of the big city where Aziz had gone. But Abbas had made good, had attended the big university, and was now an Arabic teacher at the local high school in town.

His Berber dialect, while not the same, was linguistically intelligible to those in town, but his demeanor was very different. I should have noticed it in the way he walked, but I gradually caught it in conversation as he helped me learn the local language. He was a proud man. Affable, fun, but proud. I eventually came to understand that there was a distinct sense of honor emanating from these Saharans. One day I was walking down the main street, and Abbas called to me. He was sitting at one of the local cafés with fellow teachers from the high school. Come to find out they were all from different points on the Saharan side of the Atlas. Their territorial affinity even overcame their major linguistic differences, and they were sealed together by the deep cultural estrangement they felt on this side of the mountains. These were Abbas's people.

One local reality explains much of this social division between Abbas and Aziz. This mountain city was known throughout the country for its prostitution. It was a morally dirty town, whose excesses my other friend Aziz could easily rationalize away. But my friend Abbas blushed when admitting this reality to me as a foreigner. The dignity bred in those desert regions resisted the pull from this den of iniquity. This explained his Islamic religiosity: very little participation in public ritual but a dogmatic personal identity as a "clean" Muslim. He was nothing like the puritanical movements that had emerged out of the desert over the centuries, but he claimed the same desert roots as their religious prophet, Mohammed. There was a clear pride of place.

A local like Aziz might accept Christianity, but Abbas's religious identity would never transit that religious barrier. Christianity was identified with the West and with the colonial oppression of the French. I remember the day Abbas and I were walking across the hillside behind my home, and we suddenly found ourselves walking in and out of little pits in the landscape. "What are these holes?" I asked. Abbas was embarrassed. "These were the local grave sites of the French whose caskets were dug up and sent back to France after independence." Abbas was not a violent man, but he nevertheless aligned his religious honor against any oppressive colonial modernity.

There also remained a deep Berberness in Abbas, and I learned it was the key to opening his hardened religious spirit. He would tell me over the years that I should go to see the *maraboutin* (holy ones) who crafted and sold rugs in the mountains. Interesting. These were Catholic sisters in that mountain region who made carpets as a way to employ and support local Berber tribes. I was not sure of his interest in them until he offered a story from when he was in high school and boarding in the town where these sisters had a small convent. On one occasion, he was sick and hospitalized at the local clinic where he had befriended a very young Berber girl in the bed next to his. She was waiting for her mommy to come.

Abbas tells how the day came when her mommy arrived, but to his utter surprise this mommy was one of those foreign sisters dressed in mountain Berber attire. She could speak fluent Berber, and she turned to Abbas and thanked him for caring for her "daughter." Apparently, this woman traveled with and cared for a transnational Berber tribe, and it was this indigenous, authentic expression of Christian love that had bypassed all of Abbas's defenses. He was in awe of these women who followed the Christian way.

The territory was gradually taking shape. Two men, Abbas and Aziz, situated in a single ethnolinguistic identity, classified themselves differently. Their way of constructing sameness, of including and excluding others, was self-evident to them. Their perceptions were what anthropologists might call a "folk classification." These anecdotal experiences with Abbas and Aziz were my way of beginning to discover how group identities were distinguished across this Berber terrain. This was their map, not mine, and that indigenous map shows the territory so vital for the natural diffusion of the gospel.

Some Reflections on Mapping Peoples

But let us return to our maps and, in particular, our own classification of "people groups." From my experience I want to suggest three things.

The Map of Unreached People Groups Is a Reduction, but It Is a Useful One

Essentially all maps are abstractions and leave out much detail. All maps are wrong, but some can be useful.² Accuracy is important, but their usefulness is the way they direct our attention and initially guide us. We can begin to confuse this map of people groups with actual reality. "For many people, the model creates its own reality. … We forget that reality is a lot messier. The map isn't the territory."³

The ethnolinguistic map of the Berber peoples was a place for me to begin. Remember, thinking about people groups was counterintuitive for me as an American, and this map can reaffirm an essential social reality: People will map themselves in society. This people group sensibility—though quite abstract and reductionist—forced my American eye to see the social realities of Berber peoples.

The Map of Unreached Peoples Has Strategic Limitations

> [The] first step is to realize that you do not understand a model, map, or reduction unless you understand and respect its limitations. We must always be vigilant by stepping back to understand the context in which a map is useful.⁴

People group thinking has been legitimately criticized for the way it can cause us to ignore the wider context.⁵ Admittedly, our modern taxonomic propensity can push us to overreach and invest too much in a simple ethnolinguistic model. Reaching "every tribe, language, nation and people" is certainly our end. It is a biblical promise, a biblical task, and a biblical objective. But it does not warrant a narrow strategic focus on ethnicity, groupness, and cultural homogeneity. One must appreciate the entire context God is using, what McGavran used to call the "human matrix."

For example, urbanization as a human system intersects with ethnicity and apparently seems to make inconsequential any folk classification. It is obvious that Abbas's and Aziz's children face a whole new set of conditions. The acceleration of globalization may erode their traditional maps of group identity. Modern processes of social dis-embedding, self-reflexivity, and cultural hybridity, as well as migration, poverty, and epidemics may loosen or even dissolve the social categories of their parents. Consequently, they may acquire a more modern structure of consciousness, or they could experience that pervasive homelessness that erodes their once more socially intact background. New freedoms could bring deep disaffection and malaise, and new generations will no doubt entertain options. Any counter-actualization could choose from new ideologies, indigenous art forms, or socioreligious associations that champion traditional values. Old maps are reconstructed into new maps that then recreate belonging.

All to say, we must respect the limitations of this map of unreached peoples. Every mission sending base and every training institution and curriculum must recognize and transcend the way the map may appear more real than the territory. Any effective missiology requires it.

The Map of Unreached Peoples Is Based on a Principle

The map is not the main thing. The interactions with Abbas and Aziz are not solely for pinning

---

2 Farnam Street.
3 Farnam Street.
4 Farnam Street.
5 Howell and Zehner, *Power*.

down their homogenous social affinities. The map emerges from the use of a compass, a more basic principle, and McGavran would state it in a sentence: "Men like to turn to Christ without crossing ethnic and linguistic barriers."[6] That principle might be stated a number of ways, but it will always emphasize familiarity as fundamental to the context in which people prefer to turn to Christ.

During my years in Morocco this principle was confirmed across the border in Algeria. We continually heard of an unprecedented movement to Christ—a church—among the Berbers of the Kabyle mountains—a people. I would witness this extensive fellowship when I traveled into France. But that momentum never crossed into our Berber region. The principle, it seemed, was a fairly good compass for our region of the world.

Conclusion

I like to think the Apostle Paul anticipated this entire discussion about mapping unreached peoples. His missiology of peoples appears when he speaks to those Athenians of the diverse peoples (*ethne*) of mankind (Acts 17) and the way God would determine their "allotted periods" and the "boundaries of their dwelling place" (v. 26 ESV). His motivation was not the map, but a deeper apostolic compass for reaching all peoples "that they should seek God, and perhaps feel their way toward him and find him" (v. 27 ESV). The map is an afterthought but a very strategic thought at that. It is all about peoples finding God.

Bibliography

Farnam Street. "The Map Is Not the Territory." Accessed April 13, 2024. http://fs.blog/2015/11/map-and-territory/.

Howell, Brian, and Edwin Zehner, eds. *Power and Identity in the Global Church*. Pasadena, CA: William Carey Library, 2009.

McGavran, Donald. *Understanding Church Growth*. Grand Rapids: Eerdmans, 1970.

---

6 McGavran, *Understanding*, 198.

35
Pioneer Apostleship

Twelve Principles

Daniel Waheli

The phrase *pioneer apostleship* has been used often in frontier missions circles over the past decades. The breakthrough work that the term implies, however, has been practiced since Jesus left us the Great Commission. Over the centuries, many different approaches have been employed for this type of ministry. But while strategies may change, biblical principles do not.

The purpose of this chapter is to explore some of the biblical principles involved in advancing the gospel among unreached and unengaged peoples and places with the goal of making disciples who lead to churches and movements. These principles are drawn from my reflections on Scripture and personal experiences providing oversight for pioneer field teams among unreached peoples in North and Sub-Saharan Africa, the Middle East, and South, Central, and Southeast Asia. These twelve principles are especially visible in the life of the Apostle Paul and the Lord Jesus, "the apostle and high priest of our confession" (Heb 3:1 ESV).

#1 Preparation for Ministry

As with everything in life, we need preparation if we are to have a successful outcome. Too often, in the past, knowledge was emphasized at the expense of experience and practical application. We need to emphasize all three, using Jesus as our model. He taught his disciples truth at the same time that they were learning to apply the truth in everyday situations. Some of this preparation needs to take place in local churches. One hopeful sign is the emerging collaboration of churches with specialized mission organizations and programs that specialize in training aspiring workers for cross-cultural mission. These programs include opportunities for language learning, character and leadership development, spiritual formation, team dynamics, and local outreach to local refugee and immigrant populations. Pre-field training programs like the Intercultural Studio and Launch Global, and on-field "Hub" training centers run by Live Dead, are examples of this type of integrated, experiential learning program designed to prepare workers for their journey to the nations.

#2 Power of God's Spirit

At Jesus's baptism, the Holy Spirit visibly came on him and anointed him for his upcoming ministry over the next three years (Luke 3:21–22; 4:1, 18–19). We need to follow Jesus's example. Paul said that we need to constantly "be filled with the Holy Spirit" (Eph 5:18) to strengthen the church and to advance any kind of kingdom work, especially apostolic "breakthrough" ministry (Rom 15:19).

We do not emphasize this enough. There are many fine courses on Islam, ministry among Muslims, intercultural studies, anthropology, linguistics, etc. We need to add teaching focused

#3 Abiding and Spending Time with the Father

Jesus said, "Very truly I tell you, the Son can do nothing by himself; he can do only what he sees his Father doing, because whatever the Father does the Son also does" (John 5:19 NIV). He spent nights in prayer and time alone with his Father. He knew when to dismiss the crowds and be "by himself to pray" (Matt 14:23; Mark 6:46). Sometimes Jesus "spent the night praying to God" (Luke 6:12) as when he had to make big decisions like choosing the twelve disciples or facing challenging situations as in the garden of Gethsemane.

Paul said of himself that he was caught up into paradise and saw things that he could not even express by his own words (2 Cor 12:4). He said that he prayed more in the Spirit than all the others (1 Cor 14:18). He did not cease to give thanks to God for the people with whom missionaries had been working and to lift them up in his prayers (Eph 1:6). Paul spent many hours praying alone with the Lord, the One who had appeared to him and forever changed his life. Prayer undergirds gospel advance. "Abiding" in Christ must be central in our personal lives if we are to grow in intimate knowledge of the Lord, lead others to know him, and bear fruit that endures (John 15).

#4 Team

Jesus did not work on his own. He built a "team" of disciples around himself and spent most of his time with them, teaching them and empowering them to do the same work that he was doing. As we know, the twelve apostles, together with many other trained disciples, changed the world.

Paul never worked on his own. On his first missionary journey, he and Barnabas were sent out as a team by the church in Antioch (Acts 13:1–4), and this event established the pattern for the rest of Paul's life. The apostolic work is a team effort that is most effective if all of the gifts mentioned in Ephesians 4:11 (apostles, prophets, evangelists, pastors, and teachers) are present in a team—along with other spiritual gifts, including administration, mercy, helps, and others. Because of the Spirit living within us, all Christians can be used in these gifts at various times in our lives, although most of us have one or two giftings through which we most commonly and effectively minister to others.

#5 Word and Power

John Piper says, "I count at least 17 times where miracles help lead to conversions in the book of Acts. The clearest examples are in Acts 9:34–35 and 9:40, 42."[1] In Isaiah 61 and Luke 4, we see the ministry of the Messiah described in terms of proclamation and accompanying signs. Jesus later confirmed this type of kingdom ministry in response to John the Baptist's disciples questioning whether Jesus was really the Messiah. He answered them, "The blind receive sight, the lame walk, those who have leprosy are cleansed, the deaf hear, the dead are raised, and the good news is proclaimed to the poor" (Matt 11:5 NIV). This was the Jesus way of ministry: He embodied and proclaimed the message of the kingdom and worked the signs of the kingdom.

---

1 Piper, "Signs and Wonders."

Later, Paul described his apostolic ministry, "For I decided to know nothing among you except Jesus Christ and him crucified" (1 Cor 2:2 ESV). He said that "our gospel came to you not only in word, but also in power and in the Holy Spirit and with full conviction" (1 Thess 1:5 ESV). "My speech and my message were not in plausible words of wisdom, but in demonstration of the Spirit and of power, so that your faith might not rest in the wisdom of men but in the power of God" (1 Cor 2:4–5 ESV).

The clear testimony of Scripture is that the word of God shared with the power of God has produced faith in many people's lives. It is the hearing of the word that produces faith (Rom 10:17), and demonstrations of God's power often open doors and hearts for people to listen to the word.

#6 Church Planting

Jesus told us that he would build his church and even the gates of hell would not prevail against it (Matt 16:18). Paul built his ministry on the promise that Jesus would build his church (cf. 1 Cor 3:10–15) and that nothing could overcome this work.

While churches may take different forms, they all consist of born-again believers gathering together in the name of Jesus to glorify God the Father. The book of Acts, which recounts the birth of the first church after Pentecost, gives us pictures of what a church should look like, and how it grows, and how it can be used as a key resource for apostolic teams. "They devoted themselves to the apostles' teaching and to fellowship, to the breaking of bread and to prayer. … And the Lord added to their number daily those who were being saved" (cf. Acts 2:42-47 NIV).

#7 Multiple Elders

Jesus entrusted the apostles and early disciples with the continuation of his kingdom ministry to reach the whole world. In Acts 15, we see a council of leaders that tackled challenging and difficult questions the young church was facing. Paul, or in some instances his disciples, appointed multiple elders in all the churches he founded (there is no example in the Bible of a single leader of a church).

Churches must have a structure by which they can multiply and grow through natural family connections and social networks. Historically, churches have sometimes added excessive structure, or they have eliminated all structure. Both extremes have hindered the growth of the church, either squelching initiative or eliminating biblical leadership and accountability.

#8 Depth and Breadth

The gospel impacts people's lives in both depth (transformation) and breadth (fruitfulness). Jesus spent three years working on the disciples' character, helping them become more like him. He had to inspire them, encourage them, challenge them, teach them, and rebuke them. The Holy Spirit and the new creation community helped them continue to grow.

The Apostle Paul valued the transformation God had worked in his life by grace and appealed to churches to follow him. "Be imitators of me as I am of Christ" (1 Cor 11:1 ESV). Peter urges, "Just as he who called you is holy, so be holy in all you do; for it is written: 'Be holy, because I am holy'" (1 Pet 1:15–16 NIV). Our lives must reflect and display God's character and holiness.

The Lord also wants us to bear much fruit, "thirtyfold and sixtyfold and a hundredfold!" (Mark 4:20 ESV). "This is to my Father's glory, that you bear much fruit, showing yourselves to be my disciples" (John 15:8 NIV). Our Lord is worthy to be glorified by a multitude of all tribes and nations (Rev 5:9; 7:9). "And this gospel of the kingdom will be proclaimed throughout the whole world as a testimony to all nations, and then the end will come" (Matt 24:14 ESV).

The creeds describe the church with the marks "one, holy, catholic (universal), and *apostolic*." The church is grounded in the *apostolic word*, "the faith once delivered to the saints" (Jude 3), and in the *apostolic commission*, to be co-joined with the Trinitarian God in his redemptive mission in the world. The apostolicity, the "sent-ness" of the church, is part of our very identity!

#9 Breaking New Ground

When the people wanted to keep Jesus with them, he said that he needed to move on. "Let us go somewhere else—to the nearby villages—so I can preach there also. That is why I have come" (Mark 1:38 NIV). Though his geographical reach was limited during his earthly life, Jesus always had the whole world in mind (Mark 10:45; cf. Isa 49:6). He sent the Holy Spirit to indwell and empower his disciples for the expansion of the kingdom to "the ends of the earth" (Acts 1:8)!

Paul clearly expressed his apostolic passion and purpose: "It has always been my ambition to preach the gospel where Christ was not known, so that I would not be building on someone else's foundation. Rather, as it is written: 'Those who were not told about him will see, and those who have not heard will understand'" (Rom 15:20–21 NIV).

Paul's ambition was to bring the gospel of Jesus to the ends of the earth. Sometimes the Lord redirected his plans (Acts 16:6–7), but the Spirit empowered his efforts such that he could humbly say, "So from Jerusalem all the way around to Illyricum, I have fully proclaimed the gospel of Christ" (Rom 15:19 NIV). "All the Jews and Greeks who lived in the province of Asia heard the word of the Lord" (Acts 19:10 NIV).

But Paul knew when it was time to move on to new ground. "But now that there are no further opportunities for me in these regions, and since I have longed for many years to visit you, I hope to see you on my way to Spain. And after I have enjoyed your company for a while, you can equip me for my journey" (Rom 15:23–24 BSB). The invitation to partner in apostolic ministry to unreached peoples and places still stands!

#10 Suffering

When Peter wanted to protect Jesus from fulfilling his destiny through the cross, Jesus rebuked him, saying, "Get behind me, Satan!" (Matt 16:23 ESV). Jesus knew that his death would open the doors for millions to enter paradise and spend eternity with him and the Father. Jesus's death did not make sense to Peter at that time, so he wanted to hinder it.

Suffering often does not make sense to us as well. Jesus sacrificed himself for us; as we follow his example, we aspire to say with Paul, "I have been crucified with Christ. It is no longer I who live, but Christ who lives in me. And the life I now live in the flesh I live by faith in the Son of God, who loved me and gave himself for me" (Gal 2:20 ESV).

When Paul was defending his ministry as an apostle, he listed the different sufferings that he had experienced (2 Cor 11:16–33). He did this to show that one of the marks of true apostolic ministry is suffering, suffering that reflects "the afflictions of Christ" and points to the crucified risen One we proclaim (Col 1:24).

Apostolic ministry allows the followers of Christ to add what was lacking in the afflictions of Christ: "Now I rejoice in my sufferings for your sake, and in my flesh I am filling up what is lacking in Christ's afflictions for the sake of his body, that is, the church" (Col 1:24 ESV). We know that our suffering adds nothing to anyone's salvation, of course. Christ fulfilled that for all time as he cried out on the cross, "It is finished" (John 19:30). The suffering that we are joyfully "adding," as Paul said, is the suffering "for the sake of his body," for the sake of planting expressions of his body the church all over the world! This will include any kind of suffering. Paul said that he rejoices in joining in "the fellowship of his sufferings" (Phil 3:10) to "advance the gospel" (Phil 1:12), to establish churches among all peoples, among every nation, all over the world! This is the task left over for us.

Many men and women have sacrificed their lives before us, and many will do so after us, as the "cloud of witnesses" (Heb 12:1ff.) and church history testify. Are we taking the baton in our generation and doing our part, knowing that our part will involve joyfully suffering in whatever way the Lord has prepared for us?

#11 Perseverance—Never Giving Up

There are many signs that distinguish ministry in the apostolic pattern; let us consider these two: "The signs of a true apostle were performed among you with utmost patience, with signs and wonders and mighty works" (2 Cor 12:12 ESV). We have already considered the truth that signs and wonders are part of the apostolic calling. I want to highlight the other point in this verse, which speaks about patience or perseverance. The apostolic calling never gives up!

An old song puts it this way, "I have decided to follow Jesus, no turning back, no turning back." I remember the story of the first family among the Gao tribe in India that came to Jesus. Others in the tribe told the father to renounce his faith or they would kill first his children, then his wife, and finally him. As they repeated this ultimatum multiple times, he always answered, "No turning back." He persevered in patience and faith and was willing to pay the cost. Later on, God used the martyrdom of this family to spark a revival that reached nearly a million people among the Gao, nearly the whole tribe. Apostolic ministry requires patience and perseverance and a clear decision to never give up even in the face of death.

Many of the least reached peoples in our world live in inhospitable, difficult places. As pastors, church and mission leaders, and educators, we need to ask: How can we disciple people to have the character and resilience to persevere in the hardest, darkest, most challenging places on earth?

#12 The Grave—The End Point of Our Calling

Today we live in a fast-changing, increasingly unstable world. Consider the recent wars in Ukraine, Palestine, and Sudan, not to mention the ongoing disturbances in places like Somalia. Some countries have become more open to the gospel, while others are more restrictive; governments rise and fall, and political situations change, sometimes overnight. But our calling has not changed and is not dependent on circumstance, safety, and security. We need to "go" and serve among all the unreached peoples and places in our world. Some of the greatest challenges are represented by Islam, Hinduism, and Buddhism. Many of these peoples remain bound, broken, and blinded by "the god of this world" (2 Cor 4:4).

We need to face these realities and send people from everywhere to everywhere to reach all peoples and places. Some might be called to lay down their lives for the name of Jesus. Some may be imprisoned, others miraculously saved and released (as we read in Hebrews 11 and 12, and as I myself experienced). Whatever Jesus has in mind for each of us, the apostolic calling only ends in the grave. There is no other good and honorable way to live out the apostolic calling than to finish it by death in whatever way the Lord decides is best.

Whatever our personal and varied roles in Christ's global cause, may we and our churches and ministries share the apostolic vision and ambition of the apostle,

> For I will not venture to speak of anything except what Christ has accomplished through me to bring the Gentiles to obedience—by word and deed, by the power of signs and wonders, by the power of the Spirit of God. ... I make it my ambition to preach the gospel, not where Christ has already been named ... but as it is written, "Those who have never been told of him will see, and those who have never heard will understand." (Rom 15:18–21 ESV)

Near the end of his life and before he was executed, the Apostle Paul testified (2 Tim 4:6–8 ESV),

> For I am already being poured out as a drink offering, and the time of my departure has come. I have fought the good fight, I have finished the race, I have kept the faith. Henceforth there is laid up for me the crown of righteousness, which the Lord, the righteous judge, will award to me on that day, and not only to me but also to all who have loved his appearing.

Bibliography

Piper, John. "Signs and Wonders: Then and Now." *Desiring God*, February 1, 1991. https://www.desiringgod.org/articles/signs-and-wonders-then-and-now.

36
The Unengaged

First Engage, Then Reach

Mike Latsko

One way to distinguish between the "unreached" and the "unengaged" is to understand the first as a *response* metric and the second as a *sending* one. "Reached" language identifies a people group's response to Christ, with the corollary "unreached" referring to the sad reality that few have come to him. At its core, the concept of "reachedness" is based on the presence or absence of a "viable, indigenous, growing church movement" among a people group (whatever percentage of the population one may use to gauge that response).[1]

"Engagement," however, does not measure a people group's response to Christ, but rather the global church and mission community's response to the people group. Engagement is concerned with the initial "beachhead" among a people group and not the "breakthrough" that we pray and hope will happen later. That is, we have yet to make an intentional, purposeful effort to "engage" them with the message and messengers of the gospel.

Another way to say it is: All unengaged peoples are unreached, but not all unreached peoples are unengaged. Those within *engaged unreached peoples* have a chance to hear, whether through an incipient church movement or cross-cultural worker. Some believers are in their midst. They are engaged and unreached. But *unengaged unreached peoples* have no chance to hear, for there is no gospel presence among them, whether local, national, or expatriate. They are both unreached and unengaged. They lack *access* to the gospel.

Mission leaders generally define "engagement" as involving one or more long-term teams ministering on-site in the local language with a view to indigenous movements of disciples and churches.[2] While more workers are needed among large UPGs considered "under-engaged" (i.e., insufficient workers among them), we must also pray and work toward the engagement of the unengaged unreached. Whether large or small, a people must first be engaged before it can be reached.

---

[1] "Unreached groups (UPGs) lack enough followers of Christ and resources to evangelize their own people." Note that "unreached" does not refer to "people" or "individual persons" but to "people groups," i.e., human groupings, usually but not always based on ethnolinguistic criteria. "Frontier peoples" are UPGs with virtually no followers of Jesus and no known gospel movements that still need pioneer cross-cultural workers. See joshuaproject.net.

[2] For a helpful discussion of engagement, including the original definition proposed by Jeff Liverman in 2006, see "Reaching the Unengaged" in *Mission Frontiers* (Jan–Feb 2013). IMB adds the constraint that "a people group is not engaged when it has been merely adopted, is the object of focused prayer, or is part of an advocacy strategy" (IMB, "What is an Unengaged People Group"). The determination of engagement is made by field practitioners, preferably "verified" by two or three others (cf. Leonard N. Bartlotti, "Verification: A Biblical Perspective: Toward Careful Validation of Engagement Reports," unpublished paper presented to the Vision 5:9 Network, March 7, 2022).

Why is it that fifty years after the Lausanne '74 call to cross-cultural evangelism there are still people groups without access to the gospel? There are likely several reasons.

First, the peoples among whom missionaries are currently serving still have many needs and opportunities. There is much that could and should be done to reach the lost and strengthen the churches. To look beyond the work *unfinished* to consider the work *unbegun* is often a bridge too far.

Second, our support mechanisms tend to sustain what we are doing. Most of our prayers, caregivers, short-termers, projects, money, and workers (97 percent) are focused on where the church already is. This resourcing is understandable, although severely out of balance compared to the needs of unreached and unengaged peoples.

Third, there is spiritual opposition. We know that Satan seeks to hinder all mission efforts, of course, but as a dark strategist, he is especially motivated to blunt any gospel advance. "Because we wanted to come to you—I, Paul, again and again—but Satan hindered us" (1 Thess 2:18 ESV). He knows that when there is engagement and Christ begins to build his church, "the gates of hell shall not prevail against it" (Matt 16:18 ESV).

What can be done for the estimated 133 million people in 1,586 unengaged people groups among whom no one appears to be serving?[3]

First, we must be convinced that this is God's purpose and desire. "With his blood," the Lamb "purchased for God persons from every tribe and language and people and nation." That includes these still-to-be-engaged peoples—Hindu (643), Tribal/Ethnic Religionists (428), Muslim (393), Buddhist (70), and Nonreligious/Other (52).

Second, we must be convicted by this spiritual injustice. All peoples are lost and need a Savior. "How can they believe in the one of whom they have not heard?" (Rom 10:14). Some leaders and workers may recognize that "there is no further work for me here" and like the Apostle Paul, fix their gaze on the peoples and places, near and far, "where Christ is not known."

Third, church and mission leaders must envision a way forward. Whether the sending comes from surging Majority World churches and agencies who identify the unengaged in their regions, or from traditional sending structures, or some collaboration between them, we need to explore intentional and innovative strategies. Approaches to engagement depend on the context and include incarnational ministries, engagement via diaspora segments and proximate peoples, using media and social media, opportunities in business, education, and community development, or some combination of these or other means.

Fourth, we need to embrace an eschatological missiology. The prophet foretold, "For the earth will be filled with the knowledge of the glory of the LORD as the waters cover the sea" (Hab 2:14 ESV). That time is "already, but not yet." The earth is "filled with the glory of the Lord," to be sure, but not yet "the knowledge" of that glory. So we must "go" towards those peoples who have yet to experience a personal knowledge of him.

The late Paul Eshleman, former director of the Jesus Film Project and Finishing the Task (FTT), put it this way:

---

3 For the names and locations of these unengaged unreached people groups, see the Unengaged Peoples Explorer Tool at www.unengagedpeoples.com/explorer-tool. See lists in Appendix 2.

There are more individuals living within already "reached" people groups, than there are in all the unreached people groups of the world. However, there is one major difference. Most people in the West have great access to the message of Christ through media, local churches, and believers. For 300 million people in the unengaged, unreached people groups of the world, there is no way, outside of divine revelation, to hear the message of Christ. There is no church, no missionary, and not one verse of Scripture translated into their language. How much longer will we wait until we go to these groups, and put them on our priority list for funding and manpower?[4]

We bless God's people everywhere and celebrate the efforts of those who "have fully proclaimed the gospel of Christ" in certain regions (Rom 15:19 NIV). But we need apostolic pioneers who, "assisted on their journey" by sending churches, determine to "pass through" already churched regions and direct their steps toward "those who were not told about him … those who have not heard" (vv. 21, 24 NIV). The remaining unengaged have "a God-given right to access" the gospel.[5] Let us undertake "the priestly duty of proclaiming the gospel of God, so that the Gentiles might become an offering acceptable to God, sanctified by the Holy Spirit" (v. 16 NIV). "May the peoples praise you, God; may all the peoples praise you" (Ps 67:5 NIV).

Bibliography

Eshleman, Paul. "Reaching the Unreached: It's Time to Act." *Mission Frontiers* (Jan–Feb 2013). https://www.missionfrontiers.org/issue/article/reaching-the-unengaged.

IMB. "What is an Unengaged People Group." Accessed May 1, 2024. http://www.peoplegroups.org/294.aspx.

Wood, Rick. "Editorial: The God-Given Right to 'Access.'" *Mission Frontiers* (Jan–Feb 2013). https://www.missionfrontiers.org/issue/article/editorial12.

---

[4] Eshleman, "Reaching the Unreached."
[5] Wood, "Editorial."

37

The Rise of Muslim-Background Churches

An Eleventh-Hour Workforce for the Harvest?

Patrick Brittenden and Parsa Zarin Ghalam

More Muslims have come to faith in Christ since Lausanne's inaugural congress in July 1974 than in the previous fourteen centuries combined![1] Whilst there are numerous ways to comprehend the magnitude and significance of this Believers of Muslim Background (BMB)[2] movement in the church's mission to the least reached, our guiding metaphor is taken from Jesus's parable of the workers and the vineyard in Matthew 20:1–16, in which we propose that the rise of Muslim-background churches resemble the workers in the final hours of the harvest.

The emphasis of this chapter is not only or merely on reaching Muslim people groups. Rather, we want to recognize the significance of the rise of this BMB stream of the world Christian movement, and the potential to mobilize BMB workers to reach the least reached—not just in majority-Muslim contexts but also in Western Europe, North America, and beyond. For the implications of this new development to be fully appreciated, we will need to move beyond the rhetoric of mission being "no longer from the West to the rest, but everywhere to everywhere." Instead, we suggest moving toward a posture of humility and willingness to first *learn from*, and second, *work alongside* these believers.

To guide the reader towards that goal, this chapter will first paint a picture of this new development with the help of some useful metaphors. Second, we will describe what this change looks like on the ground. Third, we will examine why the shift from Muslims as the object (or receivers) of mission to BMBs becoming the subject (or providers) in the harvest has been slow in coming. Finally, we will discuss the challenges and opportunities this "eleventh-hour workforce" presents.

The BMB Church: An Eleventh-Hour Workforce

There have been a range of different metaphors used by missiologists and historians of world Christianity that might help us to understand the rise of the BMB church. One might consider this movement as a new "series" in what Andrew Walls calls the "serial movement" of world Christianity.[3] In this sense, it might be viewed as the emergence of a new center of gravity in the world church. Or one might borrow Donald McGavran's "mosaic" metaphor, with

---

1 Patrick Johnstone suggests that the turning point is the late 1970s around the time of the Islamic Revolution in Iran. For further reference see, Johnstone, "Look at the Fields," 5.
2 Also called "MBBs" or "Muslim-Background Believers" and considered synonymous; BMB is used here to emphasis their primary identity as "Believers" first before their religious background.
3 Walls, "Mission History," 367–70.

the BMB church in the majority-Muslim world seen as its own unique tile—crafted by the divine artist and placed into the mosaic of the global church—with its own particular color and texture.[4] Or appealing to the metaphor the Apostle Paul uses in Ephesians 2:19–22, this movement might be described as a BMB "wing" in the "household of God."

This new "wing" is not fundamentally the result of any human strategy, nor is it a quaint, exotic annex or an interesting outhouse on the boundaries of the main building, but rather it is a vital part of God's purpose in growing his household (or family). While many have acknowledged and written about the growth of this new "wing," our observation is that such writing is uneven, not easily accessible, and privileges those in the West and other more powerful and affluent centers of world Christianity. This fundamental observation led us—along with a number of other highly experienced mission practitioners (both BMBs and non-BMBs)—to form the Hikma Partnership.[5] Launched in October 2022, Hikma seeks to amplify the voices and visibility of BMBs, not just for our flourishing and faithful witness in majority Muslim contexts, but also for the benefit and blessing of the whole household of God.

Given that the core theme of this book is about recovering our mission to reach the least reached, we invite the reader to consider the rise of the BMB church as an eleventh-hour workforce in the Lord's harvest among the world's neglected and forgotten peoples.[6] This metaphor is inspired by Jesus's parable of the workers and the vineyard in Matthew 20:1–16 in which a landowner hired workers for his vineyard.[7] Those hired at the start of the day worked for their agreed daily amount, but when the time for payment came, they grumbled and were resentful because those who were hired later in the day—and especially those who joined in just the last hour—earned the same as they did. The landowner rebuked them, pointing out that he is never unfair, that he is generous, and that the eleventh-hour workers—those hired at the last moment, just in time, at the final hour—were equally valuable to him as those who worked from the start of the day.

Our observation is that the rise of the BMB church is today's eleventh-hour workforce for the harvest! We can be sure that Jesus was challenging his Jewish hearers about the value of eleventh-hour Gentiles now called into the harvest.[8] Despite earlier harvest workers' lack of appreciation of the value of BMBs, and BMBs themselves not always comprehending their privileged position, BMBs are beginning to have a significant role in reaching the least reached peoples.

---

4 McGavran, *Understanding Church Growth*, 224.

5 For further details, visit https://hikmapartnership.org/en/.

6 The metaphor of the workers in the final hours of the harvest as an interpretation of the BMB movement was first introduced to us by Andy James, founder and director of Al Massira. (See James and Eric, "Islam and the Gospel.")

7 We acknowledge that some translations of Matthew 20:6 describe eleventh-hour workers as "standing around" and "idle." Our intention in referencing this passage is not to imply idleness or a lack of productivity on the part of BMBs.

8 In this there are also echoes of the parable of the lost son (Luke 15:11–32).

From Rumor to Reality

In some publications focused on global mission, descriptions of the exciting new developments in the Muslim world appear almost sensationalistic. However, there is substantial evidence to suggest that rumor has become reality: God is at work in marvelous ways. The rise of the BMB church is clear in two ways. The first is the mushrooming of church-planting and disciple making movements (CPMs and DMMs) in Muslim areas. The second is the rise of influential BMB church and parachurch organizations and networks.

Church-Planting and Disciple-Making Movements

The publication of David Garrison's *Church Planting Movements* in 1999 marked a pivotal moment when previously documented movements to Christ worldwide began to gain increased attention.[9] Jerry Trousdale's *Miraculous Movements* and Garrison's 2014 book, *A Wind in the House of Islam*, charted the dramatic proliferation of CPMs across a range of regions in the majority-Muslim world. The formation of the Motus Dei network and its first virtual global consultation in 2020 initiated the beginning of a substantial and robust missiological and theological evaluation of the movement phenomenon.[10] Motus Dei and the eventual publication of the work of that inaugural consultation, *Motus Dei: The Movement of God to Disciple the Nations*, opened the way for CPMs and DMMs to be examined via a multidisciplinary lens of biblical theology, social sciences, ethnology, anthropology, communication theory, leadership theory, and, of course, statistical analysis.[11]

In terms of statistics, the trajectory shows a remarkable growth in the number of BMBs. Conservative estimates suggest that by the mid-nineteenth century, there were around 10,000 BMBs globally. By 1925, this number had grown to between 18,000 and 28,000, with notable increases primarily in Ethiopia and among the Kabyles in Algeria. A pivotal study, *Believers in Christ from a Muslim Background: A Global Census*, revealed a surge to nearly 2 million by 1980, up from less than 150,000 in 1962.[12] By 2010, Miller and Johnson estimated the global BMB population to be around 10 million, with Indonesia contributing up to 7 million alone. This growth underscores the significant impact of CPMs and DMMs in the conversion of Muslims to Christianity.[13]

BMB Church and Parachurch Organizations

The emergence of BMB churches and parachurch organizations is making a significant impact. This is evident in BMB church and house church networks, BMB-led regional and international gatherings, evangelistic ministries, theological education institutions, and partnerships. There is

---

9 Garrison, *Church Planting Movements*.
10 For further details, visit https://www.motusdei.network/.
11 Farah, "Motus Dei: The Movement of God."
12 Miller and Johnstone, "Believers in Christ," 2015.
13 The recognition and promotion of CPM and DMM approaches to missions have not been without its critics. Discussion of the key theological or missiological fracture points in these debates is beyond the scope of this paper. Our purpose in highlighting CPMs in the Muslim world is that, whatever one's position in this missiological debate, there can be no doubt that very substantial numbers of Muslims are coming to Christ, and CPMs and DMMs are a significant part of the story. We wish to highlight the significant contributions of Warrick Farah, a scholar-practitioner, educator, author, and co-founder of the Motus Dei network, to the study of CPMs within the majority-Muslim context.

a growing trend of BMBs organizing these gatherings for encouragement, training, and teaching. For instance, the Association Chrétien Nord Africain (ACNA)[14] in France and the KhushKhabri Fellowship[15] in the UK and Asia are notable examples. Evangelistic ministries such as Pamir Ministries[16] and Lumens of Truth[17] are reaching Afghans, while BMB-led training organizations are having a substantial impact on the formation and equipping of BMBs in at least three regions where the Muslim-background church is burgeoning. Noteworthy examples include Wasla,[18] providing media for the spiritual encouragement of BMBs; Elam;[19] Pars Theological Centre,[20] training Iranians in Iran and across various diasporas; The Institute of Classical Languages[21] for Bangladeshis; and The Institute Chrétien d'Algérie for Algerians.

One of the most encouraging and intriguing BMB partnerships to emerge in the last five years is Communio Messianica (CM), also known as Ummah Al Massih (The Community of the Messiah). CM is a global family of self-governing churches consisting of members primarily from a Muslim background who, in their own words, "have been called into the faith of Jesus Christ, and thus receiving a new identity in Christ's Body, the Church."[22] Their aim is to become a global movement founded and led by BMBs in over eighty countries in both East and West. Their vision is to serve these BMBs and address the need for "a sense of *identity, belonging, and legitimization*—thus constituting a community (*Ummah*) in their newfound faith in Jesus Christ."[23] CM is on a journey towards becoming an independent and self-governing church movement, and its co-founder and joint leader, Dr. Yassir Eric, was recently consecrated CM's first bishop.

Islam, Muslims, and the History of the Least Reached?

One of the reasons why it is so difficult to comprehend the possibilities and potential of BMB churches actively joining God's harvest among the nations is that for so long in mission practice and missiological reflection, Islam and Muslims have been the "object" of mission. Certainly, it has never been difficult to make a case for prioritizing the world's Muslim population as the object or focus for the evangelization of the world, given that over 25 percent of the world's population (over 1.8 billion souls) are Muslim. Whilst there is a vast diversity in the world of Islam [sometimes referred to in the plural as "Islams" or even "islams" (with a lowercase i)], nonetheless, all of these are united in their profound allegiance to the worldwide Muslim *Ummah*.[24] Despite the obvious need, for a long time, mission to the world of Islam and among Muslims has been a relative wasteland of missionary endeavors. Additionally, this

---

14 See https://www.eglises.org/oeuvre/association-des-chretiens-nord-africains-acna/.
15 See https://khushkhabrifellowship.uk/index.php/about-us/.
16 See https://pamirministries.org/.
17 See https://www.lumensoftruth.org/about-us.
18 For further details, visit https://www.youtube.com/@WaslaMedia.
19 For further details, visit https://www.elam.com/what-we-do.
20 For further details, visit https://parstheology.org/.
21 For further details, visit https://www.ataasia.com/membership/associate-membership-list/bangladesh/.
22 For further details, visit https://www.communiomessianica.org/about.
23 For further details, visit https://www.communiomessianica.org/consecration-of-bishop-dr-yassir-eric.
24 For a thorough exploration of the implication of diversity, see Farah and Daniels, *Margin of Islam*.

has not been helped by a kind of missiological exceptionalism, which perceived Islam to be an impregnable religion immune to disciple making and church planting. This is evident in the 1910 World Missionary Conference in Edinburgh and the stark way Islam was identified as a "special case," not deemed appropriate for a "fulfillment theology" applied to most other world faiths and religious systems at that time.[25] Perhaps as a reaction to this exceptionalism, in the last twenty years there has been a move in the opposite direction, with a huge emphasis on hyper-contextualized approaches to Christian mission ministry and church planting in majority-Muslim contexts, and the emergence of the Insider Movements.[26]

As of 2024, the landscape has significantly changed for the better. Many BMB scholar-practitioners, pastors, and ministry leaders we have spoken with acknowledge that this harvest among Muslims has been a collaborative effort. It has been marked by strong commitment, unwavering prayer, and selfless service from missionaries and ministers from around the world, spanning both the Global North and South. However, they also stress that this harvest is primarily a result of God the Father's sovereignty, working through the power of his Holy Spirit to reveal his Son, Jesus Christ, in wonderfully diverse ways. Thus, this movement is less about innovative ministry strategies or missiological formulas or ideas and more about God's sovereign plan. It is crucial for our missiology to reflect Christ's ultimate example and rely on the Father, Son, and Holy Spirit. This *telos* (end or purpose) of God's glory should be paramount in our thinking. The "end" is not simply that Muslims be reached, but rather that, in being reached, the glory of God be manifest in this new community being formed *not just in or for the benefit of the Muslim world but in the whole church and for the whole world.*

Although, as outlined above, there is much empirical data and evidence for the substantial harvest amongst Muslims over the past forty-plus years, the reality is that much of the global church, especially the church in the West, still has not adjusted to both the changing demographic of this BMB stream of the world church and the implications of this BMB center of influence for the character and quality of the church's witness to the least reached.

Challenges and Opportunities of This Eleventh-Hour Workforce

Challenges
A major challenge for BMBs, CBBs (Christian or traditional historical background believers), and missionaries from both the Global North and South is recognizing the changes and transformations described above. Many traditional historic churches in the diaspora contexts of Western Europe or North America, as well as in the Middle East, are happy to trumpet BMB trophy converts and, in some cases, put them to work in the ministries of the church, but very rarely are they elevated to positions of leadership or influence within the same churches.

---

25 Stanley, *World Missionary Conference*, 227–31.
26 Though not monolithic or unified, the Insider Movements are associated with a range of other postmodern approaches and contemporary tools to evaluate church planting amongst Muslims (such as the C1–C6 spectrum). In more extreme cases, an insider might be advised to continue worshiing in a mosque, identify as a Muslim without reservation, and observe many of the five Arkan (pillars of faith). To Muslims, they appear Muslim; however, inwardly, they recognize Christ as Lord and aim to follow Christ's teachings within Islamic cultural and faith frameworks.

A major focus to date, quite understandably, has been on helping BMBs in crisis situations. This is commendable, especially when the help involves literally keeping them alive in the context of clear and present threats to life in many parts of the Muslim world, such as northern Nigeria, Somalia, Sudan, Saudi Arabia, Pakistan, Afghanistan, Iran, and more. However, the focus on helping BMBs out of various crisis situations has obscured a much greater potential of seeing these same brothers and sisters as invaluable resources to help the worldwide church understand our identity and calling to live *in* but not *of* the world. BMBs also find themselves impacted by this "donor-receiver" dynamic, "always receiving" or, as Bishop Dr. Yassir described it to us recently, stuck in the position of those who are being "babysat." As he suggested, the babysitting is being maintained by *both* foreign missionaries and organizations *and* by the BMBs themselves who have become comfortable in this more subordinate, passive role.

Opportunities

As suggested, this growing movement did not start yesterday but has been maturing for over forty years. What this means is there are seasoned, mature, and gifted BMB church and ministry leaders. Increasingly, there are also BMB theologians who are an invaluable source of wisdom and insight for the global church in our collective mission to reach the least reached, not just in the Muslim world, but throughout the whole world. As we argued above, the "end" is not simply that Muslims be reached, but rather, that in being reached, the glory of God be manifest in this new community being formed *not just in or for the benefit of the Muslim world but in the whole church and throughout the whole earth*. Here, we point the reader to the articles that emerged from the Lausanne Theology Working Group from Lausanne Cape Town 2010 in their exploration of the mandate for "the whole church taking the whole gospel to the whole world."[27] We propose that the BMB wing in the household of God has not yet been fully embraced and integrated as part of the "whole church." Part two of the article reads:

> To speak of the "whole church" is a lot more challenging than thinking merely of "all Christians," but demands that we reflect on the church's identity and calling, its very reason for existence—in history and for eternity. And as we do so, we quickly discern those places where the church is far from "whole" and we call for recognition, repentance and reformation—beginning with ourselves as those entrusted with theological leadership in the church of today.[28]

Historian of world Christianity, Andrew Walls, observes that

> Christian expansion has not been progressive, like Islamic expansion, spreading out from a central point and retaining, by and large, the allegiance of those it reaches. Christian expansion has been serial. Christian faith has fixed itself at different periods in different heartlands, waning in one as it has come to birth in another.[29]

Walls's observation about the "serial" movement of Christianity is certainly true regarding its history in Algeria and Iran, contexts with which we are both intimately connected. In contrast

---

27 Theology Working Group, "The Whole Church."
28 Theology Working Group, "The Whole Church."
29 Walls, *The Missionary Movement*, 256.

to the appearance of a steady numerical growth of Islam over time, Christianity in these now majority-Muslim regions reveals serial countercultural Christian movements that began in the disregarded margins, gained significant influence, and then fell away again later. However, today, in these same regions, once again, the church appears to be undergoing a rebirth. In this sense we are seeing not just a rebirth of the church but also a reversal of the geographic expansion of Islamic centers of influence. In both Iran and Algeria, these centers have become centralistic and imposed a particular interpretation of Islam on all peoples. The emergence of growing BMB churches is challenging and redefining the centrism of these regimes. This is benefiting not just individual Christians or the church communities who have discovered freedom in Christ but is also having an impact on other people groups and communities who have also been suffocated and dominated by these regimes. While these other non-Christian communities cannot be described as having been reached, nevertheless, they are recipients of a kind of freedom that occurs when the church begins to impact broader social, political, and cultural transformations within society.

The growth of the BMB wing in the household of God is also challenging centrism within the world Christian movement where traditional and historic centers of influence have also been imposing a particular understanding and expression of Christianity on those in the margins. This has profound implications for our challenge to reach the least reached, to reiterate, *not just* in majority-Muslim contexts *but also* across the whole world and especially across parts of the Global North, like Europe, where, unlike almost every other continent on the planet, the church is still in a recession. There are clear examples of this happening as Muslims come to Christ on the refugee highway and as BMBs settle into life in their adopted European cities. Two ministries with which we are familiar, Al Massira[30] and Come Follow Me,[31] have witnessed thousands of Muslims coming to Christ. The result is that these new BMBs are reaching not just Muslims but also atheists and nominal, backsliding, traditional Christians in these contexts.

Conclusion

The rise of Muslim-background churches (BMBs) presents a crucial moment in the trajectory of Christian mission, reflecting a profound movement of the Holy Spirit in our times. As illustrated by the metaphor of workers in the vineyard from Jesus's parable, the emergence of BMBs signifies an "eleventh-hour workforce" joining the Lord's harvest, bringing fresh vitality and diverse perspectives to the global church's mission endeavors.

However, embracing the full potential of this movement will require a paradigm shift within the global church. The historical dynamics of mission, often characterized by a "donor-receiver" relationship, must evolve to recognize BMBs as integral *participants and partners* in shaping the future of world Christianity. Challenges such as limited leadership roles and dependency mindsets need to be addressed, but the opportunities for mutual learning and

---

30 Al Massira is a now well-established evangelistic course designed for Muslims with the aim of "walking with the Prophets and meeting the messiah." For further details, visit https://almassira.org/.

31 Come Follow Me is a discipleship course written specifically for new BMBs. It is relevant to the issues they face, is rooted in inductive Bible study, and used in a regular, relational way. For further details, visit https://come-follow-me.org/.

collaboration are immense. By amplifying the voices and visibility of BMBs, the church can embody a more inclusive and holistic witness, manifesting God's glory through a renewed, unified, and mission-focused body of Christ. As we navigate this transformative moment, let us heed the call to humility, partnership, and a shared commitment, working together towards the fulfillment of God's redemptive purposes for every nation, tribe, people, and tongue (Rev 7:9).

Bibliography

Farah, Warrick, and Gene Daniels. *Margin of Islam: Ministry in Diverse Muslim Contexts*. Pasadena, CA: William Carey Library, 2018.

Farah, W., ed. *Motus Dei: The Movement of God to Disciple the Nations*. Littleton, CO: William Carey Publishing, 2021.

Garrison, D. *Church Planting Movements: How God Is Redeeming a Lost World*. Sage Publications, 1999.

Garrison, D. *A Wind in the House of Islam: How God Is Drawing Muslims around the World to Faith in Jesus Christ*. Midlothian, VA: WIGTake Resources, 2014.

James, Andy, and Yassir Eric. "Islam and the Gospel." Lausanne Europe. November 29, 2021. https://www.youtube.com/watch?v=N3xQTHqSO34.

Johnstone, Patrick. "Look at the Fields: Survey of the Task." In *From Seed to Fruit: Global Trends, Fruitful Practices, and Emerging Issues Among Muslims*, edited by Dudley Woodberry, 5. Pasadena, CA: William Carey Library: 2008.

McGavran, D. A. *Understanding Church Growth*. Grand Rapids: Eerdmans 1980.

Miller, Duane A., and Patrick Johnstone. "Believers in Christ from a Muslim Background: A Global Census." *Interdisciplinary Journal of Research on Religion* 11 (2015).

Stanley, B. *The World Missionary Conference, Edinburgh 1910*. Grand Rapids,: Eerdmans, 2009.

Theology Working Group. "The Whole Church Taking the Whole Gospel to the Whole World." Lausanne Movement. June 1, 2010. https://lausanne.org/content/twg-three-wholes.

Trousdale, J. *Miraculous Movements: How Hundreds of Thousands of Muslims Are Falling in Love with Jesus*. Nashville: Thomas Nelson, 2012.

Walls, A. F. "Mission History as the Substructure of Mission Theology." *Swedish Missiological Themes* 93, no. 3 (2005): 367–78.

38
Reimagining and Re-envisioning People Groups

Leonard N. (Len) Bartlotti

In the sweeping narrative of Scripture, the focus of God's self-disclosure is the peoples of the world. The biblical image of "the people of God" makes sense only against the background of a tempestuous mix of other "peoples," from which God selects one "holy nation" (Israel)—"you above all peoples" (Deut 10:15).[1] His ultimate purpose, however, is to dwell among a people from "*all* the families of the nations" (Pss 22:27; 96:7; Rev 7:9). "Once you were not a people, but now you are the people of God" (1 Pet 2:10 NIV). From the standpoint of creation, redemption, and eternity, a world—and throne room—full of "peoples" reflects God's beauty, creativity, and love.

Rethinking people groups does not mean eliminating the concept but reimagining and re-envisioning it in light of twenty-first-century realities. The essence of my discussion here is reflexive, consciously acknowledging our assumptions and preconceptions. It is also corrective, addressed not to critics but to those of us who embrace and advocate UPG missiology. In this article, I explore ways to reimagine people groups through an upgraded understanding of the concept itself and suggest steps to re-envision the UPG approach in order to maximize efforts to reach all peoples.[2]

Understanding "People Groups"

However nuanced in the minds of mission scholars, popularly and in practice, "unreached people groups" are primarily "ethnolinguistic" in nature. Criteria related to ethnicity and language dominate.[3] This is reflected in databases where a "people group" is defined as "an ethnolinguistic group with a common self-identity that is shared by the various members."[4]

---

1 In the social, cultural, and historical context of the Old Testament, each "nation" was distinguished by name, ethnicity, language, territory, kingship, history, and a religious system marked by lessor "gods" (idolatry) and depravity. See Köstenberger, "Nations," 676. For example, texts from Anatolia (Asia Minor) c. 1700–1200 BC point to a region inhabited by a number of distinct peoples, including the Hittites, Luwians, Palaians, Hurrians, and Hattians. In the Hittite Empire, from the fourteenth century BC, "the ethnic and cultural pluralism still increased as the political expansionism added further foreign elements to 'Hittite' culture" (Hutter, "Religion in Hittite Anatolia," 74–90). Each of these nations "had its own pantheon, and individual cult centres had their own names for deities" (Gurney, "Religions of the Hittites").

2 Portions of this article are based on my paper "Rethinking Ethnicity: Implications for the People Group Approach," presented to the Rethinking People Groups Forum, Dallas, TX, September 11, 2019. I wish to express my appreciation to the participants for their helpful comments and feedback. This chapter is a revised version of my article of the same name published in the *Evangelical Missions Quarterly*, Fall 2020.

3 The first lists were based in part on SIL's Ethnologue, a catalog of the world's languages.

4 IMB, https://peoplegroups.org/. Joshua Project also based on language and ethnicity, and the geographic distribution of such groups.

The shorthand definition has advantages. It is easily communicated and marketed. "Peoples" as "ethnic groups" can be named, profiled, objectified, enumerated, and portrayed in pictures, videos, and media. Another advantage is the appearance of an uncomplicated "this equals that" correspondence with Scripture; that is, every identifiable ethnic people and language today[5] is represented in the eschatological multitude (Rev 7:9; 5:9). This is highly motivational.

One obvious problem, recognized by Ralph Winter, is that from the beginning the "people group" concept was intended to include "socio-peoples," groups formed on the basis of other affinities like "shared interest, activity, or occupation."[6] Can we really envision these "shared interest" groups in the heavenly throng? While this is evangelistically pragmatic, I suggest it is an interpretive leap and thus an imaginative mandate.

While ethnolinguistic groups provide a helpful baseline, we need to look at the challenge of reimagining "ethnicity," "ethnic groups," and "ethnic identity" in light of more recent thinking. Given the primary UPG orientation toward "ethnolinguistics," that is the focus in this discussion.[7] Historically within the social sciences, understandings of ethnicity can be summarized into three general categories: primordialist, instrumentalist, and constructivist.

Primordialist

In this view ethnicity is understood as having a real, tangible foundation, based either on *kinship* and sociobiological factors, or on shared cultural *traits*, practices, and history. We could say that, for the former, ethnicity is "in the heart" or "in the blood," and for the second, ethnicity is "in the cultural stuff"—distinctive "traits" or "surface markers" of identity (language, dress, food, etc.). The "in the heart" or "in the blood" approach is commonly emic (i.e., how peoples see themselves). Ethnic groups are viewed as "quasi-kinship" or "extended kin" groups.[8]

Historically viewed as primordial and fixed, ethnic groups were objectified, documented, and categorized (e.g., "martial races"). Elements of their heritage and culture (including material culture) were institutionalized, sometimes immortalized, in books, journals, ethnographies, histories, memoirs, short stories, movies, and museums.[9]

---

5 The question of the historical genesis, assimilation, and disappearance of other people groups is left unanswered.

6 Ralph Winter tried but failed to prevent the reduction of "people groups" to ethnolinguistic criteria alone (Datema, "Defining 'Unreached,'" 55). Discussions of UPGs usually include socio-peoples; I concentrate on the category of ethnicity. Winter and Koch see strategic value in working with socio-peoples "for preliminary evangelism" as an "intermediate bridge to long-range church planting goals … giving a focus for ministry among a specific sub-set of the larger society as a first step to full-blown church planting." They consider ethnolinguistic groups primary because of their endurance as endogamous, multigenerational quasi-kinship groups (Winter and Koch, "Finishing the Task," 535).

7 For a helpful overview of the significant literature and issues, see Banks, *Ethnicity*; cf. Jenkins, *Rethinking Ethnicity*. "Identity" is one of the most widely researched subjects in every field of the social sciences. I use "identity" here as a social category (referring to a set of distinguishable persons), as well as a personal category (individual actors with self-consciousness) (cf. Fearon, "What Is Identity").

8 "Ethnicity," what-when-how.com. The assumption that one's identity is "in the blood" is a driver behind commercials for Ancestry.com. Discovering they have DNA from multiple sites in Eastern Europe or Africa, a person says, "I was grateful. I just felt more connected to who I am." The DNA approach reinforces the opposite: It's not really "who I am" even though one may "feel more connected." Based on test results, individuals make conscious choices, creating a symbolic ethnic representation of their reconstructed identity using identity "markers" (dress, food, etc.).

9 Anthropologists and some missiologists today acknowledge the power imbalances that shaped colonial anthropology, the colonialist paradigm of "tribe," and missionary approaches. Power dynamics continue to influence ethnicities (e.g., through the nation-state (which "names" and objectifies constituent "minorities"), international bodies, and social institutions [e.g., schools, universities]).

Instrumentalist

Fredrik Barth's seminal work *Ethnic Groups and Boundaries* marked a turning point and "shift from a static to *interactional approaches* to ethnicity."[10] Barth "abandons the notion that cultures are clearly bounded, separated and homogeneous units."[11] The focus is not on cultural traits but on dynamic interactions, ways people embrace, constrain, act on, and experience ethnicity and "imagine the ethnic community." Individuals choose and change their ethnic identity, particularly at the boundaries between groups.

In this view, ethnicity functions as a *tool*, an aspect of the way people organize themselves depending on social circumstances.[12] Individuals and groups are actors versus merely passive recipients of "culture" or heritage. They use cultural resources to pursue personal or communal advantage in particular settings and contexts. This focus reveals that "ethnic groups and their features are produced under *particular interactional, historical, economic and political circumstances; they are highly situational, not primordial.*"[13]

Constructivist

Barth's work led to greater emphasis on the *contextual* and *situational* processes of ethnic identity. Ethnicity can be mobilized contextually and situationally "in the contexts of different 'levels' and 'contextual horizons.'"[14] Identities are reconstituted, negotiated, and contested in a dynamic process of self-other interaction.

Both the instrumentalist and constructivist approaches reflect a postmodern view of culture. Identities are socially constructed, not fixed but changeable (within certain constraints).[15] Individuals maintain multiple identities and use ethnicity as a set of "diacritic" or "distinguishing markers" and tools for social engagement.

It is fairly obvious that Christian websites, mission agencies, and literature tend to display an unquestioned reliance on the primordialist ("in the blood" and "in the stuff") view of ethnicity, ethnic groups, and identity. "People profiles" have become a kind of literary subgenre![16] Unfortunately, among other problems this static approach too often rests on little or no contemporary ethnographic confirmation.

---

10 Vermeulen and Govers, "Introduction," 2 (emphasis added).

11 Vermeulen and Govers, 5.

12 Vermeulen and Govers, 2 (emphasis added), 1–9; cf. Blanton's discussion of Barth's in-group and between-group "visual signaling" (i.e., ethnic-specific behaviors constitute "a system of signals" to establish a boundary difference between groups, and to confirm belonging and commitment to the value-orientations of the community) in "Theories of Ethnicity," 9177.

13 Vermeulen and Govers, 12 (emphasis added). See Cohen, "Ethnicity: Problem and Focus," 379–403.

14 "Ethnicity," what-when-how.com.

15 Since ethnic identity involves ascription, what others acknowledge or recognize, constraints related to heritage and cultural "givens" may apply (e.g., a Punjabi is unlikely to be accepted as Afghan). Ethnicity remains relevant but may or may not be foregrounded.

16 Buttressed by stereotypic descriptions of shared "traits," some attractive (e.g., "generous hospitality," "colorful dress," "love music and dance") and others from the "dark side" (e.g., "fierce warriors," deceit, blood feuds, seclusion of women), these caricatures are presumed to be relevant to mobilization, prayer, and compassion. In one case, researchers cited Wikipedia as the major source of their information on a people group. A quick check revealed that over 90 percent of the Wikipedia citations were from newspapers and magazines. Other (readily available) scholarly sources (e.g., peer-reviewed articles, books, ethnographies, dissertations, theses, etc.) may be neglected in favor of easily digestible and promotable generalizations.

Mission thought leaders tried to account for complexity (e.g., socio-peoples, unimax, diaspora). But the above considerations are largely absent in the way the UPG movement today organizes data and conceives of peoples. Static categories veil reality and fail to convey the dynamism and fluidity of UPGs. This sometimes leads to unrefined strategies, ineffective engagements, and misplaced priorities.[17] In an interconnected, urbanized, globalized, mobile, and changing world, we need to re-envision our approach.

Re-envisioning Approaches

Brad Gill, president of the International Society for Frontier Missiology, notes the "new conditions that are pressing us to reimagine these frontiers." Gill calls for a move beyond the "subtle 'group think'" of our mission organizations, and the language and categories that may "unintentionally restrict our perception" and "blunt our imagination."[18]

Toward that end, I suggest we need a new *dynamic model of people groups* that takes into account varied contexts, changes, and affinities. We need to reimagine our understandings of UPGs in order to re-envision strategies for reaching them. I propose four conceptual steps to help us develop a re-envisioned approach: 1) multi-level model of ethnicity; 2) a dynamic, contextual view of social interaction and bonding; 3) an expanded, field-generated mission information system; 4) models of church in relation to accessibility, degrees of ethnicity, and evangelisitic potential.

Multilevel Model of Ethnicity

First, we need a reshaped model of people groups, one that enables us to understand them through multiple "lenses" rather than a single, static "ethnic" lens. Based on our earlier discussion, we can view ethnolinguistic people groups and identities through three "lenses," what could be called a *"triangular field of meaning."*[19] The same ethnolinguistic group can be understood from three intersecting perspectives, like three corners of a field. See Figure 8.

At one corner of the field, ethnicity is seen "in the heart" or "blood" and "in the traits" or "stuff" of culture. This tends to be the default emic or insider view. Since, as Geertz reminds us, "cultures are systems of meaning," we need to take these seriously. Communities find symbolic meaning in notions of heritage, land, and extended kinship, and elements like language, religion, festivals, food, dress, and music. This is the basis for most UPG "lists."

At another corner, we see ethnic identity "in the head" and "in the relationship" or "interaction." Individuals and groups are not passive victims of "culture"; they have agency. People actively use aspects of ethnic culture as tools for action, instruments to accomplish

---

17 This is not to disparage well-intentioned efforts to describe UPGs that have fostered awareness and global prayer. Some have argued that, however inaccurate or static, "Something is better than nothing! We do not have to pray 'with our understanding' in order to be heard!" The problem is what happens next: bad information—inaccurate, insufficient, un- or misinformed, distorted, stereotypical or promotion-driven—can lead to misguided agency decisions, wasted efforts and funding, unwise field initiatives, and unintended consequences among the peoples we aspire to reach.

18 Gill, "Reimagining Frontier Mission," 111–18; cf. "ISFM 2019," 161–62.

19 This phrase is borrowed from M. A. Seifrid's explanation of the Pauline phrase "in Christ" as moving within a "triangular field of meaning" between three ideas of locality, instrumentality, and modality. Martin, Reid, and Hawthorne, *Dictionary of Paul*, loc. cit.

social ends, particularly in relation to other groups. These social interactions have huge implications for evangelism and church formation.

Studies show that ethnic identity also is variable "in the context"—constructed, negotiated, contested, self-assumed, or ascribed by others. This makes us alert to the ways behaviors and social relationships associated with "ethnicity" function dynamically and variably "in the situation" and context, for example, in urban, Western, or regional diaspora versus rural and traditional contexts.

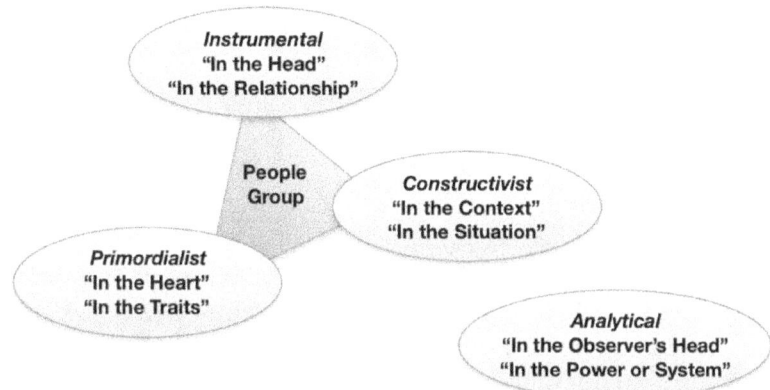

Figure 8: Multi-level Model of Ethnicity—
Ethnic identity viewed through different lenses, interactions, and contexts

In order to have a clearer understanding of UPGs, and to devise more appropriate strategies, we must be able to move subtly and adeptly between these three viewpoints. They are not mutually exclusive. Note, too, that this apparent deconstruction does not eliminate "groupness" or "ethnic identity" but rather reconfigures it more dynamically, with sensitivity to time, place, and processes of social change.

Finally, to be honest and accurate, ethnicity is also "in the observer's head" (us): We need to admit that we—any outside institution, from the UN to government, academia, and religious and mission groups—are *using* "ethnicity" as an *analytical tool* to make sense of what we see.[20] These etic understandings are appropriate, or at least useful, as long as we are aware of the power dynamics involved in our categorizations, as well as the potential for biases, unverified data, and distorted representations.

Dynamic Models of Social Interaction and Bonding

Second, we need more dynamic models of people group interaction and social bonding, especially in multiethnic, urban, and diaspora contexts.

---

20 Banks, *Ethnicity*, 185. Note the gradual "in our head" shifts in terminology from "race" and "tribe" to "culture" and "ethnic group," and (within missiology) from "homogeneous unit" to "people group." Some case studies in this volume (e.g., by field workers and Majority World leaders) reveal an awareness of (even annoyance with) the power dynamics involved in "naming" and listing groups and the apparently inflexible concepts used by conveyors of missions truth and knowledge. See the proposal below for a more ethnographically grounded, field-based, information gathering and sharing system.

For example, a Kazakh in Turkey preserves Kazakh ethnicity but constructs a Turkish Kazakh identity. This allows him/her to negotiate more advantageous social connections and a sense of belonging.[21] Migration also fosters a more fluid ethnic identity.

Minority Senegalese (e.g., Seereer) in Dakar adopt vernacular "urban Wolof" as the *lingua franca*. The process of "Wolofization" affects not only language but also ethnicity. A new "Wolof" identity is constructed, especially among the second generation. As one Pulaar-speaking elementary school teacher reported, "At home I'm Haalpulaar. When I'm in Dakar, I'm Wolof." This suggests "a new urban identity rather than a switch in ethnicity." Depending on the context and interaction, residents may reject an ethnolinguistic identifier and simply say, as did one professor, "I'm from Dakar … that's the new ethnicity now in Senegal, to be from Dakar."[22]

A similar dynamic was observed in Afghanistan. "Kabuli" (people from the capital of Kabul) describes a Persianized urban identity that, while not negating ethnic heritage, influences social relationships and values. Kabulis (Pashtun and Tajik) mix freely and have been more receptive to the gospel than their rural cousins.[23]

Case studies from South Africa, the Netherlands, Mexico, Sweden, the US, Brazil, Israel, Germany, and Singapore demonstrate strategies that transnational newcomers and students use to negotiate identity. Some adapt with "situational ethnicity" (hiding or asserting traits situationally). Alternatively, others adopt (or accept an imposed) "hyphenated identity."[24]

In each case, adaptive identities both reflect and affect an ethnic community's interaction with other peoples and the larger society. This has important implications for evangelism and church planting. These dynamics influence a group's sense of belonging, possibilities for bonding with existing fellowships, and/or the need for new movements or compound models of church.

To illustrate this, imagine from high school chemistry how an element like oxygen can combine with other elements to form molecules (atoms held together by chemical bonds) (see Figure 9). The analogy is not perfect, but similarly, we need to envision people groups in a more "combinable" way. With whom, how, when, and in what contexts members of a community "bond" with others, and develop, or reject, affinities—these are critical questions relevant to the disciple-making and church-planting process.

A pure, "tick the box" "engagement" approach to peoples is inadequate and ineffective precisely because it may miss the "bridges of God" and social connections embedded in diverse contexts. It is important not to reify or objectify ethnolinguistic identity in absolute terms. The social behavior of an individual or community varies across time and space. Receptivity, gospel access, and response also vary. From a Great Commission perspective, this realization opens promising opportunities to rethink and reimagine approaches to discipling peoples.

---

21 Kazakh ethnic identity is preserved through ethnic celebrations, meetings that maintain cultural practices, and speaking Kazakh at home, while constructing a new hybrid identity based on shared religion (Islam) and Turkic roots, and the adoption of new practices, preferences and self-identity (see e.g., Yeniceri, "Hybridization and Kazakh Ethnic").

22 McLaughlin, "The Ascent of Wolof," 142–70.

23 Internally displaced people and returnees from Iran, Pakistan, and elsewhere have swelled Kabul to over 5 million people; according to reports, ethnicity is a more salient identity among them, and the term Kabuli does not apply.

24 Hamann and England, "Conclusion—Hyphenated Identities." Note the political and power dynamics when a "hyphenated identity" is ascribed by a government or school.

So, for example, as in Figure 9, a given people group "Oxygen" (O) in some contexts may tend to bond with the "Hydrogen" (H) people. In other contexts, social bonds may develop with members of "Carbon" (C) or "Nitrogen" (N) ethnic or affinity groups—while simultaneously rejecting other elements due to prejudice or language barriers. The point is, in an interconnected, mobile, and urbanized world, the gospel can flow among a people group via any of a number of ethnic and interethnic affinities, bonds, and social networks.

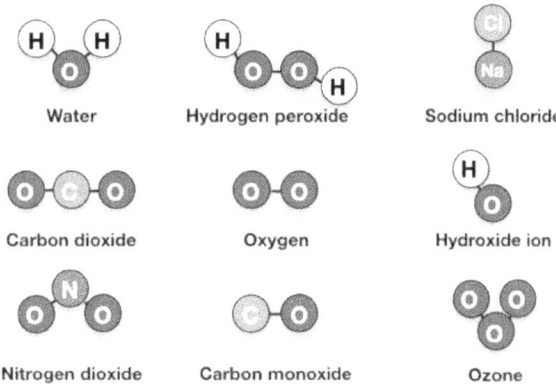

Figure 9: Social Bonding—like chemical interactions that form molecules, members of a people gropu bond with others in different ways, depending on the attractive forces and context.

Importantly for gospel advance, a new "Oxygen" believer in a diaspora fellowship in New York, Toronto, London, or Istanbul can advance the gospel *to, through,* and *with* multiple social networks, including ethnic compatriots in the homeland (e.g., O_3, Ozone).

Note that this dynamism assumes the importance of "place," sensitivity to context, and the relational and situational character of ethnicity—the "attractive forces" at work. In some contexts, e.g., rural, village, or traditional homelands, communal structures are tight. In urban and diaspora settings, people often negotiate varied relational worlds, with feelings of multiple belonging or "hybridity." Ethnic, language, and faith identities persist but may or may not be foregrounded, especially in the second and third generations.[25]

Atoms bond or break with other atoms or reactants, connecting to form molecules (see Figure 10). In a similar way, the bonds within and between communities are dynamic and varied. Social an spiritual change, like chemical changes, can be spontaneous or occur slowly over time. Think of fermentation (kimchi, sauerkraut), decomposition (garden compost), and corrosion (rust). Other reactions depend on a "catalyst" added to increase the reaction rate.

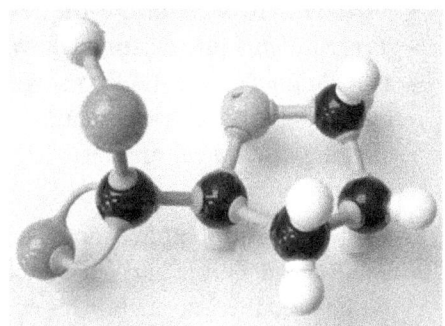

Figure 10: Multiple Affinities—the gospel advances to and through dynamic bonds and varied social networks. Image credit: "Proline model," by Peter Murray-Rust (CC BY-SA 2.5).

There are no perfect analogies, but for higher levels of data we need to deploy new conceptual images and sensibilities. We need to discern peoples, places, and populations

---

25 "A person can simultaneously hold allegiances to a neighborhood, a city, a region, a country, or a continent, or be a transmigrant in a world city or, yet, a global nomad, an employee of a transnational corporation." See https://www.sciencedirect.com/topics/computer-science/identity-construction. Cf. Jenkins who notes that globalization does not always dilute ethnic identification: local and ethnic identity "each may (re)assert itself either as a defensive reaction to, or a result of, the increasingly global context of social life" (*Rethinking Ethnicity*, 45). For the way pan-Islamist sentiments can "coexist" with local forms of Muslim identity, see Darryl Li, "Taking the Place of Martyrs," 12–39.

where the gospel has yet to exert its catalytic force. Pioneer workers must be keen observers and "barefoot ethnographers." As urban missiologist Alan McMahan puts it, we need to be better "glue sniffers" to figure out the types and strengths of "glue" that hold people together in different networks and contexts.[26]

Multiple Tiers of Data

Third, re-envisioning people groups requires "ethnographic imagination"[27] and multiple tiers of data. The shift from a reductionist, segmented model to one that is multi-perspectival, dynamic, and field based should include

- *processes*, social chemistry, and facts on the ground;
- how *commonality* (faith, city, ethnicity, nationality) is imagined or sought;
- how *difference* is encountered and dealt with;
- *intercultural* relationships, bridges, and barriers between peoples;
- *diaspora* and *transnational* connections;
- styles and modes of *communication*;
- *lessons learned* from historical efforts and previous approaches;
- current *conditions*, sociopolitical *change*, and *crises*;
- *receptivity* of subgroups (e.g., youth, immigrants) and associations;
- *proximate* cross-cultural witnesses;
- *incorporability* into existing fellowships and churches;
- associational *bridges* (believers with organic, relational connections);
- *media* and evangelistic resources;
- ongoing *assessments* and research;
- *discernment* of what the Holy Spirit is doing.

Obviously, this information is not needed for mobilization. The data we have now is sufficient for mobilization, prayer, and obedience!

We do need this information for effective field strategies and engagement. Greater detail and refinement, what we might call "Second Tier" and "Third Tier" data, take us to a deeper level of understanding and empathy. This is useful for national research, on-site strategy, outreach, and church planting. To *gather, track, share, and evaluate field-generated knowledge* will necessitate upgraded data-sharing platforms, secure communications, and greater collaboration in knowledge stewardship. This re-envisioning of information requires a broader range of inputs.[28] For security and practical reasons, we cannot "patch" this Second and Third Tier information onto our current segmented databases. Not everything fits in a spreadsheet!

This points to another glaring gap: Field workers by and large feel divorced from the missiological conversation! Many workers complain that "nobody is listening" to them. If we are to move forward, it is essential for field workers to map the context. "Often field-based personnel are in the best position to assess whether a people group is adequately engaged,

---

26 Rethinking People Groups Forum, Dallas, TX (September 13, 2019).

27 I borrow this term from Paul Willis, "The Ethnographic Imagination."

28 See Scribner, this volume. As Scribner admits, "Global people group lists, as currently conceived and structured, cannot support dynamic groupings." To be clear: Nothing said in this paper is intended to diminish the huge contribution made by mission demographers and data managers. Existing people registries have served to awaken the church to the existence of peoples currently beyond the reach of the gospel.

and their relative access to the Gospel. ... These contextual ethnographic realities ... provide important indicators for new initiatives."[29] Another way to address the disparity is through "case studies" that illuminate the complexities of pioneer church planting and provide "thick descriptions" of a people, event, or issue for analysis, training, and application.[30]

A multitiered, multi-perspectival database must be functional and flexible; view people groups from multiple contextual horizons; promote communities of learning and practice across organizational lines; and contribute to sandals-on-the-ground fruitfulness. Field accessibility is critical.[31]

Re-envisioning the People of God

Finally, we need to re-envision the church as the "people of God," with a shared consciousness that celebrates yet transcends every local identity. We mustt revitalize the image of the church in relation to three missional concepts: incorporability, multiethnicity, and church movements.

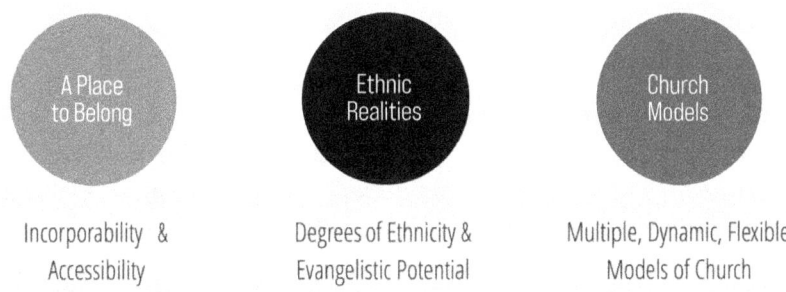

Figure 11: Re-envision People of God—Re-envision models of church in relation to incorporability, multiethnicity, and church movements.

A Place to Belong

Christian faith is "embodied" in churches. This is the *telos*, the end and purpose, of frontier missions: viable, indigenous, growing church movements among all peoples.

---

29 Bartlotti, "Refining Our Strategies," 21–26.

30 Case studies are commonly used in the social sciences, and famously, by the Harvard Business School. They can be explanatory, exploratory, descriptive, comparative, or instrumental. See Baxter and Jack, "Qualitative Case Study Methodology," 544–59. For a simple introduction to the research concept of "thick description" (promoted by anthropologists Gilbert Ryle and Clifford Geertz) and helpful sources, see Drew, "5 Key Principles."

31 After a few years on the field, many workers pursue an MA or PhD While this contributes to new knowledge, unfortunately, the knowledge tends to be individualized, constrained within publishing channels, or siloed in academia or individual ministries. There appear to be few mechanisms for translating insights into community learning and upgrading of field praxis.

The gospel cannot be said to be accessible if church is not accessible. The invitation to believe in Christ is an invitation to receive not only "forgiveness of sins" but "*a place among those who are sanctified by faith in me*" (Acts 26:17–18 ESV). The church is a place for all peoples (Isa 56:6–8; Gal 3:28; Eph 2:13–16). "A place to belong" is at the heart of the gospel!

Consequently, for mission purposes, the notion of "unreached peoples" is intrinsically linked to a concept Ralph Winter called "*incorporability*."

> Thus, for both spiritual and practical reasons, I would be much more pleased to talk about the presence of a church allowing people to be incorporated, or the absence of a church leaving people *unincorporable* instead of *unreached*. I feel it would be better to try to observe, not whether people are "saved" or not or somehow "reached" or not, but first whether an individual has been incorporated in a believing fellowship or not, and secondly, if a person is not incorporated, does he have the opportunity *within his cultural tradition* to be so incorporated.[32]

The "opportunity within his cultural tradition to be so incorporated" refers to the presence, or absence, of a truly viable, truly indigenous church. If people cannot be incorporated, if existing fellowships are not accessible—due to "barriers of understanding or acceptance"—to other peoples, then a *new version of church* is needed.

Ethnic Realities and Evangelistic Potential
Second, we must re-envision "churches" in relation to the peoples around them. In his book *Ethnic Realities and the Church: Lessons from India*, Donald McGavran, father of the church growth movement, categorized Indian churches there into nine "types." He described them based on their "*varying degrees of ethnicity*" as well as their "*evangelistic potential*,"[33] their "different relationships *to* and degrees of acceptance *by* the 'yet to believe.'"[34]

The dual concepts of "degrees of ethnicity" and "evangelistic potential" may be useful to re-envision churches in multiethnic and UPG-proximate settings. In Indonesia, an over 150,000-person multiethnic urban conglomerate with contemporary worship in the *lingua franca* Bahasa Indonesia, includes at least three thousand Muslim-background believers from a UPG![35] But to *maximize* the "evangelistic potential" of these migrant urbanites requires equipping some to *reach out* to their ethnic neighbors and training others to *reach back* to their ethnic compratiots in the homeland to catalyze vernacular movements.

Where There Is No Church
Third, we need to explore new models of church. This includes re-envisioning the connection between the frontier missions and models of "church growth" and movements among existing churches and peoples. Amidst the global flow of goods, ideas, and people, mega, multiethnic, and urban/regional house church networks are thriving from Argentina and Chile to Nigeria, India, and Indonesia, as well as the West. Despite common roots and exceptions, the two

---

32 For insightful reflections on Winter's notion of incorporability, see Gill, "Unfortunate Unmarketability of 'Unincorporable,'" from which this quote is taken.

33 McGavran, *Ethnic Realities and the Church*, 25, 64–65 (emphasis added).

34 McGavran, 2–3.

35 I am indebted to Alan McMahan for this example. It should be noted that this urban conglomerate church did not intentionally evangelize along ethnic lines or leverage ethnicity.

streams are largely disconnected professionally and missionally.[36] Reestablishing synergy and sharing resources would advance an "all peoples" vision.

UPG enthusiasts need to deconstruct categories and recognize that church movements need not be monoethnic to engage and penetrate UPGs. *Gospel freedom allows and celebrates, but does not demand, homogeneous ethnic churches.* Some church movements involve ethnic blends, with homogeneity in evangelism and heterogeneity in discipleship. Others facilitate homogeneity in smaller relational circles and heterogeneity in larger ones. Homogeneity may suit first-generation immigrants, but heterogeneity may suit the children of immigrants (e.g., pan-Asian and pan-Latino churches). Other churches have an ethnically dominant group plus mixed cultural groups (e.g., Persian, Arab). Mobilizing urban conglomerate churches, mega churches, international churches, house church networks, disciple-making movements, and proximate believers, and purposefully connecting diaspora disciple making with homeland engagements—would help revitalize movement toward UPGs.[37]

Conclusion

The concept of people groups takes us to the heart of the biblical narrative. The frontier mission movement must reimagine itself in light of global realities, the persistent needs of the unevangelized, and God's desire for a people from all peoples. We need to upgrade our understandings, envision new dynamic models, and leverage the evangelistic potential of the global church to impact the remaining UPGs.

I would invite both critics and enthusiasts to recognize, at its heart, "unreached" is a *tool to make sure we don't miss anyone.* The notion of "least reached peoples" and the "people group approach" are:

- A way of seeing the world
- A way of understanding what we/they see
- A way of organizing our knowledge
- A way of conceptualizing the task
- A way of discipling more strategically
- A way of envisioning the end

The frontier mission movement often draws its inspiration from the panorama of radiant worship in Revelation 5:9–10. As New Testament scholar Gordon Fee outlines it, the "new song" acclaims the *means* of his redeeming act ("with your blood"), the *effect* of that sacrifice ("you purchased for God"), the *breadth* of redemption ("members of every tribe and language and people and nation"), its *goal* ("made … to be a kingdom and priests to

---

36 Note, for example, that the two representative professional networks (International Society for Frontier Missiology and the Great Commission Research Network) have separate journals, conferences, and nonoverlapping attendees and speakers, despite many shared concepts, principles, and practices related to evangelistic growth, peoples, movements, accessibility, receptivity, diversity, innovative models, ethnicity, and incorporating people into the church.

37 For example, see GlobalGates (https://globalgates.info) focused on UPGs in North America's megacities. Certain "advocacy networks" focused around specific UPGs in Central Asia, West Africa, and elsewhere have also shown great promise in facilitating joint ventures in strategy, media, training, and recruiting, and placing workers in diaspora, transnational, and homeland engagement points. These would be key networks within which to pilot new multilevel, collaborative, field-based databases as described above.

serve our God … they will reign on the earth"), and the God-centered, God-ordained *climax*, "To him who sits on the throne and to the Lamb be praise and honor and glory and power, for ever and ever!"[38] We are invited to respond both with *adoring wonder*, and with faithful *cruciform witness* (Rev 6:9–11; 19:10) to "the word of God and the testimony of Jesus" (Rev 1:2; 20:4) before all nations.

Bibliography

Banks, Marcus. *Ethnicity: Anthropological Constructions*. London: Routledge, 1996.

Bartlotti, Leonard N. "Refining Our Strategies for Engaging All Peoples." *IJFM* 27, no. 3 (Fall 2010): 21–26. https://www.ijfm.org/PDFs_IJFM/27_3_PDFs/refining_bartlotti.pdf.

Baxter, Pamela, and Susan Jack. "Qualitative Case Study Methodology: Study Design and Implementation for Novice Researchers." *The Qualitative Report* 13, no. 4 (Dec 2008): 544–59. http://www.nova.edu/ssss/QR/QR13-4/baxter.pdf.

Blanton, Richard E. "Theories of Ethnicity and the Dynamics of Ethnic Change in Multiethnic Societies." *PNAS* 112, no. 30 (July 28, 2015): 9177. https://www.pnas.org/content/pnas/112/30/9176.full.pdf.

ChuckIII.com. "In What Ways Is Identity a Social Construct." Accessed May 7, 2024. http://www.chuckiii.com/Reports/Sociology/In_what_ways_is_identity_a_social_construct.shtml.

Cohen, Ronald. "Ethnicity: Problem and Focus in Anthropology." *Annual Review of Anthropology* 7 (October 1978): 379–403. https://doi.org/10.1146/annurev.an.07.100178.002115.

Datema, Dave. "Defining 'Unreached': A Short History." *IJFM* 33, no. 2 (Summer 2016): 55.

Drew, Chris. "5 Key Principles of 'Thick Description' in Research." Last modified September 5, 2023. https://helpfulprofessor.com/thick-description/.

"Ethnicity," what-when-how.com.

Fearon, James D. "What Is Identity (As We Now Use the Word)?" Stanford University, 1999. https://web.stanford.edu/group/fearon-research/cgi-bin/wordpress/wp-content/uploads/2013/10/What-is-Identity-as-we-now-use-the-word-.pdf.

Fee, G. D. *Revelation: A New Covenant Commentary*. Eugene, OR: Cascade Books, 2011.

Gill, Brad. "ISFM 2019 and the 'Reimagining of Frontier Mission.'" *IJFM* 36, no. 4 (Winter 2019): 161–62.

Gill, Brad. "Reimagining Frontier Mission." *IJFM* 36, no. 3 (Fall 2019): 111–18.

Gill, Brad. "The Unfortunate Unmarketability of 'Unincorporable.'" *IJFM* 33, no. 2 (Summer 2016): 72–76. http://ijfm.org/PDFs_IJFM/33_2_PDFs/IJFM_33_2-EditorialReflections.pdf.

Gurney, Oliver Robert. "Religions of the Hittites, Hattians, and Hurrians." Accessed May 7, 2024. https://www.britannica.com/topic/Anatolian-religion/Religions-of-the-Hittites-Hattians-and-Hurrians.

Hamann, Edmund T., and William England. "Conclusion—Hyphenated Identities as a Challenge to Nation-State School Practice?" Lincoln: University of Nebraska, 2011. https://digitalcommons.unl.edu/cgi/viewcontent.cgi?referer=https://www.google.com/&httpsredir=1&article=1109&context=teachlearnfacpub.

Hutter, Manfred. "Religion in Hittite Anatolia: Some Comments on 'Volkert Haas: Geschichte der Hethitischen Religion.'" *Numen* 44, no. 1 (January 1997): 74–90.

IMB. "What Is a People Group?" Updated May 6, 2024. https://peoplegroups.org.

---

[38] Fee, *Revelation*, 88.

Jenkins, Richard. *Rethinking Ethnicity: Arguments and Explorations.* 2nd ed. London: Sage Publications, 2008.

Köstenberger, A. J. "Nations." In *New Dictionary of Biblical Theology*, edited by T. D. Alexander and B. S. Rosner, 676. Downers Grove, IL: InterVarsity Press, 2000.

Li, Darryl. "Taking the Place of Martyrs: Afghans and Arabs under the Banner of Islam." *Arab Studies Journal* 20, no. 1 (Spring 2012): 12–39. https://ssrn.com/abstract=2262478.

Martin, Ralph P., Daniel G. Reid, and Gerald F. Hawthorne, eds. *Dictionary of Paul and His Letters.* Downers Grove, IL: InterVarsity Press, 1993.

McGavran, Donald. *Ethnic Realities and the Church: Lessons from India.* Pasadena, CA: William Carey Library, 1979. https://books.google.ae/books?id=XCaLJq3ADQgC&printsec=frontcover&redir_esc=y#v=onepage&q&f=false.

McLaughlin, Fiona. "The Ascent of Wolof as an Urban Vernacular and National Lingua Franca in Senegal." In *Globalization and Language Vitality: Perspectives from Africa*, edited by Cécile B. Vigouroux and Salikoko S. Mufwene, 142–70. London: Bloomsbury Publishing, 2008.

Vermeulen, Hans, and Cora Govers, eds. *The Anthropology of Ethnicity: Beyond "Ethnic Groups and Boundaries."* Amsterdam: Het Spinhuis, 1994.

Willis, Paul. *The Ethnographic Imagination.* Cambridge, UK: Polity, 2000.

Winter, Ralph D., and Bruce A. Koch. "Finishing the Task: The Unreached Peoples Challenge." In *Perspectives on the World Christian Movement*, 4th ed., edited by Ralph D. Winter and Steven C. Hawthorne, 535. Pasadena, CA: William Carey Library, 2009.

Yeniceri, Aslihan. "Hybridization and Kazakh Ethnic Identity Formation." MA thesis, Iowa State University, 2015. https://dr.lib.iastate.edu/server/api/core/bitstreams/15240884-7541-4e6b-847b-f28640a8440c/content.

Afterword

People Vision and the Beatific Vision

Leonard N. Bartlotti

In this book, we have heard a chorus—pastors, leaders, workers, others in the global church—raising its voice to God and to his people on behalf of the voiceless. If you have listened closely, you have also heard the oft-muffled, near-and-far heart cries of the world's neglected, forgotten, unreached, and unengaged peoples.

Taken together, these chapters present a "people vision," an eschatological vision of persons from "every tribe and language and people and nation" gathered in worship around the throne of the Lamb.

This *telos* or end is not in doubt. The sections of seats for every (audible and recognizable!) people, group, and nation in the heavenly stadium will be filled! God's redemptive historical purposes, what is written in the "scroll," will be fulfilled! This ultimate intention is guaranteed by the sacrifice of the Lamb: "with your blood you purchased for God" a people from all peoples.

The only thing not guaranteed is our response in our generation. If this hope-inspired people vision does not move us, perhaps something else is needed: A new vision of God.

I would like to suggest that our "people vision" must include a "beatific vision."

In Protestant Christian theology, the "beatific vision" has been conceived as what Moses experienced on Mt. Sinai, "seeing, in some sense, God Himself," "a spiritual, not physical sight," "the eschatological promise of seeing God face-to-face, as he is (cf. 1 Cor 13:12; 1 John 3:2) … a vision of the divine majesty," "the permanent happiness" that is "our ultimate end."[1] Jonathan Edwards writes that the pleasure of seeing God is so great and so strong that it takes the full possession of the heart; it fills it brimful, so that there shall be no room for any sorrow, no room in any corner for anything of an adverse nature from joy. There is no darkness can bear such powerful light."[2]

God in Christ has made himself visible to us. "For in Christ all the fullness of the Deity lives in bodily form" (Col 2:9 NIV). "He who has seen Me has seen the Father" (John 14:9 NASB).

We who believe have experienced a near-cosmic display of Light! "For God, who said, 'Let light shine out of darkness,' made his light shine in our hearts to give us the light of the knowledge of God's glory displayed in the face of Christ" (2 Cor 4:6 NIV). Our hope, our cry, our prayer is that persons from every people and nation might be "enlightened" to see the glory and beauty of God in the face of Jesus!

In whatever way we conceive of this unspeakable intimacy with God, in part now and in fullness then, *a new vision of Christ must be the primary motivation for our mission.* With John

---

1 Ortlund, "Why We Misunderstand."
2 Quoted in Ortlund, "Why We Misunderstand."

the Baptist, we cry, "Behold, the Lamb on the Throne who takes away the sin of the world" (John 1:29 NASB)! Behold, "the Man of Sorrows" who wipes away the tears of the world (cf. Rev 21:4)! Behold, the Lamb of God who reigns over the peoples of the world (Rev 7:9)! That is a sight for all eyes, for "every eye will see him" (Rev 1:7).

A true vision of Christ includes a vision of all those who are "in Christ, his body, the fulless of him who fills everything in every way." (Eph 1:23)

> After this I looked, and there before me was a great multitude that no one could count, from every nation, tribe, people and language, standing before the throne and before the Lamb. They were wearing white robes and were holding palm branches in their hands. And they cried out in a loud voice: "Salvation belongs to our God, who sits on the throne, and to the Lamb." (Rev 7:9–10 NIV)

The people vision is a costly vision. Although it is too-rarely said, the journey from Revelation 5:9-worship to Revelation 7:9-multitudes passes through Revelation 6:9-suffering. "I saw under the altar *the souls of those who had been slain because of the word of God and the testimony they had maintained.* They called out in a loud voice, '*How long, Sovereign Lord*, holy and true, until you judge the inhabitants of the earth and avenge our blood?' Then each of them was given a white robe, and they were told to *wait a little longer, until the full number of their fellow servants, their brothers and sisters, were killed just as they had been*" (6:9–11 NIV, emphasis added).

On a separate spreadsheet in God's database and "registry of the nations" (Ps 87:6) is another list of mostly (to us) unknown warriors and martyrs. Their wounds and witness, tears and scars, testimony and death, point to the still visible scars of the crucified risen One whose purposes they served in their generation. Our wounds reflect His. Our wounds are our witness. Our tears are our testimony. Our scars are our glory. Suffering in the way of mission reflects His power in weakness, His glory in suffering. In Johannine theology, Christ was enthroned on the cross: "And I, when I am lifted up from the earth, will draw all people to myself" (John 12:32 NIV). From that throne, salvation flows.

As we declare His glory in ends-of-the-earth witness, our lives become before the nations a visible expression, tangible outworking, and dramatic portrayal of the sacrificial, self-giving love of the God we proclaim. Because our task is not finished and so many have yet to hear, the souls under the altar have been told to "*wait a little longer, until the full number.*"

Meanwhile, sadly, the world's unsaved also "*wait a little longer, until the full number*" of God's people rise in Spirit-empowered witness. That is the heart, the prayer, the passion, behind this book.

Someday, together with children of God redeemed from every tribe and language and people and nation, the wait will be over. The "full number" of peoples will also be present, as the people vision becomes part of the beatific vision. We shall behold Him. "We shall see him as he is" (1 John 3:2). "They will see his face" (Rev 22:4 NIV).

Reflection and Discussion

Imagining Fulfillment

1. How did Gill's personal experiences in North Africa differ from his earlier thinking and expectations before he got to the field?

2. Which of the twelve principles for "pioneer apostleship" stood out to you? How do these principles align with or differ from the way missions is viewed in your church?

3. Why is it important to prioritize unengaged unreached peoples?

4. What did you think and feel as you read about Believers from a Muslim Background being a new "wing" in the household of God and "eleventh hour" workers for the harvest?

5. What are some things we need to "reimagine" about people groups, ethnic identity, unreached peoples, and models of church, as we re-envision mission to least reached peoples today?

6. Can you give examples from your experience, context, or organization of the way people from difference ethnic groups "bond" (like chemical molecules) with multiple social networks in different contexts or settings?

7. How might the proposal for "new dynamic models" of people groups, their interactions, and social bonding, help us not only understand but more effectively reach peoples?

8. What skill sets are needed for "barefoot ethnography" in new cultures?

9. How can we more effectively gather, steward, share, and use insights into peoples and cultures? How would the development of Second Tier (cultural knowledge) and Third Tier (missiological understandings) information databases help you, your workers, partners, church and organization?

10. In your context, what is being done to foster collaboration and help churches (traditional, mixed congregations, urban mega churches, house church networks, proximate believers, others) maximize their "evangelistic potential" to reach unreached peoples?

11. How does your heart respond to the vision of Revelation 5:9?

12. Write a prayer that expresses your praise to the Lamb on the throne.

Appendix 1
Frequently Asked Questions about People Groups and Unreached Peoples

Q: *Where is the idea of people groups in the Bible?*

In both Old and New Testaments, God shows His love and concern for humanity in all its diversity. Human groupings are described by a spectrum of terms referring to nations, languages, tribes, families, clans, households, and other groupings distinguished by shared characteristics like heritage, customs, language, land, religion, and common identity. These are all aspects of what we identify as "people groups" or "peoples." "God's people," in the midst of whom He dwells, are to be a blessing to "all peoples" (Gen 10; 12:1–3; Rev 5:9; 7:9).

Q: *Doesn't* panta ta ethne *just mean "Gentiles" or "non-Jewish people"?*

The term refers to non-Jewish persons in all of their diversity. That is, the reality of distinct ethne and linguistic diversity among humans was assumed. The five commissions of Jesus in the Gospels and the book of Acts to take the gospel everywhere, to the ends of the earth, to every creature, to the ethne, make this clear. The gospel must take root and Christ be honored among all of that human diversity, every compartment of humanity, that we often express in terms like peoples, tribes, or linguistic groups.

Q: *How did the early church address the tension between Jews and non-Jewish believers?*

The Acts 15 Jerusalem Council provides one model. The sharp conflict over whether Gentiles should be required to be circumcised and become Jewish proselytes resulted in a "victory of truth," the affirmation that all are saved by grace through faith, apart from works of the law, meaning you don't have to become "like them" to follow Jesus. It was also a "victory of love," as Gentiles made certain accommodations to Jewish believers that facilitated meal fellowship between them, where they could embrace as brothers and sisters in Christ.

Q: *The Bible says that "there is neither Jew nor Greek … for you are all one in Christ Jesus" (Gal 3:28), so why divide people and churches according to ethnicity in missions?*

Because God cares about "every tribe, tongue, people, and nation" being included in His kingdom, we need to care. We do not divide people along ethnic lines, but instead, encourage and celebrate the ethnolinguistic diversity of the family of God. This allows the song of salvation to be sung by new peoples in new places with new languages in new ways. We are not a melting pot but a mosaic as the family of God. As one scholar points out from Revelation 7:9, we have the unity of all being clothed in white while still displaying the diversity of peopleness, nation, tribe, and tongue.

Q: *Is the people group approach a Western missiological fad?*

While the term is a modern convention, Bible authors saw the world and humanity in terms of a diversity of nations, tribes, clans, and households; Scripture is filled with examples of each. Through Christian history, the gospel often flowed along natural social lines and relations between people. People groups are just one way of expressing these natural clusters and human groupings.

Q: *Where did the idea of planting homogeneous unit (people group specific) churches come from?*

The "homogeneous unit principle" is first an observation on evangelism: The gospel tends to flow naturally through kinship and social networks. People more often come to faith through, and join a fellowship of, "people like us." The gospel can spread through social networks without unnecessary barriers. Diverse "versions" of "church" that result are not a requirement, but an expression of gospel freedom: Believers, though one in Christ, have liberty to express their faith, worship, and life together in unique ways, based on their cultural and linguistic vernacular.

Q: *Does planting homogeneous churches perpetuate prejudice and racism among people groups?*

Prejudice, racism, and suspicion of the "other" are aspects of sinful human nature. This must be addressed in the discipleship process, through the transformation of the mind by the Spirit and word of God (Rom 12:1–2; 15:1–16; cf. Acts 11:19–21). This same process is necessary in mixed or multiethnic churches as well. In the New Testament, prejudices between believing Jews and Gentiles were openly challenged (Acts 10; 15; Eph 1–3). We affirm our unity and identity in Christ while retaining our diverse identities. New believers must be taught to believe, and live out, Jesus's high priestly prayer for unity "so that the world may believe that you have sent me" (John 17:20–21).

Q: *Shouldn't we plant multiethnic, multicultural churches with all kinds of people?*

Every church should be characterized by biblical fidelity and cultural fit. Multiethnic churches thrive especially in urban settings where the ethnic "glue" may weaken, and peoples mix easily with other ethnicities and groups based on shared interests, occupation, social class, neighborhood, generational characteristics, and affinities. In other contexts, urban compression strengthens ethnic bonds. In traditional or rural areas, kinship and language ties are primary, and churches tend to grow based on cultural and relational "bridges." These social dynamics vary according to context and affect the shape of a church.

Q: *How can we model reconciliation and the unity of the church if we encourage people group identity?*

"Unity" and "reconciliation" does not require worshiping in the same Sunday service using a dominant group's language and style. More important is what happens Monday to Saturday. Believers and diverse churches are one but can express their oneness and identity in Christ in a variety of creative and loving ways (e.g., shared celebrations, relationships and meal fellowship, collegiality between leaders, concerts of prayer, pulpit exchanges, joint outreach, etc.).

Q: *Is the frontier mission movement and UPG approach an example of "managerial missiology"?*

God is sovereign. Missions begins not with us but with the God who seeks, finds, and sends. The UPG approach is an attempt to prioritize the Great Commission and track our obedience to the mandate to take the gospel where it has not yet been fully proclaimed. While a management mentality is a temptation, at best it is an expression of stewardship (where to allocate workers and resources) and accountability (what peoples and nations do not yet have access to the gospel).

Q: *What are the main cultural blocs of least reached peoples?*

Most unreached and unengaged people groups are among Muslims, Hindus, Buddhist, and Tribal (Ethnic Religionists) peoples. Many would also include the Deaf, certain Jewish groups, and others. Frontier people groups, those unreached peoples with less than 0.1 percent believers among them, and unengaged peoples, with no intentional witness among them, are considered by many to be the highest priority.

Q: *Why do we need these numbers and "lists" of unreached people groups?*

God counts. When the good shepherd gets to ninety-nine, he goes out to find the one who is lost. But precision about numbers is not the main thing. We track them to get a better understanding of where and how many people do not have access to the gospel or an indigenous fellowship of believers. Lists are simply attempts to track the "gaps" in the global church, the "empty seats" in the heavenly stadium. The information helps us to prioritize solutions.

Q: *Doesn't every non-Christian need to be "reached"? What's different about "unreached peoples"?*

We need to "reach out" with the good news to all people. But some non-Christians have greater access to the gospel than others. Technically, in the world of missions, the term "unreached" does not refer to a neighbor or individual person, but to a human grouping with a common sense of identity. In its simplest form, "reached" versus "unreached" refers to the presence or absence of a viable, indigenous, growing church movement among a people. The initial pioneer phase of church planting aims for this missiological "breakthrough," which provides access to the gospel along the lines of natural social relationships.

Q: *Why should we make frontier missions a strategic priority in our church?*

There is a clear and well documented imbalance in the allocation of missions resources, missions sending, and the relative access people have to the gospel. Throughout the recent mission era, 85 percent of cross-cultural workers have tended to go where there are already local Christians and churches, providing training, leadership development, etc. This leaves some 3 billion people living in societies where they do not know a Christian personally and where the chances of meeting a Christian and hearing the gospel are very small.

Q: *Is disciple making and church planting among unreached people groups a greater priority than reaching my neighbors and community?*

We must do both. All people are equally lost. The difference is that UPGs do not have access to the gospel and your neighbors do. Generally, we speak the same language as our neighbors and share the culture of those in our community. There are fewer barriers to them joining a local fellowship. Lacking the gospel, the Scriptures, and a body of believers in their language, non-Christians in UPGs do not have that option. This makes frontier missions a strategic priority.

Q: *Don't we need to balance funding for frontier church planting with other mission priorities like compassion and humanitarian work, justice, social transformation, education, and development?*

The church currently spends so little on pioneer church planting among UPGs, some balance would be a very good thing! But perhaps a better way to frame the issue would be around the question of priorities. Are we addressing the spiritual injustice of those without access to the gospel? Among all the many good things the church can do, how much priority are we placing on making the gospel accessible to those without opportunity to hear and obey the good news? Needs are everywhere; where are we needed most?

Q: *Do the foreign refugees in my city count as unreached peoples?*

Many refugees come from unreached people groups in their homeland. Often migrants from major blocs of UPGs (Muslim, Hindu, Buddhist) maintain "transnational" identity and connections with family and friends in the homeland (international calls, sending money, cultural practices, visits, etc.). This underlines the importance of diaspora ministries, as the gospel may travel over these hidden highways.

Q: *Is reaching international students reaching the unreached?*

Similar to the answer above, it depends on whether or not they represent an unreached people group. Welcoming others is the Jesus style. International students need to be discipled with the understandings, skills, and tools (media, audio Scripture, etc.) to live out and share their faith if/when they return to their homeland.

Q: *What percentage of cross-cultural workers and missionaries are engaged in pioneer ministry among unreached people groups?*

An estimated 3 percent of the missionary force works among unreached people groups. Admittedly, it is much harder to know the situation among missionaries sent out from non-Western churches who may serve in proximate cultures, use business as mission, and other non-traditional but highly effective entry and disciple making strategies. The next great wave of gospel advance may come from innovative approaches and international partnerships in unevangelized regions.

Q: *What percentage of current giving to missions is directed toward pioneer ministry among unreached people groups?*

An estimated 1 percent of all missions giving goes to places that have no believers, Bibles in their language, or bodies of believers (churches). Most financial and personnel resources are directed toward ministries that strengthen the church where the church already is. The amount of money we do, or do not spend, on taking the gospel to unreached and unengaged people groups is an indicator of our level of urgency and commitment to Christ's mandate to make disciples of all nations.

Q: *Can't we use radio, TV, and social media to reach UPGs? Why do we need to send missionaries and other workers?*

Missions have for decades used radio, TV, and more recently, the Jesus Film to great effect for broad "seed sowing" evangelism. Use of the internet, social media, videos, audio Scriptures, and other media strategies is a rapidly expanding dimension of missions. However, media can never take the place of human messengers, "sent ones" who, like Jesus, can incarnate the gospel, whether they be expat, proximate, or indigenous believers. We need to connect evangelism tools and strategies (many of which reveal people who are seeking Jesus) with on-site disciple making strategies that develop, mobilize, and multiply churches, fellowships, and followers of Jesus.

Q: *Should the Western church still send cross-cultural workers when we can just let nationals reach the people groups in their country? Don't they know the language and culture better?*

The national language is not always the "heart" language of a people group. In a multiethnic country, an ethnic or minority group may cherish its identity and culture more than national identity. Thus, nationals may also have to cross linguistic, social, cultural, and prejudice barriers within their own country. Increasingly, partnerships between sending churches, agencies, local/regional workers and networks, and expatriate missionaries are proving fruitful. Every church has a responsibility to obey the Great Commission and take part in Christ's global cause.

Q: *If nationals are better equipped to reach their own people, why should the church even send cross-cultural missionaries?*

When seeking to reach UPGs, the Western church—and workers from sending churches in Africa, Latin America, Europe, and Asia—should pursue collaboration with near-culture believers whenever possible. Nationals may have a similar worldview and cultural sensitivity, while expatriate workers may bring mission experience and professional skills. In a country with multiple ethnic and language groups, sometimes the truism "near is far, and far is near" is relevant. Sometimes social, cultural, economic, and religious barriers, or a history of prejudice and conflict, make it difficult for even a local or national believer to relate and/or be accepted.

Q: *What are the main elements of a local church missions program?*

When missions and global engagement are a primary focus of a church, these elements tend to be present: (1) leadership—pastors/church leaders and missions team/leaders are educated, engaged, and have an "all peoples" strategic focus; (2) mobilization—God's heart for the nations, biblical foundations, missions education, and cross-cultural skills are integrated into discipleship, groups, and church life; (3) support—prayer for the nations, missionaries, and world situations; faithful, generous, and strategic giving; and missionary/partner care are high values and tangibly expressed; (4) sending—missional formation equips members for outreach among neighbors and nations, cross-cultural friendships, support trips, and use of their skills, professional training, and gifts for long-term involvement in the Great Commission.

Q: *How can our church become more strategic in its approach to global missions?*

When we know "the story of God's glory" at the heart of the Bible and God's purpose for a people from "every tribe and language and people and nation" (Rev 5:9), we can begin to orient our sending and going to see that goal fulfilled. Without neglecting current relationships, we place a strategic priority on those unreached and unengaged peoples and places with least access to the gospel message, the Scriptures, and an indigenous church movement. We explore partnerships with other churches, agencies, and networks for frontier engagement. Currently, only about 3 percent of mission workers are focused on unreached peoples who comprise more than 40 percent of the world's population. Pray, learn, team, and "do the math" on how your church can correct this imbalance and spiritual injustice!

Q: *What is the role of prayer in missions?*

Everything starts with prayer. In the throne room, Isaiah saw the Lord and heard His voice, "Whom shall I send? And who will go for us?" He responded, "Here am I! Send me!" (Isa 6:1–8). In prayer, the church in Antioch gave room for God to speak and for the Spirit to send the first missionary team (Acts 13:1–3). Prayer is not a strategy; it is how we come to know the Father's heart toward the least, the last, and the lost. If a local church begins to pray seriously for the nations, God will show them in how to join Him in what He desires to do.

Q: *Isn't it too dangerous to work in certain parts of the world that persecute Christians?*

Missions is risk and requires wise and discerning leadership. That said, it is always "dangerous" to take up our cross and follow Christ (Matt 16:24–26). Satan is overcome "by the blood of the Lamb and by the word of their testimony, for they loved not their lives even unto death" (Rev 12:11). God sends us even to dangerous places to show His love, redeem lost and broken people, fulfill His purposes, and display His glory to all nations so as to receive glory from all nations.

Q: *Why should we try to reach people who are resistant or hostile to the gospel?*

We cannot call someone "resistant" who has never even heard the gospel. Historically speaking, the church has made such little effort to reach most of the so-called "resistant" peoples like Muslims, Buddhists, and Hindus, that it is unfair to label them as such. Christ's mandate to "make disciples of all nations" includes "all" nations and peoples, regardless of the cost, or their real or perceived receptivity. You cannot reap a harvest without sowing seed, and sometimes you have to clear the rocks from the soil first.

Q: *Haven't forces such as globalization, migration, and the technological revolution flattened the world in such a way that people groups don't really exist anymore like they used to?*

The dynamics mentioned above affect some people more than others. Traditional people groups still exist all around the world. Among peoples in other contexts, the social "glue" has weakened. Many people today are biracial/bi-ethnic, speak more than one language, have "hybrid" identities, and may identify with their host country more than the one they left behind. The core questions remain: Does this human grouping (defined by language, heritage, affinity, etc.) have access to the gospel or not? Are members of this people group incorporable—able to become part of an existing fellowship without barriers of understanding or acceptance? If not, then they are perhaps part of a people group that requires a new engagement and disciple making strategy.

Appendix 2
Visualizing the Task
Maps, Graphs, Figures, Charts, Lists

At Pentecost the Holy Spirit empowered Jesus' body to multiply disciples among all people groups (Greek ethne). As the gospel advances, kingdom workers increase while the number of people groups without gospel access decreases. Fifty years ago, the 1974 Lausanne Congress greatly accelerated this advance by focusing attention on people groups without Christward movements.

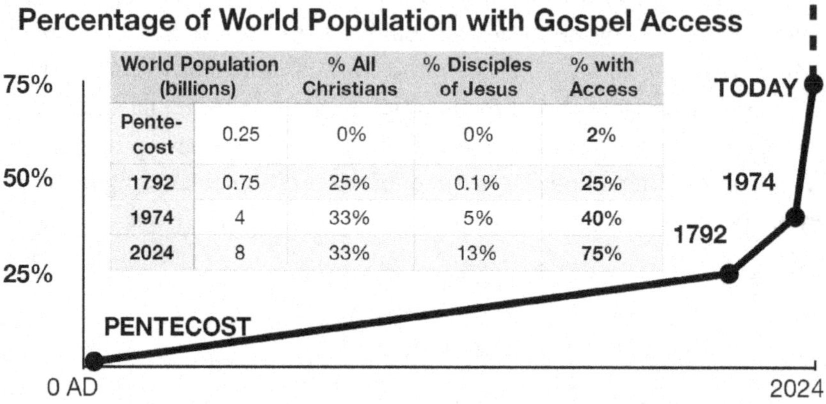

Percentage of World Population with Gospel Access

	World Population (billions)	% All Christians	% Disciples of Jesus	% with Access
Pentecost	0.25	0%	0%	2%
1792	0.75	25%	0.1%	25%
1974	4	33%	5%	40%
2024	8	33%	13%	75%

Figure 12: The Accelerating Growth of Jesus's Kingdom. Used with permission by R. W. Lewis.

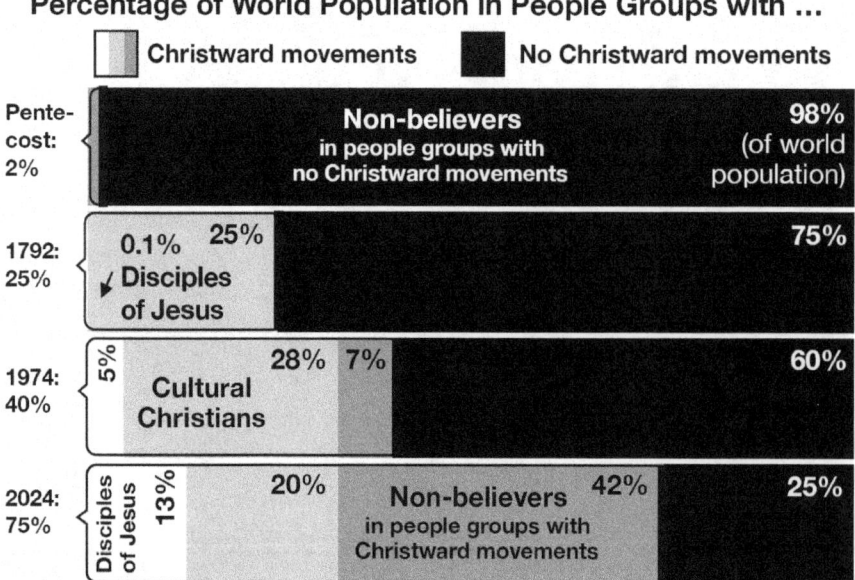

Figure 13: The Increasing Progress of the Gospel. Used with permission by R. W. Lewis.

Where Are We Sending Workers?

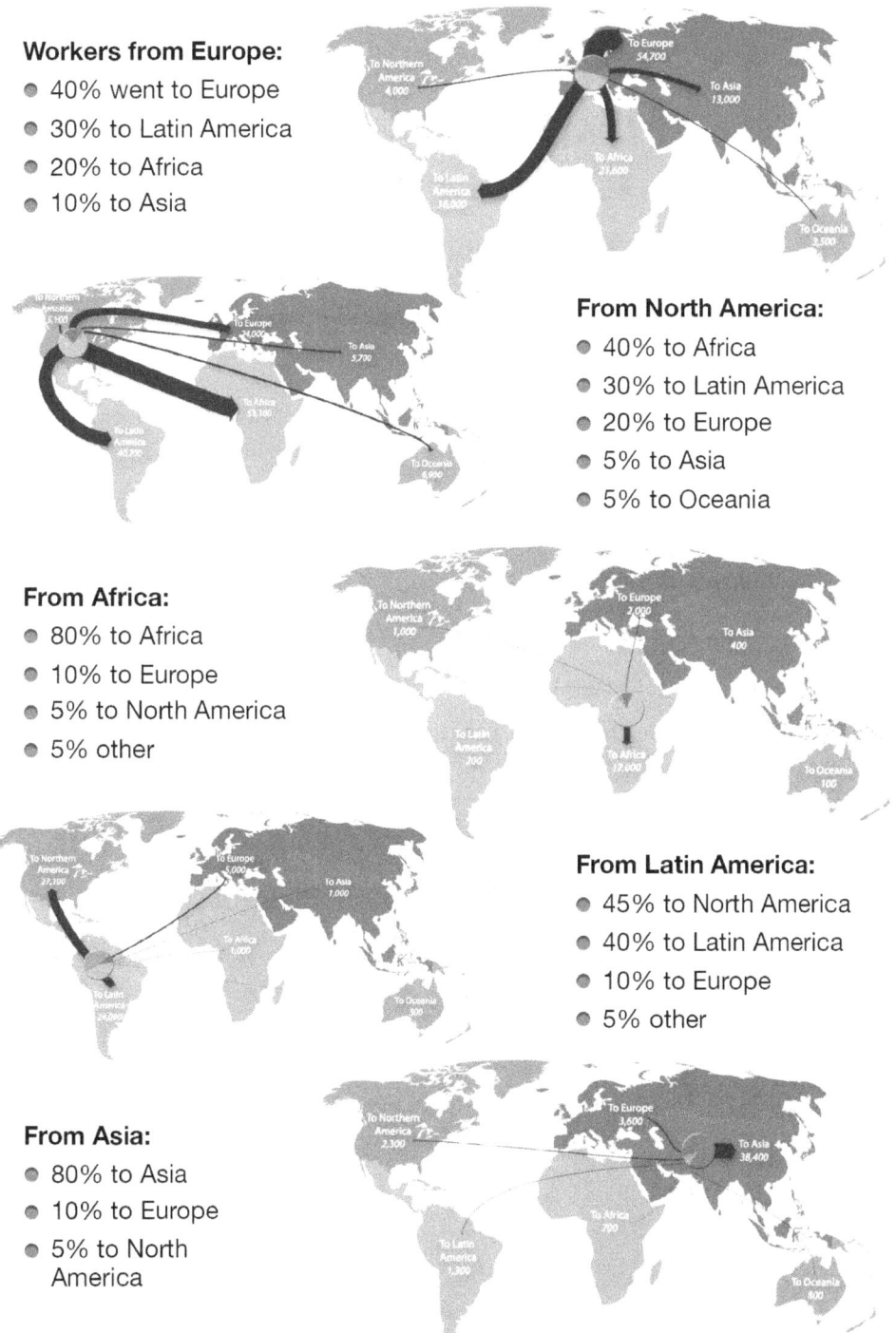

Workers from Europe:
- 40% went to Europe
- 30% to Latin America
- 20% to Africa
- 10% to Asia

From North America:
- 40% to Africa
- 30% to Latin America
- 20% to Europe
- 5% to Asia
- 5% to Oceania

From Africa:
- 80% to Africa
- 10% to Europe
- 5% to North America
- 5% other

From Latin America:
- 45% to North America
- 40% to Latin America
- 10% to Europe
- 5% other

From Asia:
- 80% to Asia
- 10% to Europe
- 5% to North America

Figure 14: 2010 Distribution oF foreign Missionaries (Oceeania omitted), from the *Atlas of Global Christianity* (Edinburgh: Edinburgh University Press), 262–63. Used with permission by Todd Johnson.

Key Languages of the Least-Reached People Groups

What languages can new workers learn for greatest access to Frontier People Groups and other Unreached People Groups? Seven of the top ten languages spoken by FPGs and other UPGs are South Asian (see figure below).

Hindi and Urdu are so similar that, although there are prejudice barriers between the two languages, learning either equips the learner to begin work among any of the 700 million people who speak one of those languages.

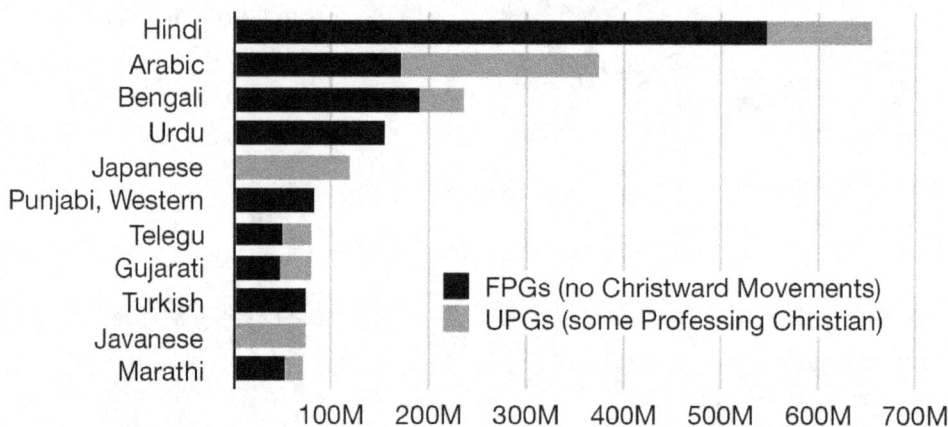

Figure 15: Top Primary Languages of FPGs and UPGs. Based on data accessed March 2024 from JoshuaProject.net/frontier/interactive. Used with permission by RW Lewis.

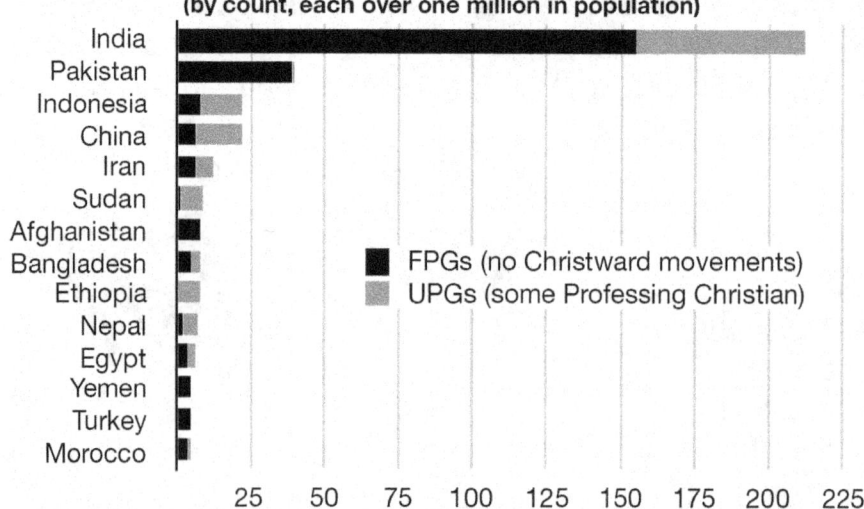

Figure 16: Top 10 Countries of Largest FPGs and UPGs. Based on data accessed March 2024 from JoshuaProject.net/frontier/interactive. Used with permission by RW Lewis.

Opportunities in Urban Centers

The 110 cities below include people from many Unreached People Groups, including Unengaged and Frontier People Groups, often isolated in ethnic neighborhoods.

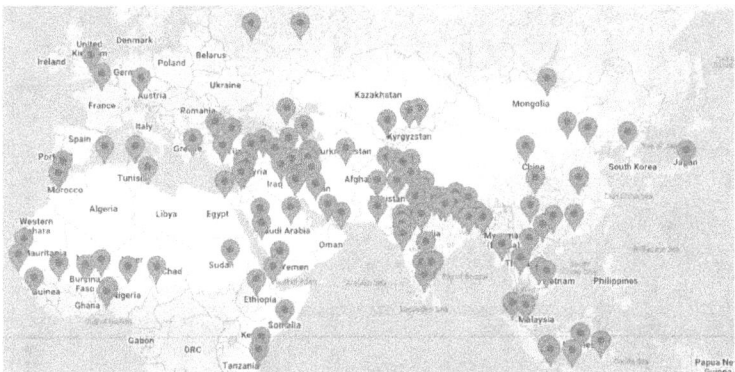

Figure 17: 110 Megacities Map accessed February 2024 on 110Cities.com/map. Used with permission.

In mega cities it is possible to gather people from reached groups into multi-ethnic churches using shared trade languages. These churches have evangelistic potential to create relational "bridges" to ethnic communities and affinity groups.

Sometimes these churches attract people from UPGs and FPGs, including Muslims and Hindus. These churches can follow Paul's example to disciple and equip some of these "God-fearers" to bring the gospel to their own people.

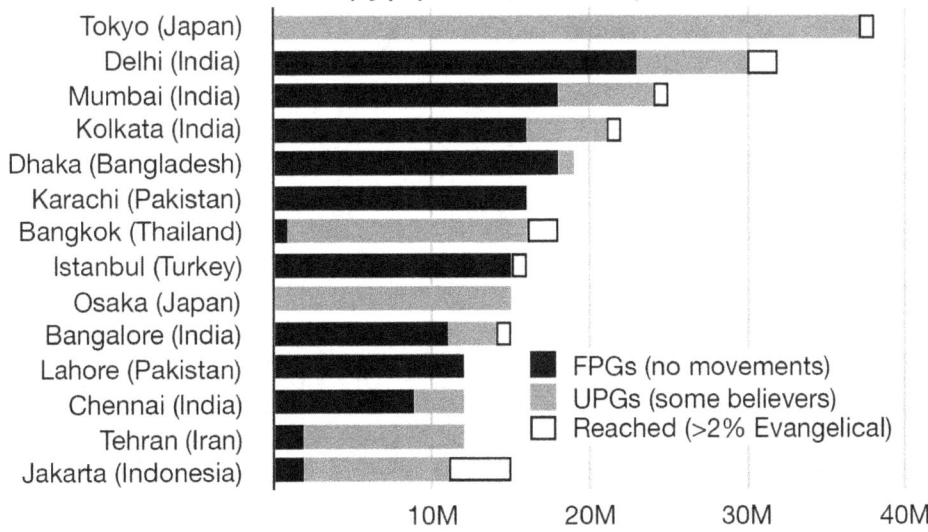

Figure 18: Top Cities of UPGs. Based on data accessed March 2024 from JoshuaProject.net/frontier/interactive. Used with permission by RW Lewis.

Layered and Hybrid Identities

People living in diaspora (outside their homeland) often have layered identities and are part of multiple social groups. Sharing Jesus *to, through and with* diaspora people can impact multiple peoples and affinity groups, locally and in the ethnic heartland.

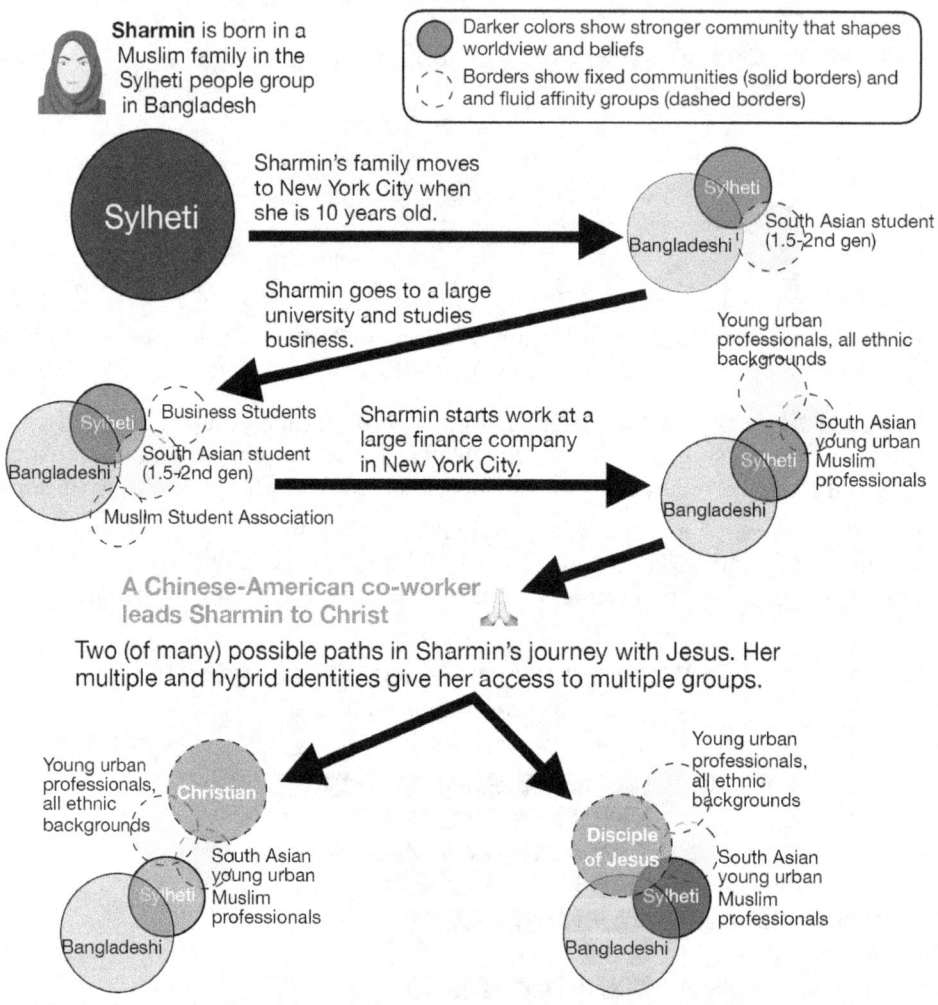

Figure 19: Layered Journey. Used with permission by Chris Clayman of JoshuaProject.net.

The Challenge of India

More people live in India (1.4 billion) than all of North America (0.4 B) and South America (0.6 B) combined, nearly as many as in all of Africa (1.6 B). The Ethnologue lists 4,000 distinct languages in India, with multiple alphabets.

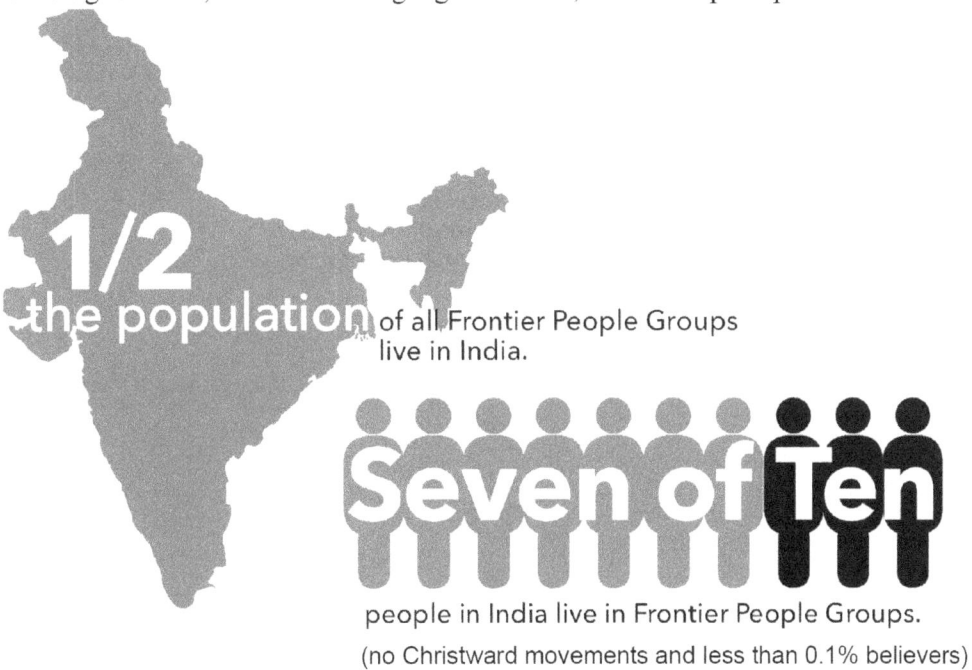

India has 1,000 times as many people in Frontier People Groups as the USA, but the USA receives 4 times as many cross-cultural workers as India.
- Outside India there is 1 international worker for every 10,000 people in Frontier People Groups.
- Within India there is 1 international worker for every 250,000 people in FPGs.
- 1 in 5,000 of all international workers globally serves among India's FPGs.
- 1 in 20,000 of those living in India's FPGs could be considered a disciple of Jesus.
- Mobilizing, equipping, and collaborating with Indian cross-cultural workers is a strategic priority.

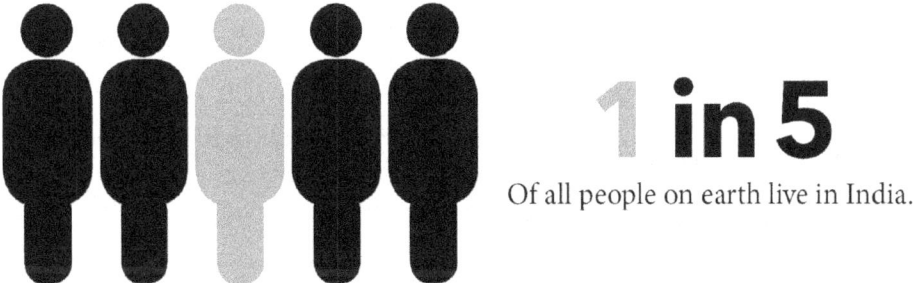

Figure 20: The Challenge of India. Adapted from the May/June 2019 issue of *Mission Frontiers*.

Global Distribution of Workers and Funding

Only 4% of international workers are focused on pioneer work among the remaining 40% of the world in Unreached People Groups. An even smaller percentage of global giving to missions goes to work among UPGs.

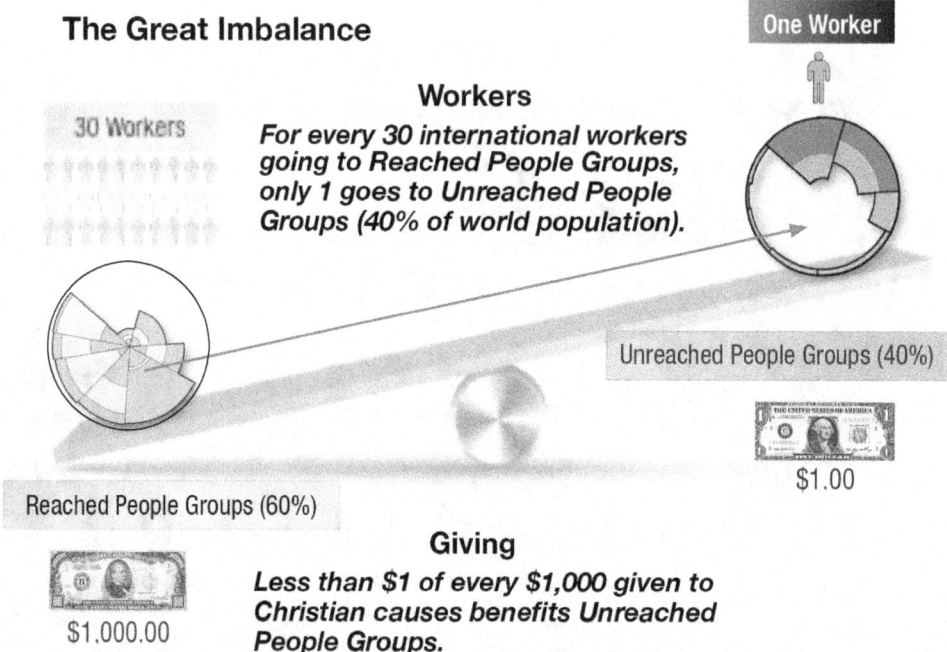

Figure 21: Distribution of Workers and Funding. Adapted from *Pray for The 31 Largest Frontier People Groups* prayer guide. Used with permission by JoshuaProject.net/the31

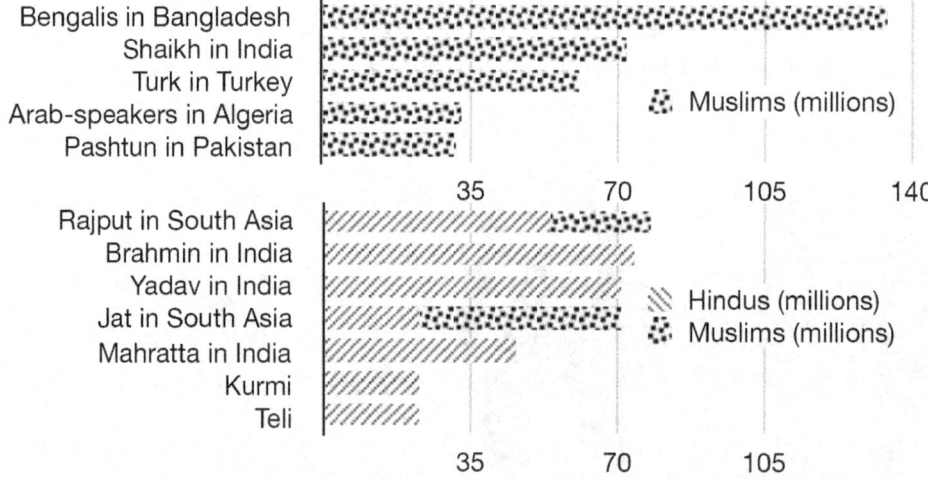

Figure 22: Largest Muslim and Hindu FPGs. Data from JoshuaProject.net/filter accessed April 2024. Used with permission by Joshua Project.

Church Movements Needed in Sub-Saharan Africa

354 Muslim UPGs (90 million) in the Sahel

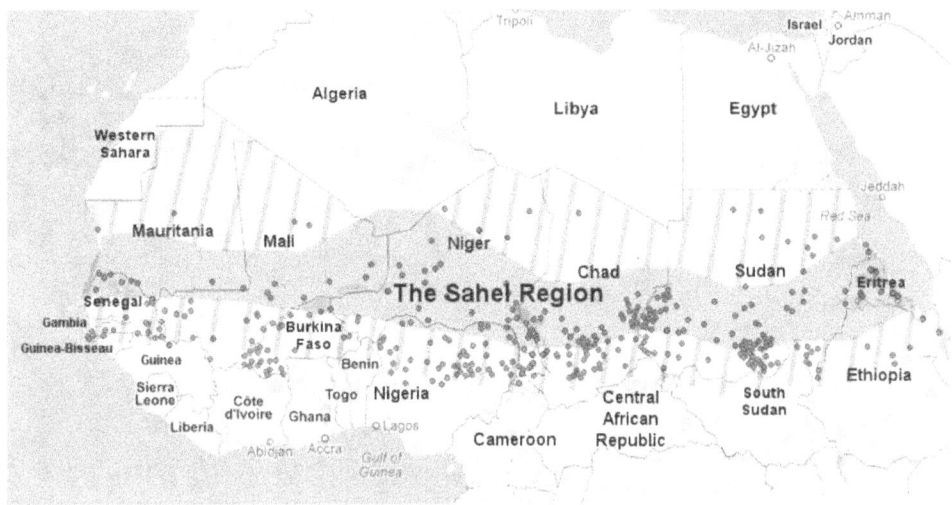

Figure 23: Church Movements Needed in Sub-Saharan Africa.
Used with permission by John Becker.
See also "The Sahel: Finishing the Task" by Patrick Johnstone
,lusanne.org/about/blog/the-sahel-finishing-the-task.

Sudan

Africa's largest country. Desert in the north, merging into grasslands and mountains in the center and tropical bush in the south. Straddling the Nile Rivers. Nuba Mountains in the center.

QUICK FACTS:

Area: 2.5 million sq km

People Groups: 141

Languages: 85

Population: 37 million

Unreached Peoples: 125

UPG Population: 36 million

Unengaged UPGs: 87

UUPG Population: 20 million

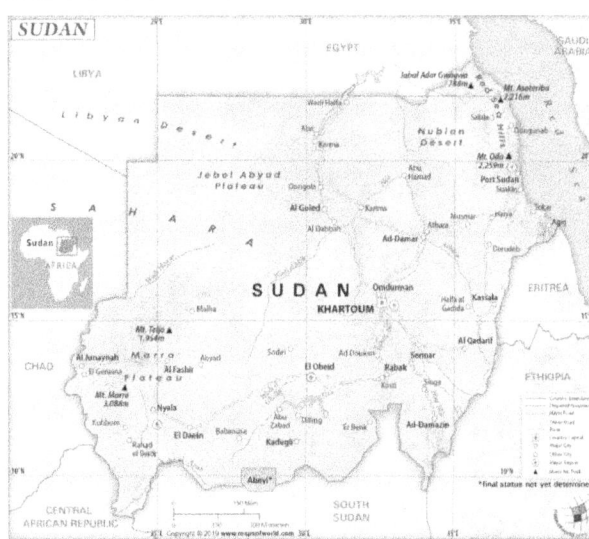

Figure 24: Sudan. Used with permission by John Becker.

Making Sense of People Groups

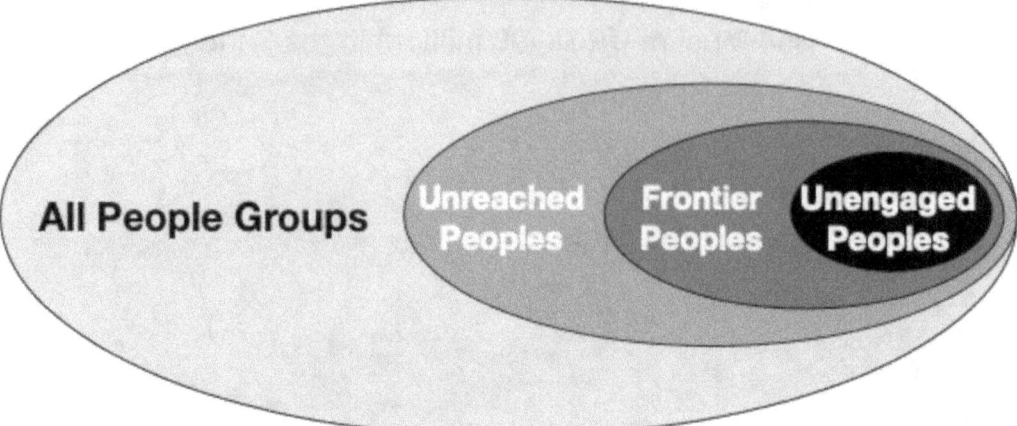

Countries with the Most *Unengaged* Unreached People Groups, by *Religion*
(Unreached People Groups with no known workers)

1. **India (729 UUPG)**
   Hindu (620)
   Muslim (83)
   Buddhist (16)
   Other (8)
   Tribal (2)
2. **China (141 UUPG)**
   Tribal (109)
   Buddhist (26)
   Muslim (5)
   Other (1)
3. **Sudan (63 UUPG)**
   Muslim (59)
   Tribal (4)
4. **Laos (53 UUPG)**
   Tribal (52)
   Buddhist (1)
5. **Chad (51 UUPG)**
   Muslim (39)
   Tribal (12)
6. **Indonesia (30 UUPG)**
   Muslim (30)
7. **Nigeria (29 UUPG)**
   Tribal (18)
   Muslim (11)
8. **Brazil (27 UUPG)**
   Tribal (27)

To explore UUPGs, visit UnengagedPeoples.com/explorer-tool

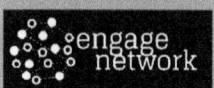

Figure 25: Countries with Most Unengaged Unreached People Groups, by Religion. Used with permission by Mike Latsko, Engage Network.

Religions with the Most *Unengaged* Unreached People Groups, by *Country*

Hindu (643 Global UUPGs)
1. India (620)
2. Nepal (15)
3. Bangladesh (3)

Tribal/Ethnic (428 Global UUPGs)
1. China (109)
2. Laos (52)
3. Brazil (27)
4. Ethiopia (19)
5. Chad (12)

Muslim (393 Global UUPGs)
1. India (83)
2. Sudan (59)
3. Chad (39)
4. Indonesia (30)
5. Algeria, Iran, Pakistan (15)

Buddhist (70 Global UUPGs)
1. China (26)
2. India (16)
3. Bhutan (11)
4. Nepal (5)
5. Thailand, Myanmar (4)

Other (52 Global UUPGs)
1. India (8)
2. Israel (4)

Figure 26: Religions with the Most Unengaged Unreached People Groups, by Country. Used with permission by Mike Latsko, Engage Network.

20 Countries with the Largest Number of Unengaged Muslim Peoples

	Country	MUUPGs	Priority Region
1	India	83	Southern Asia
2	Sudan	59	Sahel
3	Chad	39	Sahel
4	Indonesia	30	Southeast Asia
5	Algeria	15	Middle East/North Africa
6	Pakistan	15	Southeast Asia
7	Iran	15	Southeast Asia
8	Nigeria	11	Sub-Saharan Africa
9	Libya	11	Middle East/North Africa
10	SouthSudan	9	Sahel
11	Ethiopia	8	Sub-Saharan Africa
12	Afghanistan	7	Southwest Asia
13	Somalia	7	Sub-Saharan Africa
14	Mali	6	Sub-Saharan Africa
15	Oman	5	Middle East/North Africa
16	China	5	East Asia
17	Cameroon	4	Sub-Saharan Africa
18	Burkina Faso	4	Sub-Saharan Africa
19	Yemen	4	Middle East/North Africa
20	Tajikistan	4	Central Asia

Figure 27: 20 Countries with the Largest Number of Unengaged Muslim Peoples. Used with permission by Mike Latsko, Engage Network.

Appendix 3
Resources

	**Lausanne Least Reached Peoples Network** lausanne.org/network/least-reached-peoples	
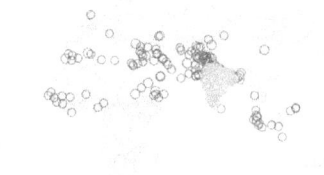	**Maps:** *Frontier Peoples-Interactive* joshuaproject.net/frontier/interactive	
	**Maps:** *People Group Maps* JoshuaProject.net/frontier/interactive	
	**Media:** *Create International* https://createinternational.com/resources/	
	**Mobilization:** *KAIROS: Christian Mission course* SimplyMobilizing.com/kairos	

 **Research:** *Global Community of Mission Information Workers*
https://www.globalcmiw.org/Links

 **Research:** *OC Research*
https://www.ocresearch.info/

 **Video:** *State of the World/ The Task Remaining*
https://www.youtube.com/WrHC7hXNoV8

 **Video:** *Understanding the Remaining Mission Task (multiple languages)*
JoshuaProject.net/frontier#videos

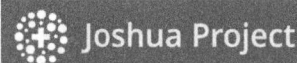 **Videos:** *Unreached Peoples*
https://joshuaproject.net/resources/videos

 **Videos:** *Prayercast*
https://prayercast.com/

Resources

 **Mobilization:** *Perspectives on the World Christian Movement* **Study Programs** *(9 global languages)*
https://www.perspectivesglobal.org

Prayer: *30 Days of Prayer for the Muslim World: Ramadan and beyond*
https://www.pray30days.org/

 **Prayer:** *31 Largest Frontier Peoples*
https://www.telosfellowship.org/go31

 **Prayer:** *Global Prayer for the Neglected*
https://allnations.international/neglectedpeople

 **Prayer:** *Operation World: Prayer Guide to Every Nation*
https://operationworld.org/

 **Prayer:** *Pray4Movement*
https://pray4movement.org/

Acknowledgments

This book fulfills a dream, a longing, a prayer. My vision and burden for "hidden" and "unreached peoples" traces back to the life-shaping experiences my wife and I had working with Dr. Ralph D. and Roberta Winter, founders of the U.S. Center for World Mission (now Frontier Ventures) from 1979-1984. We were gripped by the spiritual need of this vast, neglected sphere of peoples and swept into the forefront of the growing frontier mission movement. Dr. Winter taught us to see the world differently and to envision all peoples having access to the gospel in a way they could understand, and access to "church" in a way they could embrace and be embraced. I am grateful for his life and memory.

My wife Debi, a nurse midwife and spiritual director, friend, co-laborer, and love through over fifty years of marriage, encouraged me to take the steps of faith in ministry, field research, collaboration, and study, that lie behind this book. The sacrifices involved in releasing me to my calling and craft are known in heaven. Our children, Josh, Jeremy, and Melissa, now adults with families of their own, grew up in a cross-cultural missions ecosystem. The love, encouragement, and prayers of family have strengthened me.

Lessons learned from colleagues, field workers, agency leaders, scholar practitioners, and friends, are myriad. Paul said, "What do you have that you did not receive? And if you did receive it, why do you boast as though you did not?" (1 Cor 4:7). I cannot boast. While you are too numerous to mention by name, this book represents a stewardship of some of the insights you and I received or discovered together.

The idea for this book emerged from a series of "Rethinking People Groups" forums catalyzed by Mike Latsko (Frontiers) and Ted Esler (Missio Nexus), initially involving Greg Parsons, Tim and RW Lewis, Dan Scribner, Wilson Geisler, Kent Parks, Lara Heneveld, Minh Ha Nguyen, Alan McMahan, Dan Hitzhusen, Mike Constantz, and others. The study papers and discussions over a year and a half led to Ted's kind invitation to me to serve as Guest Editor of the "Rethinking People Groups"-themed issue of the *Evangelical Missions Quarterly* (Fall, 2020). So well received was that issue—some called it, "the best introduction to people group thinking!"—that I began to dream of a book, expanded from the initial set of articles (included here) to include a range of international church and mission voices and thought leaders—that would both represent and be accessible to a global audience.

This book would never have come into being without the strong support and encouragement of my Lausanne Co-Catalysts, Mary Ho (All Nations International) and Zaza Lima (COMIBAM/PMI), who with the encouragement of David Bennet and Tanya Van Horne of the Lausanne Movement, were instrumental in helping relaunch the moribund Least Reached Peoples (LRP) Network. Fifty years after Ralph Winter's seminal address at Lausanne 1974, the re-emergence of this UPG-focused issue network is a sign that God is stirring His people to rise up, re-focus, and reach out "to the ends of the earth." As Co-Catalysts, along with our network Steering Team of notable mission leaders, we agreed that a book of this breadth and depth was needed, and would in the process, display the panoramic engagement of the Majority World church as well as the West.

Acknowledgments

It is a privilege to labor alongside these leaders without whose contributions, along with pastors, field workers, ministry leaders, and others, this book would not be possible.

We worked with a compressed production process and deadline, with a view to the Lausanne IV Congress, Seoul 2024. I am grateful for every contributor who took time to draft articles and case studies, transparently sharing their hearts, unique perspectives, and journeys among the least reached.

Special thanks is due to Mary Ho and her Executive Assistant Clara Litzsinger of All Nations International. What we originally conceived as a simple collection turned into a complex compendium. Mary graciously donated Clara's time and expertise to serve as project manager and keep us on track. Clara's aid was invaluable, freeing me to work on editing and correspondence with authors. Bruce Pittard, Mary Ho, and Daniel Hoskins offered timely editing assistance. Robby Butler's expertise enabled us to "visualize" the task and, with input from RW Lewis and Joshua Project, represent in a small way the vast data, research, and knowledge stewarded by the community of mission information workers.

When the finish line was in sight, we faltered, but were rescued by the timely and gracious assistance of Jackie Chapman, who stepped in to provide professional copy editing and formatting of the manuscript. The missional vision and collegiality of William Carey Publishing are legendary, and we laud the work of publishing manager Vivian Doub and senior editor Melissa Hicks. I am grateful to all for their contributions to this volume.

Finally, my life experiences in Central Asia brought me into contact with people who had never heard the gospel or met a follower of Jesus—families in urban and rural settings, refugees, tribal leaders, urban professionals, villagers, and their language, customs, culinary arts, music, and oral literature. My friendships with the rugged, but ever-hospitable people in this region "put a face on" Islam and concepts like "people groups," "ethnic identity," cultural "barriers," and "access" to the gospel. One of the greatest privileges of my life was living, serving, and walking with Jesus among them. The realities of field life inform my writings, my approach to the topic of "unreached peoples," and the shape of this book.

UPGs and the "Least Reached" are not objects or concepts. They are precious people who have a right—and often delight—to hear the good news of a God who loves them more than we will ever know.

Leonard N. (Len) Bartlotti, PhD

Contributors

MIKE ADEGBILE
Movement Catalyst, Go-North Initiative; Country/Regional Director, Global Church Planting Network (GCPN) and 24:14 Global; Former Executive Secretary, Nigeria Evangelical Missions Association (NEMA)

AYCHI B. R.
Leader of disciple making movements (DMM) in the Horn of Africa; Global DMM Trainer; Founder and Director of Transformational Disciple Making Ministries; Regional Director of New Generations

LEONARD N. (LEN) BARTLOTTI (PhD)
Mission Strategist, Consultant, and Catalyst; Lead Facilitator, Vision 5:9 Global Trends; Steering Team, Lausanne Least Reached Peoples Network; Ministry in Central Asia

JOHN BECKER
Global Strategy Coordinator, AIM; Team Leader, 3P Ministries; Chairman, Strategic Partnerships, Activate Global

ROBERT A. BLINCOE (PhD)
President Emeritus, Frontiers USA

PATRICK BRITTENDEN (DPhil)
Hikma Partnership Lead; Associate Faculty, Institute Chretien d'Algerie (ICA); Ministry in North Africa and with MBBs

DICK BROGDEN (PhD)
Co-Founder, Live Dead; Pioneer worker in East Africa and the Middle East with Assemblies of God World Missions (AGWM)

ROBBY BUTLER
Mission analyst and mobilization strategist; Former personal assistant to Dr. Ralph Winter, US Center for World Mission (now Frontier Ventures)

C. C.
Church leader, The Well Community Church, Portland, Oregon, USA

CANYON HILLS CHURCH, Bothell, WA
Mobilization and Global Outreach leaders

CRISTIAN CASTRO
Executive Director, COMIBAM International (the Ibero-American Missionary Cooperation network)

SAMUEL E. CHIANG
Executive Director, Global Evangelism Network; Lausanne Catalyst for Orality; Deputy Secretary General – Ministries, World Evangelical Alliance (WEA); Former CEO of Seed Company

CHRIS CLAYMAN
Executive Director, Joshua Project; Co-Founder, Global Gates

DAVE DATEMA
Missiology Catalyst, Frontier Ventures

ABRAHAM DURAN (pseudonymn)
Latin American missiologist; Co-International Director, Frontiers; mentor and disciple-maker; former church planter and development worker in the Middle East

Contributors

RYAN EMIS
Director, Global Partnerships for Via; Mobilization Facilitator, Vision 5:9; Director of Global Consultations, Lausanne Movement; Director of the Office of the Future, World Evangelical Alliance (WEA)

TODD ENGSTROM (DEdMin)
Ministry Development Advisor and Former Executive Pastor, The Austin Stone Community Church, Auston, TX; Founding Partner, 100 UPG Cooperative

DAVID GARRISON (PhD)
Mission Researcher; Author; Global Strategist, Evangelical Advance; International Mission Board

BRAD GILL
Founding President, International Society for Frontier Missiology; Editor, *International Journal of Frontier Missiology*

MARTIN HALL
UK Muslim Ministries Ambassador & Global Collaboration Facilitator, OM; Member, Vision 5:9 Global Team

JUNGKOOK HAN
Pastor and former General Secretary, Korean World Missions Association (KWMA); Former missionary in Indonesia; pioneer in the Korean Adopt A People and UPG movements

STEVE HAWTHORNE (PhD)
Co-Editor, *Perspectives on the World Christian Movement*

MARY HO (DSL)
International Executive Leader, All Nations International; Co-Catalyst, Lausanne Least Reached Peoples Network

YAHYA ILYAS
Leader, Southeast Asian disciple making movements

ALAN R. JOHNSON (PhD)
Associate Professor of Anthropology, Intercultural Doctoral Studies program, Assemblies of God Theological Seminary; Pioneer worker in Thailand with Assemblies of God World Missions (AGWM)

MARK KIM
International Director of Global Operation, Korea; Prayer Team Leader, Vision 5:9; Former missionary in Central Asia

CÉLIA MARGARETH OLIVEIRA LARANJO
Church leader, Brazil

MIKE LATSKO
Team Leader, The Engage Network; Facilitator, Strategic Partnerships, Frontiers USA

R. W. LEWIS
Co-Founder and current CEO, Telos Fellowship; Founding staff of the US Center for World Mission and Frontiers; field service among Muslims in North Africa and India

ZAZÁ LIMA
Co-Catalyst, Lausanne Least Reached Peoples Network; President, Evangelical Transcultural Initiative (IET); Former Executive Director of PMI (Pueblos en Misión Internacional); Board Member of COMIBAM, Hikma Network, and the North Africa and Middle East Partnership

CLARA LITZSINGER
Executive Assistant, All Nations International

Bo Lundin
Senior Advisor, IBRA, media arm of the Swedish Pentecostal Church

Simon Lunt
Chairman, Diaspora Peoples in Europe (DPE); OM London; Member, Vision 5:9 Global Team

Allan E. Matamoros
Vision 5:9 Chairman; COMIBAM Internacional Field Director

Alan McMahan (PhD)
Affiliate Professor, Talbot School of Theology, Biola University; Urban missiologist; General Editor, Great Commission Research Journal; President of the Great Commission Research Network

Brian McSwain
Pastor, Middle East

Luís Fernando Nacif
Church leader, Brazil

Minh Ha Nguyen (PhD)
Co-founder and Director, Radius Global Cities Network; Creator, Shalom City Index; Member, Global Strategy Forum, WEA; Adjunct Professor, Bakke Graduate University and Vietnamese Baptist Theological Seminary; Founder and President, Southern Baptist Ethnic Research Network

O. K.
IBRA Regional Coordinator for Eurasia; Muslim background believer from Central Asia

Adeolu F. Olanrewaju (PhD)
Director of Administration, Nigeria Evangelical Missions Association

Hans Olofsson
Coordinator International Broadcasting, IBRA, Sweden

Peter Oyugi
Catalyst and Mentor, Movement for African National Initiatives (MANI)

Lisa Pak (DMin)
Finishing the Task (FTT); Operational Catalyst for Kingdom Impact Network, Wycliffe USA

Greg Parsons (PhD)
Frontier Ventures Global Connections Specialist; Curator for the Ralph D. Winter Research Center

PCC
Pastor Emeritus, Virginia, USA

Zane Pratt
Associate Professor of Christian Missions, Southern Seminary; Vice President for Field Deployment and Training, International Mission Board; Former overseas worker in Central Asia

Dan Scribner
Director of Operations, Joshua Project

Sushil Tyagi
Facilitator, Vision 5:9 South Asia; Founder and President, Nicodemus Trust

Daniel Waheli (pseudonymn)
Former International mission director; church planter and global movement trainer

Parsa Zarin Ghalam (PhD candidate)
Head of Research and Dissemination, Hikma Partnership

visit us at missionbooks.org

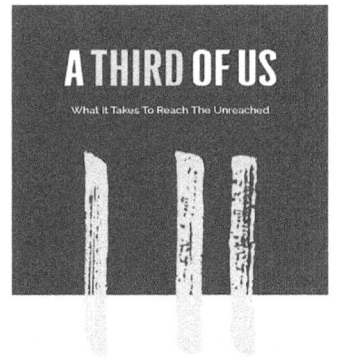

A Third of Us: What It Takes to Reach the Unreached

Marvin J. Newell

Today, over three billion people, a third of humanity, have yet to hear the good news of Jesus. In light of this staggering need, Marv Newell explores the five Great Commission passages, where Jesus methodically unfolds the essence of the disciples' task. *A Third of Us* is not just an invitation to be aware of the need, but a rally cry for today's disciples to respond. Newell casts a vision for multiple ways to get involved in reaching the unreached.

Propelled by Hope: The Story of the Perspectives Movement

Yvonne Huneycutt

The fascinating connection between the Perspectives movement, the frontier mission movement, and church planting movements is a story rarely told yet vital to understanding the spread of the gospel to unreached populations. Yvonne Huneycutt's *Propelled by Hope* unfolds the hidden tapestry of these interconnected movements through sixty personal interviews and inspiring anecdotes.

Uncharted Mission: Going to the Final Frontiers

D. C. Keane

More than the history of the founding of Frontiers, this book weaves together interviews with over one hundred missionaries who refused to accept the status quo in missions and were willing to go where no one had gone before—to the Muslim frontiers. In this inspiring true story, you'll meet pastors, engineers, artists, pilots, and others whose lives changed course when they discovered that Muslims were largely left out of historic missionary efforts.

www.ingramcontent.com/pod-product-compliance
Lightning Source LLC
Chambersburg PA
CBHW080322080526
44585CB00021B/2439